GOVERNMENT BY CONSTITUTION

The Political Systems of Democracy

HERBERT J. SPIRO

HARVARD UNIVERSITY

Government
BY
Constitution

THE
POLITICAL SYSTEMS
OF DEMOCRACY

 RANDOM HOUSE

Manufactured in the United States of America by The Colonial Press Inc.

To

Elizabeth Petersen Spiro

Preface

This book is the outcome of experience gathered while teaching courses on "Parliamentary Government," "Governments of Continental Europe," "Canadian Government," and related subjects in the field of comparative government at Harvard. It is intended primarily for use in college courses on comparative government, on the nature of the democratic process, and on constitutional government in general. But it has been written for a wider audience as well, for my colleagues in political science, for those who will be faced with responsibilities in the creating or re-making of constitutions for national or international political systems, and for anyone who is as concerned with politics as politics is concerned with him.

All our lives are today shaped by politics, and the most crucial problems confronting mankind—problems of its survival—are political ones. Accordingly, the task of political science is weightier in our time than it has ever been before. The threat of nuclear world war, the emergence of new nation-states, and the failure of established constitutional democracies make many aspects of this task novel. And this novelty indicates that new questions should be asked, where the standard ones of the past have not yielded satisfactory answers. In *Government by Constitution,* I have sought to ask some new questions. In asking these, my effort has been to employ simple language and to avoid, for the sake of undergraduates and general readers alike, overdependence upon the jargon of some of the social sciences or upon any new jargon of my own. I trust that I have succeeded.

Parts of the manuscript, in various stages of preparation, have been read by Harold J. Berman, David Riesman, and other members of the Seminar on Law and Social Relations (held under the auspices of the Social Science Research Council at the Harvard Law School in 1956); by J. Roland Pennock, David Easton, and other members of the Conference on Political Theory (held under the same auspices at Swarthmore College in June, 1957); by my former tutors and present colleagues William Yandell Elliott and Louis Hartz; and by my friend Howard C. Petersen. Samuel H. Beer, Adam B. Ulam, Nicholas Wahl, and Harry Eckstein helped to sharpen my approach to the subject while we were working together on our *Patterns of Government: The Major*

Political Systems of Europe. Carl J. Friedrich, my teacher and colleague, read the entire first draft of the manuscript. My friend and colleague Melvin Croan read the whole final version. For their constructive criticisms, my thanks go to all of these gentlemen, particularly the two last mentioned. Needless to say, any blame for the final product should go to me.

I wish also to acknowledge the help of politicians, public servants, scholars, and citizens of the eight countries with which this book deals. I appreciate the editorial guidance given me by Charles Donald Lieber of Random House. The tireless editorial contributions of David Wolfe Biller were, to apply categories used in the book, both procedural and substantive.

My strongest thanks go to undergraduates in Harvard College, from whose judgment and enthusiasm I have consistently benefited ever since I ceased to be one of them. Students in Government 112 and in my sections in Government 1 have been especially helpful. So have my tutorial students, one of whom, after graduating from Radcliffe College, concentrated her considerable critical faculties upon this manuscript. But that is not my reason for dedicating the book to her.

HERBERT J. SPIRO

Cambridge, Massachusetts
April, 1959

Contents

PART TWO : : : EIGHT POLITICAL SYSTEMS

PART SIX : : : THE CONDITIONS OF CONSTITUTIONAL SUCCESS

PART I

Politics and Policies

CHAPTER 1

The Study of Politics

"The Master Science"

"Politics is the master science." When Plato and Aristotle, the founders of the study of politics, first made this claim, they were stating what appeared to their contemporaries as an obvious fact. By "politics" they meant the affairs of the polis. This Greek "city-state," as it is now usually called, was an all-embracing community. Its members did not yet distinguish between matters public and matters private, between politics and ethics, or among economics, education, and religion. According to Aristotle, politics was that "which concerns all the citizens." Whenever an issue was raised to be decided in any one of these undifferentiated fields, that issue was political by definition. The most important events in the lives of the members of the polis—the citizens of the city—were but consequences of events in the life of the polis itself. That is why the Greeks could conceive of nothing more important than politics: politics affected everyone, in every phase and aspect of his life, and in such a pervasive manner that no human being could escape politics—no one, that is, but beasts and gods.

Can we today still consider politics the master science? Certainly no modern political system, not even a totalitarian one, is as undifferentiated or as all-pervasive as was the Greek polis. People living under modern governments are usually aware of differences among the institutions and values pertaining to politics, economics, education, religion, and other spheres of their lives. Specialized sciences or academic disciplines for the study of each of these fields have grown up over the centuries. Offhand, there would seem to be no good reason why any one of these sciences should claim preëminence. Nevertheless, it is still true that whenever an issue is raised which "concerns all the citizens," that

3

issue is as much "in politics" today as were the issues concerning Athenians two and a half millennia ago.

We are conscious, to be sure, that our lives seem to have different compartments—the state, lower and higher "social bodies" and political units, and the economy—and that we play different roles as members of these distinct and overlapping entities—as citizens, local taxpayers, members of families, and communicants of a religion: as businessmen, farmers, employees, consumers. Still, when an issue is raised for decision in any one of these compartments, it usually becomes a part of politics. This happens for two reasons. The first of these is the existence of a kind of politics within each of the different compartments. The second reason is that they are not really "compartments" at all, but are overlapping and mutually interdependent phases. The political character of issues becomes particularly evident, therefore, when they arise out of relations between two or more of these spheres—when, for example, a decision has to be made about the role of government in the economy, or of the churches in education.

To reassert the primacy of politics, then, does not necessarily imply any arrogance on the part of politicians or of political scientists. Rather, it means that nothing is more important for men than awareness of the scope and limits of their capacity to shape the fate of mankind. The most dramatic illustration of this importance is the danger in our time that all or most of mankind might be wiped out. Surely nothing can be of greater concern than this, because if the end of human life itself is not prevented, no other forms of human activity will remain. A nuclear holocaust can be prevented, as it can be brought about, only through politics, that is, through the process by which men deal with the issues that concern them in the communities in which they live. Of these communities, the totality of mankind is the greatest.

Mankind as a whole is only now becoming conscious of facing issues that concern all human beings. At present, because technology has shrunk the globe, all men together do confront such issues, and many people are acutely aware of this. But they have not yet learned how to deal with these issues one by one as they arise, and much less how to set up machinery designed to handle them over a long period of time.

For smaller human communities, however, such machineries have been established and have operated with varying degrees of success. At these lower levels of human organization, some modern constitutional democracies in particular have dealt efficiently with the problems they confronted. They have adapted their politics to changes in these problems; they have been stable over time; and they have marshaled wide popular acceptance for their policies. Because of their success, they provide the best models from which lessons may be drawn about the *do's* and *don'ts* for constructing political institutions of global scope. But this is neither the only nor the main reason for studying politics at the levels at which it has been successful. The fact that governments created by men have been more successful in some instances than in others, coupled with the recurrent need to create new political systems and to reform old ones, provides an equally urgent reason for this study.

Constitution-Making

If we look at politics as the process by which men in groups make decisions about issues arising out of the common problems they face, we can understand why political activity would be ranked highest in the hierarchy of human activities. At the same time, we could also set up an internal hierarchy for different types of political activity. Some problems are clearly more important because they affect more people than other problems, and do so in more basic terms. Consequently, decisions about issues arising out of these wider and more basic problems are of special importance. In this sense, those decisions are of the highest importance which deal with the creation of a new political system or with the fundamental reform of an old one. These may be likened to fundamental choices made by the individual—of ethic, career, or mate—that will shape his or her entire future and are always to some extent irreversible.

In the life of a political system, such fundamental decisions are made at the time of its founding. They are expressed in documents like the Declaration of Independence and the Constitution of the United States. Decisions of highest importance may also be made in the course of a violent or peaceful revolution, or as the result of a war. Many decisions of such basic importance have had to be made all over the world, especially during the last hundred years: recently they have had to be made with increasing frequency.

Since the end of World War II, about forty states, including some old ones and some newly created ones, have given themselves new constitutions or have changed their governments fundamentally by other means. Of the countries discussed in this book, this has been true of Germany and Italy, and doubly true of France with her two postwar constitutions. It also applies to all the countries that have come under Communist domination since the war, although their constitutions have little practical significance today. All of the countries that have emerged from colonial domination in Asia, Africa, and the Near East acquired new constitutions as they achieved independence. Indeed, more than half the member states of the United Nations have undergone some kind of fundamental constitutional reform since 1945. And the adoption of the Charter of the United Nations itself, as the constitution of an organization meant to be global in scope, affords another example of a document expressing basic choice. Decisions of this type affect all the members of the political system. They affect them in their everyday lives to a much greater extent, and for longer periods of time, than other types of political choice. That is why constitutional decisions are the most important ones. Since constitutions themselves are the product of political decisions, there is a real and urgent need for the comparative study of politics.

Comparative Government

Outside of the comparative study of government, men who engage in constitution-making have no means of finding out what devices can best help them overcome obstacles that stand between themselves and their goals. Historians, whose outlook on time is retrospective, may ask of the past of any one country how it came to be the unique combination it is today of things and people, of institutions and values. Students of politics, who are trying to provide knowledge for the architects of political systems, have to look forward in time as well. Once they have gained the historians' understanding of "how things came to be this way," and have clearly formulated goals for the future, they must ask: How can we approach these goals? Since their nation (if it is a nation) has not reached the goals, something must be lacking—and that something may perhaps be provided by an institution to be found elsewhere.

In this way, Americans have often sought to realize the goal of honesty in the public service and have searched for institutions designed to curb corruption. Some Frenchmen, in pursuit of the goal of cabinet stability, have advocated the adoption of devices believed to provide such stability in Great Britain. Again, in Germany, where as many as thirty political groups had been represented in parliament before Hitler came to power in 1933, variations of election laws of other countries were introduced after 1945, in order to prevent this kind of fragmentation. On the international plane, in an effort to avoid failures similar to those experienced by the League of Nations, the Charter of the United Nations contains many departures from the Covenant of its unsuccessful predecessor. In these and many other cases, specific institutions were deliberately "engineered" into being as the means for realizing goals.

Usually, the new institution was copied more or less accurately from some other political system. Only rarely did the inventive genius of a "constitutional engineer" create something really unprecedented. In most cases, the men concerned with constitutional decisions seek to get some inkling of the probable effects of the introduction of a new institution into their country. In order to find this out about proposed innovations such as the merit system, or about contemplated changes in procedures for parliamentary dissolution or proportional representation, they compare the functioning of these institutions or processes in comparable circumstances. This would not be necessary if political institutions could be tested in laboratories. But since this is possible only in a metaphorical sense—e.g., the states as political laboratories for the wider federal system—the comparative method is best suited for giving answers to the kind of question constitution-makers have to ask.

The primary importance of politics and the frequent need for constitutional engineering thus combine to define the task of the comparative study of politics. This task is by no means new. Many great talents have addressed themselves to it, ever since Aristotle collected 157 constitutions of the Greek world of his day. In the modern West in general, and in the United States in particular, comparative government has attracted some great minds and many thorough ones. These scholars usually favor one of two main methods, the *determinist* or the *institutional,* unless they combine the two in the *functional* approach. This book is an attempt to link systematically certain valid insights of each of the methods. Before outlining the comparisons that will be made here, we should therefore take a critical look at the prevailing schools of thought.

The Determinist School

Those who follow the determinist method see political institutions only as reflections of underlying causal factors, which they view as determining all that happens in politics. The primary interest of the determinists goes to the "substructure," as it is called by the Marxists, who belong to this school. For the Marxists, it is the mode of production that makes everything else move. To them, the substructure is generally identical with the economy. Society, government, and intellectual activity are parts of the "superstructure" and therefore mere reflections of the all-important determining factor.

Other determinists focus on other factors—geography, national character, social structure, cultural tradition, or some combination of these. At any rate, they usually deny that a people can rationally, deliberately, and purposefully "give" itself a constitution and thereby set the guidelines for its future development. For example, when a nation, like France under the Fourth Republic, has trouble in arriving at much-needed decisions, the determinists attribute this to one of the causes just cited. The French constitution or parliament they consider mere consequences of these underlying determinants.

The determinists may be right when they assert that men cannot shape their own fate through the building of constitutions, although none of them is capable of proving that his particular "first cause" is the prime factor. The possible truth of their assertion, however, does not obviate the inescapable need to create new constitutions from time to time; nor does it abolish the belief of many men that they are making meaningful decisions when they do give themselves a new constitution. All sorts of determined factors may indeed have conspired to doom the French to have unstable and inefficient government. Nevertheless, there have always been many Frenchmen—and there are many of them today—who firmly believe that constitutional change could at least alleviate these troubles. And this conviction itself makes a difference for French politics. This was particularly evident at the end of World War II, and again when General de Gaulle returned to the premiership in 1958. On both occasions, opportunities presented themselves to scrap the existing constitution. At such times, people's knowledge of the constitutional provisions of other, apparently more successful, systems also has significant effects.

Few men will let determinist arguments persuade them into the docility of complete inaction. Ample proof of this is provided by the activism frequently displayed by adherents of such deterministic philosophies as Marxism and Calvinism. At some moments in history, men simply have to make constitutional decisions. At the time they become aware of making such decisions, they at least think that they are going beyond determinism. Those of us who have to make constitutional decisions ourselves, or who want to help others make theirs wisely, must therefore reject as inadequate the determinist approach to the comparative study of government.

The Institutional School

Where the determinists compare data of the substructures of systems, the institutionalists compare constitutions and their component parts. They ascribed France's ills of the 1950's to the constitutional weakness of the premier, to the lack of discipline in the National Assembly, or to the failures of the electoral system of proportional representation. Similarly, they explained the political health of the Federal Republic of Germany, contrasted with its predecessor, the Weimar Republic, and its neighbor, the Fourth French Republic, in terms of constitutional provisions for judicial review of legislation, for a weakened presidency, or for the "constructive vote of no-confidence."

Scholars who belong to the institutional school are usually much more optimistic about the feasibility of constitution-making than their determinist colleagues. The latter, explaining the failure of the Weimar Republic to survive Hitler's rise, would say that this experiment was foredoomed from the outset, no matter how clever its architects may or might have been. "German national character is antidemocratic," or, "Inflation and depression were so severe that totalitarianism was bound to win out," they would say. The institutionalists, on the other hand, find the cause of the collapse of the Weimar Republic in some error committed by the constitutional authors at Weimar in 1919. They claim that the founding fathers at Bonn three decades later were more successful, because they avoided similar errors.

In its more naïve forms, the institutional method is no more helpful for our purposes than that of the determinists. Just because the United States version of the separation of powers seems to have worked out reasonably well, for instance, there is no reason to assume that the same constitution would be equally successful in the Canadian, German, French, Japanese, or Russian contexts. Again, the achievements of cabinet government in Great Britain are not entirely unconnected with the existence of a traditional "governing class" in that country. Since no similar class can be found in the United States, British cabinet government transplanted to America would be likely to yield rather different fruits.

The institutional school is even less helpful when its adherents consider institutions comparable simply because they happen to bear the same label. When functions are analyzed, it becomes evident that the presidents of the United States, France, Germany, Switzerland, and Mexico share little in common but their title. The same holds true for the cabinets of Britain, Sweden, Germany, and the United States. Even party systems in different countries often do not perform the same functions. We might do better to compare French political parties with British interest organizations than with British parties. In many cases, it is misleading even to compare two historical periods of the very same institution in one political system, because its function in the political process —and the problems and issues with which that process deals—have changed radically over the years. The British Crown may serve as the most obvious illustration, but the party system of the United States is similarly a case in point: its role in the nation in 1820 simply was not the same role it played in 1920. To focus on institutions alone, without regard to the environment within which they operate, is bad enough. To compare institutions which perform different functions in the political process and which are, therefore, not comparable, is worse.

The Functional School

The functional approach sometimes combines the shortcomings of the other two schools. For example, its followers may assume that "the executive" performs the same functions in all political systems, that the French Premier (prior to 1959) was the French executive, and then reason as follows: "Only a stable executive can be efficient. The best way to insure executive stability in a parliamentary system is to give the premier the power to dissolve parliament. French Premiers have not had an effective power of dissolution for eighty years. French national character being what it is, they will never really get it. Therefore, France will not get an efficient executive." This method not only makes the mistake of assuming that all "executives" perform the same functions; it also overlooks differences in the dominant values of different political systems. It is at least conceivable, for instance, that many Frenchmen did not consider Cabinet stability particularly valuable and that other goals were more important for them. Prevailing values—the goals in pursuit of which people act in politics—affect the functions of seemingly similar institutions. More than that, dominant values shape the very raw material of politics: the problems that the political system is facing.

Problems are obstacles between men and their goals. They are the raw material of politics. Politics is the process of making *decisions* about *issues* arising out of the problems faced by human communities. There are different types of problems, and different kinds of decisions are made in the course of politics. The main purpose of the comparative study of politics is to gauge the usefulness of various institutions and procedures as instruments for the attainment of common goals.

In order to find out what effects an institution has on the context in which it is operating, one can compare either different institutions in similar environments, or the same environment before and after introduction of a new institution. One will not obtain any useful information from comparing institutions that are functioning in wholly dissimilar contexts. The context of a political system is shaped by the problems that it is facing. Even similar problems, however, whether they be economic, cultural, external, or constitutional, should not be compared as separate, isolated phenomena, in quantitative terms. Economists and some other social scientists may make comparisons of this kind; political scientists should not.

We have to consider also the dominant values of the time. This is particularly applicable to economic problems. These may not be problems at all for a society which does not value prosperity or economic efficiency. Some primitive tribe, for example, may be suffering from dire sub-subsistence poverty, and what little production and distribution goes on within it may be badly disorganized. But the tribe does not pursue the goal of prosperity, and the possibility of reorganizing its economy has never occurred to any of its members. Consequently, for all practical purposes, its politics presents no economic problems.

Differences in dominant values are often overlooked by followers of the functional school of thought. For example, in giving advice to constitution-makers in Ghana today, they might suggest, as a model, the constitution of another country in its first stage of independence from colonial domination, e.g., the United States after the American Revolution. But there is a vast difference between the economic goals pursued by the two sets of founding fathers. To cite only one difference, ours believed firmly in private property, while those in Ghana are quite willing to experiment with various forms of social control and state ownership. This colors their perception of the economic problems that their country is facing today, and it affects their notion of what sort of political machinery is needed for processing their economic problems.

The same is true for constitutional problems. Since many countries that acquired new constitutions in the present century have been unable to make them work properly, one might reasonably ask: Why do revolutionary regimes and governments of countries that have recently achieved independence persist in futile constitution-making? Why this "great modern fallacy that a constitution can be made, can be manufactured by a combination of existing forces and tendencies"? [1] The answer is very simple. Every self-respecting nation on the face of the earth *wants* to have a constitution if it does not already have one. And, with the notable exception of Great Britain, most states that have constitutions would not mind improving their existing ones. Constitutionalism in this sense is one of the dominant values of our time, all over the world. And no matter

[1] Jacob Burckhardt, *The Civilization of the Renaissance in Italy,* Modern Library, p. 68.

how often it seems to have been disproved by history, the belief persists that a deliberately constructed constitution is the best means available for assuring achievement of the common goals of a community.

The Separation of Powers

Many of the best students of constitutional government have shared this belief. The fact that they came to its study "from the inside," as it were, has shaped the questions with which they have approached their work. This has been particularly true of the functional school, which has traditionally classified the functions of government under the headings provided by the separation of powers: legislative, executive, and judicial. Americans are particularly used to this classification of political functions, because their Constitution is based explicitly upon it. In the United States, there have been many controversies arising out of allegations that one or another of the three branches overstepped the limits set for it by the Constitution. In recent years especially, the Supreme Court has often been accused of engaging in legislation. These controversies suggest that this classification harbors many disadvantages for an understanding of politics even in the United States. For other systems, which are not based explicitly upon the separation of powers, this approach is bound to cause misunderstandings.

Every government does much more than to make and execute laws and to judge actions in terms of these laws. But even if we assumed that a particular government performed no functions other than the legislative, executive, and judicial ones, a description of its workings based upon these three categories would be quite unsatisfactory. Some contemporary students of politics have recognized this. They focus on the policy-making process and emphasize that no absolute distinction can be made between "making" policy and "executing" it.[2] Policy is still being made even in the last moment of its implementation. For example, the city council may pass an ordinance designed to curb jaywalking. The chief of police begins the "execution" of this law or policy when he issues instructions concerning the way in which policemen in his traffic division are to apply the ordinance. Under the traditional executive-legislative classification, the cop on his beat would be viewed simply as putting into effect what the city council made into law. Actually, however, in deciding which pedestrian to stop, how to address him, and whether or not to give him a ticket, the cop is still acting in the same policy process that began, not when the city council passed the ordinance,

[2] Carl J. Friedrich, *Constitutional Government and Democracy*, 1950, pp. 360 ff.

but when someone recognized the problem of jaywalking, focused public attention on it, and thereby converted the problem into an issue of politics. The traffic judge, too, is still acting in the same flow of policy when he questions offenders, their counsel, or the assistant district attorney, when he dresses down a jaywalker or criticizes an overzealous policeman, and finally, when he convicts or acquits individuals who have been charged with violating the ordinance.

Thus, even if government performed no functions other than those meant to be described by the tripartite separation of powers, this classification would fall far short of the job of any classification: to distinguish things that differ, and to put things that are alike into the same class. The trouble with this old classification is twofold: Legislature, executive, and judiciary are alike in that they all make policies, and the making of policies is their main function. But what distinguishes the types of policies they make is not the same as what distinguishes legislation from execution of laws, nor is it the same as what distinguishes either of these from adjudication.

A Look Ahead: The Plan of the Book

Because of these shortcomings of determinist, institutional, and functional methods, a new approach to the comparative study of politics will be developed in Chapter 2. There the questions will be asked to which we will try to get answers in the remainder of the book: What are the problems faced by the eight countries whose politics we are studying? What similarities and what differences are there among these problems? How are the problems handled in successive phases of the political process?

In order to break down these questions into manageable proportions, we will develop classifications both of the problems and of the decisions made about the problems. Throughout the book, we will be looking for guidelines for constitution-makers, who must always ask themselves: How can we make sure that our constitution and its parts will accomplish the intended results and thereby bring us closer to our goals? Indeed, it is the main purpose of the comparative study of politics to find answers to this question. But this applies only to the analytical side of the undertaking—the side in which we try to divorce ourselves from values and in which we take an uncritical view of the particular goals that any one political system happens to be pursuing.

This cold question of the constitutional engineer may be asked by the builder of a totalitarian system as well as by the founders of a constitutional democracy. In fact, the totalitarian is more interested in this question, because he seeks to engineer the whole society, the total system—hence the term "totalitarianism." Moreover, he has much greater confidence in his capacity to shape the future for centuries than does the constitutional democrat—witness Hitler's "Thousand-Year Reich," and Khrushchev's conviction that "we socialists will bury you capitalists."

There is another side of the undertaking, however. If we define the success of constitution-making purely in terms of achieving the results intended by the authors of a constitution, then we would leave unanswered a very important question: Is there any basis on which we can evaluate the results that the founders of a constitution want to achieve, any ground on which we can accept or reject the goals toward whose attainment a political system is dedicated? In Chapter 3, in order to answer this question, we shall try to formulate a set of norms that go beyond success in terms of intentions—norms that may be used to judge the intentions themselves. These norms also go beyond the problems confronting political systems and, in some instances, even beyond ideological differences. They may serve as a lowest common denominator of values on which agreement is possible among all adherents of constitutional democracy and, in addition, among many Marxists and among most others who are heirs to the "Western political heritage."

These norms can provide questions that can be asked in a comparative way of concrete political institutions and procedures, and they can yield concrete answers more useful than the usual criteria of freedom, equality, security, and the like. These values will be derived from the basic norm of individual responsibility. This formulation will give a useful normative dimension to an approach that is otherwise mainly analytical. From it, we will also derive our four criteria for evaluating the performance of constitutional systems: stability over time, adaptability to changes in the environment, efficiency in dealing with problems, and effectiveness in gaining acceptance for policies from the population.

The chapters of Part II contain brief descriptions of the eight political systems on which this study is based: Sweden, Switzerland, Italy, Germany, France, Great Britain, Canada, and the United States. They are arranged in reverse order of the reader's probable familiarity with them. Each chapter will begin with a sketch of the constitutional history of the country and its present constitutional structure. It will outline the major problems the system is facing in our time, and then discuss the most important issues figuring in its contemporary politics, together with the groups concerned with the resolution of these issues. Each of these chapters will end with a preliminary evaluation of the performance of the political system, in terms of the four criteria just cited. Throughout Part II, we will be isolating similar problems faced by these nations. In the course of doing this, we will find that some problems, although they seem to be almost identical in two political systems, are treated in very different ways; that is, they give rise to different types of issues, generate controversies of different intensity, and are resolved in different ways. These differences *may* be due to constitutional factors, or their causes may lie closer to the determinists' substructure.

Part III, on "Political Style," will analyze in greater detail differences in the treatment given to similar problems in the politics of our eight countries. The political style of a country comprises the manner in which issues are formulated, fought over, and eventually disposed of. First, we will give a typology of political style under five headings: Purposive Interest, Pragmatism, Violence, Ideologism, and Legalism. This will be followed by an attempt to account for differences in political style, especially with regard to ideologism and legalism.

Up to this point, most of our attention will have been devoted to the problems faced by the eight countries. In Part IV, we will shift to the institutions and procedures that have been designed for solving these problems. We will examine the methods by which deliberation of issues is carried on and the means by which the resolution of issues is achieved. Finally, as to the personnel that participates in both deliberation and resolution, we shall seek to discover what kind of men and women, with what sorts of background and training, perform these functions in the different political systems.

Since most of the people who have specialized political jobs in modern democracies are thought of also as representatives, Part V will deal with "Representation." We will inquire why there is a need for representation, and why the groupings with which people identify themselves for purposes of representation vary a great deal in different systems. This will lead us to a comparison of channels of representation, including interest organizations and political parties. The comparison of party systems will involve theories of consensus, or agreement, since strong consensus has often been used to account for the accomplishments of successful party systems in countries whose people seem to have few disagreements among themselves.

Part VI, on "Conditions of Constitutional Success," will bring us back to the most important questions of political science: How can politics succeed? What are the prerequisites for the success of a constitutional system? How much agreement, and what kind of agreement, is required in order to reduce violence in the settlement of disputes? Where do we find the "true constitution" of a successful political system—in documents, "in the hearts of the citizens," or somewhere else? Can such a true constitution, and agreement on it, be created where it does not already exist?

In our Conclusion, finally, we will apply some lessons for constitution-makers in general, drawn from the experiences of these eight constitutional democracies. In it, we will raise questions about the applicability of these lessons to constitution-making at the two levels where it is most urgently needed in our own day: the so-called "underdeveloped" areas and that other area which, constitutionally speaking, is the most underdeveloped area of all, namely the global community of mankind.

CHAPTER 2

Problems and Policies

In paradise or some other utopia, there would be no politics. Indeed, there would be no problems in paradise, since—by definition—no one would see any obstacles between himself and his goals. All the inmates would have attained their goals, including those goals concerning relations with their fellows. Without problems, there would be no issues; and without issues, no politics. All this would be true despite the fact that there would, of course, be power in paradise—God's power. This suggests, incidentally, the inadequacies of the method that considers power central to politics and claims that politics deals with the distribution of power.

Types of Problems

Here, we will view politics as a flow of decisions about issues that arise out of problems. A decision is made when one of several alternative courses of action is selected. The alternatives are contained in the issue that is up for decision. Issues normally—but not always—arise out of problems. Problems are obstacles between men in their present condition and their goals. In this sense, problems are the raw material of politics. The function of a political system is to deal with or to "process" its problems. Problems are the "input" of the political "machine" or "organism." Its "output" consists of policies. Policies are made up of series of decisions.

Problems, as the raw material of politics, may be classified in any convenient fashion, such as that given in the Preamble to the Constitu-

17

tion of the United States: "to form a more perfect Union, establish justice, insure domestic tranquility, provide for the common defense, promote the general welfare, and secure the blessings of liberty." Each of these headings constituted a goal. For instance, the Founding Fathers wanted their Union to be *more* perfect than it was, and they wanted to *insure* domestic tranquility—which suggests that it was in need of insuring at the time of the Constitutional Convention. This lack of perfection in the Union and the relative lack of tranquility were among the problems faced by the thirteen American states in 1788. For our purposes, we will distinguish four main classes of problems: (1) economic, (2) cultural, (3) external, and (4) constitutional.

Problems do not necessarily give rise to issues. In order to generate issues, a problem must first of all be recognized as an obstacle between people and their goals. Then there must be disagreement on how to solve the problem. In the United States, for example, there is wide agreement that traffic in narcotics should be controlled by the federal government; as a result, this problem does not usually give rise to any issues in American politics. Problems of this kind stay in the prepolitical stage, because they do not enter into politics. But once problems are recognized, as the result of a decision, if further decisions are made by individuals or groups that they favor differing means of dealing with the problems, then issues become formulated, and such problems are in politics.

The eight countries with which we will be dealing in this book all face a variety of problems. That is one reason, though probably not the only one, why each of them falls far short of paradise—though envious citizens of less successful states may not always think so. These countries are political systems because they are confronting problems, their members are aware of this, and their members disagree among themselves about the proper means for handling their problems. Of course, they do not all face the same problems, though there are similarities in many respects. We must take the differences into account since these are bound to be reflected in the issues which play important roles in their politics and in their relative success as problem-solving "machines" and as constitutional democracies. In other words, we must not ascribe differences in success merely to constitutional differences, when they could be due to the "input" of their problems. Thus, if two automobiles perform very differently, it may be because one has a more efficient engine than the other. Or the first car may outperform the second because, with an identical engine, it is being driven on better roads. Or, finally, both of these reasons may combine to account for the difference. To change the metaphor—and to assuage readers who object to mechanistic analogies—the first of two cows may produce more and better milk than the second, either because it is in better health, i.e., has a better "constitution," or because it grazes on superior pasture, or again for a combination of these reasons. The point is that every comparison of systems of government should start with the nature of the problems that they have to handle. What sort of questions does this lead us to ask?

1. Economic Problems: These refer mainly to "who gets what, when," both for the system as a whole and within it. They call for questions about the level and extent of industrialization, the scope of the transport and communications systems, the foreign-trade balance, standard of living, distribution of income among different sectors of the economy as reflected in social security institutions, the labor and employers' organizations and their activities, and so forth. Under the heading of economic problems, we will probably find the strongest similarities among our eight countries. Of course, Great Britain and Italy, or the United States and Canada, do show marked differences with regard to their relative degree of industrialization, among other items. But the relative stage of economic development is not too relevant to the nature of the issues to which economic problems give rise. This is so because income is not being distributed relative to an absolute standard of prosperity as it prevails, say, in the United States. Rather, it is being distributed relative to the total national-income pie. The issues concern the size of the slices of that pie which different groups are going to get. These issues have been resolved differently in various countries. Thus, Sweden, with its highly developed social security system and years of socialist government, has pursued one kind of economic policy; the United States, with its vast resources and traditions of "private free enterprise," has pursued another.

Marxists would say that all these countries are at fairly similar stages of capitalist development. And so they are—at least when compared with China or Iraq. Moreover, they all have had some similar economic experiences, especially in connection with the two World Wars and the Great Depression. This has affected the goals they seek to realize. These goals or values in turn contribute to shaping the demands in terms of which they will recognize economic problems and formulate issues about them. In this respect, the similarity of economic problems is also attested to by the existence in most of these countries of interest groups and political parties with similar economic orientation: socialist, communist, and liberal parties among them; and labor unions, employers' associations, small merchants' groups, and the like. Where there are differences, such as European peasants' organizations, which have no clear counterpart in United States farmers' lobbies, these are clearly identifiable, they can be accounted for by obvious historical differences, and their reflections in politics can be seen readily. In general, however, because of broad similarities of economic problems, this area is useful for comparative studies.

2. *Cultural Problems:* These refer to ethnic, religious, intellectual, and similar cleavages in a society. They call for questions about the number and types of groups that exist, and their internal cohesion. By asking these questions, we find out, for instance, that multilingual Switzerland, which is also divided between Roman Catholics and Protestants, confronts cultural problems quite different from those of Sweden, where virtually everybody speaks the same language and belongs to the same Lutheran state church. The United States and Canada, their populations made up of successive waves of immigrants and their descendants, of different ethnic backgrounds, face cultural problems for which there are few equivalents in the Old World. West Germany today, whose population is about evenly divided between Protestants and Catholics, has problems that are not the same as those of the earlier Weimar Republic in Germany, in which Protestants outnumbered Catholics by a ratio of 2 to 1. France, with her still unsolved problem of relations between the state, the church, and the schools, has to deal with a whole set of issues produced by these problems and by memories connected with them. These issues, in turn, are lacking in Great Britain, where religious problems were largely resolved even before the time of the French Revolution. In Italy, on the other hand, because Rome is simultaneously the physical capital of the Roman Catholic Church and the capital of a national state that was finally unified only in 1870, issues to which few Englishmen would give a second thought tend to dominate political debates, even when these debates are supposed to be dealing primarily with economic, external, or constitutional problems. When we compare the role of issues of this kind in the different countries, and the efficiency of their constitutional systems in dealing with them, we must not forget these differences at the level of problems.

3. *External Problems:* These involve defense and foreign relations. With regard to these problems, students of international politics traditionally ask questions about "power." What is the military strength of a country? What are its economic resources for supporting the military

establishment, in war or in peace? What is its geographic position, from a strategic viewpoint? What potential allies or enemies does it have in terms of its "national interest"? However, there is much more than power in this sense involved in gauging the external problems of any political system. Thus Sweden and Switzerland, because of their traditional neutrality, simply do not face some of these problems today, partly because they earlier made the basic choice that they did not want to face them. The United States, as one of the strongest states left in the world, has a unique set of external problems, but the nature of these problems is determined not solely by brute strength, in military terms. Among the remaining countries, there are great similarities in external problems. The differences frequently are no more important than those in standards of living, discussed under economic problems, because all of the European countries are heirs to similar military and diplomatic traditions. These traditions affect the way in which European countries handle such problems, and the kind of personnel specializing in diplomatic and military activities. As a result, the issues arising out of external problems may be more alike from one country to the next than the content of the problems would lead us to expect. Only Germany is in a unique situation, because it was occupied by the victors of World War II and has been divided into two parts ever since. The two German states have been "sovereign" for only a relatively short time. The desire for reunification is primary in German politics today, or at least in political oratory and literature. Moreover, the problem of the division of the country is not only an external, but also a constitutional one. Because of its crucial character, it colors to some degree virtually all issues. This must be borne in mind by anyone who compares the success of recent constitutional engineering in West Germany with its counterpart in France and Italy, neither of which is divided by an iron curtain.

4. Constitutional Problems: The postwar creation of new constitutions best illustrates this class of problems. They concern the way in which other problems are to be handled—the "rules of the political game." Questions about constitutional problems should first ask how much of a constitution had to be brought into being or was to be reformed. They should inquire about the types of constitutional provisions that were needed, and the kinds of semiconstitutional rules that may have been in use in the country and could be adapted in the course of constitutional engineering. Constitutional problems are most difficult to solve when they involve the creation of a new system, as in the case of the founding of the United States, or the revolutionizing of an old one, as in that of the

French Revolution. Britain, the United States, Canada, Sweden, and Switzerland solved their more serious constitutional problems before the beginning of the twentieth century. France, Italy, and Germany did not. This accounts for many of the present-day differences between the two groups of countries. It also makes the study of the last three, and comparisons among them, particularly worth while, because it makes possible isolation of the effects of the introduction of new political institutions and procedures.

When we make comparisons for this purpose, we must consider not only that constitutional problems played a recent role in these countries, but also the timing of major sets of problems and the order in which they had to be dealt with. In Britain, for instance, the religious, constitutional, and industrialization problems came up in that order, each of them after the previous one had been largely solved. In France, by contrast, they arose almost simultaneously, which may account for the fact that none of them has ever been as successfully solved as its parallel across the English Channel.

Problems become a part of the political process as the result of decisions. They are "digested" by the political system as the result of more decisions. In the end, a "healthy" system, at least, finally disposes of each problem as the result of further decisions, and thereby makes room for the processing of new problems. This means that ideally no memories are left of any bitterness that disagreements about the proper solution to the problem may have generated. But the successful disposal of a problem should leave memories of the means used in solving it. In other words, the system learns from processing its problems, just as each of us learns from experience. The farmer who drives a car in New York City for the first time may have a few close shaves and be cursed at by cabbies. A normal man will soon forget about the cab drivers' imprecations, but his driving technique will be improved, and he can put this improvement to good use when he drives in Chicago the next year. The point is that both individuals and political systems profit from having to deal with a constant flow of varied problems. In this sense, politics itself has positive value.

The Flow of Policy

In order to be able to compare political systems with an eye to finding out which institutions perform which functions, a classification of decisions is needed that can follow a problem all the way from its initial recognition to its final removal from politics. For this purpose, the following five steps are suggested:

1. Recognition of Problem: This could be further broken down into decisions about recognizing our four types of problems, since these decisions differ. It takes one kind of choice, for instance, to recognize poverty and another to recognize the need for constitutional reform. In some countries, this function is not yet highly institutionalized and therefore has to be performed in an informal manner, possibly from the "grass roots," as by means of expressions of popular discontent or petitions. In others, it is regularly performed by stably organized interest groups. Under totalitarian regimes, some kinds of problems are regularly recognized by intelligence reports of the secret police, while in most democracies this same job is done partly by the press.

2. Statement of Issue: When people decide that there is something wrong with their present condition, that is one thing. When they or their politicians decide that there are different means of dealing with this problem, that is quite another. Moreover, an issue is often formulated which does not arise out of any "real" or objective problem. Some politicians are specialists in creating such artificial issues, perhaps for the purpose of differentiating their stand (or their followers') from that of their opponents. In some countries, artificial issues play a more important role than real issues—a situation related to what we will later describe as a highly ideological political style. Thus, for example, when the Nazis made the preservation of the purity of the "Aryan" race a principal issue of German politics, they created an artificial issue that bore little relevance to any concrete problems Germany was facing at that time.

There are different ways of stating an issue arising out of a problem. For example, the number of alternative courses of action can vary, from two to infinity. If the issue is formulated in terms of only two alternatives, these may be diametrically opposed to each other, or they may be fairly similar. In addition, the dimension of time plays a role in the formulation of issues. For example, some parliaments use procedures under which a problem, once recognized, has to be dealt with right away or not at all. Procedural and institutional peculiarities, along with the background of the personnel of politics, influence the way in which issues are stated.

This stage of stating the issue by formulating alternative solutions to a recognized problem provides opportunities for creativity to enter into the flow of policy. This is so because problems never automatically generate issues on their own, and because the specific formulation of an issue is rarely dictated by the nature of the underlying problem or by the political environment. Occasionally, an inventive politician thinks up entirely new alternatives. Pierre Mendès-France may be said to have done this when he tried to deal with some of France's economic ills and the cultural problem of alcoholism by starting a campaign to further the drinking of milk—not that he was very successful with this particular effort.

3. Deliberation: After the different alternatives have been formulated, deliberation begins. Deliberation consists of the weighing of alternatives and their likely consequences. It involves a number of closely related decisions, which are not always made in the same order and may indeed be made almost simultaneously: Both individual citizens and politicians have to select the particular alternative each is going to favor. They have to justify, both to themselves and others, the stand they take on the issue. And they may want to elicit support for their stand. In choosing the policy they intend to favor, citizens use different methods of making up their mind, depending on whether they think that their choice is one of program, representation, a government, means of expressing protest, and so on. Each of these types of choices can again be broken down further. Voters who believe themselves to be choosing among programs will go about their choice one way when they confront two or three very general programs and another when they confront a dozen highly specialized ones. This difference is illustrated by the deliberation that precedes British and French general elections. In choosing a representative, it makes a difference whether the candidates are thought of as geographical, economic, or racial representatives. In choosing a government, awareness of voting for a single leader or for part of a coalition similarly influences the method of deliberation.

In the course of deliberation, one also weighs how to justify the choice he is about to express, or may already have made. Thus, opting in favor of milk in the French case could be justified in a number of ways: national standards of health, the protection of minors, raising standards of the dairy industry, curbing activities of the winegrowers' lobby, raising the prestige of France in international politics, and perhaps still others. These decisions are strongly influenced by such historical factors as ideologies, the legal and educational system, and the type of personnel active in politics. This is also true of the choices made, especially by politicians, about eliciting support. The basic choice is between making or not making an effort to get support for one's stand; then one considers different ways of going about this. For instance, a politician who has selected a particular alternative course of action, mainly because he expected it to be the most popular one ("There goes the mob, I am its leader, I must follow it!"), might not consider it worth while to launch a campaign on its behalf. If he did want nevertheless to secure widespread popular support, he would have to make up his mind what sort of media to use—personal speeches, visits with his supporters or his opponents, press, radio, television, statements of foreign politicians, and so forth.

4. Resolution of Issue: While the weighing of alternatives that goes on during deliberation does not yet involve the exercise of "will," resolution does. In the flow of policy, this is the phase at which the transition is made from thought to action. It therefore calls for distinctive qualities in those institutions and persons who have to resolve issues. These qualities are popularly referred to as decisiveness, resoluteness, or resolution. They differ considerably from those needed in the course of deliberation. The importance of this distinction will become clear when we describe the unhappy confusion of the two functions—deliberation and resolution —in French and other Continental parliaments. In most constitutional systems, the method for resolving issues is firmly institutionalized. Decisions of this type may be made by referendum, as often in Switzerland and occasionally in Sweden; in general parliamentary elections, as in Great Britain; or in parliamentary voting, as in France before the Fifth Republic. In some countries, France among them, the decision is often made not to resolve an issue—and this too is a kind of decision.

5. Solution of Problem: The earlier illustration of the jaywalking ordinance suggests that solution requires another distinct method of making decisions. Usually, the solution of a problem involves decisions of increasingly greater detail at successively lower levels of the bureaucracy. As the detail increases, the scope of the bureaucrat's discretion narrows. The police chief may have added some general instructions to the ordinance passed by the city council before he sent it on down to the head of the traffic division. The latter could not go beyond the limits of these instructions, but had to decide in greater detail which of his men, on which shifts, whether mobile or stationary, were to apply the ordinance;

and so on down the line. If the political process operates efficiently, its problems will ultimately be solved. The problem of jaywalking would be alleviated after a period of sustained enforcement of the policy of the city council. Similarly at other levels of politics: A flood hits the New England states; the disaster problem is recognized by everyone involved, but in terms of statewide scope mainly by the governors of these states, who apply to the federal government for disaster relief, which is granted and distributed by departments of the federal government through their field agencies. The coincidence of several natural disasters in different parts of the country leads to recognition of their recurrence as a nation-wide problem, and on the initiative of congressmen, an act is passed setting up a permanent fund for disaster relief. So long as later natural catastrophes do not exceed the resources of this fund, the problem of aiding areas struck by recurrent disasters has been removed.

However, just because the problem that first gave rise to an issue has been "objectively" removed, the issue need not die. For this to happen, removal or solution of the problem has to be recognized. This may be done either tacitly or explicitly. Countries in which this function is performed poorly usually suffer from a high incidence of artificial issues —issues that are petrified memories of long-solved problems, but that still make for divisive cleavages among the population and distract attention from the real problems, present or future.

These, then, are the steps or phases through which any problem passes, as policy is made about it. The distinction between one phase and the next may not always be clear. This is true especially of very urgent problems, like an unexpected foreign attack, when all five phases appear compressed into one. But problems arising out of events in the past and those expected to arise out of events in the future both make for a slower moving flow of policy. How slowly or quickly the process moves, and how regularly, depends upon both the constitution of the system and the nature of the problems it is handling. The important thing to bear in mind is that the problems are being subjected to a *flow* of decisions. They are not being shifted mechanically from one compartment to another—from legislature to executive to the courts. If we wish to use analogies, that of a clocklike machine is no longer appropriate. It suited the notions the American Founding Fathers had about their Newtonian universe and the "machinery of government." In our own time, an electronic calculator might give a better picture of the political process. At the beginning of the process, camera-like or radar-like devices scan the horizon for new problems. These are then fed to the calculator in terms of categories with which it can work—this is how the constitution shapes the statement of issues. The solving of previous problems has "stored" in the calculator certain memories it can use in solving the current problem. It matches the issue against alternative solutions and then resolves the issue in the best possible way. At the output end of the calculator, other electronic or automation equipment may be hooked on to effect the removal of the problem. While the solution is being taken care of, the calculator continues to monitor it, until it recognizes the final disposal of the problem, whereupon it can begin to process the next one. The main respect in which the calculator differs from political systems and individuals is that it lacks inventiveness or creativity.

Individual Decisions

For the first phase of the policy flow—the recognition of problems—we can ask for the locus in time of the event about which the decision has to be made. The problem may lie mainly in the past, as in the case of some arbitrarily drawn state boundaries in the Federal Republic of Germany. Or it may be expected in the immediate future, as in the case of Premier Khrushchev's correspondence during the Middle East crisis of 1958. Or it may lie in the more remote future, as in the case of the effects of economic assistance to underdeveloped areas. The main point here is that for each phase of the policy flow, and for each kind of decision classified under the aspect of time, different methods are best suited for making the corresponding decision.

This also applies to decisions made by individual human beings. Often, we have to make a decision about an event which lies in the past: Did I misplace my book, and where? The answers amount to decisions. The question is asked after recognition of the problem. In arriving at an answer, I use methods of investigation and reasoning that differ from those I would use when deciding how to hit a tennis ball, how to drive a car, or which key to hit next on a typewriter. For the last three kinds of decisions, I use standards that I decided earlier to accept and to apply to problems requiring a more immediate and urgent solution than that of the lost book. These standards are being applied by me, perhaps because they were "built into" me, or perhaps because I formulated them myself in anticipation of later encountering the problems and having to decide about them. The faculties through which I recognize these urgent problems have to operate much more quickly than those employed in connection with my forgetfulness. Knowledge plays a role in both, but the types of knowledge differ. In the case of individual decisions about events anticipated in the future, things are again different. The methods used for making such decisions vary, as does the degree of care with which they are made. If it is a problem of tomorrow's menu, it will not be handled in the same way as next summer's trip to Europe, the selection of a home, or the purchase of a thirty-year life insurance policy.

Analogies

Before proceeding further, it may be well to anticipate—and reject— a criticism that may be raised here or at later points in this book by readers who object to "organic" analogies, to comparisons between political systems and the individual. In the first place, as used here, these analogies do not seek to establish any identity between states and individual human beings. Secondly, where decisions are made, they are ultimately made by individual men and women, because it is precisely our consciousness of our capacity to make decisions that distinguishes human beings from the rest of creation—a point the next chapter will elaborate. And thirdly, the time seems to have arrived in the evolution of the social sciences for turning the tables on the psychologists, from Plato to Freud.

It was the psychologists who began to project down to the plane of the individual categories originally used to describe society. Thus, in the classic instance of this kind of operation, Plato divided man up into "elements," which might be either harmonious or "warring." The reason for this projection must have been the same as that for projecting other social categories, such as the legal term "cause" (*aitía*), up to the planes of nature and the universe.[1] This projection was made by the same early philosophers, for whom the most important entity was not the individual but the polis, as mentioned at the outset. They projected both upward and downward from their image of the political system, because man became conscious of it before he became conscious either of man or of nature as entities distinct from the undifferentiated political system. This was entirely excusable in the case of the ancient Greeks, but it is no longer excusable for the moderns. Nowadays, society is much more obviously differentiated than the individual, who is, after all, still one unit— even when schizophrenic. The main respect in which individuals and

[1] See Werner Jaeger, *Paideia: The Ideals of Greek Culture*, 1939-44, vol. I, pp. 160 ff.

political systems resemble one another is as devices or organisms that are aware of facing problems and of having to make decisions about these problems.

To say that man is a political being means that man is a problem-facing and problem-solving being. He wants to overcome his problems and reach his goals, and he knows that he can do this only in common with other human beings. Hence he lives in communities and is a part of the political process. The more successfully a community enables its members to overcome their common problems and to become responsible for their future, the closer it comes to the goals of constitutional democracy.

CHAPTER 3

Responsibility

The Task of Political Science

The fact that men in groups are aware of facing common problems brings communities into being and sets for them the tasks of political systems. It also defines the task of political science, which is threefold: to study the realities of politics, to formulate goals, and to build bridges from the realm of reality to the realm of goals. In this chapter, we will be concerned with the second aspect of this task—the formulation of goals, values, norms, or ideals in which a community believes or, according to political philosophers, ought to believe. Any statement of prevailing values or proposal for the adoption of new goals or ideals should be made in a clear manner, which makes reference to concrete reality easy. Many of the values discussed in the literature of contemporary political science do not meet this requirement—terms like "freedom," "security," "equality," "peace," or "initiative," often mean quite different things to different men.

Unless goals are stated in clear and concrete terms, the other two aspects of the task of political science are difficult to carry out. One can hardly make systematic inquiries about political reality unless one knows what he is looking for, and this knowledge will be lacking in the man who does not know where he is going. It is even more obvious that vagueness about goals will retard efforts to close or narrow the gap between men's present condition and their aspirations. That is why the founders of political science, in addressing themselves to its triple task, devoted great efforts to value theory. It was also their reason for considering politics the most important task given to man. Similar conceptions motivated the great political scientists of later ages—men like Thomas

Hobbes, Jean Jacques Rousseau, the authors of the Federalist Papers, Jeremy Bentham, or Woodrow Wilson. By contrast, whenever either the first (analytical) or the second (normative) part of their task has been neglected, as by medieval theologians or modern positivists, the product has been relatively worthless. Mediocre political science has usually been turned out in periods when politics was not considered a very important activity. This was true, for instance, during the Middle Ages, when even philosophy was looked upon as handmaiden to theology. It was true in many places during the nineteenth century, when economics —the "dismal" science, as it was called—reigned supreme in the minds of many, because they saw business activity as the main road to human progress. In our own time, politics is again coming to the forefront, if for no other reason than the feasibility of the destruction of mankind. Because of the return of politics to preëminence, a clear statement of its purpose is needed.

Power and Legitimacy

But how can agreement be found on the purpose of politics? Traditionally, students of politics have agreed that the functions of politics revolve around "power." That is why the analytical study of politics has concentrated on phenomena of power—its pursuit, its concentration, controls upon its exercise, its distribution, and so on. The main question for political philosophy, as the corollary of power, has been that of legitimacy: How can obedience to governmental power be justified? Today, these terms no longer appear useful.

"Power" has already been criticized once in passing, on our detour to paradise. As an analytical concept, it has lost much of its former attractiveness, and for two reasons: In successful constitutional democracies, power has been stabilized to such an extent that we can learn little about a country by looking at its power structure—even assuming that agreement could be reached on the meaning of the term. Hobbes provided its classical definition, "present means to obtain some future apparent Good." And this leads to the second reason—drawn from contemporary world politics—for the lowered usefulness of the term. In an age of intercontinental ballistic missiles, even brute military strength has ceased to be "power," because a nuclear world war would clearly bring no "good" to either side.

Legitimacy, too, is no longer a central question, and for similar reasons. People simply do not ask themselves—at least in the constitutional democracies we are studying here—"Why do I obey the government?" They do ask themselves, "How were central political decisions made? By whom? Will I be exposed to their effects? Did I have any opportunities to contribute to them? Will I have opportunities to contribute to central decisions to be made in the future?"

Policy and Authority

Because of these changes, the concepts of power and legitimacy should be replaced by the concepts of *policy* and *authority*. The notion of policy as a series of decisions was explained in the last chapter. Authority is here conceived of as the normative counterpart of policy. It is concentrated at those points in a political system where its dominant values are reflected in the most representative fashion. These are the points at which are made decisions or policies that will be accepted by those people who will be affected by their consequences. Much of what happens to human beings, of course, is not due to decisions at all, but is the outcome of a "concourse of natural causes." And much of what does happen to them as a result of human decisions is not the direct product of their own decisions, but of the decisions of others. Authority is a kind of "additive" to policies about our fate, which leads us to accept them, even though they are made by others. But is there some content of authority on which fairly general agreement could be achieved? In other words, even if we do get agreement that the *function* of politics consists of making policies about problems, could we get a similar consensus on the *purpose* of politics? We certainly need some such consensus, if we are to establish criteria in terms of which to evaluate different constitutional systems.

In searching for agreement on the content of authority, we may find a clue in the increase in constitution-building itself. A great deal of this went on in classical antiquity, but very little in the Middle Ages. Since their end, as Jacob Burckhardt pointed out, constitutional engineering has been constantly growing in frequency and scope.[1] He noticed it in the Italian Renaissance mainly because of the *frequency* of constitutional tinkering. The construction of constitutions of *scope,* in the modern sense, however, had its beginnings in the English Civil Wars of the seventeenth century. Preoccupation with constitution-writing comes to the fore especially in the Putney Debates, in which Oliver Cromwell and representatives of his regiments discussed the Agreement of the People; the first though abortive attempt at an English written constitution; and in Cromwell's speeches about his Instrument of Govern-

[1] See footnote, p. 11.

ment, England's only and short-lived written constitution. The next wave of constitution-making occurred during the American struggle for independence—in the Declaration, the state constitutions, the Constitution of the United States, and some of Chief Justice Marshall's early opinions. During the same period, the French Revolution set off even more constitution-making in Europe. And since then, it has been going on all over the world.

Cromwell and his followers were the first to cut themselves off from the old fountain of legitimacy when they used brute power to cut off King Charles's head. The old fountain of legitimacy had been tradition. Cromwell could not appeal to it, since he had so dramatically violated tradition. Therefore he appealed—among other sources that he tried to tap—to the consent of the governed. Cromwell and his followers, as the new rulers, wanted the governed to share with them the new responsibility they had assumed for the course of England's future. And why had they assumed this responsibility? Because new values that had become dominant after the Reformation no longer let people accept as inevitable a natural, unplanned, unengineered course of events. Men were beginning to believe then, as they still believe today, that they could shape their fate, mold their future, and become responsible for themselves to a very large extent, and certainly to a greater extent than in earlier times.

The Increase in Responsibility

In this sense, one can look at modern history as the history of man's increasing responsibility for his future. There can be no doubt that today much more is subject to human choice, to the making of decisions, than in any past epoch. This is true of nature, of society, and of the individual. In primitive societies, men accept most of what happens to them as lying completely beyond their control. They react, but do not act, in pursuit of any goals that could be termed long range. Things were not quite that bad in the Middle Ages. Nevertheless, the contrast between this pre-constitution-building period and our own is marked. Today, men in the West and in other spheres of influence of Western philosophy—and that includes the Marxist orbit—think that virtually all problems can be subjected to decisions, to policy. We believe that practically everything about individuals, society, and nature can be changed, shaped, molded, influenced, channeled, or in some way subjected to human choice. Individuals can make decisions previously considered impossible about their health, appearance, their friends and mates, their children and careers, and their location on the globe—or in outer space. Communities nowadays make analogous choices, and when they do, it is—by definition—through the political process.

The "Situation of Responsibility"

This increase in human responsibility has come about as the result of the creation of more—and more meaningful—alternatives, of better control over natural and social resources, and of superior knowledge about the consequences of human actions. Men can become responsible for their future to the extent that three conditions are met: First, there must be alternatives among which to choose. Second, resources must be given with which to implement the choice. And third, there must be some foreknowledge of the probable effects of the decision. A perfect "situation of responsibility," in this sense, is impossible. Persistent limits are set to the alternative courses of action we can choose. Our resources are always restricted. And our foreknowledge of the outcome of our actions must always remain merely probable. Only adherents of ideologies—closed, comprehensive, consistent systems of knowledge purporting to provide solutions to all questions—would deny this last restriction on our capacity for responsibility. Only fools would deny that our resources—physiological and psychological, social, institutional, and natural—are always limited. And no one but a madman could deny the first restriction, because we never can have the alternative (among other unavailable ones) to undo the past.

Despite this unattainability of the perfect situation of responsibility —and partly because of it—this concept can serve as a useful standard for judging political systems. The increase in constitution-making itself, which has just been sketched, suggests that the value of responsibility is central to theories of constitutional democracy. The same indication comes from the great number of prominent thinkers who could agree on this as the lowest common denominator of values, although they are often in radical and even violent disagreement on other questions and although they come from a great diversity of specialized fields of study: Reinhold Niebuhr, Karl Barth, Martin Buber, Erich Fromm, Jean-Paul Sartre, José Ortega y Gasset, Karl Mannheim, Alfred Weber, Chester I. Barnard, Stuart Chase, Hans Kelsen, Philip Selznick, Karl Jaspers, Carl J. Friedrich, Karl R. Popper, and many others.[2] All of them could agree that the individual should, within the limits of the possible, seek to be-

[2] See Herbert J. Spiro, "Responsibility in Citizenship, Government, and Administration," *Public Policy,* vol. IV (1953), pp. 116-33.

come responsible for his own fate. As a member of vast human organizations, he can assume this responsibility only by contributing to those central decisions whose consequences will in turn affect him. The norm of individual responsibility thus demands that citizens be given such opportunities for policy contributions and, further, that these contributions be proportionate to the extent to which the contributors will be affected by or exposed to the consequences of the policies.

Even Robinson Crusoe on his island, before the arrival of his man Friday, was living in an imperfect situation of responsibility. These limitations are multiplied many times by the complexity and internal interdependence among the parts of modern political systems, where a great many decisions have to be made centrally. The increasing centralization of the making of decisions seems an inescapable process. And in terms of the norm of individual responsibility, some of its concomitants seem desirable. Thus, in a laissez faire economy, decision-making about economic problems is highly decentralized. Individuals, therefore, appear to exercise a high degree of responsibility for their economic future. But depressions and inflations have demonstrated that the choices they make are among a multiplicity of unclear alternatives, with unsatisfactory resources for implementation, and virtually no foreknowledge of the consequences. In the end, great unemployment or some similar economic catastrophe may occur, in which millions of individuals are in effect held accountable for something that was none of their responsibility, for a course of events that they did not deliberately help to bring about. In the United States, measures such as establishment of the Securities and Exchange Commission and passage of the Employment Act of 1946 have helped to improve the individual's situation of responsibility in this respect.

Measures like these have often been interpreted as steps on the road to collectivism or socialism, and the increase in constitution-making could be interpreted in the same way. This would lead to the conclusion that political systems, as collectivities, do indeed exercise greater responsibility now than in the past, but that this increase in communal responsibility has been accompanied by a decrease in individual responsibility. The Soviet Union could be cited as an example to support this contention. Under collectivism, Russia has certainly been better able to plan its future, but many individual Russians face fewer alternatives today than before the Revolution. Yet even the Soviet Communists assert, along with other, less totalitarian Marxists, that it is their aim to establish perfect individual responsibility in the classless society of the future, "in which the free development of each is the condition for

the free development of all," in the concluding words of the program-
matic section of the *Communist Manifesto*. In terms of final aims, therefore, the Communists could agree with the norm of individual responsibility. But we would disagree with them about the collectivistic means
by which they propose to reach the goal. Whether particular policies,
like the Employment Act, are acceptable from the point of view of the
norm of individual responsibility has to be determined on the basis of
questions derived from the norm itself.

Another factor commends the concept of the situation of responsibility even more than our interpretation of increase in constitution-
making or the advocacy of individual responsibility by contemporary
thinkers. It is the fact that from this concept we can derive concrete
questions to ask of concrete political institutions and procedures in order
to compare the extent to which they fulfill the demands of constitutional
and democratic values. Moreover, the norm of individual responsibility
is such that very few of our contemporaries would reject it—at least
publicly. Even most Marxists would accept it as an ultimate goal. Only
fascists and other avowed elitists, and adherents of certain non-Western
fatalistic or nonindividualistic philosophies, would reject it. For these
reasons, we may be hopeful that wide agreement can be achieved on the
authority of policies that are made in conformity with the demands of
the norm of individual responsibility. But what kind of questions should
we ask in order to find out about this?

1. Alternatives: What kind of choices are available to citizens? The
spectrum of possible political systems in terms of this question runs all
the way from the totally regimented state, in which no alternatives would
be available, to a condition of anarchy, in which alternatives would be
virtually unlimited—and in which men would probably go mad as a
result. These are extremes that have never existed in reality, but some
strongly bureaucratized states have gone far toward the choiceless extreme, while some periods of chaos and anarchy have approached the
opposite pole of unlimited choices.

Constitutional democracy lies at the midpoint between the two
ends of the spectrum. It provides alternatives in different forms: policies
to be chosen in elections, referenda, plebiscites; the choice of governors
or representatives; the choice of membership in organizations devoted to
the general or some special interest; the alternatives of protest or non-
participation; and others.

The individual citizen has many opportunities to make decisions on
alternatives. Some of them may not be "political" at all. Each of us as-

sumes responsibility for his own fate in all of his or her choices—most obviously in the more important ones, some of which have been mentioned by way of analogy: choices of ethic, career, husband or wife, residence, and so forth. But as the society grows tighter and its component parts more and more interdependent, our most important decisions are increasingly about contributions to a centralized process of making policies, through alternatives of the kind just enumerated.

2. *Resources:* What are the resources available for implementing these choices? To begin with, there is once more the "raw material" of the political system, which is also the soil out of which its problems grow —the problems about which decisions have to be made. Thus, in the United States, the frontier created problems of communication, largely of an economic nature, as obstacles between the pioneers and their goal of civilizing virgin lands. Along with these problems, however, the frontier also presented them with many of the resources through which they could implement their choices and realize their goal: rivers, horses, lumber, and eventually iron with which to build railroads and coal to serve as fuel.

Resources may, therefore, be classified under the same headings as problems themselves: economic, cultural, external, and constitutional. Under this last category would come the institutional resources available for implementing policies—parliaments, parties, bureaucracies. In centralized modern political systems, those institutional resources are very important through which the persons to be affected can hold to account the makers of central policy decisions. In this connection, we would also want to ask about the distribution of resources available for the implementation of choice within the system. For example, farmers are especially affected by agricultural policy, though they are of course not the only citizens who benefit or suffer from the consequences of centrally made policy in this field. This raises two sets of questions, one about the availability of channels through which farmers can implement choices made by them about farm policy, the other about the proportion or balance between these institutional resources and the extent to which farmers are especially affected. This is of interest, because the availability of excessive resources to any special interest could be no more condoned, from the point of view of the norm of responsibility, than insufficient resources.

Resources and alternatives mutually limit each other, since no choice would be meaningful that fails to take into account the limits set to resources with which the decision can be implemented. These limits to resources are always given, and any choice which fails to take them into consideration would be irresponsible. Conversely, available resources not used in the service of policy-making might as well not exist at all, just like problems that remain unrecognized.

3. *Knowledge:* This mutual interdependence also applies to the third condition of sound situations of responsibility: foreknowledge of the likely consequences of one's choice. Without any attention to these effects, the choice would be meaningless—it would not, in fact, be a choice at all. The knowledge is about the "behavior" of the resources. It, too, is always less than complete, especially when it is knowledge about human responses to human decisions. Only adherents of ideologies —total systems of knowledge—pretend to have certain foreknowledge of the consequences of human actions. That is why choices based upon ideologies have to be rejected as irresponsible. For instance, the Marxists who supported Hitler's attack on the constitutional democracy of the Weimar Republic, because they "knew" that fascism was the last stage of monopoly capitalism—before the proletarian revolution and socialism —were acting irresponsibly, because they assumed themselves in possession of perfect knowledge.

The two components, resources and knowledge, overlap in the realm of law, particularly in the sphere of fundamental constitutional law. The rule of law and the stability of the rules of the political game provide citizens with foreknowledge of the likely consequences of their own actions and those of others. Here the spectrum runs from the fully bureaucratized state, in which the whole future is foreordained, to either anarchy or perfect totalitarianism, with constitutional democracy once more at the midpoint. Under the model form of complete bureaucratization, citizens would have perfect knowledge of the future, but no opportunities whatsoever to make any choices. Under anarchy, there would be no way of anticipating the results of one's choices, for which infinite alternatives would be available. Perfect totalitarianism—from the point of view of its subjects, not of its rulers—would also exclude any foreknowledge of the consequences of one's actions, which in its case would be based on a minimum of alternatives. Under totalitarian regimes, actions that earn official commendation today may be condemned as criminal or treasonable tomorrow. Neither of these models of extremes has ever existed. They show the mutual interdependence of the two components of responsible action: knowledge and alternatives. They also point up the midway position of constitutional and democratic government. There, the rule of law provides foreknowledge. A high degree of pub-

licity enables citizens to anticipate the consequences of alternative policies. Strongly developed social sciences—and especially political science
—also help.

Responsible Action

Responsible action, therefore, is based upon a choice among alternatives, with use of the available resources, in anticipation of its likely
consequences and the readiness to accept them. A sound situation exists
for the individual when he has optimum opportunities to make such
choices in contributing to central decisions whose consequences will in
turn affect him—and in a measure proportionate to the extent that he
will be affected. The basic goal of constitutional democracy is here conceived of as the creation of better situations of responsibility. In terms
of this goal, we can evaluate the intentions of the builders of modern
constitutions, as well as the effects of institutions and procedures operating within political systems. One could also judge specific policies by this
criterion, because it is the observance of procedures of responsibility
that lends authority to policy. In this book, however, we are less interested in the content of specific policies than in the methods by which
different governments make policy. Specific substantive policies are intended to solve specific and relatively transient problems, such as an economic recession or a foreign threat. The consideration of problems of
this kind and subsequent decisions is not, for our purposes, a profitable
task: immediate problems, and decisions with regard to them, are subject to far more rapid change than are the *methods* by which a political
system deals with the various situations that require action on its part.

From the norm of individual responsibility, we will draw the questions to ask about political systems, when we compare them with one
another. This means that we will have to examine them under all three
aspects—alternatives, resources, and knowledge—keeping their mutual
interdependence in mind. This should give us a double advantage: It will
enable us to make the comparisons in concrete terms, systematically relating determined and created factors. And it will enable us to refer
constitutional politics back to the individual human beings, without whom
there would be no values in the world.

Critique and Defense of Responsibility

Before returning to our main task from this excursion into the field of
normative theory, we should deal with an objection that may be forming

itself in the mind of the critical reader. It relates to the admitted un-attainability of our ultimate standard of evaluation, the perfect situation of responsibility. The critic would agree that, as a goal, our concept of individual responsibility seems desirable. His difficulty with it, however, would be twofold. In the first place, he would question whether a system of government genuinely dedicated to the full realization of individual responsibility could survive in a struggle with others based on the sup-pression, exploitation, and collectivization of the individual. Specifically, in the contemporary struggle between the West (consisting largely of an alliance of constitutional democracies) and Soviet totalitarianism, he would question whether continued pursuit of the goal of individual re-sponsibility would make the Western countries less efficient than their collectivist opponents. And secondly, he might attack the norm itself as wholly unrealistic. As a matter of fact, the critic would probably con-tinue, most individuals in the world today do not want to bear the bur-den of responsibility you would impose upon them for their own fate and that of their fellows. They are afraid of this responsibility, seek to escape from it, do not want to have to make choices, and prefer to exchange the uncertainties of the persistently limited knowledge of which we have been writing for the certainties of modern ideologies, like communism and fascism. That is why they have repeatedly in the last half-century handed over to a great leader, who would not be account-able to them, the determination of their destinies.

How can we counter these two objections? As to the first, concern-ing the alleged inefficiency of responsible government, there is the histori-cal fact that constitutional democracies have defeated totalitarian dicta-torships in the past, notably in World War II. Throughout the following chapters, we will have occasion to test the relative efficiency of responsi-ble and unresponsible governments. We will ask, for example, about the advantages and disadvantages of letting individuals who have some spe-cial interest in a field of policy contribute to that policy, of letting indi-viduals make decisions alone or in committees, e.g., in cabinets. These tests will lead us to the conclusion that responsible methods are indeed more efficient.

As to the second objection, about the yearning of the "mass man" —as our critic would call the individual in contemporary "mass soci-eties"—we can reply that it is precisely the reaction to the catastrophic consequences of dictatorial leadership that has generated all the current advocacy of the norm of individual responsibility. The thinkers we men-tioned seem to agree that the great economic and political catastrophes of the twentieth century might have been averted if individual citizens had not resigned their own fate into the hands of men like Hitler, accountable only to that vague entity, History. Thus, it is the disastrous effects of the very assumptions of those who deny the individual's capacity to become responsible for his own fate that lie at the roots of the current flood of "responsibilitarian" literature.

Our critics will consider these justifications of our conception of the basic value of constitutional democracy rather flimsy, beause they sound too pragmatic. After all, perhaps it can be demonstrated that nonresponsible government *is* more efficient. And whether the depression and the two World Wars could have been prevented simply by more responsible conduct is doubtful, to say the least. Suppose, then, that all our arguments failed. Would we still adhere to our view of the citizen's capacity for responsibility? The answer is a firm *Yes.* If necessary, we would continue to adhere to it purely on the basis of faith—a faith that, in rational terms, is neither more nor less defensible than our critics' attacks. On the basis of this faith, to put it very bluntly, we prefer to see people go to hell under their own steam than to see them taken to paradise or some other utopia when they themselves cannot be responsible for their ascent.

"Success" of Constitutions

Part II will consist of descriptions of the political systems on which this study is based: their constitutional history and present constitutional structure; their major current problems and the main issues in their politics. Before we begin these descriptions, we should again fix in our minds what it is that a political system does, and also what any government that claims to be constitutional and democratic ought to seek to accomplish. A political system deals with the problems its members believe themselves to be facing. The purpose of constitutional democracy is to do this in a way that will make for sound situations of responsibility for all concerned, by enabling citizens to make responsible contributions to the policy flow. In order to achieve this, the system must be *stable, adaptable, efficient,* and *effective.*

Our initial comparison, in the thumbnail sketches that follow, will be cast in terms of these four criteria. By *stability,* we mean continuity over time. In this sense, the American Constitution has been more stable than the French. Stability is, therefore, a condition for the element of foreknowledge of the norm of responsibility. By *adaptability,* we mean the capacity to adjust to changes in the environment. Great Britain was more adaptable in her colonial policy than France. By *efficiency,* we mean the relation between the "input" of problems and the "output" of policies. In this sense, the Federal Republic of Germany has been more efficient than the Weimar Republic which preceded it. And the federal bureaucracy in the United States is more efficient now than it was in 1900. Without efficiency, the component of resources would detract from the individual's capacity for contributing to policy. By *effectiveness,* finally, we mean the acceptance given by the citizenry to the constitutional order and to the policies it produces. In this sense, the Canadian constitution is more effective today than it was during the years up to World War I, when many French-Canadians accepted it, and pro-British policies made under it, with great reluctance. Ineffective government is often due to the feeling, on the part of those who do not accept it, that they are not being provided with adequate alternatives for choice; thus, in the case just cited, many French-Canadians refused to accept conscription for military service. They felt that alternative policies had not been given fair consideration.

We will compare these eight governments in terms of their stability, adaptability, efficiency, and effectiveness—the four measures of the "success" of any constitution. Our main purpose for doing this is to determine contributions made to success or failure by deliberately created, rationally engineered institutions and procedures. Our central focus is the feasibility of constitutional engineering. Meanwhile, we should not forget that success in constitution-building in and of itself is not necessarily desirable. It may produce the stability of stagnation, or of Pharaonic Egypt. It may adapt itself to the recently dominant value of racial hatred. It may provide the efficiency suggested by the self-image of Himmler's SS—in running concentration camps, in terrorizing and liquidating millions. Or it may result in the effectiveness of governments during the Middle Ages, which were accepted simply because the possibility of alternative governments never occurred to anyone. This is why we have had to try to formulate our values clearly, so that we would be able not only to compare in terms of success and of realization of the intentions of constitution-makers but also to judge these intentions themselves in terms of the universal goals of constitutional democracy.

PART II

Eight Political Systems

CHAPTER 4

Sweden

Constitutional History

The roots of both the Swedish people and the Swedish state lie deeply imbedded in the past. They are roots that can easily be traced to their "seedtime," because they are relatively unentangled with other peoples or other states. Besides, Sweden has enjoyed a very steady constitutional evolution, jolted by very few radical changes—none of these since the sixteenth century (at least there has been no civil war in Sweden since 1598). "Radical" means "going to the roots," and there may be readers who do consider "radical" some of the constitutional changes in Sweden since that time. Whether this view has merit, and just what it is that amounts to basic constitutional change—these are questions that will have to be deferred until we reach a discussion of "Consensus" in Part VI. What concerns us here is the general pattern of constitutional development in the eight countries under study, of which Sweden is the first. Comparison of this pattern will enable us to consider explanations of differences among them.

If one were to project the general pattern for each nation onto a graph, employing a smooth and rising curve to indicate that the political system dealt successfully with successive sets of problems, Sweden's line would be one of the smoothest and longest. It would be smooth because there has been little wholesale constitutional engineering and few revolutions. And it would be long because of the deep roots of both people and state. In both respects, Sweden is obviously older than the United States of America, whose system of government dates from 1788, and whose territory began to be settled by Europeans in the 1600's. When Pilgrims and Puritans landed in America, the Swedish kingdom had already been a going concern for three centuries, and its people were conscious of their descent from ancestors who had lived continuously in Sweden even longer.

Consciousness of continuity with a long past, in this sense, is naturally stronger in all of the European countries than in either the United States or Canada. But it is particularly strong in Sweden, because of its peninsular location on the rim of the Continent. This protected it against the frequent invasions and consequent intermixing of tribes and peoples, a repeated occurrence in Germany, France, and Italy. Only insular Britain has been similarly shielded, but the late union of Scotland and England, at the beginning of the seventeenth century, gave that political system at least two trunk roots, contrasted with Sweden's one. The valleys of the Swiss Alps were also like islands, so that the same families have lived in the same valleys for centuries. However, because of the slow accretion of the Swiss Confederation, the feeling of continuity of people and state does not reach as deep there as it does in Sweden.

This feature of historical continuity should be remembered in judging the success of the Swedish constitution. It means in effect that there was much less of a job to be done when the Swedes did get around to adopting written constitutional documents than was the case, for example, in the United States or in Germany. When the first national German constitution was created, in 1871, one of its most important tasks was to provide a framework of institutions for a diversity of previously independent states with different traditions. No Swedish constitution ever faced this task.

The present Swedish constitution consists of four documents, the oldest two dating back to 1809 and 1810. It is, therefore, usually called the second oldest written constitution operating in the world today. The oldest, of course, is that of the United States. But the fact that the birth dates of these two constitutions were only twenty-two years apart does not by itself suggest much resemblance between them, since the American Founding Fathers had to start so much more nearly from scratch than their Swedish contemporaries, who could not properly be called founding fathers at all.

The earliest of the four documents comprising Sweden's constitution, the Instrument of Government of 1809, was adopted after the deposition of King Gustaf IV Adolf, following Sweden's defeat in war by Russia. In many respects, it brought up to date earlier Instruments of Government of 1719 and 1720—once more a sign of the continuity of the Swedish constitution. The Swedish word we translate as "Instrument of Government" is *grundlager,* which does not mean "constitution," but comes closer to the German *Grundgesetz,* the "Basic Law" that governs the Federal Republic of Germany today. *Grund* in both cases is related to the English word "ground." The Instrument of Government of 1809 does lay down ground rules for relations among the most important organs of Swedish government—the King; his council; and Parliament, which is usually referred to by the Swedish word *Riksdag.*

The second part of the constitution, the Act of Succession of 1810, was adopted when Napoleon's Marshal Bernadotte was elected Crown Prince of Sweden; under it members of the Bernadotte dynasty have succeeded to the Swedish throne ever since. Third is the Riksdag Act of 1865, which in effect amended parts of the Instrument of Government dealing with Parliament. Until adoption of the Riksdag Act, the Swedish Parliament had consisted of four chambers, one for each of the four estates of the realm: nobles, clergy, burghers, and peasants. As the result of its passage, the Riksdag became bicameral—as are all the other parliaments with which we will be dealing.

While the Riksdag Act was adopted only after considerable controversy, at times bordering on violence, passage of the youngest of the four constitutional documents was relatively uncontroversial. This is the Freedom of the Press Act of 1949, the latest in a series of such Acts, dated 1812, 1810, and 1766. This building on old documents, and on unwritten customs that are often even older, is the main characteristic that emerges from either a cursory or a detailed study of Swedish constitutional history. Important changes have been few and far between and, in the last two centuries, each one has been brought about without the use of violence.

Constitutional Structure

Sweden is a constitutional monarchy, as are two others among our eight countries—the United Kingdom and Canada. The Swedish King— according to the Act of Succession, only males may inherit the throne— reigns but does not rule. Day-to-day government is carried on by the Cabinet, whose Premier is selected by the King. Members of the Cabinet need not be members of Parliament, and there have been so-called "Cabinets of experts" consisting of nonmembers. The Swedish Cabinet, unlike that of France or of England, is not dependent for its survival in office upon the support of a parliamentary majority. Although the Cabinets usually represent a coalition majority in the Riksdag, Cabinets have often continued to hold office in the face of an adverse majority. Under the terms of the constitution, the King may dissolve either or both houses of Parliament. In practice, this has been done rarely out of season since 1921, and only on the request of the Premier. Regular elections to the popular chamber occur each leap year; when dissolved in advance, a special election is held, but the new chamber then merely serves out the remainder of this four-year term.

The popularly elected chamber consists of 230 members. Reversing usual practice, this lower house is in Sweden called the "second" chamber. Its members are elected directly, under a system of proportional representation introduced in 1909. There are twenty-eight constituencies, each of which has anywhere between three and twenty-four deputies. The 230 seats are reapportioned among the constituencies every four years on the basis of population changes.

The 150 senators of the upper, "first" chamber of the Riksdag are elected indirectly, for eight-year terms, by provincial assemblies. These assemblies are grouped in nineteen senatorial constituencies, and these in turn make up eight groups, each of which elects its senators in successive years, so that roughly one-eighth of the upper chamber is renewed every year. The provincial assemblies that perform these elections are themselves directly elected every four years. The upper and lower chambers have equal powers, in contrast with all the other countries but Italy.

Referenda, which are constitutionally possible, are held occasionally, but not at the same time as parliamentary elections. Constitutional amendments must be passed by two successive parliaments, with a general election intervening.

Problems

Sweden probably faces fewer and milder economic problems than any of the other seven systems. One important reason for this is her slow and gradual industrialization; another is the still predominantly non-urban distribution of the population (only 35 per cent live in cities of more than 25,000). By American standards, most Swedish industrial employers operate on a small scale, the average enterprise employing fewer than fifty workers. The Swedish standard of living is the highest in Europe and one of the highest in the world.

There are few serious cultural problems facing the Swedes in the middle of the twentieth century. More than 99 per cent of them speak Swedish as their mother tongue. Practically all belong to the Lutheran state church; in a total population of over 7 million, there are only about 26,000 Roman Catholics in the whole country. The average level of schooling is very high. So is the incidence of alcoholism, divorce, and illegitimacy, which seem to be the only serious contemporary problems that should be considered under this heading.

Sweden used to be one of the "great powers." Today, her external problems are defined by the close proximity of the Soviet Union. While the two countries do not share a common boundary, Sweden's neighbor, Finland, has been exposed militarily to the Soviet Union since its defeat in the Russo-Finnish war of 1939. In addition, there are thousands of miles of Baltic coastline to guard against possible attack from Communist countries bordering on the Baltic Sea. These include Poland, East Germany, the Soviet Union itself, and the three former Baltic republics incorporated into it after World War II—Lithuania, Latvia, and Estonia. Defense against her western neighbor, Norway, is no problem, since relations between these two Scandinavian kingdoms have been excellent; in fact, they shared the same king until the beginning of the present century. Relations with Denmark have also been good. Nevertheless, both of these neighboring sister realms could potentially create defense problems for Sweden, as they did under German occupation between 1940 and 1945.

Sweden faces no constitutional problems at this time. For all practical purposes, there is no opposition to the monarchy. The existing relations among King, Cabinet, Riksdag, parties, and electorate are widely accepted. People generally believe that their constitutional system is best suited for the tasks it should perform for them.

Issues and Politics

In view of this paucity of serious problems, we should expect a similar paucity of divisive issues in Swedish politics. In fact, the logic of our approach would lead us to expect Swedish politics to be rather dull. And so it is—by far less lively than in any other country discussed in this book. However, Swedish politics has not always been so dull, nor has it been that way for very long. The heated controversy preceding reform of the Riksdag in 1865 has already been mentioned. After adoption of the Riksdag Act, things went on in a very animated fashion. The major issues were reorganization of the defense establishment, the tariff, extension of suffrage, temperance legislation, electoral law, the royal prerogative, and accountability of the Cabinet to the Riksdag. Universal manhood suffrage was not extended until 1909, after a prolonged struggle. Universal male and female franchise, without property qualifications, for voting in both local and Riksdag elections did not come until after the end of World War I. It was during this war, in which Sweden was neutral, that the issue of the King's prerogative in defense matters was also finally settled, not in his favor. The settlement was not reflected in amendments of the Instrument of Government. Not until the 1950's was a commission appointed for the purpose of bringing the constitution up to date with practice. And in 1959, after four years of studying the problem, this commission reported in favor of further postponement of formal amendment.

New problems became the raw material for Swedish politics in the 1920's. Most important among these were economic and external ones, in that order. By 1920, the Social Democrats were the largest party represented in the Riksdag, and the problem of ownership of industry was introduced as an issue by them. They also advocated construction of a comprehensive system of social security. On both of these issues, they were opposed by the Conservatives and the Liberals, who were mainly concerned, respectively, with economy in government and strengthening national defense. The fourth major Swedish party, the Peasants, took their stand wherever they thought it would help the farmers. Cabinets were unstable during this period; most of them were supported by minorities in the Riksdag and resigned because of defeat in one or both of its chambers.

The Great Depression changed this. It began to affect Sweden in 1931, with the result that the election of 1932 brought gains to the Social Democrats and the Agrarians. A Socialist minority government was formed, which stayed in office until 1936. During the beginning of its term, the main issues arose out of the economic problems of the Depression. These were dealt with successfully, whereupon new issues became central, among them laws governing strikes, and then defense policy once again. For a period of three months in 1936, a minority Cabinet of the Peasant party was in office, to be replaced by a Socialist-Peasant coalition. Since then, the Social Democrats have dominated all cabinets— alone or in coalition either with the Peasants or with all three other major parties during the war years. The main issues have concerned economic and social security. World War II did not materially change this. But the seriousness of the problems has declined, and with it the intensity of feeling on the issues.

Nor did World War II increase the importance of issues arising out of external problems. Sweden had remained neutral in the first World War. One reason for this was the unsettled condition, in 1914, of the controversy about the defense establishment, which had played a divisive role ever since reform of the Riksdag. More important was the genuine and fairly widespread desire not to become embroiled, a desire which was all the stronger because many Swedes had friendly relations with both Germans and British. (Sweden also fortunately lacked the ethnic minority problems, the imperial rivalries, and the geographical proximity that drew some of the other Continental countries into the war.) Neutrality raised many supply questions during World War I years, but these were more or less successfully dealt with by making concessions, at one time to the Central Powers, at another to the Allies. (Indeed, on balance, Sweden's economic gain from the war was a substantial one, incidentally.)

After the Russian Revolution, the Swedish government permitted Swedish volunteers to join the Finns in their fight for independence from Russia, which was a fight against the Red Army, and issues arising out of this action were debated for some years thereafter. Though some Conservatives tacitly sympathized with Imperial Germany, people were by and large agreed on the neutrality policy. The defeat of Germany and her allies undoubtedly contributed to the full-fledged establishment of democracy in Sweden after the end of the war.

During World War II, even this vestige of divided sympathies was lacking, especially after the German invasion and occupation of Denmark and Norway. No National Socialists were ever elected to the Riksdag. The Swedes dealt with the problems arising out of the war by forming a broad coalition cabinet of the four major parties and by trying to maintain their neutrality as best they could. This involved the making of considerable concessions to Germany on several occasions, but in the end it achieved its goal. Neutrality has been maintained since then, even in the age of nuclear weapons. Sweden, unlike Switzerland, has joined the United Nations—and indeed provided its second Secretary-General—but she has stayed out of the North Atlantic Treaty Organization. Although Swedish sympathies lie definitely with the West, this issue did not generate a great deal of partisan debate. The more recent problem, whether to provide the Swedish armed forces with nuclear weapons, was treated in a characteristic way. Such armament was planned for, but parliamentary resolution of the issue was postponed for as long as possible, while the issue was still potentially explosive. When the debate does start, fairly strong agreement on what to do about this problem will probably exist.

There are still some problems with which the Swedes believe they have to deal. Alcoholism is one of these, and there have been several referenda since the end of World War I about issues arising out of this: whether to have prohibition, what kind of liquor rationing to have or keep. And although in the past prohibition parties have been active in Swedish politics, this is no longer a truly partisan issue today. The same applies to the problem—perhaps it should be classified as cultural—of left-hand driving. Sweden is one of the few countries in the world that still maintain this nonconformist custom. The issue of changing the law was submitted to the voters in a referendum in 1955 and defeated.

Political parties and interest organizations play roles of apparently equal importance in the first three stages of the Swedish political process, that is, from recognition of problems through deliberation. Often it is difficult to distinguish between a party and the interest organization associated with it. This question is further complicated by the "joining" habit, which is strongly developed among the Swedes. In 1949-50, the memberships of the Swedish Federation of Labor, the Central Organization of Salaried Employees, and the Swedish Farming Organization together accounted for more than three-fourths of the gainfully employed population.[1] In addition to these groups, there are numerous strong cultural organizations, such as church and educational associations and temperance societies. The Federation of Labor is closely allied with the Social Democratic party, some of its affiliated unions providing for automatic membership in the party for their members. Similar relations exist between the consumers' coöperatives and the Social Democrats. The employers' associations naturally tend to favor the Conservatives. The Liberals' electoral support largely overlaps that of the temperance and sectarian societies, and in the 1920's one branch of the then-split Liberal party was actually referred to as "Prohibitionist." There is also an overlap between the officers of the parties and the interest organizations, to the point that leaders of interest groups become Cabinet ministers.

The relative strength of the political parties has been fairly stable in recent years, with the total popular vote divided more or less along the following lines:

Party	per cent
Social Democrats	45
Liberals	20
Conservatives	15
Peasants	10
Communists	5

The Communists have been marginal and have achieved little influence either among the parties or through the trade unions.

[1] Dankwart A. Rustow, *The Politics of Compromise*, 1955, p. 154.

The function of resolving issues has been performed jointly by Riksdag and Cabinet, except on issues submitted directly to the electorate by referendum. Since a Cabinet that is defeated in the Riksdag need not resign, it holds the upper hand when it comes to resolution. The solution of problems is taken care of by the very efficient bureaucracy, which has ancient traditions of honesty and legality (Dag Hammarskjöld, the Secretary-General of the United Nations, is one of its products). Partly because of this efficiency, when issues are once resolved they are automatically removed from politics and hardly ever live on artificially.

Success

The Swedish political system must certainly be judged successful, by our standards and almost any others. The constitution has been remarkably stable. What major changes it has undergone were the result of prolonged deliberation. Each of them was effected only after it had commanded wide consensus. In this respect, the main criticism that could be made is of the slowness of adaptation: often the change did not occur until long after far-reaching agreement had been achieved. But the divisiveness generated by constitutional issues was never such that violence broke out before their settlement.

Swedish politics has also been extremely efficient. It has always in the past century recognized the real problems facing the country, and has done so on time. It has made for rational debate of the issues arising out of these problems, and then has solved them in what must be considered the most practicable way. This was true, to cite only one example, of the Great Depression in the early 1930's, which led to the end of democratic constitutionalism elsewhere in Europe. This threat never arose seriously in Sweden, which indicates that her politics deserves just as high a grade with regard to effectiveness. The constitution is unquestioningly accepted by all parts of the population, a fact to which the weakness of the Swedish Communist party bears witness. It is true that, in 1946, the Communists received 11 per cent of the popular vote, but this was in part due to sympathies aroused by the Soviet-British-American alliance during World War II. Moreover, Swedish Communists do not make as vicious an impression as most of their counterparts in other Continental countries.

The only major criticism of the Swedish political system that might be offered in conclusion is that its operation is so dull. It presents no corruption, little heat of feelings, no excitement. Similar judgments have been made by foreigners of Swedish life in general. This pervasive dullness has been used as an explanation for the emigration of many able young Swedes to countries, such as the United States, where they can find more rewarding employment for their talents. It has also been taken to account for riots in Stockholm in recent years, during which young men attacked the police without any evident provocation: They just wanted to do *something*—anything exciting. But any people with constitutional and democratic institutions gets the kind of politics it wants and deserves. Swedish politics affords its citizens excellent situations of responsibility and is, for that reason, just as stable, efficient, effective—and dull—as they have made it.

CHAPTER 5

Switzerland

Constitutional History

Switzerland is popularly thought of as one of the oldest and most stable democracies in the world and is often referred to as the classic democracy. These popular notions are true only to a very limited extent, i.e., when applied to the three communities around Lake Lucerne—Uri, Schwyz, and Nidwalden—which joined in an "eternal league" by a written compact in 1291 A.D. From this nucleus, the Helvetic Confederation (the official title of the Swiss state) took its start. These "arch cantons" were governed by the democratic assembly of their arms-bearing males in the thirteenth century, as a few of the Swiss cantons are still governed to-day.[1] The Swiss Confederation—the contemporary political system—is much younger than that, however, and the traditions of neither the whole nor all its component parts have been democratic for very long. What was said about the deep roots in the past of both the Swedish people and the Swedish state, therefore, applies less to the Swiss people and their state.

The birth of the modern Swiss political system coincided with the French Revolution. Between 1291 and 1789, an intricate network of treaties had been spun like a cobweb among the sovereign states that were later to become member cantons of the Confederation. In 1789, these were replaced by the Constitution of the Helvetic Republic, made in Paris, and so unitary in its intent that it abolished boundaries between cantons in its very first article. It was replaced five years later by the "Act of Mediation," which was drawn up on the order of Napoleon Bona-

[1] See page 303.

parte, "First Consul of the French and President of the Italian Republic," by four French senators and fifty-odd representatives of the cantons. It consisted of separate constitutions for each of the cantons (then nineteen), plus a federal constitution. The latter provided for the common defense and specified the number of troops and amounts of money to be contributed by each canton, down to the last man—Bern, 2292 men; Uri, 118. The Napoleonic constitution lasted as long as Napoleon's dominance in Europe.

One of the products of the Congress of Vienna was the Federal Treaty of 1815. It was given the title "treaty" because it established a league or an alliance rather than a political system calling for a constitution. Although the Mediation Constitution had established central organs of government, the Treaty of 1815 did not. This turned out to be its major shortcoming, which began to be subjected to increasing criticism starting in 1830, set off by France's July Revolution of that year. During the same period, several cantonal constitutions, dating from the pre-revolutionary era, were revised to make them more democratic. A draft of a new federal constitution was prepared and debated in 1832 and 1833, but it was not acceptable to a majority of the cantons. As a result, discussions of a revision of the Federal Treaty dragged on fruitlessly over the next decade. Just how divided were the views was shown at a convention of the League in 1844, at which no less than nine mutually contradictory drafts of revisions were debated.

One of the causes of this incapacity to find constitutional agreement was the cleavage between the Protestant and the Roman Catholic cantons. This led to a brief and relatively bloodless civil war in 1847, in which the armies of the Protestant cantons defeated their opponents in a campaign lasting for only twelve days. Thereupon, a committee of revision was established, whose draft of a new federal constitution was ratified by fifteen cantons and one half-canton in 1848. With this, the modern Swiss political system came into being. The Constitution of 1848, whose federal aspects were in part modeled on the Constitution of the United States, set up a bicameral Federal Assembly, an executive Federal Council, and a Federal Court with limited jurisdiction and part-time judges. The Federal Assembly was made up of the National Council, popularly elected, and the Council of Estates, in which each canton was represented by two councilors.

The Constitution of 1848 provided that its own complete revision (*Totalrevision*) should, under certain conditions, be submitted to a referendum, and could be requested by a popular initiative bearing 50,000 signatures. It also left the furnishing of the army up to the individual cantons, and in general assigned relatively few functions to the federal government.

With the national unification of two of Switzerland's neighbors, Italy and Germany, and the Franco-Prussian War of 1870-71, strengthening of the defense functions of the federal government began to be advocated. Moreover, many of the cantonal constitutions had been further democratized during preceding years by such provisions as the popular initiative, popular election of the cantonal government, and obligatory referenda on legislation. A *Totalrevision,* taking these changes into account, was therefore submitted in a referendum in 1872, but was defeated by a popular vote of 261,071 to 255,609 and a cantonal vote of thirteen to nine. The principal objection appeared to be the excessive centralism of the draft. A new draft, toned down, was ratified in 1874 by a popular vote of 340,199 to 198,013, and by a cantonal vote of 14½ to 7½, becoming the federal constitution that has survived to this day.

It has survived, but not without many changes. Between 1874 and 1891, it was amended five times. In the latter year, popular initiative for consitutional amendments was introduced. Between 1891 and 1947, the constitution was amended thirty-eight times. Just how fundamental these changes were is a question that will be deferred until Chapter 22. At this point, it suffices to mention that they included such matters as legal uniformity, proportional representation for elections to the National Council (1918), terms of office of National and Federal Councils (1931), Swiss membership in the League of Nations, and recognition of Romansch as one of the "national languages" of the Federation (the others are German, French, and Italian).

Constitutional Structure

The complete revision of 1874 did not change the basic outlines of Swiss constitutional structure. The federal system still consists of nineteen cantons and six half-cantons (the half-cantons came into being when three of the twenty-two cantons were split in two). The Federal Assembly still consists of two houses, the Council of Estates, in which each canton is represented by two councilors, each half-canton by one; and the National Council, which usually has 196 members. Members of the Council of Estates are popularly elected in all of the cantons but four (where cantonal assemblies elect them). Members of the National Council (one for every 22,000 inhabitants) are elected popularly and directly for a term of four years, from cantonal constituencies.

The Federal Assembly—the two houses jointly—elects the Federal

Council, "the highest executive and leading organ of the Confederation," which consists of seven members, who head the seven departments of the federal government. The Council elects from among its members the federal President for a term of one year only—he may not succeed himself. (Their choice is usually the member who has served as Vice-President during the previous year.) The President as such performs certain representative functions, but is in other respects the equal of his colleagues. The Federal Council is a truly collegial body, in the sense that it makes its decisions as a committee of equals. The federal character of Swiss government emerges in the fact that constitutional practice has given permanent representation on the Federal Council to three cantons —Zurich, Bern, and Vaud—and to one other non-German-speaking canton aside from Vaud. Its term is four years, but individual members of the Federal Council frequently are reëlected; some serve for twenty or thirty years.

Swedish Cabinets, as has been noted, rarely resign upon losing a vote in the Riksdag; the Swiss Federal Council, which performs many of the usual functions of a cabinet, never resigns. As a corollary of this, neither the Federal Council nor any other organ of government can dissolve either house of the Federal Assembly.

A Federal Court with wider jurisdiction than its predecessor was established by the Constitution of 1874, but it is not nearly as important as its counterparts in the United States, Canada, or the Federal Republic of Germany, because the Swiss court does not review legislation for its constitutionality. Its role in criminal cases is severely circumscribed. In this connection, it should be mentioned that the Federal Assembly issues amnesties and pardons, and resolves jurisdictional conflicts among federal administrative agencies. These are functions which would normally be described as executive or judicial.

Problems

Switzerland's economic problems have never in the present century been as serious as those of its larger neighbors—Italy, France, and Germany— or those of Austria, whose proportions are closer to those of Switzerland. Only in wartime, when the neutral country was to a large extent cut off from the foreign supplies on which it is dependent, did the economy suffer. Like Sweden, Switzerland was subjected to industrialization relatively gradually. Because there are few basic natural resources other than water power, there is little heavy basic industry. As a result, the number of employees in the average Swiss industrial enterprise is low.

Yet the income pyramid is steeper in Switzerland than in Sweden. Industry accounts for only about two-fifths of the gainfully employed population, with agriculture and "commerce, hotels, and transport"—i.e., tourism, to a large extent—accounting for one-fifth each. Because of the limited natural resources, the Swiss balance of trade is usually unfavorable. But this foreign-currency deficit is more than made up for by tourism and the banking, insurance, and other commercial services that Switzerland performs for the international economy. Externally, the prosperity of the Swiss is demonstrated by the stable strength of their currency, and internally, by fairly constant full employment. There is no real poverty and little serious crime. American tourists find evidence of this crimelessness when, much to their surprise, they see thousands of dollars worth of the currencies of all the countries of the world being tossed about in Zurich banks or exchange booths, with never a guard or an armored truck in sight or in existence.

The cultural problems the country faces today are "normal" in terms of Swiss experience, but more manifold and potentially more divisive than those confronted by the other seven political systems, with the possible exception of Canada. First, there is the linguistic division. Of the four national languages, German is spoken by about 3,600,000 people, French by about 1,000,000, Italian by about 300,000, and Romansch by 55,000. Second, there is the religious division. About 57 per cent of the population are Protestants, 41 per cent Roman Catholics, and about 0.4 per cent are Jews. The main linguistic division does not coincide with the main denominational division—the German speakers are not uniformly Protestant and the French speakers uniformly Catholic, or the other way around. In fact, there are predominantly Protestant and predominantly Catholic cantons in both of the major language regions. The distribution among the languages and between the religions has remained virtually constant over the past century, so that changes in this respect at least have not created any new problems—as has been the case, for instance, in the Canadian province of Quebec.

Half the population of Switzerland—its women—do not have the vote in federal Swiss politics. One may choose, of course, to consider this as a cultural problem or as a constitutional problem. Indeed, there are some antifeminists who may be inclined to deny that it is a real problem at all, treating it rather as an artificially created issue. That they are quite wrong was shown during the campaign that preceded a referendum on women's suffrage, held in 1959. The proposed constitutional amendment was rejected by a popular margin of almost 2 to 1.

Switzerland's external problems also present certain difficulties, although to a lesser extent than in the past. The cultural attraction exerted on the several ethnic groups by the neighboring nation-states used to be considerable and used to present at least the danger that this might influence attitudes on foreign policy. For example, a great deal in the life of the German-speaking Swiss, in the years before World War I, was modeled on Imperial Germany. All of Switzerland's neighbors at that time— Germany, Austria, Italy, and France—were much stronger militarily than she could ever hope to be. Moreover, there was always the threat of war between some of these four countries that surround the Swiss Confederation. That the importance of the defense problem had earlier been considered great is shown by the prominence given defense provisions in each of the constitutional documents discussed above. Switzerland, like Sweden, has dealt with this problem in part by declaring her neutrality. But, again as in the Swedish case, both World Wars showed that neutrality could be preserved only by maintaining a strong and therefore expensive military establishment. Even with such a defense establishment, Switzerland, surrounded by Nazi German forces on all sides, was obliged to make a few concessions, although not as many as the Swedes made in very similar circumstances.

Switzerland has been confronting constitutional problems of sorts throughout the history of the Confederation. Just how serious these problems have been in recent decades is another question. That there has been a high incidence of them, however, cannot be denied. The very frequency with which referenda on constitutional amendments are held supports this—between 1874 and 1947, forty-three amendments were approved, and another thirty-eight were defeated. In addition, another complete revision—such as the one that brought the present constitution into being in 1874—was voted upon in 1935, but overwhelmingly defeated. The content of these amendments has in some instances affected important features of the constitution, as in the case of the introduction of proportional representation in 1918. Similarly, in 1949, an amendment reducing emergency legislative powers of the Federal Assembly, introduced by popular initiative, was passed in a referendum, although the Federal Assembly had opposed its adoption. It bore the title "People's Initiative for the Return to Direct Democracy," which in most countries would sound inflammatory. In addition to this type of amendment, there have been many others, ranging from the federal role in the economy, through regulation of alcoholic beverages and gambling casinos, to prohibition of decorations in the army and of inhumane slaughter of animals. Finally, there is the recurrent problem of women's suffrage. Thus Switzerland's constitutional problems seem to be both more numerous and more serious than those of Sweden.

Issues and Politics

As we would expect, Swiss politics is much more interesting than Swedish. The issues range over many fields and are often strongly disputed under wide participation of the citizenry. One reason for this is the constitutional provision requiring a referendum on every constitutional amendment and allowing for popular initiative on amendments. Another is Swiss federalism, under which, as in the United States, individuals hold dual citizenship: in their canton and in the Confederation. Elections must be held in both. So must referenda. As a result, citizens often have to go to the polls several times in the course of a single year. In some countries, this might be expected to lead to apathy. In Switzerland, it never has, and electoral participation is quite high.

One unusual aspect of Swiss politics is the fact that so many problems are debated in terms of the constitution as much as in terms of, say, economics or foreign affairs. The variety of types of constitutional amendments, just cited above, is both an illustration and an explanation of this. It offers an explanation for this peculiarity of Swiss political style, because popular initiative—for which 50,000 voters must indicate their support by signature—applies only to constitutional amendments, not to ordinary legislation. This means that a group desiring some change, making no progress through normal parliamentary channels, can always try to achieve its goal by means of the initiative. Another reason for this tendency to convert substantive problems into issues about the constitution is federalism. We find similar tendencies in the other federal systems with which we will deal—Germany, Canada, and the United States.

The first problems the Confederation faced in 1848 were constitutional questions, involving federalism in the main. Here another similarity with the United States and Canada emerges. In young federal systems, the dominant issue during the period before and after the founding is whether to accept or reject, to strengthen or weaken, the federation. The basic reason for one's stand on this issue may be—indeed, it is likely to be—not constitutional, but economic or cultural. This was true in Switzerland, too. The Civil War of 1847 had been fought by Liberals and Radicals against the Roman Catholics. For forty-four years thereafter, the Catholic Conservative People's party was not represented in the executive Federal Council, which was monopolized by the Liberals and

Radicals. Of these two parties, the Radicals were the more progressive and gradually they became much the stronger of the two. But it was not until 1891, when the last Liberal member of the Federal Council retired, that the first People's party representative was elected to the Federal Council. Thus, this acceptance of full participation in government by the original opponents of Confederation occurred only seventeen years after the complete constitutional revision of 1874, which itself had been ratified only because of the concessions its second draft had made to the anticentralist groups in the country.

Not all the problems that first gave rise to Confederation have been solved. Nor have all the issues arising out of some of the solved problems been entirely removed from the political arena. The problem of federal-cantonal relations, as in all non-stagnant federal systems, has been a persistent one. And some of the issues arising out of the religious conflict still come to the fore in public debate from time to time. Thus, the Jesuits were excluded from the country by the Constitution of 1848, and this exclusion was retained in 1874. Some Swiss Catholics resent this, and from time to time there is talk of a constitutional amendment to drop this article. However, no popular initiative to that effect has ever been made. This suggests one of two conclusions: Either the Catholics have accepted this solution of the Jesuit problem; or they do not want to reopen the issue until they have some hope for success. This last alternative is the more likely one, because of the virtually constant ratio of Protestants to Catholics over the last century.

By and large, the more serious cultural problems of the middle of the nineteenth century have been solved. As evidence for this we may take the lack of the kind of recrimination about the Civil War still common in United States politics. The very fact that Southerners refer to this conflict as the "War Between the States," and that textbooks used in Southern schools treat it differently from otherwise identical textbooks used in the other states, suggests the nature and longevity of this recriminatory issue. The success of the Swiss Confederation in dealing with the centrifugal influences of the language problem is demonstrated by its sustained policy of neutrality. This dates back to the period of the Congress of Vienna and beyond. It has been made easier by the country's geographical position in its "Alpine Redoubt." But it has not always been in the interest of Switzerland's more powerful neighbors, especially in times of war. Moreover, neutrality has been the expressed policy of an overwhelming majority of people and parties. No matter how close the cultural ties of any one of the different groups with its ethnic fellows across the border, the strongest loyalties go to the system that reconciles their own cultural differences within the Confederation, that is, to the constitution.

Departure from the policy of neutrality, therefore, has not been an important issue. About the proper consequences to be drawn from Swiss neutrality, on the other hand, there has been occasional disagreement. This was true, for example, with regard to the issue of joining the League of Nations. Switzerland did join as the result of a 1920 referendum on this issue. In the next year, another successful referendum, this one on popular initiative, required that international treaties of indefinite or fifteen years' duration be subject to the referendum, whenever this is demanded by an initiative with 30,000 signatures, or by eight cantons. After World War II, Switzerland did not join the United Nations.

As a concomitant of this zealously guarded neutrality, the defense problem has always been a serious one for Switzerland, as already indicated. The threat to Swiss security from her militarily strong neighbors was one of the reasons for the *Totalrevision* of 1874. The solution provided by the new constitution was so successful that related issues have come up only rarely since then. In 1895, reform of the military provisions of the constitution was rejected in a referendum. In 1921, the same fate befell an initiative for the disestablishment of military justice. In 1931, an initiative forbidding the award or wearing of decorations by military and civil officers of the Confederation was passed. And in 1939, an amendment subjecting private armaments production to federal control won in another referendum. In other respects, however, the 1874 constitution's eleven articles governing the military establishment have been preserved intact and have not given rise to any important issues. The constitution does not allow standing troops; Article 18 provides that every Swiss citizen is subject to defense service and will be provided with his first uniform and equipment free. His weapon remains in his hands, even when he is not on active duty. And this is most of the time, since basic training lasts for only a few months, after which the citizen-soldiers return to duty for brief annual training periods with men from their own canton. As an intended result of the operation of this system, Switzerland has not developed a professional military caste. A commander-in-chief is appointed, by the Federal Assembly, only in the event that body decides to mobilize the country, and then only for the duration. (Such a mobilization occurred during World War II.)

While cultural and external problems have thus generated few issues for Swiss politics, economic and constitutional problems have generated a great many. The stand taken by the parties on these issues can generally be deduced from their names, traditions, and programs. As in Sweden, the overlap between political parties and interest groups is marked. The Liberals, who have received only a small proportion of the popular vote in recent decades, and the Radicals, who have averaged about one-fourth, have already been mentioned. The Radicals are a democratic, "bourgeois" group in the classic sense, and the major opponents of the Social Democrats, whose program is Marxist but just as mild as that of their Swedish namesakes. They, too, have averaged about one-quarter of the popular vote since the 1930's, as has the Catholic Conservative People's party. The strongest of the remaining parties is the Party of Peasants, Artisans, and the Middle Estate, which has averaged between 10 and 16 per cent. It is as closely identified with the corresponding interest organizations as the Social Democrats are with the trade unions. In the former case, the relevant groups are the Swiss Union of Peasants and the Swiss Union of Arts and Crafts. There is also the Swiss Union of Commerce and Industry, the sympathies of whose members would be predominantly with the Radical or Catholic Conservative parties.

Another noteworthy group, which began as an interest organization, later became a political party as well. It illustrates the difficulty of distinguishing between these two types of organizations, which political science normally treats as different and distinct. The "Migros" chain was founded in 1935 by an enterprising businessman named Duttweiler, in order to fight the high cost of living by means of something resembling a series of coöperative supermarkets. Duttweiler was first elected to the Federal Assembly as an independent, but his Democratic party then elected six National Councilors (out of 194) in 1943, and a few more in subsequent elections. In 1957, their initiative led to a referendum on an antitrust amendment, which was defeated. Finally, there are the Communists, who were outlawed in 1940, but reconstituted themselves under another label in 1944. They normally elect between four and seven National Councilors.

It is a peculiarity of Swiss politics that the relative strength of the different groups in the National Council is not reflected in the seven-member Federal Council. The late accession of the Conservatives to this cabinet-like body has already been mentioned. By 1919, the Federal Council consisted of five Radicals and two Conservatives. In 1929, one of the Radicals was replaced by a representative of the "Peasants, Artisans, and Middle Estate." But although the Social Democrats were the second or third strongest party, in terms of electoral support and representation in the National Council, between 1919 and 1943, they did not participate in the Federal Council. Only in 1943 did one of their leaders become a Federal Councilor. In the election of that year they were the strongest of the parties, yet they were outnumbered 6 to 1 by their "bourgeois" opponents in the Federal Council.

The disproportion in the party composition of the Federal Council, together with the long continuity of service of its individual members, suggests that it has to do more with the solution of problems than with the resolution of issues. In this it is efficiently supported by the federal bureaucracy, whose task, it should be noted, is not as broad as that of bureaucracies in nonfederal systems. The cantonal governments and their bureaucracies perform many tasks that elsewhere—in Sweden, for example—would be the responsibility of the central bureaucracy. This is also true, in a more general way, of federal systems viewed as problem-solving devices. Many of their problems are left to be dealt with by state politics, so that the pipelines of the federal political process need not be clogged with local issues.

Since the Federal Council—the "executive,"—does not perform the resolving function, who does? The answer is not a simple one, since this function is highly decentralized in Switzerland. It may be performed by the Federal Assembly, one of whose houses, it must be remembered, is representative of the cantons, which have either their own assemblies or direct democracy. Or it may be performed by the male voters in a referendum, together with the cantonal assemblies, the concurrence of a majority of which is also required for passage of constitutional amendments subjected to the referendum.

What is unique, at least among the countries studied in this book, is the possibility of performance of the functions of recognizing problems and formulating issues by anyone who can muster 50,000 signatures—1 per cent of the present total population—for a constitutional initiative. This means, in effect, that every phase of the Swiss policy flow up to and including the resolution of issues, is much more decentralized than in other countries.

Success

This type of decentralization in the political process does not, however, mean that the making of policy in Switzerland is also disorganized and, therefore, inefficient. On the contrary, the Swiss constitution must be judged at least as successful as the Swedish, especially in view of the higher incidence of more serious problems faced by the Swiss, notably in the cultural and constitutional spheres. We will work our way toward an explanation of this success throughout the remainder of the book. Meanwhile, we will have to conclude by backing up our preliminary, favorable judgment on the success of the Swiss system.

With regard to constitutional stability, Switzerland at least *seems* to make a poor showing, in terms of the number of attempted and adopted constitutional amendments. However, the basic structure of government has not been changed greatly. Some things have remained remarkably stable. But we will have to delay determining how essential these are to the "true constitution" until we have formulated criteria for isolating the content of the true constitution of any political system.

Swiss politics has certainly been adaptable and efficient. Problems have always been recognized in time. Indeed, it might be said that the opportunities afforded by the constitution for recognizing problems are open to so many institutions and groups that this is the most efficient stage of the process. These opportunities, nevertheless, do not result in "crackpot" artificial issues; the difficulties of seeing an issue through initiative and referendum, and the good common sense of the Swiss voters, discourage the cranks. (One special peculiarity of Swiss politics—the relatively small number of cranks—will be discussed in a later chapter.) Finally, the Constitution of 1874 has been effective. One evidence of its effectiveness is the utter failure by the Communists—and, in the 1930's, by the Fascists—to achieve support. Another is the defeat of the attempted *Totalrevision* of 1935, by 511,000 to 196,000 votes. The latter figure seems substantial, it is true, but it is remarkable that the issue left no bitterness among the defeated proponents of this corporative scheme —the more so because of the harsh constitutional conflicts taking place in Germany and France about the same time.

The Swiss constitution is not only successful, it also provides its citizens—at least the men—with excellent situations of responsibility. They are presented with many, but not too many, and meaningful alternatives: in cantonal and federal elections, through the initiative and in referenda, by way of the many organizations which they can join or support. The resources available for implementing their choices are similarly manifold. This is as true of the strictly political resources, such as the federal and cantonal bureaucracies, as of the economic and cultural resources available to citizens, among them one of the finest and most highly developed educational systems in the world. In this connection, it should be mentioned that Swiss emigrants are less motivated by domestic boredom than Swedish emigrants. Switzerland is so much smaller and more limited in her resources that it would become overpopulated without emigration. Moreover, the high proportion of Swiss emigrants, and

SWITZERLAND : : : *67*

even emigrants' children, who retain their federal and cantonal citizenship bears witness to their loyalty to, and satisfaction with, their homeland. Finally, citizens have good foreknowledge of the probable consequences of the contributions they make to both centralized and decentralized decisions.

In this sense, therefore, the world-wide reputation that Switzerland enjoys as *the* model democracy may be justfied. This does not mean that other countries should ape her institutions, as Uruguay did—with relatively poor results—when it copied the collegial "executive." Nor does it overlook the past denial of political rights to many of Switzerland's men, or the continued denial of rights to its women today. It does suggest, however, that there is *something* that has made constitutional democracy work well in Switzerland in the face of grave obstacles, chief among them the fact that a century or two ago the people of this state would not even have been considered a "nation" according to the accepted definition of that word. Part III will undertake to identify this *something,* to determine what it is that accounts for this success, and to inquire whether it can be transplanted to other countries.

CHAPTER 6

Italy

Constitutional History

By beginning this descriptive part of the book with Sweden and Switzerland, very high standards of steadiness of constitutional evolution have been set. On a comparative graph representing growth of constitutions, these two countries would have curves that ascend steadily with but few oscillations. The Swiss curve would be somewhat less steady than the Swedish; Sweden's would be longer, because it covers a greater period of time. The Italian line on the graph would be in sharp contrast: the ups and downs in Italian constitutional history have been many, and on the whole there have been more downs than ups. Moreover, the national state of Italy was founded only in 1861, as a monarchy. The Italian Republic came into being much more recently, in 1946. In this sense, it is the youngest of the political systems with which we are dealing, since the contemporary Federal Republic of Germany at least had a republican forerunner during the Weimar period, from 1918 to 1933.

This comparative youth of the present Italian political system must be borne in mind to avoid misunderstandings that are likely to be caused by thinking of Italy in terms of geographical continuity with the Roman Empire, or of Rome, "the Eternal City," as somehow identical with Italy. This latter is true to an even lesser degree than would be the assumption that New York City is identical with the United States. American visitors to Italy are usually impressed by the tangible presence of the dimension of time in Rome, where they can see physical deposits of the centuries one upon the other, like geological layers in the cross-section of a mountain: the Roman Forum, medieval Christianity, the Renaissance, and then century after century, in the form of buildings and monuments. Of course, the Romans of today are, if any-thing, at least as conscious of continuity with their ancestors as are the Swedes or Swiss with theirs. But this city of Rome, which was the capital of the Empire, and was and is the capital of the Roman Catholic Church, has been the capital of Italy only since 1870. The Italian Kingdom had come into being nine years earlier, against the opposition of the Papacy, but its capital could not be moved to Rome until the process of national unification had been completed in 1870.

This late date of national unification—it virtually coincides with the same event in Germany—accounts for much of the roughness of Italian constitutional development. Until 1861, the Spanish Bourbons ruled in southern Italy and the island of Sicily, Austria controlled large parts of northern Italy, and the Papacy owned much of the territory around Rome. The nucleus of the unification movement was provided by the Kingdom of Savoy, based on Piedmont in the north. The course of unification involved a war by Piedmont and France against Austria, and a revolution against the Bourbons in the south. Piedmontese forces defeated a Papal army. Eventually, French troops garrisoned Rome to protect the Papacy against the Italian Kingdom, and it was not until their removal that national unification of Italy was completed. But this situation was not viewed as creating the need for a new constitution, as did its parallel in Germany one year later. Unified Germany then needed a new constitution, because of the federal character of the new Empire. Italian unification was not federal, hence the Piedmontese constitution of 1848, called the Albertine *Statuto* (after King Charles Albert, who granted it), was simply continued in effect as the "Fundamental Statute of the Kingdom of Italy."

This constitution had been modeled on the French July Constitu-tion of 1830 and the Belgian Constitution of 1831, both of which were meant to copy much from constitutional monarchy in Great Britain. It provided for a bicameral Parliament, which consisted of a Senate, whose members were nominated by the King, and a Chamber of Deputies, whose members were elected, in the beginning, on the basis of a very limited franchise.

The *Statuto* remained in effect until 1946—at least in constitutional theory. One hundred years under the same constitution could be consid-ered an enviable record of stability, if many radical changes had not taken place behind this façade. In fact, the precise content of the Italian constitution was hard to determine, because it did not provide for any distinction between ordinary legislation and constitutional amendments. As a result, any law that diverged from the *Statuto* had the effect of a constitutional amendment. Accordingly, it was possible to pass from the Piedmontese constitutional monarchy of 1848, with its small electorate, through unification and the gradual broadening of the suffrage, on to Benito Mussolini's Fascist dictatorship and the Lateran Treaty and Concordat with the Vatican, to the fall of Fascism—all under the same constitution. Indeed, doubts may be raised whether one document capable of covering such a variety of political situations may properly be called a "constitution."

Italian constitutionalism did not become democratic until just before World War I, when nearly universal male suffrage became a reality. In 1882, when the electorate was quadrupled to include 2 million voters, the population of the country amounted to about 30 million. In any case, for the three decades around the turn of the century, Italian government was either ineffective or unrepresentative, or both. This was in part due to the inability of Papacy and Kingdom to come to terms, which had the result of keeping Roman Catholics who were loyal to the Church from participating in national politics. The Vatican changed this policy only in 1904 and 1909, and it was not until then that the large Church-loyal segment of Italy's almost 100 per cent Catholic population was adequately represented. Related to Catholic abstention was another reason for the poor performance of Italian government during this period: the practice of *trasformismo,* under which cabinets were supported by shifting majorities in the Chamber of Deputies—majorities that were based purely on patronage and bore little if any relevance to the interests supposedly represented by the deputies.

During and after Italy's not very rewarding participation in World War I, cabinets became increasingly unstable and incapable of dealing with the grave economic problems of those years. A series of strikes was followed by the outbreak of open violence, and in October, 1922, the King put an end to a situation bordering on civil war by commissioning Mussolini, as leader of the Fascist movement, to form a cabinet. Victor Emmanuel III continued to reign, and new laws continued to be proclaimed in his name. Indeed, it was nominally the King who deposed Mussolini in 1943. While the *Statuto* thus remained in effect throughout the period, the structure of the constitution changed more than once. Mussolini altered it in 1928 by establishing the Grand Council of Fascism, which joined the Fascist party with the government. Mussolini, as Chief of Government, headed the Grand Council. Previously, by an act of 1925, Mussolini had had the position of Prime Minister strengthened by combining it with the office and functions of "Chief of Government," a constitutional novelty. It was not until 1939 that the Chamber of Deputies was abolished, to be replaced by the Chamber of Fasces and Corporations. This was to provide the capstone for a corporatist structure of representation, whose lower supports had been constructed during previous years.

But all of this collapsed, to return to the constitutional *status quo ante,* when the King sent the dictator packing after the Fascist Grand Council had turned against Mussolini. The *Statuto* served its purpose once more until a referendum in 1946, in which Italian voters—now including women for the first time—were asked to decide between monarchy and republic. By 54 per cent against 46 per cent they voted in favor of the new Italian Republic, whose constitution was prepared by a Constituent Assembly, elected when the constitutional referendum took place. The new constitution went into effect in 1948. It incorporated the two agreements negotiated by Mussolini with the Papacy: the Lateran Treaty, recognizing the Vatican as a sovereign state inside the city of Rome; and the Concordat, giving the Roman Catholic Church extensive rights in connection with education and with the solemnization or dissolution of marriage. This went much further than previous Italian practice, despite Article 1 of the *Statuto,* which read: "The Catholic, Apostolic, and Roman religion is the only religion of the State. All other cults existing at this time will be tolerated in conformity with the laws." For this reason, the agreement with the Vatican amounted to constitutional change, and its explicit inclusion in the new Republic's constitution served to confirm this fact.

Since the new constitution went into effect in 1948, flesh has had to be put into and around the skeleton it was meant to provide for Italian government. But this process of growth has been neither even nor easy. One provision, for the creation of a constitutional court, was not acted upon for seven years. Another, an article calling for the creation of nineteen regions with their own councils, had been fulfilled only to a very limited extent even by 1959.

Constitutional Structure

The republican Parliament, as its monarchical predecessor, consists of a Chamber of Deputies and a Senate. The Chamber has some 575 members, who are elected according to proportional representation, on the basis of an electoral law that has been manipulated by the incumbent majority before every general election. The Senate is about half the size of the lower house, and its members are elected by a somewhat more complicated system of proportional representation, from different constituencies.

It has equal powers with the Chamber, but its constitutional term of office runs to six years, by contrast with the Chamber's five. In practice, this constitutional difference has been inoperative, because for the parliamentary elections of 1953 and 1958, both houses were dissolved at the same time by the President of the Republic. The constitutionality of this presidential action was questioned on both occasions, giving rise to fairly acrimonious constitutional controversy. To elect the President, the two chambers, meeting in joint session, are supposed to be joined by three representatives from each of the regional councils. But since no regional councils had been established, the first and second Presidents of the Republic were elected by Parliament alone. Presidential functions closely parallel those of the President of the former Fourth French Republic.

The Italian President was ahead of his former French colleague (until 1958) by controlling the appointment of five of the fifteen judges of the Constitutional Court. Five of the remaining ten judges are appointed by the other courts, and five by Parliament meeting in joint session. The Constitutional Court is supposed to review legislation and administrative action for its constitutionality, as does the Supreme Court of the United States, which served as a model. This made it a novelty in Italian experience and led Italian Premiers to the interpretation that presidential appointments to its bench were to be made on nomination of the Cabinet. Because the first President, Luigi Einaudi, did not share this view, there was a lengthy delay—until 1955—in getting the Constitutional Court into operation.

Cabinets require the support of a majority in both houses. Both chambers may be dissolved by the President, acting on the request of the Prime Minister and after consultation with their presiding officers. By 1958, the Chamber of Deputies had not been dissolved before expiration of its regular term, but the Senate, as already mentioned, was dissolved one year ahead of schedule in both 1953 and 1958.

Problems

Italy is the poorest of the countries discussed in this book. Its standard of living is the lowest. Except for water power, and recently discovered oil and natural gas, it has virtually no basic resources. Its economic problems are further complicated and aggravated by the uneven geography of industrialization. The north is relatively highly industrialized and has a number of large and efficient manufacturing concerns, including world-famous firms such as FIAT and Olivetti. The south, by contrast, remains relatively untouched by the Industrial Revolution and is so backward economically that it may rightly be called an underdeveloped area. Because of deforestation and erosion, and absentee ownership of uneconomically large landed estates, its agriculture is miserably poor. These economic problems of the south in particular, and of the whole country in general, were worsened by the ravages wrought by World War II. Much more than Sweden and Switzerland, Italy is and has always been a country dominated by cities—this goes back to the Renaissance era of rich city-states. Nevertheless, about half the population makes its living from agriculture even today. Both city and country have traditionally suffered from overpopulation. Roman Catholic opposition makes difficult any solution based on birth control. Much of the surplus population used to be siphoned off by emigration, but immigration restrictions in the United States and other countries have interfered with this process in recent decades. All of these factors have combined to give Italy a higher rate of chronic unemployment than is found in any of the other countries. Distribution of wealth and of income is very uneven and presents the picture of a very steep pyramid. There is evidence of poverty all over the country, especially in the south.

Italy's main cultural problem is that of relations between the Vatican and the Italian state. All the great Italian lay political thinkers, from Dante and Machiavelli on down to our own times, have addressed themselves to this problem, and most of them have sided with secular governments against the Church. This may come as a surprise, since Italy is as solidly Roman Catholic as Sweden is Lutheran. (The total population—nearly 50,000,000—includes only some 80,000 Protestants and 50,000 Jews.)

The root of this problem goes back to the role of the Bishop of Rome—the Pope—as temporal ruler of the extensive Italian territories formerly held by the Church. Since the Papacy opposed the rising tide of nationalism in the nineteenth century, and did not acquiesce in the establishment of the national capital in its own "Eternal City," Rome, the estrangement between the new political system and citizens loyal to the Vatican was almost inevitably bitter and long lasting. In fact, it was not repaired until the first decade of the present century, when a new Pope withdrew official opposition to political participation by Catholics. The founding of the Catholic Populist party, the *Popolari,* by Don Luigi Sturzo, himself a priest, eventually followed. This eased the problem somewhat, although it left the new group wide open to accusations of being an instrument of the Vatican.

Under the Fascist regime, political activity by Church groups was prohibited, and a struggle took place between Mussolini and the Catholic Action organization. After Mussolini's deposition, men who had been associated with Sturzo and Catholic Action became the founders of the new Christian Democratic party, which, fifteen years later, is still subject to similar attacks of clericalism. Although the Lateran Treaty and the Concordat became a part of the republican constitution, the problems created by the physical presence in Italy of the capital of the worldwide Roman Catholic Church still generate many issues for Italian politics.

Only one ethnic minority group presents a serious cultural problem: German-speaking Tyroleans around Bolzen, in territory that was formerly Austrian. Because they are a distinctly different group, the regional council provided for by the constitution has been established in this case—as also in the island of Sicily. But because the area was combined with a neighboring Italian-populated one to form this region, there have been complaints from the German-speaking citizens that the Italian government was trying to "swamp" them. Occasionally the Austrian government protests to Rome on behalf of its brethren south of the Brenner Pass.

External relations with Austria have otherwise recently been friendly, as also with Italy's other northern neighbors, France and Switzerland. This was not true of relations with Yugoslavia, with which Italy contested possession of Trieste in the forum of the United Nations. In World War II, Fascist Italy was an ally of Nazi Germany. After the defeat of German and rather inferior Italian forces in North Africa, the Allied armies first invaded the Continent via Sicily and southern Italy. In World War I, Italy belatedly joined the Allies against Germany and Austria-Hungary, only to be badly defeated by the Central Powers. Both before and after this war, Italy engaged in colonial ventures that, as military operations, did not crown her with glory. In 1896, some 10,000 Ethiopians defeated more than twice that many Italians in one of the worst military disasters in the history of modern colonialism. Italy did acquire Libya and, in 1936, made up for 1896 by defeating and "conquering" Ethiopia, so that Victor Emmanuel III was styled "King of Italy, Emperor of Ethiopia."

In general, the history of Italy's foreign relations suggests that her external problems are shaped by her exposed position in the Mediterranean Sea and, so far at least, by her chronic inability to muster military forces of a quality comparable with that of her European neighbors. In the period of the Cold War, this has been complicated by Italy's identification with the West, her proximity to Yugoslavia and that country's unique position in the Communist camp, and the large size of the Italian Communist party, which is the strongest in Western Europe.

The main constitutional problem is the novelty of the republican constitution itself. The closeness of the referendum on retaining or abolishing the monarchy—54 to 46 per cent—has already been mentioned, as well as the failure to fill in all the gaps in the constitutional structure. These factors by themselves would not be very serious, because the difference between constitutional monarchy and republic has not been especially significant for Italy. Much more serious is the opposition to the parliamentary regime itself, which is presumably shared by all those Italians who cast their votes for the Communist party. Any government which feels—as did the Italian government in recent elections—that its survival requires the massive support of the Church and of a foreign power, the United States, clearly still has a serious constitutional problem on its hands.

Issues and Politics

Italian politics revolves around many issues on which the public is deeply divided—issues which are debated vigorously and often violently, and which are seldom resolved to anyone's satisfaction, not even that of the group which has apparently been the winner. The violence that frequently marks contemporary Italian politics may be taken as a continuance of a tradition exemplified in the methods by which unification was achieved: revolution, civil war, and war between dynastic states. In the past, violence occasionally also occurred as the expression of pure desperation by men who felt that they had nothing to lose, as in the southern peasants' uprising of 1860-65. At other times, violence was employed by the police on behalf of the regime that happened to be controlling the state, as under Prime Minister Francesco Crispi in the 1890's, against agricultural unions in Sicily and against the Socialists. The violence and terror that reigned during the years preceding Fascism's advent to power have been noted. The Fascists themselves extolled the use of force as a matter of principle, although Mussolini did not go quite as far on this score as Hitler, in either theory or practice. After Mussolini's deposition and while only northern Italy was under German military control (the rest of the country was already in Allied hands) Italian partisan resistance fighters fought bravely and ended up by killing *Il Duce* and mutilating his body. Since that time, there have been a number of violent or near-violent strikes. The incidence of violent crime is also high in Italy.

Averting the next eruption of violence, or fixing the blame for the last one, is therefore a frequent issue. Parliament is not an ideal place for conducting debates on this issue in a decorous fashion, since the deputies themselves frequently engage in public fisticuffs. This is also true of the persistent issue of corruption, because of the frequent involvement of leading politicians in scandals arising out of graft, bribery of public officials, and the like. The Montesi scandal, which enriched the tabloids of the world from 1953 to 1958, may serve as an example. Set off by the fatal drowning of Vilma Montesi, it led to the resignation of the Foreign Minister, whose son was suspected of murder. The case involved prominent politicians, members of the Italian and Vatican nobility, and a grandson of the late King of Italy. In its course, the Roman chief of police was accused of trying to cover up the crime and of accepting bribes from the central figure in the plot, an alleged black-marketeer with a false title of nobility, who was also accused of being a dope peddler and procurer for Roman café society. When the case finally came to trial in 1958, key witnesses claimed that they no longer remembered what had happened, the public prosecutor withdrew the charges, and the court acquitted the defendants.

The roots of corruption, as those of violence, go back at least to the unification period. Corruption at the local level often operated through the provincial prefect, an appointee of the Ministry of Interior. As chief law-enforcement officer, the prefect also supervised elections. At the national level, the practice of *trasformismo,* introduced by Prime Minister Agostino Depretis in 1876, constituted a form of corruption on a large scale. For forty years, under *trasformismo,* Prime Ministers built, or rather juggled, their parliamentary majorities by dispensing official patronage to any deputies, regardless of party or local origins, who would support them in the Chamber. This practice undoubtedly made its contribution to the death of constitutional government in Italy under the monarchy. Mussolini promised not only to put an end to the instability of Cabinets but also to clean up corruption. But the Fascist regime turned out to be about as corrupt as its predecessor, mainly because of the opportunities for graft presented by its many economic activities. The organization of the economy along vertical, "corporate" lines, with Fascist party functionaries in charge of each corporation, made the continuation of old habits easy for the men who were running the new regime, especially since they were no longer subject to public criticism.

The return of constitutionalism has not helped matters very much, although attempts to reduce corruption have been made. One of these attacked the problem through tax legislation, by requiring people to file sworn statements of their income. Until this was done, in 1951, the Italian income tax, which accounted for only about one-tenth of total tax revenues, was levied on the basis of estimates of the taxpayer's income, made by a bureaucrat and subject to bargaining. Naturally, this system was wide open to abuse.

Italy's economic problems have generated a number of divisive issues. A persistent one among these since World War II has been land reform in the south, which has been carried forward by the Christian Democratic governments, but criticized as inadequate by the Communists. On several occasions, the refusal of peasant squatters to leave formerly uncultivated land belonging to absentee landlords has led to bloodshed. The problems of unemployment and overpopulation have also been contested issues, involving questions of foreign policy because of disagreement on the acceptability of United States aid under the Marshall Plan and its successor programs. Foreign and defense policy itself has been hotly debated between the strong Communists and their Christian Democratic opponents, who have been supported by the other proconstitutional parties. Italy's membership in the North Atlantic Treaty Organization has been one such issue. Earlier, the best means for regaining control of Trieste was another, which involved the question as to which side in the Cold War—the Western powers or the Soviet Union—would be more likely to help Italy achieve this goal. The Italian Communist party naturally follows the line laid down in Moscow, which means that issues of advantage to the Kremlin are often introduced into Italian politics, even though they appear to bear little relevance to the immediate problems confronting Italy. The problems of Western European Union—the European Coal and Steel Community, Euratom, the Common Market—have been debated along similar lines.

The constitution itself has been an issue, both in the broad sense already mentioned and in some of its various parts. The issues of dissolution of the Senate and appointments to the Constitutional Court have been cited. A similar issue was raised by changes made in the electoral law before the general election of 1953. These changes were designed to help the proconstitutional parties achieve a parliamentary majority and to discriminate against the Communists and their left-wing Socialist allies. The constitutional propriety of this measure was hotly debated, as have been similar steps in France and West Germany. In the campaign of 1958, constitutional questions raised by the trial of a Roman Catholic bishop in a state court played an important role. The Bishop of Prato had denounced a couple, who had been married only in a civil ceremony, as living in "scandalous concubinage," although the Concordat recognizes civil marriages as legal. Subsequently, the couple were treated as outcasts by their fellow townspeople and sued the bishop for criminal libel. In a sensational trial, he was found guilty and fined: he then appealed the case and was acquitted, whereupon the couple appealed to the Constitutional Court. The consequence for the campaign was to raise the whole constitutional issue of the relations between the Vatican and the Republic. At the same time, General de Gaulle's return to the premiership in neighboring France, which occurred during the campaign, was used by Italian politicians to dramatize the need for either strengthening the constitution to prevent parliamentary deadlock, or for voting Communist in order to prevent a "Fascist coup à la de Gaulle."

In every postwar Italian parliamentary election, the label of clericalism has been pinned on the Christian Democrats, and not by the Communists alone. The Italian Christian Democratic party, by contrast with its West German namesake, is an avowedly Catholic party; although its links with the Vatican are not as close as were those of its forerunner, the *Popolari,* it naturally invites this charge. This does not seem to have interfered excessively, however, with its electoral fortunes. In the first republican election, in 1948, the Christian Democrats won more than half the seats in the Chamber of Deputies. In 1953 and 1958, they did not do quite as well, but their popular strength has hovered between 45 and 50 per cent. The Communists, together with their allies, the left-wing Socialists, have regularly polled about one-third of the vote. The right-wing Socialists, who have generally supported or even been in coalition Cabinets with the Christian Democrats, receive approximately 7 per cent of popular support. The remainder is taken up by small monarchist and neofascist groupings on the anticonstitutional right, and several very small parties supporting the Christian Democrats in the center, among them the Liberals and the Republicans.

The state of Italian political opinion is shown not only in the quinquennial parliamentary elections, but also in local elections and in the elections of the Sicilian regional council. More important indicators than these, however, are the elections of works councils in industry, in which the Communist-dominated General Italian Confederation of Labor competes with its anti-Communist opponents. Italian industrial labor is comprehensively organized, as are the employers—in the latter case, partly a carryover from the days of Fascist corporate organization. The Church also maintains a vast network of religious organizations. Nevertheless, at least when compared with Sweden and Switzerland, self-governing associational life is not as rich and varied in Italy, and the individual citizen is not as likely to belong or to participate in a variety of organizations at the same time. Thus, his membership in the Communist party is all-embracing—trade union, youth groups, sports association, and so on. To a somewhat lesser extent, the same is true of other groupings.

The composition of the Italian electorate has remained fairly stable under the republican constitution. Italian Cabinets, on the other hand, have been unstable. Although all of them have been dominated by the Christian Democrats, individual Prime Ministers and their Cabinets have rarely lasted much more than one year at a time. The first President of the Republic was a Liberal, who was succeeded by a Christian Democrat. Because that party has such a large following, it comprises many different shadings of political opinion. Accordingly, a change from one Christian Democratic Premier to another may be accompanied by real shifts in policy, as well. It may also make for something resembling a genteel tug of war between the President and the Prime Minister, when these two, even though members of the same Christian Democratic party, are identified with different wings.

Yet the resolution of most issues other than those decided in general parliamentary elections has to be performed somewhere between Parliament, the Cabinet, and the President, if it is to be performed at all. All that parliamentary elections really decide is whether the constitutional regime is to be continued or is to be replaced by something else dominated by the Communists. So far, Christian Democracy, with its allies, has survived these tests. But the composition of the Parliaments emerging out of these elections has been such as to hamper the deliberative process. Because of the Christian Democrats' frequent dependence on the very small parties in accumulating a parliamentary majority, the importance of these groups, and also that of shifting factions within the leading party, has been exaggerated out of proportion to their electoral support. These conditions in turn have prevented sustained policies from being made or put into effect. The oversized and not very efficient bureaucracy, some of whose members are antipathetic to the policies under which they are working, has also interfered. All of this together frequently results in the persistence of old issues, the failure to solve old problems lying back of them, and the consequent failure to recognize more urgent new problems. Moreover, the commitment of the strong Communist party to goals that contradict those of constitutionalism means that many issues are introduced into Italian politics designed more to obstruct than to make for a smooth flow of policy. At the same time, the inability of the governing parties to present a record of real achievement tempts them to deflect public attention from their failings by overconcentrating on the Communist threat.

Success

Italy's degree of constitutional success is assuredly unimpressive when compared with that of Sweden and Switzerland. How she compares with Germany and France will be seen in the next two chapters. The comparison with Germany will be particularly useful, because the two countries achieved national unification within a year of one another. Since that time, the Italian constitution has been unstable, unadaptable, inefficient, and ineffective. It failed to gain the acceptance, during the first three decades of its existence, of both the Church-loyal Catholics, who excluded themselves, and the great masses of the population, urban and rural, who were excluded. This, combined with inefficiency—the failure to find solutions especially to economic problems—led to the victory of Fascism. That regime in turn, while somewhat more efficient—Mussolini made the trains run on time, as is always said, and he did drain the Pontine Marshes—was accepted by ever fewer Italians, to the point where it was based on the force of German occupation troops alone. To replace constitutional monarchy, the Republic was established, with something less than widespread popular enthusiasm. Since then, roughly one-third of the electorate has been supporting parties opposed to the constitution. This is a poor record of effectiveness.

The present constitution has been relatively stable so far as formal amendments go. But because of the failure to fill in the framework it provided, as in the case of regional councils, not everything its authors intended has been stable: something that does not exist cannot be called stable. In any event, the present constitution has been in effect for only ten years, and in seeking a better judgment of constitutional stability, we should look at the period of one hundred years since the unification struggle. In that perspective, the conclusion must be that the Italian state has had a very unstable constitution ever since it came into existence.

It has also been very inefficient. True, the problem of competition with the head and headquarters of the Church is uniquely difficult, and Italy is naturally poorer than any of the other countries. Nevertheless, the various political processes by means of which these problems were handled have not advanced them very far toward solutions, considering the length of time available. One reason for this inefficiency has been inadequate adaptability. When new problems arose, obsolete or inefficient processes have too often been retained to deal with them, instead of being discarded. This has been true especially of the bureaucracy and—no more disastrously, although more dramatically so—of the military.

Italians are in poor situations of responsibility. The only meaningful choice they can make in parliamentary elections is between the alternatives of constitutionalism or communism. This gives them few opportunities to contribute to the central decisions of their government on other matters. Their resources, both institutional and material, for implementing any decisions are insufficient. And even if they were better off in terms of these first two criteria, their foreknowledge of the consequences of any contribution made to the policy flow would also be poor, because of the instability of Cabinets and the irrelevance of changes in Cabinets or policies to changes in voters' views.

The seriousness of Italy's economic and cultural problems, compared with those of Sweden or Great Britain, could be used to explain this relative failure of Italian politics. This is how it has been explained by adherents of various determinist schools of thought. In order to test the correctness of this interpretation, we will next turn to a political system that has been confronted with similarly grave problems, Germany.

CHAPTER 7

Germany

Constitutional History

Germany, like Italy and unlike Switzerland, was unified from above and in a brief span of years. This process was concluded in 1871 in the Hall of Mirrors at Versailles. It was there, at the end of the Franco-Prussian War, that Bismarck proclaimed William I, the King of Prussia, as German Emperor, in the presence and with the concurrence of the princes of the other German states.

During the preceding years, by military means, Prussia had defeated Austria, her rival for hegemony over the German Confederation, she had acquired new provinces as the spoils of her victory over Denmark, and she incorporated the Kingdom of Hanover. German national unification was thus brought about through dynastic wars at home and a united effort by the German states, under Prussian leadership, against France. Earlier, in connection with the 1848 liberal uprisings all over Europe, German liberals had attempted to bring about unification from below; their Frankfurt Parliament had disbanded when the effort failed. The success of unification by Prussia expressed this earlier liberal failure in constitutional terms, however, by making the new German Empire (Reich) a federal system, in reality a federation of princes. It was made up of twenty-five states: four kingdoms (Prussia, Bavaria, Saxony, Württemberg), five grand duchies, thirteen duchies and principalities, and the three "Free and Hanseatic Cities" (Hamburg, Lübeck, and Bremen).

While the member states retained their previous constitutions, which were quite diverse, the constitution of the Reich was based on that of the North German Confederation, established in 1867 as the forerunner of the Empire. As its main federal organ, the new constitution provided for a Federal Council, in which the heads of the member states were represented. For all practical purposes, its composition gave Prussia control of this upper house of Parliament. The lower house, the Reichstag, was popularly elected by male suffrage. Each district was represented by one deputy, chosen by a majority on the first ballot or by a plurality in a run-off. The cabinet was headed by the Reich Chancellor, who was also head of the Prussian government, appointed by and accountable to the Emperor. Nominally, the Chancellor should also have had the support of majorities in the Reichstag and the Prussian State Diet, but in fact he was dependent upon the Kaiser alone. This was shown by Bismarck, during the nearly twenty years he held the post and, as well, in 1890, when the new Kaiser ordered him to resign.

The Imperial Constitution remained stable until Germany's defeat in World War I. During its last two years, a kind of military dictatorship prevailed. The Armistice was preceded by revolutionary uprisings modeled on the successful Russian Revolution of 1917. In November, 1918, the Kaiser was forced to abdicate and flee the country, and a provisional government, under pressure from "soldiers' and workers' councils" in Berlin, proclaimed the Republic. A constituent National Assembly was elected and convened at Weimar, and the constitution it wrote took its name from that historic center of German culture. The Reich retained its imperial title, but became a republic in which monarchy was abolished at all levels.[1] Federalism was retained, but the predominant position of Prussia, although by far the largest and most populous state, was reduced in the Federal Council. Further, the personal union between the Prussian and Reich chancellorships was eliminated. The Reich Chancellor was to be effectively accountable to the Reichstag, now elected quadrennially by universal suffrage on the basis of proportional representation. The Reichstag could be dissolved by the President, and it could overthrow the cabinet by expressing lack of confidence in it.

The Reich Presidency was the most novel provision of the Weimar Constitution. The President was popularly elected for a term of seven years—for three years longer than the Reichstag. He appointed and dismissed the chancellor, and he was given extensive emergency powers under the constitution's famous Article 48. Thus the President could use

---

[1] The word *Reich* does not necessarily imply imperial aspirations, and related words are used to denote matters of state by other countries with Germanic languages—the Netherlands, Denmark, and Sweden.

virtually any available means—including the army and suspension of civil rights—to restore order in an emergency.

Neither governments nor the constitution were stable under the Weimar Republic. Cabinets were in office for an average of about eight months. As for the constitution, its content was more difficult to determine than that of the Italian *Statuto*. It could be amended by a two-thirds' vote of the members of the upper house and by a two-thirds' majority of a Reichstag quorum. Since the quorum in the Reichstag was two-thirds of the total membership, this meant that constitutional amendments could be passed by four-ninths—less than half—of the members of the Reichstag. As a result, any bill passed by a majority greater than that required for amendments could be considered a constitutional amendment. This also applied to so-called "Enabling Acts," by which Parliament gave more or less unrestricted powers to a Cabinet, usually for a limited period of time. It was by means of such an Enabling Act that Adolf Hitler, having been appointed Chancellor by President Hindenburg in January, 1933, was given full powers for an unlimited time. In this sense, all the decrees and laws afterward issued by Hitler could be considered constitutional.

Prior to Hitler's appointment, proconstitutional Cabinets had been unable to cope with the effects of the depression. From 1930 to 1932, a Cabinet headed by Dr. Heinrich Brüning of the Catholic Center party had relied heavily on the presidential emergency powers of Article 48, with the Reichstag in recess most of the time. In 1932, two Reichstag elections and one presidential election (plus its run-off) were held. Hindenburg was reëlected and then dismissed Brüning, one of whose two brief successors used Article 48 in conjunction with dissolution of the Reichstag. Meanwhile, millions were unemployed and violence reigned on the streets, with National Socialists and Communists terrorizing each other, as well as all those unlucky enough to find themselves between these two extremes. In this situation, Hindenburg finally called upon Hitler—who had the previous year opposed him as a presidential candidate—to form a Cabinet. Thus the Weimar Republic died or, as some put it, committed suicide.

During the next twelve years, until Germany's total defeat at the hands of the Allies, the German political system became the very model of a modern totalitarian dictatorship. Although Hitler kept up a façade of legalism—not entirely unjustified in terms of the Enabling Act—constitutionalism in Germany had obviously come to an end. Then, with defeat, with the occupation of the country by the four victorious powers, and with the division of the country brought about by the Cold War, the German political system itself, as it had existed since 1871, came to an end. The founding of the Federal Republic of Germany in 1949, and shortly thereafter of the German Democratic Republic in the Soviet zone of occupation, brought into being two new political systems. Both of them claim continuity with the Reich, although the western state undoubtedly has the better claim. Nevertheless, both the Federal Republic and the Democratic Republic are new units, facing new problems and dealing with them by means of new institutions.

The German Democratic Republic employs for this purpose the proven methods of Soviet Communism, slavishly copying every change in party line from Moscow. For this reason, we will not directly concern ourselves with it in this book. The Federal Republic, on the other hand, consciously built on the Weimar tradition, earnestly endeavors to correct all of the presumed shortcomings of the Weimar Constitution which were believed to have contributed to the rise of Hitler. Its "Basic Law," as the constitution is called, was drafted on orders of the military governors in the three Western zones of occupation. They had instructed the ministers-president of the states in their zones to have a constitution prepared. The ministers-president—heads of the state governments—in turn convened a "Parliamentary Council," composed of representatives of the state parliaments, which wrote the Basic Law. It was ratified by all the state parliaments but one, the Bavarian, and the first elections under it were held in 1949.

Since then, much greater progress has been made with filling in its interstices than during roughly the same period in Italy. For instance, the Federal Constitutional Court provided for by the Basic Law was activated after a much shorter delay than its Italian counterpart. The Basic Law has been amended in order to give a constitutional basis to the new German defense establishment, which had not been envisaged by the demilitarizing Occupation Powers at the time of constitution-making. To amend, a two-thirds' majority of both houses of Parliament is required. As a result, the Basic Law itself has been quite stable.

Similar stability has not prevailed in electoral law, which has been modified before each federal and most state elections. The territorial structure of the Federal Republic has also been altered, through the combination of three states into one, designed to eliminate state boundaries arbitrarily drawn by Allied occupation zones. In addition to the changes actually made, there is constant discussion of further constitutional change. Since the Basic Law was so called in order to emphasize its tentative nature—in view of the division of the country that the founders hoped would not be permanent—debates of constitutional change appear as quite proper to German politicians. Moreover, whenever prospects for reunification brighten, people begin to discuss the constitution of a reunited Germany.

Constitutional Structure

The Basic Law reflects throughout the preoccupation of its authors with the errors committed by their forerunners in the National Assembly at Weimar. Thus, the powers of the new Federal President were drastically reduced. He is elected for a term of five years—one year longer than the lower house of Parliament—by a joint session of both houses, supplemented by an equal number of electors from the state parliaments. There are nine of these states now—before territorial reform, there were eleven —and none of them outdistances the others nearly to the extent that Prussia used to do. The states are represented in the Federal Council, the upper house of Parliament, by three, four, or five members of their governments, depending on population. These votes are cast as one unit. The Bundestag, which replaced the old Reichstag, has had between four and five hundred members. These are elected under a new system. Since 1953, 50 per cent of them have come from single-member constituencies, on the basis of a simple majority system. The remaining 50 per cent are elected from the member states, as constituencies with several deputies each, on the basis of proportional representation. The Bundestag elects the Federal Chancellor, normally by an absolute majority of its members. It cannot overthrow the Chancellor unless a majority of its members agree beforehand on his successor. This is the adroit innovation of Article 67 of the Basic Law, which is likely to become even more famous than Article 48 of the Weimar Constitution. It was designed to prevent Cabinet instability, of which there has been none in the Federal Republic. In total, the position of the Chancellor has been greatly strengthened as compared with that of his Weimar predecessor. For this reason, the emergency powers the Basic Law gives to the Chancellor, which are hedged in by requirements of controls on the part of the Federal Council, have not had to be used.

The Federal Constitutional Court was one outcome of the retrospective orientation of the authors of Bonn's constitution. Its purpose is not only to serve as the umpire of the federal system, but also to protect the basic rights of citizens under the Basic Law, and to ensure the constitutionality of legislation. Half its members are appointed by each of the two houses of Parliament, and bargaining among the parties with regard to these judicial appointments delayed the court's operation, though not by as much as in the Italian case. Since it began functioning, the court has been doing a land-office business. When it became evident that its original structure hampered efficient operation, the court requested a revision, which the Bundestag has made.

Problems

As the Germans themselves saw things at the end of World War II, constitutional problems were not of primary importance for them. Economic problems were. Their cities and industries had been laid waste by Allied strategic bombing; their economy had been exhausted by the efforts of total war; and the productive capacity of their agriculture was being strained beyond the breaking point by an influx of some eight million refugees and expellees. The economy thus laid waste was being further disorganized by its division into separate occupation zones and, later, into distinct western and eastern portions.

The primacy of economic problems was recognized by the Western Occupation powers, too, when they created an Economic Council as the first German organ of self-government with greater than state-wide scope. In the years after 1945, outsiders would thus have agreed that economic problems were the most urgent ones facing the Germans. Many Germans felt the same way before their national unification in 1871, of course, but this would not have been as obvious to others then. The North German Customs League, which preceded the North German Confederation—itself the immediate forerunner of the Reich—gives an indication of the importance of economic problems in the eyes of many Germans of that time. As in the case of many federations before and since, its members did not have the resources adequate for dealing with the new problems they were facing. These problems arose out of the Industrial Revolution, whose full impact was then beginning to be felt in the German states. Railroads had to be built, together with the coal, iron, and steel industries needed for that task and for the armaments race among the big powers, which was about to begin.

National unification served these purposes well and had the result that Germany was industrialized much more rapidly and more thoroughly than France or Italy. Germany, by contrast with Italy, had the necessary natural resources, especially iron and coal. And the two provinces she took as spoils from France in the war of 1870-71, Alsace and Lorraine, were of considerable help.

After Germany's defeat in World War I—as a result of which, incidentally, these provinces returned to France, and Germany lost industrially valuable territory elsewhere and had to pay millions in reparations to the Allies—economic problems were, if anything, of even greater importance. But they were overshadowed by the constitutional problem. The great inflation of 1923 followed—not necessarily as the effect of her war losses—and wiped out the savings, and in many cases the self-respect, of the middle classes. Next, after five years of relative prosperity and economic progress, came the Great Depression of 1929, with its vast numbers of unemployed. Ever since then, many Germans have believed that constitutional democracy is possible only if it rests upon a firm basis of economic stability, and that another great depression would result in another victory for totalitarianism, in Germany and elsewhere. This is one reason for their postwar preoccupation with economic problems; it also helps to explain the West German government's leading role in the movement for European economic union—once more because the existing states do not have the resources to deal with their economic problems in the middle of the twentieth century.

National unification created sizable cultural problems. For one thing, the new Reich contained several large ethnic minorities—Poles, Danes, Alsatians. For another, even the "Germans" themselves were very diverse in their make-up. The less educated among them spoke such different dialects that they could barely communicate with one another. Finally, the founding of the Reich united within the same national state the two antagonistic denominations of Christendom, which had fought the great religious wars on German territory: Protestants and Roman Catholics. Since the Peace of Augsburg (1555) gave recognition to the principle *cuius regio, eius religio*,[2] most of the German states had been predominantly of one or the other denomination. The new Reich combined them, so that Protestants outnumbered Catholics by a ratio of 2 to 1. From this resulted the first great parliamentary struggle of Bismarck's two decades as Reich Chancellor, the Kulturkampf, or culture struggle, between him and the Center, a Catholic political party. The Kulturkampf lasted from 1871 to 1883, when it ended more or less in a draw. In its course, the Jesuits were expelled, and they and, later, other religious orders were dissolved and civil marriages made mandatory. During the Weimar period, such cultural problems were not of as great importance. Hitler's attacks on the Catholic and Protestant Churches brought them to the fore again, as did his anti-Semitism, which resulted in the extermination of most German Jews, who made up 1 per cent of the total population. After the war, the change of relative strength between

[2] "Whose region, his religion"—i.e., the religion of the ruler determined the religion of his subjects.

Protestants and Catholics to virtual parity in the Federal Republic called for new approaches to this problem.

External problems have played an unusually important role in German, and particularly in Prussian, history. One reason for this was the fact that Prussia became a dominant state largely by means of her excellent army. Another is the exposed position of the German lands on the Continent—much more exposed than any of the three countries discussed earlier. In this way, Napoleon gave early impetus to the movement for unification, not only by eliminating many of the petty states, but also by making it obvious that a disunited Germany might continue to be easy prey to invasions from across the Rhine. Unification itself, as we have seen, was achieved as the direct result of military ventures. And the monarchy fell as the direct result of the military disaster of World War I. The cloud of defeat under which the Weimar Republic was born —its first government had to assume responsibility for the Treaty of Versailles—helped to prevent it from getting the kind of popular acceptance that would have been necessary for its survival when it was being attacked by enemies of constitutionalism from the right and left. Finally, Hitler launched World War II in an effort to solve Germany's other problems by dealing with her external ones by force.

The victors were bent upon eliminating "German militarism" once and for all. But soon the Western Allies found that they needed a West German army in order to prevent the further expansion of Soviet military power, and they initiated West German rearmament, within the framework of Western European Union and NATO. At the same time, the Soviets were arming the Democratic Republic, their satellite. Meanwhile, the country had been divided in two. Reunification had become the single most important problem for all German politicians. This was so obviously an external problem, since it could not be solved without participation of the United States and the Soviet Union, that practically all issues in contemporary German politics are in some way related to questions of foreign policy.

We have already seen that the main constitutional problem, namely that of creating a new constitution, was heavily influenced by the problem of division. The very title of the Basic Law was devised in order to emphasize the desire for reunification, which is also mentioned prominently in its preamble. By itself, the need for a new constitution would have provided substantial difficulties for Bonn's Parliamentary Council. Division made their task even more formidable, and it was further complicated by the deep awareness, on the part of the authors of the constitution, of the failure of Germany's first democratic constitution, and by their varying interpretations of its causes. Despite all this, the record of the first ten years of the life of the Federal Republic indicates that they solved their constitutional problem very well.

Issues and Politics

West German politics since the founding of the Federal Republic in 1949 has been dominated by issues which differ in several ways from those prominent in Weimar and Imperial days. Issues due to economic problems have not been as important, nor have they been fought over as violently as in the past. An obvious reason for this—but not the only one—has been the success of the "social market economy" of Professor Ludwig Erhard, the Christian Democratic Economics Minister, in dealing with economic problems. Ever since his Occupation-supported currency reform of 1948, Germans and envious citizens of neighboring victor states of World War II have been speaking of the West German "economic miracle." In these circumstances, the Social Democratic Party, which admittedly was not too eager for socialization of private property even during the Weimar Republic, has considerably toned down its Marxist ideology. The trade unions have staged very few strikes.

Another type of issue that used to plague German politics, although it is still raised from time to time, has decreased in importance: historical recrimination. In the Weimar Republic, for example, die-hard monarchists never forgave the founders of the Republic and kept the issue of restoration alive until Hitler came to power. Die-hard nationalists never forgave the founders of the Republic for allegedly "stabbing in the back" the military at the end of the war and signing the Versailles Treaty. The Social Democrats carried grudges against all parties to the right of them for delaying the establishment of constitutional democracy for as long as they did—and this despite the fact that the Social Democrats shared in political responsibility during the Weimar period with the two other parties of the "Weimar Coalition," the Center and the Liberals. In contemporary West German politics, there would be many additional causes for this kind of recrimination: by the proconstitutional parties against former Nazis, who persecuted them under Hitler; by former Nazis for having been "denazified" by the constitutionalists in collaboration with the Occupation Powers; by many Germans against the Occupation Powers for Allied bombings of great urban centers, or for the policy of dismantling industrial plant as reparations payments. Yet relatively little recrimination is to be noted.

The religious cleavage has also become less of an issue, at least in federal politics. In state politics, on the other hand, it is often the single most important issue. One reason for this is the changed demography of the Federal Republic. At least as important, however, has been the deliberate assignment of the function of dealing with cultural problems to the states rather than the federal government. School systems especially are controlled by the states. As a result, recurrent and divisive controversies over state support to denominational or "Christian community" schools are fought out at the level of the states. The Christian Democratic Union, West Germany's strongest party, whose leader, Dr. Konrad Adenauer, has been Federal Chancellor from the beginning in 1949, is a mixed Catholic and Protestant party, in which the two denominations are about equally represented, in terms of electoral support if not leadership. This contrasts sharply with the major religious party of Imperial and Weimar days, the Center, which was explicitly Roman Catholic.

Foreign and defense policy, and the constitution, have provided the major issues for West German politics, at least since full self-government was restored to the Germans by the Occupation Powers—and that did not really happen until 1955. Before that year, the Western Allies still retained a veto power over German legislation in those fields. Until 1949, the Allied High Commissioners even had to issue licenses to German parties wanting to participate in federal campaigns, to certify them as bona-fide democrats. This, incidentally, was one explanation for the absence of recriminatory issues: Politicians opposed to the new constitutional order or identified with the Nazi regime were simply not licensed. When the Allies began to take the lid off the West German political kettle, external and constitutional problems began to generate increasing amounts of steam. The division of the country accounts for this. Of course, the desirability of reunification itself has not been an issue. The best means for achieving reunification, however, has been strongly controverted. Here two broad alternative policies have been competing.

The winning policy, thus far, has been that followed by Dr. Adenauer's Christian Democratic government, which is closely identified with United States policy toward the Soviet Union. It has involved the admission of the Federal Republic to the Schuman Plan, Western European Union, NATO, and the various steps on the road toward establishing a six-state federal union in Europe, consisting of France, Italy, the Federal Republic, Belgium, the Netherlands, and Luxemburg. It has also meant the rearming of the Federal Republic as a member of NATO, and the eventual provision of its forces with atomic weapons.

The other alternative, pushed by the Social Democratic party, has favored a broader European union, which would include the countries with strong socialist parties—the United Kingdom and the Scandinavian countries. It has opposed joining NATO, been skeptical about, though not in principle against, rearmament, and it has fought tooth and nail the furnishing of German defense forces with nuclear weapons. The Social Democrats have even accused Adenauer of being unenthusiastic about reunification, because it might put an end to the majority position of his party—the territory of the Democratic Republic used to be a stronghold of the Social Democrats before 1933.

These issues have often been debated in constitutional terms. The amending provision of the Basic Law provides one explanation. Rearmament called for constitutional amendments, for example, and the Adenauer coalition did not command the needed two-thirds' majority in both houses of Parliament. The Social Democrats therefore had an interest in creating issues which could be resolved only by constitutional amendment. This would enable them to block any policy with which they disagreed, especially by casting the votes of Social-Democratic-controlled state governments in the Federal Council, where these amounted to the required one-third. The Basic Law specifies that the three, four, or five votes of each state in the upper house of Parliament shall be cast as a unit. Most of the state governments, which require the support of majorities in the state parliaments much as does the federal Cabinet in the Bundestag, have been coalitions, of virtually every conceivable grouping. Some coalitions, for example, have included all the parties active in the politics of a state; others have consisted only of the two major parties opposing each other on the federal level, Christian Democrats and Social Democrats. In the first years of the Federal Republic, the composition of a state coalition depended mainly on the relative strength of alignments with regard to what seemed to people the most important problems in their state—economic problems in the industrial heartland of North Rhine-Westphalia, for example, and cultural problems in Catholic, traditionalist, and almost separatist Bavaria. But as a result of the need for an amending majority in the Federal Council, state election campaigns, which take place at irregular intervals between Bundestag elections, have increasingly been fought over federal issues, and especially foreign policy.

The predominance of the reunification problem may also go far toward explaining the comparatively mild new tone of West German politics. In East Germany, the West Germans face unanimity, albeit artificially created. This has made for a kind of yearning for unanimity on their own part, expressed in parliamentary resolutions about the need for reunification, which are passed from time to time. In part, this may also be due to their recent experience with National Socialist totalitarianism, the recurrence of which most Germans are agreed must be prevented at almost any cost. The same revulsion against Nazi lawlessness also accounts for the frequent conversion of conflicts about material interests into cases before the Federal Constitutional Court, which symbolizes the very antithesis of lawlessness, charged as it is with guarding the constitution. In the same connection, we should note the absence of violence and the very low incidence of corruption in the politics of the Federal Republic, since both violence and corruption characterized the Nazi regime and the last few years of the Weimar Republic.

Under the Empire and the first Republic, from twelve to over thirty political organizations competed in parliamentary elections. The Federal Republic has so far elected a new Bundestag in 1949, 1953, and 1957. In the first of these, nine parties placed deputies; in the second, six parties; and in the third, only four parties. The strongest of these has been the Christian Democratic Union—in alliance with its Bavarian ally, the Christian Social Union—which progressed from less than one-third of the popular vote to more than half of it. The Social Democratic party has received about one-third, with slight increases from one election to the next. The Free Democratic party, which started out with 52 out of 402 deputies in the first Bundestag, has declined to 41 out of 497 in the third. Its program is based on political liberalism and nationalism of the nineteenth century, and economic liberalism of the twentieth. While it participated in Adenauer's coalition cabinets until 1956, it split into two wings that year and joined the opposition after the next election. The German party has maintained a stable strength of between 15 and 17 deputies. Its support is strictly localized in northern Germany, and it has participated in all of Adenauer's Cabinets. The Bavarian party has been similarly localized, but has failed to elect any deputies after 1949. The Refugee League, not licensed as a party for the first election, placed 27 in 1953, but none in 1957. The Communists elected 15 in 1949, but none in the 1953 elections; the Federal Constitutional Court declared their party anticonstitutional after that year.

In Germany, as in the other countries, there is a great deal of overlap between political parties and interest organizations. The latter naturally play a role in politics, even though the Basic Law says that only "political parties participate in forming the political will of the nation." In general, each interest group tends to be closely identified with one of the parties. In the Weimar Republic, for example, the Social Democratic, Center, and Liberal parties each had their affiliated trade union. This is no longer the case since the founding after the end of the war of the German Trade Union Federation, whose constitution declares its neutrality in partisan politics, and whose leadership combines Social Democrats with Christian Democrats in a ratio of about 4 to 1. The organizations of big industry in the Rhineland are believed to be close to the Free Democrats, as are professional groups with predominantly Protestant membership. Among other examples are the peasants' and artisans' associations, which have firm relations with the Christian Democrats. Within the Christian Democratic Union, an assortment of groupings has been organized to cater to the various social and economic statuses—professionals, white-collar employees, workers, peasants, civil servants, youth, women, and others. Similar groupings have also developed within the other parties.

Under the Weimar Republic, such groups often succeeded in electing their candidates directly into the Reichstag. This was one reason for the great number of parties, and therefore one reason for the instability of Cabinets. With the brief exception of the Refugee League, this has not occurred in the Federal Republic. But even if it had, cabinets might still have remained as stable as they have been: the same man has been Chancellor since 1949, with few changes in his coalition—and this even though he was first elected by the barest majority: 202 out of 402. The requirements of Article 67, according to which lack of confidence can be voted only if a majority agree on a successor to the incumbent Chancellor, must go far, though not all the way, toward explaining this Cabinet stability. It has had the effect of leaving to Parliament mainly deliberative functions, after the election of the Chancellor, and leaving to the Chancellor the resolution of issues other than constitutional ones and those decided in a general election. In the process of solving problems he has the support of his Cabinet and of the efficient and honest bureaucracy. Problems are recognized by parties and interest organizations. Issues are usually formulated at the parliamentary level.

Success

Over the long run, since 1871, the German political system has been anything but stable—monarchy, the "Revolution" of 1918, Weimar, Hitler, and now the Federal Republic *and* the Democratic Republic. Even the present Basic Law is at least potentially very unstable. But each of these four regimes, with the exception of the Weimar Republic, was relatively efficient in dealing with the problems that it considered of greatest importance. Yet, each of the systems that preceded the present one failed to adapt itself to changes in these problems, and this brought about its downfall in every case. The Empire failed to adapt itself to increasing demands for more democracy, both inside Germany and abroad. This steadily reduced its effectiveness, precisely at the time of maximum stress, during World War I. The Weimar Republic, partly because of overconcentration on these constitutional problems of the previous regime, failed to adapt itself to the grave new economic problems. With millions of unemployed on the streets, its effectiveness began to wither away in the face of Hitler's onslaught on constitutionalism itself. Nazi totalitarianism, while widely accepted by the German people in its early years, because it succeeded on the economic front where the Republic had failed, became the captive of its own ideology. This led to such excesses in the "solution" of Germany's cultural and external problems that Hitler lost both the support of the German people and the war.

The constitution of the Federal Republic of Germany, in terms of ten years' performance, must be adjudged a success—even a brilliant success. The Basic Law has been stable in the face of many temptations to tamper with its stability. Politics has been efficient in disposing, within the limits of the possible, of the real problems confronted by West Germany. And the constitution is almost universally accepted, as are the policies produced under it. Moreover, citizens in West Germany are in sounder situations of responsibility than Germans have ever been. They can make meaningful contributions to central decisions other than those which at present lie beyond German influence, i.e., about the division of their country. They can do this because they can choose among meaningful alternatives, presented in state and federal elections and through the many organizations they can join or support. Their resources for implementing these choices are good in every respect. And the stability of the constitutional order and the rule of law provide them with solid knowledge of the likely consequences of their choices.

Most remarkable, perhaps, is that all of this is true despite the problems of unprecedented gravity that the Germans were facing in the years following their colossal defeat of 1945. How much praise for this success should go to the constitution-makers of Bonn?

CHAPTER 8

France

Constitutional History

In 1959, the Fifth French Republic, engineered by General Charles de Gaulle, succeeded the Fourth. The Fourth Republic itself was brought into being within the memory of most readers, after France's liberation from German occupation at the end of World War II. Before that, there had been the four years of Marshal Pétain's Vichy regime, tainted by collaboration with the Nazis. It had succeeded almost eighty years of the Third Republic, whose Parliament voted Pétain into power in Bordeaux in 1940. The average life of cabinets in the Third Republic was about seven months. In the Fourth, it was even shorter. For all these reasons, Americans especially are likely to think of France as the very model of constitutional failure. But we should not let ourselves be deceived by the contemporaneity of events into overlooking certain long-term patterns of stability, adaptability, efficiency, and effectiveness that can be found beneath reports in the daily press.

Of the five Continental countries under study, France is the oldest, both as a nation and as a state. Thus it was that Machiavelli, in bemoaning the divided condition of his Italy, asked his compatriots to emulate the French monarchy, which was already a strongly centralized state. And—to skip over the centuries—when Italy and Germany were finally achieving national unification, around 1870, France was founding her *Third* Republic—the third, that is, after the great French Revolution set the example for constitutional engineering all over Europe. France herself has had perhaps a dozen constitutions since then. The story is told of a man who walked into a Paris bookshop after the Revolution of 1830 —or was it the one of 1848?—and asked for a copy of the constitution.

"Sorry, Monsieur," the reply came back, "we do not carry periodical literature." Nevertheless, however many constitutions France may have had since the Revolution or before, they have all been constitutions of the same France, providing a political framework for a territory and a population that have not changed significantly, at least when compared with those of Switzerland, Italy, and Germany.

The First Republic followed the decapitation of Louis XVI, in 1793, and was eventually succeeded by Napoleon's Empire. By 1814, another Bourbon King, Louis XVIII, was restored. After another revolution, in 1830, there came the eighteen years of the so-called "July Monarchy" of Louis Philippe. This led to still another revolution in 1848, and the establishment of the short-lived Second Republic, which was relieved by the Second Empire of Louis Napoleon, nephew of the first Emperor of the French, in 1852. The Second Empire ended with Louis Napoleon's defeat by the Prussians at Sedan in 1870, whereupon a revolutionary mob in Paris proclaimed the Third Republic, whose constitution, however, was not completed until 1875. In the interim, Paris passed through another bloody uprising, the Commune of 1871.

The constitution of the Third Republic consisted of a series of "Organic Laws," which defined relations among the most important organs of government: the President; the Chamber of Deputies and the Senate, which together formed the National Assembly; and the Ministers. The Chamber of Deputies was elected directly by universal male suffrage, which had been introduced earlier by the Second Republic. The Senate was indirectly elected. The President was elected for a term of seven years by the National Assembly. His actions were to be countersigned by Ministers accountable to the Chamber of Deputies. He could dissolve the Chamber with the consent of the Senate.

The right of dissolution was used only once, in 1877, when Marshal MacMahon, the President, ordered a new parliamentary election when the Chamber opposed his royalist Ministers. But the subsequent election returned an even stronger opposition, and MacMahon ultimately resigned before his term had expired. MacMahon's action proved so unpopular, largely because it was reminiscent of antirepublican coups by the two Napoleons, that it turned out to be the last dissolution in the whole history of the Third Republic. Even in the Fourth, the lower house was dissolved only once before its full term had expired, and on that occasion not very long before its normal end.

The Third Republic worked with these same institutions until it installed Marshal Pétain as "Chief of State." It passed through a number of constitutional crises on the way, but managed to survive each one.

First, in 1889, there was the threat that General Boulanger, who demanded reform of the constitution, would rally enough popular support behind himself to become dictator. Next came the Dreyfus Affair, which lasted from 1894 to 1906, and shook the Republic to its very foundations. It involved civil-military relations, continuation of the century-old struggle between defenders of the Old Regime and the Great Revolution, anticlericalism, and anti-Semitism. It ended with the exoneration of Captain Dreyfus, who had been wrongly accused and convicted of espionage. One of its consequences was the complete separation of Church and State, in 1905.

From then until 1934, the republican constitution had clear sailing. In that year, the Stavisky scandal, which exposed many politicians who were involved in corruption, brought about serious antirepublican riots. This led Premier Doumergue, an ex-President, to propose constitutional reform aimed at reducing the instability of ministries by making dissolution of the Chamber of Deputies the necessary consequence of the fall of a cabinet. During subsequent years, several premiers were granted the power of legislating by decree, since the Chamber found itself just as unable to agree on positive policies as had the Reichstag during the years preceding 1933. Finally, after France surrendered to victorious German armies in June, 1940, Parliament voted Pétain full powers by virtual unanimity—569 votes to 80.

While General de Gaulle was leading the Free French forces from England, discussions of constitutional reform had already begun. After Liberation, the voters were asked in a referendum whether to continue with the Third Republic or to have a new constitution prepared. They voted overwhelmingly against the Third Republic, and subsequently elected a Constituent Assembly, whose draft constitution was submitted to another referendum and rejected by a narrow margin. A second draft was accepted, but only by a slim majority. This is how the Fourth Republic was born. It was to live for only twelve years—about equal to the life span of the Weimar Republic. Since the constitution of the Fifth Republic was ratified by the French electorate only in 1958, we will here describe the structure of its forerunner. In doing so, the main questions to be remembered will be: What caused the failure of this constitution? How did interpretations of this failure influence the construction of the constitution of the Fifth Republic?

Constitutional Structure

The Fourth Republic borrowed heavily from the Third, and even where deliberate departures from its traditions were made, practices somehow returned to those of "the good old days"—so much so that the result has been described as an "easy return from the Fourth Republic to the Third." To begin with, there were some changes in nomenclature. The former Chamber of Deputies was now called the National Assembly, and in fact the constitution concentrated in it most of the functions previously performed by the two houses that together formed the National Assembly of the Third Republic. The old Senate, in keeping with its reduced powers, was to be known as the Council of the Republic, and the two chambers together simply as Parliament. In order to give representation to France's overseas possessions, the constitution established the French Union, with its own separate Assembly, half its members to be delegates from the French Parliament and half from overseas assemblies. It also provided for a consultative Economic Council.

Many of the members of the Constituent Assembly directed their major efforts to correcting what they believed to have been the greatest weakness of the Third Republic: instability of Cabinets. The usual argument was used, and the usual conclusions drawn. The argument was based on comparisons with politics in Britain, where Cabinets are stable. The conclusions attributed this stability to two main factors, the Cabinet's power to dissolve the House of Commons when it loses a vote of confidence there, and party discipline. The lack of discipline among French parties, in turn, was believed to be due to the electoral system that prevailed during most of the Third Republic. This was based upon very small single-member constituencies, in each of which the candidate receiving a majority in the first election, or a plurality in the run-off, was declared elected. This system was said to make for "village pump politics," since relations between deputies and their constituents were so close that voters were motivated by local rather than national issues.

These considerations led to the use of a system of proportional representation for the election of the Constituent Assembly and of later National Assemblies. Instead of the single-member *arrondissement,* the larger *département* now made up the basic election district, from each of which between five and nine deputies were elected to the National Assembly. But the provisions for the method of electing the lower chamber were not included in the constitution; they were left instead for a separate election law, which would be easier to amend—and which was, in fact, to be amended before later elections.

The interpretation that linked Cabinet stability with an effective power of dissolution, on the other hand, was reflected in the constitution itself. The Council of Ministers, i.e., the Cabinet, was now given the opportunity to dissolve the National Assembly and call for the election of a new one, but only in certain severely restricted circumstances. These restrictions were written into the new constitution because not all the members of the Constituent Assembly wanted to avert Cabinet instability. The Communists, for instance, preferred to have Cabinets at the mercy of the National Assembly, where they expected to play a leading role—as indeed they did. Other politicians of the left, who identified themselves with the traditions of the Revolution, also believed in establishing a *régime d'assemblée,* under which the Assembly itself would govern, using the Cabinet merely as an intermediary, "executive" instrument in the narrowest meaning of that word. The resulting constitutional compromise provided that the Cabinet could dissolve the National Assembly eighteen months after the last parliamentary election, but only if two Cabinets had been overthrown by absolute majorities during the eighteen months preceding dissolution.

A comparison of the constitutional documents alone would have suggested that the new National Assembly would be stronger than the old Chamber of Deputies, at the cost of weakening the new Council of the Republic compared with the old Senate. The Cabinet was strengthened, too, mostly at the expense of the President of the Republic. The latter was to be elected by both houses of Parliament, meeting in joint session, for a term of seven years, but could not act without the countersignature of a Minister.

The constitution was hard to amend. Unless two-thirds of the National Assembly, or three-fifths of both the Council of the Republic and the National Assembly, supported an amendment upon its second reading, it had to be submitted to a referendum. This procedure was never used, and the few amendments that were passed were of little importance, except for one which restored some of its former functions to the old Senate.

Problems

The Third and Fourth Republics faced very different sets of major problems, but both attempted to deal with them by means of very similar methods. The process of industrialization took much longer in France than in Germany. It started before the Third Republic came into being, and it continued throughout most of that Republic's life, yet industrialization never went as far as it did in Germany or, for that matter, as in Great Britain. Alongside the great steel and coal industries that France developed before World War I, she retained a large part of her older economic structure: preindustrial, essentially commercial, and based on the small shopkeeper and artisan. Similarly, French agriculture continued in the main to be based on peasants with small landholdings, although larger and more efficient agricultural enterprises existed in some parts of the country.

Until 1914-18, at least, when great battles brought ruin to much of the countryside—and death to many of her young men—France was rich in natural resources. With a population smaller than that of Italy, her productive agricultural area was about four times as great. In large part because of this natural wealth, there was relatively little demand for economic activity by the state, in contrast with the German situation during the same period. For the same reason, too, politics could be considered as a sort of sport, which was of no real significance in the lives of those who participated in it.[1] This condition began to change during the interwar years, when the great international economic upsets had their effects on the economy in France, as everywhere else. Since World War II, it has changed almost completely. The war itself cost France almost as dearly as the first one, in both men and resources. In its aftermath, France, like Britain, was to lose some of her more profitable overseas possessions. But because the French did not "preside over the liquidation" of their empire as efficiently as did the British, because they became involved in a series of colonial wars, first in Indochina and then in Algeria, their economic problems were heightened. American aid ameliorated a number of crises, but no postwar French government proved able to deal adequately with the problem of inflation. Nor was any one of them successful in effecting reform of the many problematic economic habits of the French, such as persistent overproduction of wine, hoarding of gold, and evasion of tax payments.

France's main cultural problem goes back to the conflict between the Revolutionary French State and the Roman Catholic Church. Ever since the Revolution, the defenders of the revolutionary tradition have been anticlerical, and the Church and many of those Frenchmen (and

---

[1] "France is a happy land where the soil is generous, the artisan ingenious and wealth evenly distributed. Politics are the pleasure of individuals but not the condition of their lives." Robert de Jouvenal, *Republique des Camarades,* as quoted by André Siegfried, *Switzerland,* 1950, p. 166.

more Frenchwomen) loyal to the Church have been antirepublican. There are no other serious cultural problems, despite the presence of a German-speaking minority in Alsace and Lorraine and the influx of millions of immigrants during the interwar years. The capacity of French culture to assimilate foreigners seems remarkable in this respect, although it has not been as successful recently in assimilating several hundred thousand Algerians, most of whom come to France only in order to earn francs to send or take home. The Church-State problem was "solved" a number of times, sometimes in favor of one side, sometimes in favor of the other. Until the birth of the Fourth Republic, if not thereafter, the losing side never did accept the solution. Even under the Fourth Republic, the problem of state support for Catholic schools gave rise to major parliamentary debates and resulted in the overthrow of cabinets.

France's external problems have always played an important role in her politics, mainly because her position on the Continent is almost as exposed as that of Germany. The three German wars fought by France, on French soil, between 1870 and 1945, suggest how preoccupied with external problems the French should reasonably be. France has maintained a strong military establishment throughout modern times. In fact, many of the traditions of the French army, as those of the bureaucracy, go back to the glorious reign of Louis XIV. And even though the French Revolution brought about the first mass conscription in history and the Napoleonic wars the greatest glory to the French army, the attitudes of many French military leaders have been antirepublican. At least, their loyalties to France have been greater than their loyalties to the Republic —whichever Republic it might happen to be at the time. When these military men—and the same may be said of many bureaucrats—have felt that the republican regime was not protecting the French "national interest," they have often supported movements for the abolition or at least the drastic reform of the Republic. Such problems of civil-military relations are likely to arise in any political system which has to maintain a large military establishment. In this way, external problems create constitutional problems as by-products, as it were.

Since Liberation, France would have had very serious problems of defense and foreign relations even without these complications. Of her colonial possessions, she lost outright Indochina, Morocco, and Tunisia. Her mandates from the League of Nations over Syria and Lebanon came to an end. And in Algeria, France has been fighting the Arab nationalist movement in what is constitutionally considered a part of Metropolitan France, that is, not a colony. At home, along with the other Western European countries, France has faced the threat of Soviet Communist aggression, with which none of the European countries could deal alone. This has raised the problem of what kind of alliances to enter into. Throughout this period, France has had to become accustomed to her new status in international politics as a second-rate power—a downgrading that has called for new approaches to diplomacy on her part. This has been made doubly difficult for many Frenchmen by the renaissance, especially economically, of West Germany. The usual domestic activities of the French Communist party, continuously the strongest single party in the National Assembly, have in no way helped these external problems toward solution.

Finally, there is the problem of the constitution—a problem, as already noted, that has been in the forefront of French politics ever since the Revolution. Under the Third Republic, to be sure, the proportions did not become truly serious until the latter years. For the Fourth Republic, founded as it was with little positive public enthusiasm, the constitution has always been the single most important problem. The reason for this is simply that people explained their government's poor performance in handling its other problems in terms of the constitution. Thus, General de Gaulle resigned from the provisional Presidency in January, 1946, because he opposed the first constitutional draft then being prepared by the Constituent Assembly. He opposed the first and second drafts in the campaigns on the referendum, and his *Rassemblement du Peuple Français* was founded with the goal of constitutional reform. Other French politicians constantly kept alive the issue of constitutional reform. Yet, except for the one major change in the electoral law mentioned above, only minor amendments were actually adopted. When the Fourth Republic was in what turned out to be its death throes, the problem was once more under attack in Parliament. Three specific reforms had been proposed by the Cabinet. One involved a new electoral law. The second would have made it impossible for deputies to propose increases in expenditures. And the third would have required that any negative majority opposed to a policy proposed by the Cabinet would have to form a positive majority, by agreeing on an alternative policy, before it could vote lack of confidence in the cabinet—a modification of Article 67 of the West German Basic Law, which shifted emphasis from the premier to policy.

In the end, in 1958, disagreement on solutions to the constitutional problem had grown too strong to be contained within the constitution of the Fourth Republic. De Gaulle became Premier and drafted the kind of constitution for the Fifth Republic that he had wanted the Fourth to adopt twelve years earlier. But even then, there was no unity among the opponents of the incumbent constitutional system. Many of the leaders of the Algerian uprising that returned De Gaulle to power preferred to abolish the Republic outright and felt that he was betraying them by merely replacing one Republic with another.

Issues and Politics

Roughly until the 1930's, many issues important in French politics became increasingly petrified. In other words, the controversies debated in Parliament and during electoral campaigns bore less and less relevance to the real problems that France was facing, at least in the judgment of "objective" outsiders. This was true particularly of the great historical issue, the Old Regime versus the Revolution. There was little practical point in debating in the 1890's an issue that had been pretty well settled a full century earlier; even if a majority of Frenchmen had wanted to return to a prerevolutionary state of affairs—and no majority of them ever did—they clearly could not have undone the vast changes that had been wrought since the Revolution. Yet many debates sounded as though this kind of return to the past were a practical possibility. It is apparent, of course, that debates of this kind were often used to obscure very concrete material interests in the present rather than the past. Thus, the old nobility, the army, and the Church, which are usually considered the three pillars of "reaction," had very definite interests to protect in the Third Republic. So did the peasants and those segments of the bourgeoisie who had been the main beneficiaries of the Revolution. And both sides often took recourse in the verbiage of the revolutionary issue as an effective weapon of debate. This occurred, for example, during the Dreyfus Affair.

Early alignments in Parliament were mainly based on such historical issues. The opposition to establishing the Third Republic was composed of groups supporting the pretenders of the Bourbon, Orléans, and Bonaparte dynasties. On the other side of the fence, there were Conservative and Radical Republicans. These were soon joined by the nascent Socialists, whose party was outlawed for some years and suffered several splits. But the Socialists, although they were also interested in a historical issue like the Commune of 1871, did address themselves more directly than the other parties to the contemporary economic problems that accompanied increasing industrialization.

These same problems were also being attacked by a growing trade-union movement, although labor organization was not legalized until 1884. The unions grouped themselves into the General Confederation of

Labor in 1895, but unlike their counterparts in Germany and Great Britain, they opposed "political action"—through the parties and Parliament—as a matter of principle. Instead, they sought to destroy the capitalist state by means of "direct action"—sabotage and strikes, including the instrument of the great general strike. Before World War I, a number of major strikes took place, among them one against the state by post-office employees, and another against the privately owned railroads. They were suppressed more or less violently by the government.

In addition to the recurrence of violence, periodic exposures of corruption by public officials created issues for French politics. In 1887, for example, the son-in-law of the President of the Republic was discovered to have been selling medals of the Legion of Honor. In 1892, a number of politicians were found to have been bribed by the then-bankrupt Panama Canal Company in connection with a promotion scheme. Forty years later came the Stavisky Scandal, and there were many in between. The crises brought about by such scandals and by the Dreyfus Affair often drew the upholders and the enemies of the Republic into two great opposing camps. This happened several times after World War I, but by that time economic problems began to give rise to the most divisive issues.

During this period, the French party system consisted of a number of political groups, of which all but the Communists and Socialists were loosely organized. From left to right, there were the Communists, the Socialists, the Radical Socialists, the Popular Democrats, the Republican Democratic Alliance, and the Republican Democratic Federation. The farther to the right, the less disciplined were the parties. Indeed, the two last-mentioned groups should not really be described as parliamentary parties, but rather as electoral organizations only. Even farther to the right were some ultranationalist and royalist groups; these did not normally sponsor candidates for election to the Chamber of Deputies, but instead staged more or less violent demonstrations.

All of this ended with the German victory of 1940, after which Marshal Pétain's "French State" replaced the "French Republic," on postage stamps and in political reality. But throughout the German occupation of first half and then of all France, the Resistance organizations inside the country and General de Gaulle's Free French abroad were discussing the reforms that should be undertaken after Liberation. During the war years, there was great hope that the experience of the Resistance itself would forge a new national unity for French politics and that the useless squabbling of the old parliamentarians would be replaced by a more realistic and more efficient political system.

For a brief honeymoon period after Liberation, it appeared that the hopes for national unity might have been justified. This was the period of *tripartisme,* when the three parties mainly identified with the violent Resistance against German occupation received approximately three-fourths of the total popular vote cast in elections. The three parties were the Communists, the Socialists, and the Popular Republican Movement, which was descended from the much smaller Popular Democratic party of the Third Republic, a Catholic group but one with no antirepublican clerical connections. All three were well disciplined and, therefore, helped by the new electoral law. Moreover, the two remaining large political groupings, the Radicals and the Conservatives, had not entirely escaped the taint of the Vichy regime or of collaboration with the Nazis. Many potential Conservative candidates and voters, especially, could not even take part in the first elections, because they had been deprived of their political rights as collaborators. Collaboration with the Germans, incidentally, was to add another historical issue to the more ancient ones which continued to crop up in the Fourth Republic. After Liberation, thousands of collaborators were tried and sentenced, among them Marshal Pétain, who died a prisoner, and his Premier, Pierre Laval, who was executed. Their posthumous exoneration was debated from time to time —one Frenchman's hero can still be another's traitor.

As the memories of the occupation grew dimmer, the parties that had not been identified with the Resistance grew stronger. Thus, the Conservatives got half a million votes more in the election of November, 1946, than they had in that of June, 1946. The National Assembly elected in November, 1946, served until the next election, held in June, 1951. By that time, De Gaulle's *Rassemblement du Peuple Français* had entered the field. The Communist party and the R.P.F. accounted for almost half the votes cast, while the Socialists and Popular Republicans together received fewer votes than the Popular Republicans alone had received in June, 1946. De Gaulle permitted the R.P.F. to disintegrate soon thereafter, but in the next parliamentary election, another new organization entered the competition. This one had been founded by Pierre Poujade and was designed to attract the support of France's numerous small shopkeepers and artisans and of anyone else who was dissatisfied with the parliamentary regime.

Throughout the 1950's, cabinet instability grew worse and worse, and ministerial crises longer and longer. Internal cohesion of all the parties, except for the Communists, weakened continually. Debates within and among the parties on issues generated by the new economic and external problems grew ever hotter. There were deep splits in almost all the proconstitutional parties on the issue of ratification of the European

Defense Community, which had been designed to help meet the Soviet threat through the rearmament of West Germany as part of a supranational European army. The National Assembly rejected EDC in 1954, and soon thereafter similar splits were created over Western European Union. This was finally ratified, with the result that Germany was rearmed, but with its army and that of each of the members retaining its national identity. The prosecution of the Indochinese war was an equally divisive issue. In 1958, the issue of the Algerian war was, next to De Gaulle's "constitutional revolution," the most burning issue in French politics. Meanwhile, the inflation continued, more or less violent strikes occurred at fairly regular intervals, and Cabinets tumbled one after the other.

During these eventful years, interest organizations have of course also been active in French politics. But they operate differently from their counterparts in the Bonn Republic or in Italy. The trade unions' rejection of political action has already been mentioned. This policy was changed by the largest of the three labor organizations in contemporary France, when the Socialists split off from it in 1946, leaving the Communists in control. The new Socialist and the Roman Catholic unions attracted many members of the Communist union, precisely because of the latter's stronger partisan affiliation. The links between the Popular Republicans and the Catholic union, and between the Socialist party and union, have continued to be much looser.

Other pressure groups include the National Confederation of French Employers, representing big business, and the General Confederation of Small and Medium Business. They have traditionally applied "pressure" at the levels of the ministries and the bureaucracy. Because of the lack of party discipline on the French right, it is not easy to identify these organizations with any one party. This can be done only when a group, whose nucleus at least would be considered an interest organization in the United States or Great Britain, elects its own candidates to Parliament, as was done by the Poujadistes.

The relations between interest organizations and parties also becomes clearer by studying the officers of pressure groups who are also party politicians. Of these, there are many in France, just as in Germany. The two countries differ in that it is not as easy in France to tell which interest group meshes with which party. Alignments and alliances shift much more frequently in France than in Germany. A comparison of the Federal Republic and the Fourth Republic also suggests that French interest groups bargain harder than their German counterparts and are readier to use extreme measures, such as strikes and violence. The Germans are more likely to heed reminders about the general interest or the public welfare. Incidents like taxpayers' strikes, winegrowers' road barricades against the national government, and mob scenes in front of the Parliament building, which are frequent in France, simply have not happened in West Germany.

An explanation of these differences will be sought in a later chapter. At this point, however, one possible reason for this frequently disorderly behavior of the French citizenry may be suggested. Perhaps Frenchmen feel confused and frustrated because they do not know which organs in their politics are supposed to perform which functions. For example, who recognizes problems? Under the Fourth Republic, the fact has been that some of the most vital problems have gone unrecognized until it was too late for sensible action. Issues have normally been formulated at the parliamentary level, but often in a way so unsatisfactory to so many people that men from outside the National Assembly's "closed arena," as it has been called, have advanced radically new alternatives, as did Poujade and De Gaulle. Next, one may ask who resolves the issues. The answer must be that just as many problems go unrecognized, so do many issues remain unresolved almost permanently. Their resolution is dragged from one coalition cabinet on to another, of slightly different make-up, on to a third, which may resemble the first, and so on. The only hopeful glimmer in this flow of policies is presented by the phase in which problems approach their solution. There, France's civil and military servants put in an efficient and, on the whole, honest performance. But because they do this without decisive directives from public, Parliament, or cabinet, and because they often have to make their decisions quickly when no further procrastination is possible, these administrators and generals in effect sometimes perform all the functions of the political process—from recognizing to solving the problems.

The French bombing of a Tunisian border village in 1958 may serve as an illustration. The endless succession of cabinets in Paris had never made up its mind about the proper means for dealing with the problem of rebel infiltration into Algeria from across the Tunisian border. Vague or contradictory directives had been given to the French command in Algeria. The vagueness and contradictions were an accurate reflection of French public and parliamentary opinion on the Algerian problem. As a result, after a particularly strong raid had been carried out by the rebels from across the border, a colonel on the spot decided to retaliate by bombing a nearby Tunisian village, which was believed to have served as a staging area. The Cabinet then found that it could not disavow the action, even though it evoked protests in France and from

France's allies abroad. Subsequently, neither the current Cabinet nor its successor was willing or able to deal decisively with the new problems that flowed from the colonel's decision made in the field: whether to withdraw French military forces from Tunisia, to order the army in Algeria to follow a consistent policy of "hot pursuit," or to prescribe some third alternative. And this was only one incident on the road to the insurrection of the French colonists and military in Algiers, to their call for the overthrow of the Republic, and to General de Gaulle's return to power as France's savior and the latest in a long line of constitutional engineers.

Success

But one must not hastily record the French political system or systems, as they have functioned since 1871, as utter failures. Despite the frequent changes of Cabinet, despite even the drama of 1958, the French constitution has still been more stable than those of both of her major Continental neighbors, Germany and Italy. The Third Republic operated on the basis of the same set of organic laws until 1940. The Vichy regime can be viewed as a foreign-dictated interlude much more reasonably than the Nazi or Fascist regimes can be considered merely episodic in their respective contexts. And the Fourth Republic has been certified as a virtual continuation of the Third.

In a comparison of efficiency, France's rating is lower. Until the 1930's, the problems were not so serious that inefficiency in finding solutions for them really mattered. But with the troubled period that began with the Great Depression, this happy era of the relative unimportance of politics came to an end in France, as it had in less fortunate lands twenty and fifty years earlier. Decrease in the acceptance accorded the constitution and governmental policies also became marked in the early 1930's. Inefficiency was no longer considered bearable by many Frenchmen; such low effectiveness resulted that defeatism opened the road to German victory and disillusion led to the overwhelming rejection of the Third Republic in the post-Liberation referendum. When the constitution-makers of 1946 nevertheless produced nothing better than another installment in the serial which had been running since 1871, one should not be surprised that it turned out to be the last installment— the last, that is, if De Gaulle succeeds in overcoming the chronic constitutional *malaise*.

Again by comparison with their neighbors on the Continent, French citizens until recently were in superior situations of responsibility. This was certainly true before dictatorships were established in Italy and Germany, and even more so while the great dictators were in power. During that period, most Italians and Germans could make no meaningful contributions to central decisions at all, because they had no alternatives among which they could choose—unless it be those of joining, submission, emigration, imprisonment, or death. The French, during the same years, could choose among a multiplicity of parties and other organizations and had many other avenues for realizing their personalities and individualities, many of them not strictly speaking "political," but quite effective because of the then relatively limited effects of politics on citizens' lives. France was still comparatively rich, so that the resources were there, too. True, foreknowledge of the consequences of their political choices was poor. They could never know which of the parties would enter what kind of coalition, yet they could be reasonably sure that no drastic changes would result in any case and that the bureaucracy would carry on in its wonted efficient way.

In the dying years of the Third Republic and since the founding of the Fourth, all this has changed. Now the alternatives had become meaningless. The choices could not be implemented. And the rapid succession of stark new problems that France simply *had* to face at home and abroad had become so bewildering, and of such great effect upon the everyday lives of all the people, that Frenchmen could no longer be satisfied with uncertainty about the morrow. So they turned for relief to a man who promised them yet another democratic constitution, yet another Republic. The perplexing thing is that all of this happened to a democracy in a constitutional framework. Justice Oliver Wendell Holmes once expressed the view that if the people of the United States want to go to hell, there is nothing in the Constitution to keep them from it. And this is what seems to have been happening in France. The indecisiveness of the political process reflected the irresoluteness of the French people. Even the best-designed constitution—and France did not have it—cannot by itself generate energy and determination, where there is lethargy and apathy. But whether a better designed constitution than that of the Fourth Republic could have prevented things from coming to their present pass, that is another question. We shall try to answer it later, in Chapter 24.

CHAPTER 9

Great Britain

Constitutional History

England's roots as both a people and a state reach farther back in history than those of any other European political system. For the continuity of the state is the same as that of the Crown, which dates at least from the Norman Conquest in 1066 A.D. Continuity as a people goes much beyond that, but the same date is significant in this respect, too, because no important immigration has occurred since then, nor any successful invasion from outside the British Isles. Constitutional continuity was disturbed only once, during Oliver Cromwell's Protectorate of short duration; even then it was not broken, and was soon restored.

It should be noted at the outset that, strictly speaking, the continuity described above applies only to England, and not to the present political system, which is officially called "the United Kingdom of Great Britain and Northern Ireland." Ireland—sometimes parts of it and sometimes all of it—was won and lost over the centuries. Today Northern Ireland's status is a dual one: it has its own Parliament and it also elects members to the British Parliament. The rest of Ireland has a republican constitution and maintains a tenuous status within the British Commonwealth. Wales was added shortly after the Norman Conquest. Scotland was brought under the British Crown after its King James VI became England's James I, in 1603. Down to this day, Scotland has a legal system which differs from that of the rest of Great Britain, in that it is based on the Roman law rather than the English common law. And yet the absorptive and adaptive qualities of English political processes have been such that these additions of land and people have never brought about quick, revolutionary change, but only slow, evolutionary modification.

These qualities of English politics are also suggested by two other facts. The first of these is the remarkable success achieved by British political procedures when exported by the British themselves to America, Asia, and Africa. We will see case studies of this in Canada and the United States. Some of the former British colonies, to be sure, have experienced difficulties as newly independent nations in trying to make British processes work—Pakistan, for example, or Ghana. But none of them has encountered as much trouble as the former colonies of France, Italy, or the Netherlands.

The second evidence of the uniqueness of the British constitution is the fact that the success of British politics, at least since the eighteenth century, has generated so much "envy of less happier lands," in Shakespeare's phrase, that British institutions and procedures have become the most widely copied in the world, by far. The French constitutional monarchies of the nineteenth century were modeled on the British pattern. Constitutional monarchy elsewhere in Europe, as we saw in the Italian case, also attempted to emulate Great Britain, either directly or indirectly. The copying has not been confined to the institution of constitutional monarchy; indeed, the widespread adoption of the system of parliamentary procedure in use at Westminster is especially significant. The influence of this kind of borrowing on the procedures used by international assemblies, such as those of the League of Nations and of the United Nations, is really incalculable and, in terms of present world problems, may well turn out to be of much greater importance than other forms of imitation.

Only in the last hundred years has the Constitution of the United States become an export commodity that has been giving considerable competition to Great Britain in this "market." The Latin-American countries and others wanting either a popularly elected president or a federal system, or both, have generally followed the model of the United States. Swiss federalism provides a limited illustration of this. But so many of the subtler, and for that very reason more fundamental, features of American political processes are also adaptations of the British archetype— this will be a principal theme of our description of government in the United States—that copying them sometimes merely amounts to second-hand borrowing from England.

But what *is* "the British constitution"? The standard answer to this question emphasizes the word *unwritten*. But this is not quite accurate. True, Britain has no single constitutional document as do all of our other systems except (British) Canada and Sweden. The Swedish constitution, it will be recalled, consists of four documents. Similarly, the

British constitution could be said to consist of a series of documents. First in the series is Magna Carta (1215), in which King John's barons forced him to accept a number of restrictions on his power *and* on that of his heirs. Magna Carta was followed by others, among them the Petition of Right (1628), in which King Charles I assented to even more far-reaching concessions demanded by his Parliament. This was followed by the Bill of Rights (1689), which was passed by Parliament after the so-called Glorious Revolution of the previous year, and many of whose provisions were repeated in the Bill of Rights of the Constitution of the United States. The Act of Settlement (1701) did the same thing for the British Crown that the Act of Succession, a century later, did for the Swedish Crown. The Reform Acts of 1832 and 1867 extended the suffrage. The acts granting the suffrage to all men in 1918, and to all women in 1928, would also be considered constitutional. The Parliament Acts of 1911 and 1949 reduced the functions of the House of Lords. Some students of the British constitution would extend this list, and it is unlikely that all would agree as to which documents should be included.

This, then, is one reason why Britain is said to have an unwritten constitution.

In studying Sweden, we could distinguish between acts of the Riksdag that are, and those that are not, part of the Swedish constitution, because constitutional acts can be amended only if passed by two successive Parliaments with a general election intervening. This is not true in Great Britain, where any Parliament could make the most fundamental change —one which would certainly be considered constitutional in Sweden or the United States—by a simple majority of the House of Commons and of the House of Lords and with the assent of the Monarch. The remarkable phenomenon is that constitutional amendments, in this sense, have never been passed by such simple majorities or without full and prolonged debate of the issue. As a result, there seems to be only one method for deciding which documents should be considered parts of the British constitution: the measurement of their effective longevity as parts of the operative constitution of which people and politicians are conscious, and of the proportions of the debate that preceded their adoption.

This test leaves certain difficulties, one of them being the second reason for calling the British constitution unwritten. Most of those institutions and procedures, which occupy the most prominent places in written constitutions, are not mentioned in the great constitutional documents that have just been listed; in fact, they are not mentioned in any law at all. Just think of the detail with which the United States Constitution defines the functions of the Congress and of the President, and relations between them. British constitutional documents, by contrast, do not define the functions of the House of Commons at all; they specify only a number of things which the House of Lords and the Monarch must *not* do; and they say very little about relations between the Monarch and the two Houses of Parliament. And the Cabinet, which is usually considered the keystone of the arch of British government, is mentioned nowhere at all, except for the Standing Orders of the House of Commons, that is, its rules of procedure. Nevertheless, the more important aspects of Cabinet government, especially the dependence of the Cabinet upon the confidence of Parliament, have been stably established since the eighteenth century. Since they are not written down in any Act of Parliament, they could be changed overnight. Yet no British politician would even think of proposing anything of the sort. This puzzling state of affairs is another reason why we will have to inquire later on into the content of the "True Constitution."

Parliament evolved slowly out of the Great Council that the medieval English Kings convened from time to time. When Edward I summoned the so-called "Model Parliament" in 1295, it was made up not only of barons, the clergy, and knights, but also of burgesses, i.e., townspeople. However, by contrast with Sweden, peasants were not represented. Toward the end of the 1300's, it had become custom for the barons and the upper clergy to meet in one assembly, the knights and commoners in another. The House of Commons began to originate grants of money, the levying of which had been the initial reason for adding commoners to the Great Council. Bills of petition to the King were coupled with grants of money, and the King, in order to get the money, would grant the petition in an Act, the first sentence of which, from the fifteenth century on down to the twentieth, has invariably read: "Be it therefore enacted by the King's most Excellent Majesty, by and with the advice and consent of the Lords Spiritual and Temporal, and Commons, in this present Parliament assembled, and by the authority of the same. . . ." Parliament's share in the government of the realm increased during the struggle between Henry VIII and the Roman Catholic Church. The ultimate outcome of this struggle was a national Reformation in England and the establishment of the Church of England with the King as its head.

In the seventeenth century, under James I and Charles I, the problem of the relation between King and Parliament arose and was settled by means of the Civil War (1642-49). The royal side lost, Charles was executed, and Oliver Cromwell ruled as Lord Protector under the Instrument of Government (1653), the only written constitution in Britain's history. By 1660, monarchy had been restored, in the person of Charles II. His successor, James II, reopened the issue of Catholicism, which led to the "Glorious Revolution" of 1688 and the definitive establishment of the "supremacy of Parliament."

When German-speaking Hanoverian Kings began to occupy the British throne, in 1714, active government gradually devolved upon the Cabinet, partly because George I and II did not speak English. Throughout the eighteenth century, constituencies for the House of Commons were very unevenly distributed, and there was a great deal of corruption through patronage dispensed by the Cabinet acting on behalf of the Crown. The struggle over reform lasted for more than a century and was not rewarded until passage of the Great Reform Act of 1832, which provided for a very limited extension of the suffrage and the greater equalization of constituencies. The last couple of years of the debate were accompanied by sporadic eruptions of violence. The King had to threaten to create enough new Whig peers to outvote Tory opponents of the reforms in the House of Lords, before the upper chamber capitulated. After this concession, Cabinets generally would not resign after losing a vote in the House of Lords, although they needed to win majorities there in order to pass bills. Except for the extension of the suffrage, still to a very limited electorate, no other changes truly constitutional in nature occurred during the remainder of the nineteenth century.

In 1909, a serious constitutional crisis—one which was widely recognized as such—began with the refusal of the House of Lords to pass the budget proposed by the Chancellor of the Exchequer, Lloyd George. Again the country seemed on the verge of violence and again the King was persuaded to threaten to pack the House of Lords. This made possible passage of the Parliament Act of 1911, which eliminated for practical purposes the Peers' former ability to obstruct passage of money bills voted by the Commons. But the Parliament Act went even beyond this by providing that the House of Commons could override the Lords' veto on ordinary bills by passing them in each of three successive sessions of Parliament during a period of at least two years. This had the effect of making amendment of the British "constitution"—whatever it may consist of—about as difficult as amendment of the Swedish constitution. Subsequently, there were the final extensions of the suffrage already cited and, after the great victory of the Labour party in the election at the end of World War II, the elimination of the remaining electoral inequities, such as the double voting privilege of university graduates (each of the great English universities had until then elected one member to Parliament). The Parliament Act of 1949 reduced the delaying effects of the Lords' veto to one year. And in 1958, the House of Lords was once more reformed, this time in its composition rather than its functions, by adding members for life—nonhereditary "life peers"—including women peers for the first time in history.

Many other important changes have occurred since 1832, but whether they should be considered constitutional or not is a question we are not yet equipped to answer. There was, for example, the reform of the civil service in the middle of the last century, which did away with inefficiency, ignorance, and corruption by reducing the number of positions filled by patronage. At the beginning of the present century, the post of Prime Minister was filled by a member of the House of Lords for the last time, and it is now understood that only a member of the House of Commons may hold that position. The theory of the "mandate" was somehow introduced, according to which neither the Lords nor the Opposition would obstruct passage of a bill dealing with an issue on which the electorate had clearly expressed itself in the previous general election. And finally, there were the many economic changes, especially those transforming the right of private property, which were brought about by the Labour government after 1945. These have been referred to as an "economic and social revolution" and should, therefore, perhaps be included in any catalogue of constitutional changes.

Constitutional Structure

The House of Commons has more than six hundred members; they are elected from single-member constituencies by a plurality system. General elections follow the dissolution of the House, whose normal tenure is five years. The Monarch calls upon the parliamentary leader of the majority party to form a Cabinet. When no single party can command a majority, as happened frequently during the interwar years, the Monarch has some choice in the selection of the party to which this task is entrusted. The same procedure applies when the majority party does not have an obvious parliamentary leader. The Prime Minister then forms his Cabinet, which must have the support of a majority in the House in order to remain in office. If it loses a vote of confidence, the Cabinet can do one of two things: The Prime Minister can resign and let the leader of the Opposition form a Cabinet, which then similarly requires majority support in the House. (Sometimes, the incumbent leader of the majority party simply resigns in favor of another, as Anthony Eden did in favor of Harold Macmillan after the 1956 Suez Canal crisis.) Or he can ask the Queen to dissolve the House of Commons and thereby "go to the country" in a general election on the issue on which he suffered his parliamentary defeat. The Queen, according to present usage, has to grant the request.

A vote of confidence has not actually been lost in British politics since the end of the three-party system in the early 1930's. What has occurred is the informal loss of confidence in their Prime Minister by members of his own party, leading to his resignation in favor of another leader of the same party, as in the Eden case just cited and also in the resignation of Neville Chamberlain in favor of Winston Churchill in 1940. Since 1924, dissolutions of the House of Commons have occurred only at or after the end of its five-year term—the House elected in 1935 served until 1945, because no election was held during the war—or when the Cabinet felt that dissolution before that time would be to its electoral advantage. Thus, the slim Labour party majority resulting from the election of 1950 enabled the Conservatives to harass the Cabinet in Commons to such an extent that it dissolved the next year. (Labour lost the ensuing general election, however.) In 1955, the Conservative Cabinet got a dissolution one year before expiration of the five-year term, because it thought the time propitious—as indeed it turned out to be, for the Conservatives increased their parliamentary majority by twenty-four seats.

Constitutionally speaking, the Cabinet itself is the active part of the Queen's Privy Council. Its members, as Privy Councillors, take an oath to observe secrecy about the Cabinet's business. This provision facilitates the collective accountability of the Cabinet to Commons and helps to make it more of a collegial group than its Italian, German, and French namesakes. The Monarch's role is roughly equivalent to that of the presidents of these Continental countries, whose offices were modeled on that of the British King. But the Monarch has many advantages over them, not the least being deliberate preparation for, and uninterrupted service in, the office.

Since Britain has no clearly defined constitution, there is no place in her politics for the judicial review of legislation. However, this function is performed for many of the overseas members in the British Empire and Commonwealth by the Judicial Committee of the Privy Council. The membership of this body overlaps with the so-called Law Lords. Until 1958, the Law Lords were, except for Bishops of the Church of England, the only members of the House of Lords appointed for life, since all others inherited their titles. The Law Lords performed the judicial function of the upper house, which is the highest court of appeal. They are presided over by the Lord High Chancellor, who is also the presiding officer of the House of Lords in its parliamentary role and is also a member of the Cabinet. The Lord Chancellor, in other words, performs executive, legislative, and judicial functions, if one were to apply the categories of the American separation of powers to his office. The only office provided for by the Constitution of the United States with any degree of similarity is that of the Vice-President, as successor to an incapacitated President and as presiding officer of the Senate. The British model influenced the design of this American institution.

Problems

In the course of the last four hundred years, Great Britain has had to deal with a series of problems very much like those the major Continental countries have had to face. But in Britain the timing with which they have arisen has been different. The sixteenth century brought to the fore the religious problem and, by and large, saw its solution in the establishment of the Church of England. Later attempts—the last one in the Glorious Revolution of 1688—to reopen the issue of Roman Catholic predominance or even equality have failed. In the seventeenth century, the constitutional problem set off England's last civil war and the brief experiment with a written constitution. It, too, was finally settled by the Glorious Revolution, which was hardly a revolution in the sense of the American and French upheavals of the next century. This cannot be said of the Industrial Revolution, which took place in Great Britain before it spread to the remainder of the European world and to the United States. The Industrial Revolution brought economic problems to the forefront of British politics during the latter part of the eighteenth and all of the nineteenth centuries, and they still play the most important role today. Britain's early industrialization also made her the most powerful state in world politics during the nineteenth century. It lay behind her position as arbiter of what has been called the *Pax Britannica,* and the acquisition of her vast colonial enterprises. In the twentieth century, the most important issues of British politics have arisen out of economic and external problems, not out of constitutional or cultural ones.

At the end of World War II, the British had to come to terms with increasing demands for independence from their colonial dependencies—on the Indian subcontinent, in Africa and the Caribbean Sea, among others. They had to adjust themselves to the new international situation, in which their strength would not measure up to that of either the United States or the Soviet Union. They had to try to make up for the vast material losses caused by the war—the wiping out of British credits with the countries that were formerly their debtors, the loss of most of the British merchant fleet, the damage due to German bombings, and the excessive strain placed on their industrial plant by the demands of war production. In addition to all this, Britain's human resources had been hurt even more by the war than by the preceding years of depression and tremendous unemployment. How were these problems handled, and with what results?

Issues and Politics

British politics dealt with these problems in very much the same fashion in which it had been dealing with all its varied problems during the previous century. What distinguishes this process above all is the much greater clarity, as compared with the Continental countries, that has always prevailed in Britain about the most important issues of any given period. This kind of clarity exists in Italy, Germany, and France only during times of acute constitutional crisis, when the main issue is the survival of the constitution itself. In Britain, by contrast, the order of importance of various issues seems self-evident even in periods of great political calm. This has been true at least since 1832, when the increase in the electorate was followed by the firmer crystallization of two great political camps, which permanently opposed each other inside and outside of Parliament. Before extension of the suffrage led to electoral organization, Tories and Whigs had comprised very loose and shifting alliances inside Parliament. After the Reform Act, the shifting of factions inside Parliament became less frequent, and there was greater consistency between the organized campaign appeals of the two parties and the conduct of their Members of Parliament. (It was also during this period that the terms "Tory" and "Whig" were replaced by "Conservative" and "Liberal.") While in the Continental countries several political parties were pursuing a variety of goals—and disagreeing about their proper order of priority—in Great Britain only two parties were fighting over one major set of issues at a time. The contribution this constant opposition between two comprehensive alternative programs is believed to have made to the success of British politics is, of course, the reason why so many politicians and political scientists have wanted to introduce versions of the "two-party system" in less fortunate countries.

The great issues of the years following the adoption of the Reform Bill can easily be listed in chronological order. In the middle 1830's, it was factory legislation and the Poor Laws, both designed to deal with new problems brought about by increasing industrialization. In the 1840's, it was the reform of the tariff, leading to repeal of the Corn Laws in 1846. Free trade remained a central plank in the Liberal platform and was accompanied by some opposition to the expansion of the Empire, of which the Conservatives were the great protagonists. From time to time, throughout the second half of the nineteenth century, and into the twentieth, the Irish Question became the central issue in British politics. During the first decade of the present century, issues of trade-union organization played an increasingly important role. From 1909 until passage of the Parliament Act in 1911, reform of the House of Lords was crucial.

Meanwhile, successive steps on the road to achievement of universal suffrage had given the vote, by 1928, to ever more members of the lower economic strata. Together with the growing trade-union movement, this led to the founding of the Labour party, which initially supported the Liberals in return for legislation favorable to labor. After World War I, the Labour vote in parliamentary elections grew at the expense of the Liberals. From 1922 until 1935, the House of Commons contained members of three major parties, and in some Parliaments during the first half of that period, none of these controlled a majority of seats. This might have had the effect of diluting the customary clarity about the most important issues, had it not been for the counterbalancing effect of the obvious primacy of the economic problem, which resulted in a great general strike in 1926 and increasing unemployment. In the general election of 1929, the Labour party for the first time defeated the Conservatives. Since then, one or the other of these two parties has always held a majority of the seats in Commons.

The elimination of the Liberals as an effective parliamentary party suggests another explanation of the two-alternative treatment of issues in British politics: Once this method has been in use for a long period of time, it somehow survives changes that occur within each of the two great camps. Something similar happened in the United States, when the Civil War destroyed the existing party system, which was soon afterward replaced by a new alignment in two great camps—an alignment that is still with us today. Canada has had very similar experiences more recently. The self-perpetuating qualities of the two-alternative method are further backed up by another fact of British parliamentary history. When Winston Churchill formed a coalition Cabinet, which included members of all three parties and which was backed by all three parties in the interests of prosecuting the war against Germany, a Liberal member of Parliament became the official Leader of His Majesty's Opposition. This salaried position is usually occupied by the leader of the minority party in the House of Commons, and its existence facilitates efficient debate, as our study of parliamentary procedure will show. During the war, however, no one seriously wanted to oppose the coalition Cabinet, certainly not the man who was appointed Leader of the Opposition. Nevertheless, the method of carrying on debates between two opposing sides had become so entrenched that the British could not countenance a no-alternative system any more than they had previously countenanced a three-alternative system. Government without an opposition was just as inconceivable for them as government against two oppositions.

The main issues between Conservatives and Labour have been about the limits to which the welfare state should be carried. After winning a clear mandate on this issue in the election of 1945, the Labour Cabinet put into effect its comprehensive National Health program. It nationalized several industries, notably coal, steel, and transport. It also put the finishing touches on the equalization of the franchise, as already mentioned, and further restricted the functions of the House of Lords, two measures which the Conservative party opposed. Finally, Labour engineered the relatively smooth transition of India and other parts of the Empire from colonial to self-governing status. When the Conservatives were returned to power, they denationalized the steel industry but retained virtually all features of the welfare state. Since then, disagreements on foreign policy, such as those on the Suez and Jordan landings, have generated the most heat. Proposals for the reform of the educational system, designed to provide better opportunities for children of working class parents, have also been controversial.

Aside from these issues, which flare up for only brief periods at a time, there seems to be far-reaching agreement on the goals that the British political system should be pursuing, and even on the best means to attain those goals. This deflects disagreements—the perpetuation of which is guaranteed by the party organization—to the question of which group of leaders is best qualified to apply these agreed means for reaching the agreed goals.

The range of problems on which the parties are agreed also enhances the importance of interest organizations. Of these, there are just about as many as in the other European countries. Some of them are even more closely linked with one or another of the parties than are their Continental counterparts. Thus the Trade Union Congress is directly affiliated with the Labour party, at whose annual conferences it controls about five times as many votes as do the constituency organizations. Before Members of Parliament began to be paid by the government—in 1911—trade unions gave their few M.P.'s the equivalent of a salary. And, currently, a large number of Labour parliamentary candidates have their campaigns financed by trade unions. The unions are not alone in this practice. Many other interest organizations are "represented" by their members or officers in the House of Commons. But the representation is hardly a real one, since party discipline and the rigidly controlled timetable of the House give their M.P.'s few if any opportunities to play a role other than that of a Conservative, Labour, or Liberal Member of Parliament. In this respect, they differ sharply from their parallels on the Continent, as we will see in greater detail in the discussion of parliamentary committees.

A practical consequence of this difference is the greater concentration by British interest groups on contacts with the bureaucracy. In other words, they are more active in the solution phase of the policy flow than in deliberation or the resolution of issues. Ministries at all levels, and the boards of the nationalized industries, actually seek the advice and opinions of affected interest organizations, and this kind of consultation has been institutionalized. Thus the solution of problems is taken care of not only by the bureaucracy but also by these outside organizations, which on the Continent are more active in the earlier stages of the political process.

In Britain, the major issues are resolved in general elections, in terms of alternatives formulated in the House of Commons, about problems recognized by the political parties—usually by their parliamentary leadership. Problems that were not at issue during the last election but have arisen subsequently are normally recognized in the House of Commons. The issues arising out of them, as also other minor issues not debated in the general election campaign, are resolved by the Cabinet, which also gets them started on their road to solution. The British Cabinet thus performs more functions than do any of the Continental Cabinets. But it does this—especially resolving noncampaign issues—under constant exposure to its supporters and the Opposition in the House of Commons. Since Cabinets often take into account the advice and criticism voiced there, Members of Parliament can at least make some contributions to these decisions.

Success

In later chapters, when we compare experiences with constitutional engineering, we will ask questions about the degree to which the intentions of the makers of a particular constitution were realized. In the British case, this question would make no sense, because there are no intentions, there is no single group of authors, and there is no made constitution. But there are institutions and procedures that are the equivalent of those established by created constitutions in other systems, and they have been more stable than those of any of the other countries studied in this book. The Parliament at Westminster is the oldest in the world (if we disregard the Icelandic one, as perhaps we may). Some of the procedures it uses are older than the modern consciousness of men's capacity to make rather than to find law—older, that is, than four hundred years. And yet they are still being used in the making of decisions of all kinds, every Monday through Friday while Parliament is in session. Institutions have been modified significantly over the centuries, but they have undergone change only very gradually. Therefore, no matter what we may finally decide upon as the content of the "True Constitution," it has been very stable in the United Kingdom.

The stability has not been one of stagnation—and this is a statement that need not be backed up by particulars. The English constitution, and especially its forms, has been adapted to ever-changing problems. Nor have these forms been mere formalities. Rather, as proven methods for dealing with certain types of problems, they have affected the very substance of these problems and their solutions. Thus, the presence of a Leader of the Opposition made a difference for the conduct of World War II. In the case of Italy, we found that the same procedures had been used over the last century to deal with a variety of problems. There, the trouble was twofold—the procedures were inefficient to begin with, and they were not adapted to changing circumstances. In the German case, we found that the Empire, the Weimar Republic, and Nazi totalitarianism each used procedures that were more or less efficient when applied to those problems each regime considered the most important. But they were deficient in that they failed to elicit sufficient acceptance for their own survival and, therefore, failed to provide stability. In Britain, by contrast, the most useful features of procedures that were efficient to begin with have been adapted in order to deal in each period with the problems considered most important by those people whose acceptance then mattered. Not since the seventeenth century has the British constitution been ineffective, except in Ireland. Only Sweden and perhaps Switzerland, of the seven other countries, could boast of less violence than Great Britain has known during the past one hundred and fifty years. Today, there are no serious opponents of the constitution anywhere in the United Kingdom. The government's policies, so long as they have been made by constitutional means, are accepted even by those who may have fought tooth and nail against their adoption.

Both the effectiveness and the stability of the British constitution have been explained in terms of the British people's "agreement on fundamentals." We will analyze this interpretation later. Here, we may offer another tentative explanation: the efficiency of British politics. It has almost invariably recognized the real problems on time, indeed, ahead of time, while the politics of other systems have often refused to face up to a problem even after it had been long upon it. The slow preparation of the Indians for self-government and the grant of independence to India and Pakistan thus stand in marked contrast to France's treatment of her North African dependencies. Once recognized, problems have been stated as meaningful issues, containing realistic alternatives, and facilitating optimum deliberation. In the course of deliberation, the relevant information and knowledge is brought to bear upon the issue. There is a resoluteness in British politics that simply does not permit of procrastination. The final solution of problems is helped by this resoluteness and also by the fact that bureaucrats get clear directives.

These conditions seem to provide British citizens with a very favorable situation of responsibility. They can contribute to the flow of central policy at every one of its stages. They know that those men who make the most important central decisions are periodically accountable to the electorate and continuously exposed to deliberation by those who supported their election and by those who opposed it. In general elections, they have the choice between two (or three) comprehensive sets of policies and the knowledge that each of these is practicable. At other times, they can make contributions through interest organizations. This gives them the resources to implement their choices beyond election time. They also have a highly professionalized, efficient, neutral, and scrupulously honest bureaucracy. They know not only that the Cabinet will be able to live up to its election promises but also that the rules of the British constitution will be fundamentally the same when they die as when they go to the polls for the first time.

This evaluation is not meant to paint the picture of a Utopian political system. British politics has its drawbacks, too. For example, the alternative programs presented by the two parties are practicable because there are only two of them. This means that the full range of possible policies may not be made available. The Cabinet's capacity for resolute action may tempt it into precipitate action in a situation in which hindsight may find it a blessing to have been hamstrung. And Great Britain's economic resources are dwindling. Unless efficient and inventive politics manages to develop substitute sources of power for coal and oil, for example, British industry will have very dim prospects. At this time, Britain seems to be concentrating successfully on developing the peaceful uses of nuclear energy for that very reason. But the most efficient political system cannot make something out of nothing, just as the well-constituted cow of our earlier analogy will not produce milk unless she is fed.

There is, moreover, one aspect of the success of the British political system that must be profoundly disturbing to anyone who is looking for guidelines to constitution-making, as we are here. That is the unmade character of the British constitution. If we compare the five systems that have been described so far, we could well conclude that the more engineered a constitution is, the more likely is it to fail. Conversely, the more naturally grown and unplanned a constitution, the more likely is it to succeed. We should keep this tentative conclusion in mind as we cross the Atlantic to look at two engineered constitutions, the first of which was virtually transplanted from Great Britain, while the second, that of the United States, was meant to break with the British past in order to make a new beginning in a New World.

CHAPTER 10

Canada

British Statutes, 30 Victoria, Chapter 3.

An Act for the Union of Canada, Nova Scotia, and New Brunswick, and the Government thereof; and for Purposes connected therewith.

[*29th March, 1867.*]

WHEREAS the Provinces of Canada, Nova Scotia, and New Brunswick have expressed their Desire to be federally united into One Dominion under the Crown of the United Kingdom of Great Britain and Ireland, with a Constitution similar in Principle to that of the United Kingdom;

And whereas such a Union would conduce to the welfare of the Provinces and promote the Interests of the British Empire;

And whereas on the Establishment of the Union by Authority of Parliament it is expedient, not only that the Constitution of the Legislative Authority in the Dominion be provided for, but also that the Nature of the Executive Government therein be declared;

And whereas it is expedient that Provision be made for the eventual admission into the Union of other Parts of British North America:

Be it therefore enacted and declared by the Queen's most Excellent Majesty, by and with the Advice and Consent of the Lords Spiritual and Temporal, and Commons, in this present Parliament assembled, and by the Authority of the same, as follows. . . .

Thus reads the Preamble to the British North America Act of 1867, whose passage by the British Parliament created the modern Canadian political system. It brought into one federal union the provinces of Ontario, Quebec, Nova Scotia, and New Brunswick. Since that time, six other provinces have been added, from British Columbia on the Pacific Ocean to Newfoundland in the North Atlantic. The much-amended British North America Act is still considered Canada's basic constitutional document, but for an understanding of the Canadian constitution, we must take into account much more than the Act and its amendments and go far beyond 1867 in the past of both Canada and Great Britain —and also of France.

Constitutional History

The Constitutional history of Canada begins in the France of Louis XIV. For a hundred years before 1760, when the British conquered Quebec, "New France" was under a system of royal government. Designed by the "Sun King," this scheme was to shape future French-Canadian notions of politics, but it is just as interesting for what it tells us about the constitution of the Old Regime in France. For, its three principal officers were the governor, the bishop, and the intendant, representing the three pillars of the monarchy—the army, the Roman Catholic Church, and the bureaucracy. Land grants were made by the Crown on a feudal basis to the Church and to individuals, usually impoverished noblemen. In return for receiving their *seigneuries,* the *seigneurs* served as military officers and performed functions of local government. Their own tenants, the *habitants,* in turn paid feudal dues to the *seigneurs.* The social structure of New France was hierarchical. There was no self-government.

With the British conquest in 1760, most members of the small upper crust that had ruled Quebec left for France. Only the clergy stayed behind, taking upon themselves many of the functions previously performed by other members of the elite. The British put the province under military government, to be administered by a Governor appointed by the Crown. He was assisted by his Executive Council, whose members the Governor appointed, and a Legislative Council, whose members were also appointed. These provisions were formalized by the Quebec Act of 1774, which also granted Roman Catholics freedom of worship and left in effect French-Canadian civil law, based on the Continental tradition of the Roman law. The British conquest thus brought neither the English common law nor self-government to French Canada, although Nova Scotia had achieved an elective Legislative Assembly in 1758. And to the South, in Virginia and Massachusetts, colonial self-government had started more than a century earlier.

The War of American Independence brought self-government to Canada in its aftermath. This came about when many United Empire Loyalists—opponents of independence in the thirteen colonies who emigrated to Canada—settled in Quebec. They demanded the institutions and the legal system to which they had been accustomed. The result was the Constitutional Act of 1791, which divided the territory into two provinces, Lower Canada (later Quebec) and Upper Canada (later Ontario). Lower Canada was predominantly French and was again granted religious freedom and retention of French civil law. Upper Canada was English. And both provinces were now given their own Governors and elective Legislative Assemblies. The Governor ruled with the assistance of his executive council, still an appointed group. The legislature consisted of the appointive Legislative Council, which provided most of the members of the Governor's Executive Council and was drawn from a small circle of wealthy families. The Legislative Assembly had relatively few functions and often did not even control the purse strings, because the Governor had other sources of revenue, like the vast Crown lands in Lower Canada. Both Canadas became increasingly discontented under this system and eventually, in 1837, separate rebellions took place in the two provinces. But before that happened, the French-Canadians had at least become familiar with the procedures of British politics, with freedom of the press, and with the rights of British subjects under criminal law: trial by jury and habeas corpus.

The rebellions led to the dispatch to Canada by the British Cabinet of the Earl of Durham, who had been one of the leaders in the agitation leading to passage in 1832 of the Great Reform Bill. "Radical Jack," as he was known, was to be Governor General and to make a full report on the causes of the rebellions and recommendations for the future of the Canadas. His report should be ranked with Alexis de Tocqueville's *Democracy in America* as a brilliant analysis of society and politics in the New World. He made two major recommendations: "amalgamation of the races," i.e., the French and the English, through reuniting the two provinces; and the grant of "responsible government." The first of these was acted upon at once in the Union Act of 1840, and was proven unwise by subsequent events. The second was not to come for another ten years, and then turned out to be the model for the devolution of self-government to British colonies all over the world on into the present time. More than that, Durham's recommendation for responsible government was one of the first reasoned statements by an Englishman of the theory of cabinet government in Great Britain. It seems that, because the British have never had to reconstruct their own constitution from scratch, they have been forced to rationalize its operation only when trying to transplant it into one of their overseas possessions. Hence, the study of Canadian government is of interest, not merely on its own merits, but also because of what it teaches about the government of the mother country.

According to Lord Durham, the grant of responsible government would result in "administering the government on those principles which have been found perfectly efficacious in Great Britain." What were these principles?

> Every purpose of popular control might be combined with every advantage of vesting the immediate choice of advisers in the Crown, were the Colonial Governor to be instructed to secure the co-operation of the Assembly in his policy, by entrusting its administration to such men as could command a majority; and if he were given to understand that he need count on no aid from home in any difference with the Assembly, that should not directly involve the relations between the mother country and the Colony. This change might be effected by a single despatch containing such instructions.[1]

And that was exactly how the change was effected, in 1848, reflecting the British reluctance to engage in wholesale constitutional engineering. When the Governor's Council in United Canada lost a vote of confidence in the Legislative Assembly, it resigned and was replaced by a new one. This set off a period of inefficiency in Canadian politics. Both sides resented the forced marriage which Durham's recommendations had brought about between the French and the English. The Legislative Assembly of United Canada was split by the racial cleavage and many other divisions, so that some eight distinct and ever-shifting factions could be distinguished in it. During a period of ten years prior to Confederation, ten cabinets succeeded one another. And the resources of the province, as also those of the Maritime Provinces—Nova Scotia, New Brunswick, and Prince Edward Island—were insufficient for realizing the goals their citizens had set for themselves.

These troubles led to the movement for Confederation, which was achieved in 1867. In the course of this movement, some debates took place not unlike those which occurred later in the various Continental constituent assemblies, and very much like those of the American Founding Fathers in the Constitutional Convention at Philadelphia in

[1] Sir C. P. Lucas, ed., *Lord Durham's Report*, pp. 279-80.

1788. The Canadian Fathers of Confederation carefully considered the United States model of federalism and, because of the Civil War that was just then coming to an end, rejected it. As a result, the British North America Act did not set up a federal government with powers delegated to it by the states—provinces in the Canadian case. It reversed this concept by delegating powers of the federal government to the provinces. Indeed, the British North America Act contained the provincial constitutions.

Since the British Parliament passed the British North America Act in 1867, it has explicitly amended it a number of times, always at the request of the Canadian Parliament. Thus, in 1871, the Parliament of Canada was given the power to establish new provinces. In 1915, the composition of the Senate was altered. In 1940, unemployment insurance was added to the list of legislative fields under control of the federal Parliament. In 1949, the British Parliament amended the British North America Act to transfer to the Canadian Parliament the power to make its own amendments of the Act in the future, "except as regards rights or privileges by this or any other Constitutional Act granted or secured to the Legislature or the Government of a province, or to any class of persons with respect to schools or as regards the use of the English or French language. . . ." As a result, an amendment of 1951, giving the federal Parliament control over old-age pension legislation, was again passed by the British Parliament, while an amendment readjusting representation in the Canadian House of Commons was passed by the Canadian Parliament in the next year, this time without recourse to Westminster.

Constitutional Structure

Today, Canada is just as much a constitutional monarchy as Great Britain or Sweden. Since the Queen resides in England, her functions are performed for her by the Governor General, whom she appoints on the recommendation of her Canadian Cabinet, which functions almost exactly as its British model. Reading the British North America Act would give no hint of this:

> There shall be a Council to aid and advise in the Government of Canada to be styled the Queen's Privy Council for Canada; and the Persons who are to be Members of that Council shall be from Time to Time chosen and summoned by the Governor General and sworn in as Privy Councillors, and Members thereof may be from Time to Time removed by the Governor General.

In other words, even twenty-seven years after Lord Durham formulated the principles of Cabinet government, none of the Canadian or British contributors to this constitutional document saw any reason for putting these provisions down in black-on-white, nor have they to this day. Nevertheless, the Canadian Cabinet is just as dependent upon the support of a majority in the House of Commons as is the British Cabinet. The Canadian Prime Minister is selected in the same way, and he can ask the Governor General for a dissolution of the House of Commons, just as the British Prime Minister can ask the Queen. The only significant difference between the two Cabinets is the traditionally "federal" make-up of the Canadian, that is, the presence on it of politicians from the various provinces, according to a recognized formula.

The House of Commons at Ottawa is elected from single-member constituencies just like those which elect the House of Commons in Westminster. It has about 263 members. Its full term also runs for five years. The Canadian Senate, however, seems considerably more obsolescent than the House of Lords. Its members are appointed for life on recommendation of the Cabinet. As in the House of Commons, seats in the Senate are apportioned among the provinces according to a prescribed pattern. Nevertheless, the Senate in no way performs federal functions in the sense that this is done by the upper chambers of the Swiss, German, and United States legislatures. In recent decades, the Canadian Senate has been most useful as the repository for aging or otherwise unwanted supporters whom Prime Ministers wish to "kick upstairs."

The Senate does perform one useful function: as a divorce court. Quebec civil law makes it virtually impossible to obtain a divorce. Residents of Quebec desiring a divorce, therefore, petition the Canadian Parliament to pass a private bill to that effect. A committee of the Senate hears these cases, in which only proven and uncondoned adultery is accepted as sufficient grounds. The committee reports back to the Senate, which passes the bills, whereupon the House of Commons normally passes them also, without debate. Thus the Senate relieves the much busier House of this time-consuming "judicial" burden. Its procedures are quite well suited for this, because the British Parliament, from which they were copied, was a court for centuries before it became a "legislature," as the discussion of parliamentary procedure will show.

The most notable differences between the Canadian and British constitutions are due to Canadian federalism. The subordinate position of the provinces to the federal government has already been mentioned. The method designed to achieve this subordination is interesting for two reasons; first, because it put into effect Alexander Hamilton's foiled plan for establishing a similar superiority of the Union over the states in the United States; and second, because it set up a pattern of provincial-federal relations, which was the same as that of Canadian-British relations before Canada achieved complete self-government. Just as the British Cabinet appointed the Governor General for the "Dominion" (as it is referred to only rarely nowadays), so the federal Cabinet appoints a Lieutenant-Governor for each of the provinces. The provinces have their own Legislative Assemblies and Cabinets headed by Premiers—as they are called in contradistinction to the federal Prime Minister—who need the support of an assembly majority. But the Lieutenant-Governor today can still do something which the Governor General used to be able to do: He can in effect veto or delay bills passed by the provincial Legislative assembly. He normally does this on the initiative of the federal Cabinet, which appoints him and pays his salary, on the ground that the provincial bill goes beyond the power (*ultra vires*) of the provincial government, in terms of the British North America Act. He can delay adoption by either "reserving the bill for the pleasure of His Excellency" (the Governor General, but actually meaning the federal Cabinet) or by referring it to the Supreme Court of Canada. The Supreme Court, which serves as umpire of the federal system, gives advisory opinions, unlike its counterpart in the United States.

The British North America Act does not provide for a Supreme Court, which was nevertheless established in 1875, originally with five, now with nine justices. Until 1949, however, it was not the last court of appeal for civil cases arising in Canada. This function was performed by the Judicial Committee of the British Privy Council, which consists of the five Law Lords, who are occasionally joined by a judge from one or another of the dominions. When they function as the Judicial Committee, they are formally only advising the Monarch in the exercise of his prerogative on appeals by his loyal subjects in his "Dominions beyond the Seas." Formally, therefore, they are not functioning as a court, but the only difference this makes is that they do not wear wigs, as British judges otherwise do. In fact, the Judicial Committee reviewed Canadian federal and provincial acts, and decisions of Canadian courts, for their constitutionality. No British court has ever done this for acts of the British Parliament, as we saw in the last chapter. But the King can review the constitutionality of acts of dominion parliaments, since these are mere creations of the British Parliament, deriving their authority from it. Moreover, while there is no single constitutional document in terms of which acts of the British Parliament could be judged, the British North America Act is such a document for judging the constitutionality of acts of the Canadian Parliament. And so the Judicial Committee of the Privy Council was the last court of appeal for Canada, in criminal cases until 1931, and in civil cases until 1949.

Today, the Supreme Court of Canada plays this role alone, and it continues to help shape the federal system, as does the Supreme Court of the United States. In at least one respect, however, it faces a more difficult task: The content of "the constitution of Canada" is not much clearer than that of the constitution of Great Britain. The only thing that is certain is that the Canadian constitution *begins* with the British North America Act of 1867 and its explicit amendments. However, a great deal must be added to this, first of all "the British constitution," since the Act of 1867 was to give Canada "a Constitution similar in Principle to that of the United Kingdom." In addition, the Colonial Laws Validity Act of 1865 had the effect of making Canadian acts void if they conflicted with acts of the British Parliament, but this ceased to be applicable after the British Parliament adopted the Statute of Westminster, in 1931, by which Great Britain gave complete self-government to her dominions. (Until 1931, much British legislation was automatically applicable in Canada.) Those provincial constitutions which are included in the British North America Act should also be considered parts of the Canadian constitution—and they may be amended by the provincial legislatures, "except as regards the Office of Lieutenant-Governor."

Thus, the precise content of the Canadian constitution is about as hard to fix as that of the British constitution, except for its federal provisions, which are specified in great detail in the British North America Act. But in this connection another difficulty has arisen, because the British Parliament turned over most of the amending function to the Canadian Parliament. The provincial governments want to share in this function, but no agreement on this question has been reached so far. This unsolved constitutional problem, which will be discussed below, means that there is no agreement in Canada on the locus of the "constituent power"—the power to create or alter the constitution. This situation would prove upsetting indeed for scholars of jurisprudence in a Continental country. It is bad enough when they cannot locate "the sovereign" or "sovereignty," which is said to lie with the office or body which "has the last word" in the state. Since the sovereign is hard to find in constitutional democracies, they have substituted the concept of the constituent power for it. Canada today does not even have that, which would make almost impossible the analysis of its politics according to the usual categories of political science.

Problems

The Dominion of Canada was founded mainly because none of the four
provinces that first entered into the Confederation had at its disposal the
resources required for exploiting or settling the rich half-continent to the
north of the United States. Settlement and exploitation was their goal,
but between it and their condition in the 1860's stood many sizable obstacles; these were the problems that led to Confederation. The economic
problems are indicated in the British North America Act itself. The
finances of the provinces were in bad shape at the time; hence the Act
provides that the Dominion should assume their debts, collect certain
taxes, and provide annual subsidies for provincial expenses. They needed
foreign investment, mainly British at the time: therefore "the Regulation
of Trade and Commerce," banking, interest, bankruptcy and insolvency,
and many related matters were put under "the exclusive Legislative
Authority of the Parliament of Canada." These provisions were designed
to make for uniformity all over the territory of the new Dominion, in
order to make Canadian investments more attractive to foreign capital.
The British North America Act also stated that "it shall be the Duty of
the Government and Parliament of Canada to provide for the Commence-
ment within Six Months after the Union, of a Railway connecting the
River St. Lawrence with the City of Halifax in Nova Scotia, and for the
Construction thereof without Intermission, and the Completion thereof
with all practicable Speed." Solution of the problems of transportation
and communication lay beyond the separate means of the provinces and
could be approached only through the pooling of their resources.

Many of the original economic problems were solved as a result
of Confederation, as the founders had promised themselves. Manitoba,
Saskatchewan, and Alberta were added, first as territories, then as provinces. British Columbia, on the Pacific Coast, joined, and after World
War II, the previously independent Dominion of Newfoundland became
the tenth province. But the solution of old problems was accompanied
by the creation of new ones. Thus, the wheat farmers in the prairie
provinces have been faced by the unsteadiness of wheat prices in the
world market, their dependence on eastern Canadian capital, and more
recently the "dumping" of wheat by the United States. With the demise
of Britain as the great creditor country, Canada has become worried
about the great share of United States investments in her growing basic
and manufacturing industries. Along with their growth has come the
organization of labor and, during the Great Depression, great unemploy-

ment. In the province of Quebec, the agricultural and traditionalist way of life was transformed as the result of industrialization, bringing new groups of people to a more active participation in politics.

Canada's single most important cultural problem, at the time of Union and before and since, has been the concentrated existence, mostly in Quebec, of a large French-Canadian population, the descendants of the original settlers who were conquered by the British in 1760. The proportions of this problem are best described in the words of Lord Durham's report:

> I expected to find a contest between a government and a people. I found two nations warring in the bosom of a single state: I found a struggle, not of principles, but of races; and I perceived that it would be idle to attempt any amelioration of laws or institutions until we could first succeed in terminating the deadly animosity that now separates the inhabitants of Lower Canada into the hostile divisions of French and English.[2]

His solution was amalgamation, which failed. Unitary Canada could not deal with the cultural cleavage between the French-speaking Catholics and the English-speaking Protestants. Federal Union was designed to separate the two groups insofar as their geographical distribution made this possible, and to prevent the chronic generation of issues arising out of this problem by assigning to the provincial legislatures exclusive powers over "Solemnization of Marriage" and "Laws in relation to Education," and by giving the English and French languages equal status in the federal and Quebec legislatures. This helped to push the problem down to the provincial level, where it could be more adequately dealt with. At the same time, however, because of the relative increase of the French over the English population in Quebec, this series of problems has tended to give rise to very controversial issues that are debated in constitutional terms. Canada has also absorbed large numbers of immigrants without acting as a "melting pot" to the extent that the United States has. Their failure to let themselves be assimilated has therefore also created problems, except in the case of immigrants from the United Kingdom, who easily adapt to British-Canadian ways.

Alcoholism also presented a serious cultural problem at one time, as in many frontier societies. In *Russell* v. *The Queen* (1882), the Judicial Committee of the Privy Council upheld a federal law providing for local option, because this measure was of importance to public order and safety. Much later, in 1925, judicial interpretation of the British

[2] *Ibid.,* p. 16.

North America Act was favoring the provinces, and permitting the Dominion government to interfere in provincial affairs under the "peace, order, and good government" clause of the Act only in grave national emergencies. This led Lord Haldane to deliver a famous opinion, in *Toronto Electric Commissioners* v. *Snider:*

> Their lordships think that the decision in *Russell* v. *The Queen* can only be supported today . . . on the assumption of the Board [the Judicial Committee] apparently made at the time of deciding the case of *Russell* v. *The Queen,* that the evil of intemperance at that time amounted in Canada to one so great and so general that at least for the period it was a menace to the national life of Canada so serious and pressing that the National Parliament was called on to intervene to protect the nation from disaster. An epidemic of pestilence might conceivably have been regarded as analogous.

As to external problems, Canadian territory had twice been invaded from the south—during the Revolutionary War (1775-76) and the War of 1812—and the Fathers of Confederation were justly concerned lest the release of United States troops from their Civil War duties might lead to another invasion. This gave added impetus to their movement. The separate provinces could not deal with this problem, nor could they expect sufficient aid from the British Empire. Tension between the United States and Great Britain led to fear of an American attack on Canada and the dispatch of more than ten thousand British reënforcements. Solution of their external problems consequently was one of the important results hoped for through Confederation. Success in this respect also helped Canada to approach ever closer to a position of equality with the mother country—a position now fully achieved. Today, the main external problems are the maintenance and strengthening of Canada's own identity against the economic and cultural attractions of the United States to the south, and of Canada's defenses against the threat of Soviet Communism from across the polar icecap to the north. Beyond that, Canada has as much of an interest in preserving world peace and preventing a third world war as all other nations.

In the 1860's, the great constitutional problem was simply the need for a federal constitution and its specific content. That problem was solved, but because the solution was a federal one, it has constantly bred new problems: What should be the share of the provinces in federal revenues, and how should it be distributed among them? How should representation in the House of Commons be apportioned? How should the federal and provincial governments share the burdens presented by new demands for social security? Finally, and most important, by what procedures should decisions about changes in federal-provincial relations be made? This is the problem of amending the British North America Act. Since the British Parliament devolved this function upon the Canadian Parliament—with the exceptions noted above—the provinces have claimed a right to participate in the amending process, somewhat as the states participate in amending the Constitution of the United States. At a conference held in 1950 for the purpose of devising an acceptable procedure, six categories of constitutional provisions were laid down. Specific sections of the North America Act could be amended (1) by the federal Parliament alone; (2) by the provincial legislature concerned alone; (3) by the federal Parliament and the provincial legislature concerned, acting together; (4) by the federal Parliament and a certain number of provincial legislatures; (5) by the federal Parliament and all of the provincial legislatures; and (6) sections that could not be amended at all. When representatives of the federal and the provincial governments next tried to classify all of the sections of the British North America Act in terms of these categories, they found that they could not reach agreement. Accordingly, there continues to be no accepted procedure for amending the Canadian constitution.

Issues and Politics

Before Confederation, eight different factions were operating in the Canadian Parliament. One of these was most concerned with strengthening Empire ties, another with westward expansion, a third with radical agrarian reforms, a fourth with maintaining the unity of French Catholic culture, a fifth with promoting the anticlerical spirit of the European revolutions of 1848, and so forth. The Confederation movement changed this. Federal Union now became the primary problem and the central issue of politics. After the Dominion was founded, strengthening or weakening the federal government remained the most debated issue for some time. This was a relatively clear-cut problem, and even before Confederation, the eight factions melted down into two: those in favor and those against. The old antagonisms between French- and English-Canadians were subordinated to this major concern. The Conservatives, who had been the great protagonists of Confederation, formed the first Cabinet and stayed in office until 1896, except for the years between 1874 and 1878, when they lost a general election after exposure of a corruption scandal involving the Canadian Pacific Railway. Railways and the tariff provided the main issues until 1896.

From 1896 until 1911, the Liberals were in office. Cultural problems had come up before this time, for example in connection with the control of schools in the new province of Manitoba, and when a French-Canadian with some Indian blood had led two rebellions against the government in the West. External relations figured in politics, too, as in the debate on the extent of Canadian participation in the Boer War. Because some French-Canadians felt more sympathy for the Boers, whom they regarded as a British-oppressed minority like themselves, the cultural problem infused some bitterness into this issue.

From 1911 until 1917, a Conservative Cabinet was in office, to be joined in a coalition government by a group that had split off from the Liberal party. The Liberals divided because their predominantly French wing in Quebec objected to the coalition's World War I conscription policy—again because they did not want to "fight the Empire's wars for it." The long-term onus of the conscription issue fell upon the Conservative party, however, and their alienation of Quebec's French-Canadian voters enabled the Liberals to return to power in 1921 and to continue to control the Cabinet until 1957, except for the years between 1930 and 1935, when the Conservatives returned to inaugurate Canada's "New Deal."

World War I also broke the monopoly of the two federal parties on seats in the House of Commons. Growing discontent among the farmers of the prairie provinces had led to the formation there of agrarian groups which first gained control of the provincial governments and then, in 1921, returned the second largest group to the federal House of Commons. Ever since, Alberta has been run by parties other than the two major federal ones—the United Farmers of Alberta until 1935, and the Social Credit party since then. Since 1944, Saskatchewan has had a Cabinet consisting of members of the Coöperative Commonwealth Federation, which models itself on the British Labour party. These two parties together have also sent up to forty-one members to the federal House of Commons. Meanwhile, the Legislative Assembly in Quebec has been controlled by a French-Canadian "nationalist" group, the Union Nationale, since 1942. This party does not participate in federal election campaigns, although it leans toward the Conservatives.

The Canadian party system is thus quite different from those of the other countries so far described. At the federal level, the two major parties have alternated in office. The smashing victory of the Conservatives in 1958 proved that the pattern is unlikely to change in the near future. But at the provincial level—and most Canadian provinces are as big as "sections" or "regions" of the United States—different parties have frequently had majorities for long periods. The only remotely analogous situation prevails in the Federal Republic of Germany, where Bavaria and other states have active parties that have been unable to elect deputies to the Bundestag. This suggests that we should examine any possible connection between federalism and these special Canadian conditions when we discuss party systems in Chapter 21.

All sections of Canada have a very active organizational life, with a multiplicity of farmers', business, religious, labor, and other organizations. Until the American Federation of Labor and the Congress of Industrial Organizations merged, Canada had two labor unions affiliated with these United States "international" organizations. Since the merger, the two Canadian groups have also joined. Some of their member unions have been directly affiliated with the Coöperative Commonwealth Federation, an avowedly socialist party, which has so far scored electoral successes mainly in Saskatchewan. In 1958, the C.C.F. and the labor union began to lay the groundwork for organizing a Socialist Canadian People's Party with wider appeal. In Quebec, there is a separate Catholic trade union, the only one in North America.

There are other important features that make Canadian politics different from both British and United States politics. Communism and anticommunism have not been as critical an issue in Canada as in the United States. Thus, Canada has recognized and permits trade with Communist China—but Canada is also a leading member of NATO and has constructed jointly with the United States the Distant Early Warning radar line on her territory. When the British landed troops in the Suez Canal zone in 1956, Canada took a leading role in the United Nations against this intervention. The kind of xenophobia and isolationism that occasionally crops up in United States politics is very rare indeed in Canada, except for Quebec. "Socialism" is not as widely frowned upon there; witness the existence of the Coöperative Commonwealth Federation, which at one time got more than 15 per cent of the national popular vote. Certain types of intellectuals are much more likely to show up in leading positions in Canada than in the United States. Mackenzie King, whose twenty-one years as Prime Minister constituted a record for length of such office in any British dominion, had been an economist. Lester Pearson, the Nobel-Prize-winning Minister of External Affairs, had been a university lecturer in history. And many other illustrations could be cited.

Some of the differences between Canadian and United States politics cannot be explained by way of differences between the problems faced by the two countries, or between the make-up of the population. Compare, for example, the treatment given to the problems of the one-crop economies of the two Middle Wests. Both areas were hit by this at the same time. The ethnic composition of the populations is very similar, and there has been a great deal of migration back and forth across the International Boundary. The initial response to the farmers' problem after World War I was similar, too, but in the long run Canada gained two additional parliamentary parties at the federal level from this experience, while the United States retained a party system that was not affected. Again, the problems of Communist subversion and espionage were quite similar in the two countries. Thus, the first Soviet spy ring was uncovered in Canada and a Canadian Communist Member of Parliament was convicted in the trial that followed its exposure. Yet anti-communism has never been an important Canadian issue. Later we will therefore want to ask to what extent constitutional differences may have contributed to bringing about these "un-American" peculiarities in the politics of Canada.

The Canadian constitution does make for a distinctive flow of decisions. Unlike Britain, problems in Canada are usually recognized not only at the central parliamentary level, but often also at the provincial level. This seems to be true of many federal systems. In the Canadian case, it can help explain the rise of new parties of provincial scope in times when the federal parties and government seemed to be responding inadequately to the special needs of one region. When a group like the United Farmers of Alberta, which was as much of an interest group as a political party, took over the provincial government, it soon found out that regional problems could not be solved without federal coöperation. As a result, it elected members to the central Parliament. The Social Credit movement passed through the same two phases fifteen years later, to be followed by the Coöperative Commonwealth Federation. But— and here another difference with Britain arises—these provincially based parties were not absorbed by the Conservatives and the Liberals, nor does any of the new parties threaten to replace one of the old ones. One result of this situation is the dispersal of the issue-formulating function. This can go on at the central parliamentary level, but often it is done by a provincial government, negotiating directly with the federal Cabinet. Sometimes the issue is formulated through litigation before the Supreme Court of Canada or, until recently, the Judicial Committee of the Privy Council. Deliberation also takes place at all of these levels.

The most important issues are decided in elections of the federal House of Commons. Here, something resembling the British theory of the mandate prevails. Again, it is not as clear-cut as in Great Britain, because provincial governments can obstruct the actions of the Dominion

CANADA : : : 141

government. National issues arising between general elections are resolved by the Canadian Cabinet, unless they involve the individual provinces, in which case the provincial governments participate in the resolution of issues. Both the federal and the provincial Cabinets and their respective bureaucracies look after the solution of problems.

The qualities of the civil service vary widely among the provinces. The federal bureaucracy, influenced strongly by its British model, has often been troubled by requirements to give to French-Canadians a share of positions proportional to their strength among the total population. In some cases, this has resulted in personnel practices not unlike "featherbedding" in American industries with strong labor unions. Nevertheless, the over-all performance of the Canadian federal bureaucracy has been quite good.

Success

The Canadian federal constitution has been quite stable since adoption of the British North America Act in 1867. In the foreseeable future, it promises to become even more stable, because of the lack of agreement on the procedures by which it can be amended. Formal amendments affecting federal-provincial relations are likely to be avoided in favor of more informal changes. This stability has evidently not been one of stagnation, because of the great territorial expansion and immigration that has been absorbed by the constitutional system. It has, on the whole, also been an efficient constitution, though it has handled some types of problems much more satisfactorily than others. Efficiency in the solving of the old cultural problem has been the lowest. This was shown during World War II, when the electorate was asked in a nation-wide referendum whether it would release the federal Cabinet from its promise not to ship conscripted soldiers overseas. In the verdict outside Quebec was 79 per cent in favor of release from the promise; in French-Canadian Quebec, it was 71 per cent against, but there were no violent riots as there had been over a similar issue in World War I.

Since the war, the cultural cleavage has come up again and again in conflicts between Ottawa and Quebec, although the trend over the long run seems to be a constant lessening of tensions. If this continues, the Canadian constitution will also gain in effectiveness. As things stand now, the continued cohesion, with very little violence in this century, of the two races that Lord Durham had found warring in the bosom of a single state must be considered quite an achievement. Along with the great popularity of the British royal family, even among French-Canadians, it calls for an explanation. This will be offered in connection with the discussion of "Consensus," in Chapter 22; meanwhile, we may tentatively conclude that the British North America Act did "conduce to the Welfare of the Provinces"—and did possibly even "promote the Interests of the British Empire." Throughout the history of their present political system, Canadian citizens have been living in sound situations of responsibility—even while they were still British subjects without having their own citizenship recognized. The choices through which they can contribute to central decisions have been and are manifold, and the fact that many decisions are decentralized to the provinces directly concerned gives them a further advantage. No minority group has been denied such choices, as have Negroes in the United States.

Since Canada began to build up her own civil, foreign, and military services in good time, before she was put entirely on her own by Great Britain, adequate institutional resources are available for implementing central decisions. And the structure of interest and party organizations is such that individuals can implement their choices. Moreover, the potential of Canada's natural resources is of vast proportions. Constitutional stability and the constant accountability of politicians to their electorates provide sound foreknowledge of the consequences of citizens' choices. Only for the province of Quebec do we have to make an exception to this judgment. There, majorities based on the more ignorant rural population have been used, sometimes together with corruption and violence, to keep in office a government that has done anything but improve situations of responsibility. But this is not likely to last forever, as similar experiences in the United States suggest.

CHAPTER 11

The United States of America

Constitutional History

The Constitution of the United States is the oldest written constitution in the world that still provides the framework for a political system in our own time. It was produced in four months of work by the Constitutional Convention, which met in Philadelphia during the summer of 1787. The convention had been called by the Continental Congress, itself based on the Articles of Confederation of 1777, which had been adopted by the thirteen former British colonies in their War of Independence. The delegates to the convention came from every state but Rhode Island. They were deeply conscious of their opportunity to give the new country a permanent constitution. At the same time, they were also aware of the tremendous obstacles to true success. That is why, in the last of the Federalist Papers, Alexander Hamilton quoted David Hume:

> The zeal for attempts to amend, prior to the establishment of the Constitution, must abate in every man who is ready to accede to the truth of the following observations of a writer equally solid and ingenious: "To balance a large state or society [says he], whether monarchical or republican, on general laws, is a work of so great difficulty, that no human genius, however comprehensive, is able, by the mere dint of reason and reflection, to effect it. The judgments of many must unite in the work; experience must guide their labor; time must bring it to perfection, and the feeling of inconveniences must correct the mistakes which they *inevitably* fall into in their first trials and experiments." These judicious reflections contain a lesson of moderation to all sincere lovers of the Union, and ought to put them upon their guard against hazarding anarchy, civil war, perpetual alienation of the States from each other, and perhaps the mili-

tary despotism of a victorious demagogue, in the pursuit of what they are not likely to obtain, but from time and experience. . . . The establishment of a Constitution, in profound peace, by the voluntary consent of the whole people, is a prodigy, to the completion of which I look forward with trembling anxiety.

The Founding Fathers were perfectly clear in their minds about the goals of the new nation. Their every utterance since the Declaration of Independence in 1776 shows this, and the Preamble to the Constitution enshrines the goals they sought to secure "to ourselves and our posterity." The obstacles in the path of realizing these goals were also perfectly obvious. During the War of Independence, when the primary goal consisted of cutting the ties with Great Britain, the main problem was military, bringing the colonies together under the Articles of Confederation. After Great Britain recognized the independence of the United States in 1783, economic problems replaced external ones as most important. But throughout the entire period, because both external and economic problems faced in common by a new community can be solved only through politics, the Founding Fathers knew that the key to solving all their problems was solution of the constitutional problem.

The Articles of Confederation had failed to provide such a solution. They had been written too much in the shadow of the war to be useful in dealing with the problems of peace. They left to the states problems that, individually, they lacked the resources for handling. They were also too inflexible to be adapted to the changed emphasis in goals of the newly independent states, because they could be amended only if the "alteration . . . be afterwards confirmed by the legislatures of every State."

The constitution-makers at Philadelphia, as others ever since, searched all over the globe and all over history for models that might help them in designing the new structure. This kind of search was to become much easier for later constitutional engineers, simply because there came to be more models to copy from as time went on. The difficult thing about the task of the American Founding Fathers was that theirs was the first attempt "to balance a large state or society . . . on general laws," in Hume's words. Theirs was the first deliberately designed constitution for a large political system. This limited to five main types the models whose comparative study they could apply to their own efforts: First, for the federal aspects of their work, they referred to leagues and confederations of all kinds, both classical and modern. For the internal structure of the national government, they relied on four remaining types of models: constitutions of classical antiquity, some of which had been rationally designed; the unplanned constitutions of postmedieval states; the young, engineered constitutions of their own thirteen new states; and the British constitution. The British constitution played a special part in the deliberations at Philadelphia. This was, after all, the constitution under which they and their forefathers had been living. The colonial charters, the constitutions under which the North American colonies had been governed (including Nova Scotia, as we saw), had followed the pattern of the British constitution of their time as much as the constitution of New France had followed that of the Old France of Louis XIV.

Of all that the Constitutional Convention borrowed from the past, more came from the British constitution than from any other single source. The best-known illustration of this is the separation of powers— even though Britain did not in fact have it. James Madison, in Number 47 of the Federalist Papers, wrote of the separation of powers: "The oracle who is always consulted and cited on this subject is the celebrated Montesquieu." And then:

> The British Constitution was to Montesquieu what Homer has been to the didactic writers on epic poetry. As the latter have considered the work of the immortal bard as the perfect model from which the principles and rules of the epic art were to be drawn, so this great political critic appears to have viewed the Constitution of England as the standard, or to use his own expression, as the mirror of political liberty; and to have delivered, in the form of elementary truths, the several characteristic principles of that particular system. That we may be sure, then, not to mistake his meaning in this case, let us recur to the source from which the maxim was drawn.
>
> On the slightest view of the British Constitution, we must perceive that the legislative, executive, and judiciary departments are by no means totally separate and distinct from each other. . . .

Madison understood the British Constitution better than Montesquieu, the French "oracle." Indeed, Madison and his colleagues more than *understood* British political procedures: They lived and breathed them to such an extent that most of the time they were not even aware of conducting politics "the British way," and of writing "the British way" into the Constitution of the United States. And when they were aware of copying from their former mother country, they could do so without resentment, because they had won their independence five years earlier, after a war in which they had considered their own interpretation of the British constitution right, and the British interpretation wrong.

Besides the borrowed institutions and procedures, there was of course much in the Constitution which was pure and ingenious innovation. This was true especially of many of the federal provisions, governing relations among the states and between them and the central government. But perhaps the most important constitutional invention of the American Founding Fathers was Article V, which sets forth the procedure for amending the Constitution. Article V provided the solution to the most perplexing of all constitutional problems, the problem of combining stability with adaptability, permanence with flexibility. Unwritten constitutions do not face this problem. It is peculiar to written ones, especially when they are new. Oliver Cromwell discovered this after the English Civil War. He tried to bring about revolutionary changes by giving the country a written constitution, his Instrument of Government. Having done that, he wanted to keep this new structure of government stable or, as he put it, "standing" and "unalterable." His Parliament, on the other hand, kept on trying to alter what he considered the "fundamentals," pushing toward instability and flux. We have seen how the easily amendable written constitution of the Weimar Republic also failed to provide stability and even facilitated its own transformation into totalitarianism, which is a condition of permanent flux.

Instability is one horn of the dilemma faced by constitutional engineers. The other is rigidity. The problem of rigidity exists for unwritten constitutions as well. For if any constitution fails to adapt itself to changing problems, its politics will become inefficient. If it fails to adjust to new goals of the population, one of which may be efficiency, the constitution will cease to be accepted. Inefficiency in the face of changing problems had been the main trouble with the Articles of Confederation, which could not be amended except by unanimous agreement among the thirteen states. The Articles of Confederation were now to be superseded by the new Constitution, once it was ratified by special conventions—not by the legislatures—in only nine of the states. Thereafter, and this was the great innovation, stability was to be provided by making its amendment *difficult,* and adaptability by making its amendment *possible.* If two-thirds of both houses of Congress vote for an amendment, which is then ratified by the legislatures of three-fourths of the states, it becomes a part of the Constitution.[1]

Both permanence and flexibility were further buttressed by another, more famous invention of the Founding Fathers, "the rights of the courts to pronounce legislative acts void, because contrary to the Constitution,"

---

[1] Since it has never been used, we here ignore the second method, under which the Congress, "on the application of the legislatures of two-thirds of the several states, shall call a convention for proposing amendments," which must then be ratified by the legislatures of, or conventions in, three-fourths of the states.

which Hamilton explained in Number 78 of the Federalist Papers. The stabilizing function of the exercise of judicial review by the Supreme Court was emphasized by one of the delegates to the Constitutional Convention, sixteen years later, when he had become Chief Justice of the United States. John Marshall decided:

> That the people have an original right to establish, for their future government, such principles as, in their opinion, shall most conduce to their own happiness, is the basis on which the whole American fabric has been erected. The exercise of this original right is a very great exertion; nor can it nor ought it to be frequently repeated. The principles, therefore, so established, are deemed fundamental. And as the authority from which they proceed is supreme, and can seldom act, they are designed to be permanent.

The ingenuity of this passage from *Marbury* v. *Madison* becomes apparent when we consider that this was the first decision holding a congressional act unconstitutional. And the Act expanded the functions of the Supreme Court by giving it original jurisdiction over cases that, according to the Constitution, came under its appellate jurisdiction. Marshall therefore not only guaranteed the permanence of the Constitution; at the same time, he laid the foundation for the Court's role as interpreter, adjuster, and expander of the Constitution.

Because the Supreme Court had performed this function, formal amendments to the Constitution have been passed only rarely and, with the exception of the plunge of the Civil War, the curve of American constitutional development has been a very smooth one. The first ten amendments, the so-called Bill of Rights, should not be considered constitutional changes at all, because they had been promised to the states during the campaign for ratification. Besides, the first eight of them are mainly restatements of the rights of Englishmen, contained in various British constitutional documents. Of the other amendments adopted before the Civil War, only the Twelfth was important; it required that electors cast separate ballots for President and Vice-President. This was made necessary, because the original procedure had turned out to be one of those mistakes of constitution-makers "which they *inevitably* fall into in their first trials and experiments," according to David Hume.

This was not the only error committed at Philadelphia, but the others did not have to be corrected, or at any rate not by constitutional amendment. An example of this is the President's "power, by and with the advice and consent of the Senate, to make treaties." The phrase, obviously taken from the British political vocabulary, led President Washington to seek the advice of the Senate, by actually consulting with them in the Senate chamber. The Senators, however, were reluctant to speak up, whereupon the provision fell into disuse. In other respects, the authors of the Constitution prevented its frequent amendment by leaving problems to the states for decision, as was done with the question of qualifications for voting in elections of members of the House of Representatives and presidential electors. As a result, the extension of the franchise to all free male adults, which was such a revolutionary issue in Europe and was not completed in the United States until the 1830's, could be handled by each state as it saw fit.

While the constitutional problem of the franchise could be solved by the states, and the resulting controversies contained within these "compartments," the constitutional problem of slavery could not. Its ramifications had already threatened the success of the Constitutional Convention. Some of the most delicate compromises written into the Constitution revolved around this problem. They made the Constitution in effect the lowest common denominator of goals—and of means to reach those goals—upon which agreement could be secured in 1787. This lowest common denominator served its purpose well while the political and economic unity of the young system was being built up, and while it was expanding over vast new territories to the west.

Gradually, however, the divergence over goals between the Southern and the Northern States increased, partly because of the importance of slavery to the cotton economy of the South. Various means of resolving the issue within the framework of the Constitution were tried, only to fail. Congress decided the issue first in the Missouri Compromise of 1820, and again in the Compromise of 1850. In 1854, the Kansas-Nebraska Act left the slavery issue in those new territories to be settled by their population, which led to bloodshed. In 1857, the Supreme Court held the Missouri Compromise unconstitutional, in its Dred Scott decision. Starting in 1854, at the latest, decisions of this kind were no longer being accepted as authoritative by those who disagreed with their substance. By 1861, agreement broke down about the proper procedures by which disagreements should be settled. The Constitution ceased to be effective. The South no longer wanted a "more perfect Union." The will to remain in a single political system had broken down. The Civil War ensued.

When people refuse to accept decisions arrived at by regular procedures, power becomes the *ultima ratio,* as it has often been in international politics. The effectiveness of the Constitution was restored by force of arms. The Thirteenth, Fourteenth, and Fifteenth Amendments were the resolution to the slavery issue. Yet they were to create new constitutional problems that have been generating issues for United States politics ever since. One of them, the Fourteenth, in the hands of the Supreme Court, was slowly turned into an instrument for applying to the states the same prohibitions the Bill of Rights placed on the Congress; its eventual effect was to help reduce the apparently basic difference between federalism in the United States and in Canada. By now, anyone who is not aware of the formal constitutional difference would never realize that the central government in the United States has only powers delegated to it by the states, while Canadian provinces have only powers delegated to them by the Dominion.

Of the remaining amendments, only the Seventeenth, providing for the popular election of Senators, resulted in a significant constitutional change, one which the Founding Fathers had not left open to revision by the states. The Prohibition Amendments hardly affected the machinery of government, although they may have flavored the fuel powering it. Extension of the vote to women solved this particular problem in the way it was being solved all over Europe, with the notable exception of that ancient "democracy," Switzerland. Restriction of the President to two terms was an act of recrimination against the late President who had been elected four times. Compared with such British constitutional changes as the Parliament Acts, this latter amendment is of trivial significance.

Constitutional Structure

The United States is a federal system of fifty states, thirty-seven of which have been admitted since ratification of the Constitution by the thirteen founding members of the Union. Like the Swiss Confederation, which learned much from the United States, but unlike Germany, each of the component units has its own system of courts. Each has its own bureaucracy, which is also true of the Swiss cantons and the Canadian provinces, but again not of the West German states. The governors of the states are elected directly, not by state parliaments as in Canada and Germany. The Constitution intended that the states should participate in the federal government through the Senate, in which each of them was to be represented by two Senators, originally elected by its legislature. As a result of adoption of the Seventeenth Amendment, the voters, rather than the legislature, in each state today have this opportunity for participation through their Senators. Other channels are available for state governments, e.g., by way of the federal bureaucracy or through governors' conferences, both nationwide and regional. It also frequently happens that former governors are elected to the Senate or appointed to the President's Cabinet.

The 437 members of the House of Representatives are elected directly from single-member constituencies. The number of Representatives to be elected from each state is determined by the Congress after each decennial census, but their apportionment within each state is regulated by its legislature. The functions of House and Senate differ in three major respects: First, "All bills for raising revenue shall originate in the House of Representatives." Second, treaties made by the President are subject to approval of the Senate alone, requiring the concurrence of two-thirds of the Senators voting. Third, presidential appointments of judges, ambassadors, and other high officers of the United States require approval by majority vote in the Senate. Two-thirds of the votes in both houses can override a presidential veto, which can therefore have a delaying effect somewhat similar to that of the House of Lords or the constitutional amending procedure in the French Fourth Republic.

The Presidency is the single office combining a greater number of functions than any established by the other written constitutions discussed in this book. Actually, the President today exercises many more functions than those provided for by the Constitution. He initiates most policy and, although he needs the support of the Congress in order to have his bills passed and to get the funds necessary for their implementation, a number of techniques for circumventing this need have been developed. Thus, the requirement for the Senate's concurrence on treaties has often been evaded by means of so-called "executive agreements." More commonly than this, however, the President uses all the vast means of persuasion at his disposal in order to elicit congressional support. He also makes, and is expected to make, concessions on his part in order to obtain similar concessions from congressional opponents of any particular measure. This general expectation leads to a constant bargaining process, in which both sides overstate their demands at the outset in order to get more of what they want at the end.

Some of the sources of the central position of the Presidency in the American system are constitutional. Unlike most Continental presidents, he has no prime minister to compete with, and the Congress cannot get rid of him: No President of the United States has ever resigned. His term runs for four years, while that of the House of Representatives runs for only two; Senators serve for six years, with one-third of their number elected every two years. Moreover, the President is one man, the Constitutional Convention having deliberately opted against a "plural executive," as Hamilton explained in Number 70 of the Federalist Papers. All the European Cabinets, except that of West Germany, are much more collegial or committee-like in their operations. And the Congress consists of 537 men and women, none of whom can hope to compete effectively with the President, especially since there is no institution of the leader of the opposition. The congressional leaders of the opposition party come close to playing this role only when the President's own party is in a minority. But even then, they do not present the kind of alternative program with which the British leader of the opposition challenges the Prime Minister daily in the House of Commons.

The nonconstitutional reasons for the President's preëminence are at least as important as the constitutional ones. They are connected with the party system for which, of course, the Founding Fathers made no provision at all. The main function of the party system is the election of the President. The Constitution provided that this should be performed by special electors: "Each State shall appoint, in such manner as the Legislature thereof may direct, a number of Electors, equal to the whole number of Senators and Representatives to which the State may be entitled in the Congress." Again, the problem of the franchise was pushed down to the level of the states. The electors soon became mere intermediaries, whose votes were almost invariably cast for the presidential candidate who had received the majority of votes in the state. The presidential candidates, in turn, were nominated at national conventions of the parties. Since the end of the Civil War, when the present party system was established, or reëstablished, the Republican and the Democratic parties have held their national conventions every four years; without exception, the nominee of one of the two parties was subsequently elected President. This procedure is so regular and so firmly established that it must be considered just as much part of the constitution as the procedures of Cabinet government in Great Britain. It is, moreover, a distinctive feature of the American constitution: party leaders in the other countries are usually selected by the parliamentary delegation of a party rather than by an extra-parliamentary assembly like a convention. Only in Canada has the decision on selection of a party leader who subsequently became Prime Minister been made by a convention, and there only rarely, since national party conventions take place at long, irregular intervals. In the United States, the nationwide nominating and campaign process, combined with what is for all practical purposes the direct popular election of the President, has made his office into much more than the authors of the Constitution intended it to be.

The Supreme Court, whose nine justices are appointed for life by the President with the consent of the Senate, has been playing the role the Founding Fathers presumably intended for it, sometimes with more vigor, sometimes with less. Since the Court early refused to give advisory opinions and since it exercises much discretion in selecting the cases it will review, it has had better opportunities to shape its own role than its younger replicas in Canada and the Federal Republic of Germany. The Supreme Court reviews and can reverse the decisions of lower courts, both state and federal. And it reviews and can reject as unconstitutional both state and federal legislation involved in cases appealed to it. Occasionally, after a measure has been held to be unconstitutional, the Congress reënacts it in a form that overcomes the Court's objection. As a last resort, it can initiate an amendment to the Constitution in order to create new standards of constitutionality, as it did with the Sixteenth Amendment (1909), which established the constitutionality of a federal income tax struck down by the Court in 1895.

Problems

During the War of Independence and since World War II, external problems constituted the most serious ones faced by the United States. During the founding period and the decades before and after the Civil War, constitutional problems were of the greatest importance. During most of the remainder of the one hundred and eighty years of the life of the Republic, people have been preoccupied with economic problems, with cultural ones taking the center of attention for occasional intervals. Once independence had been achieved and the Constitution safely launched, the young nation could concentrate on forming a more perfect economic union: improving transportation and other means of communication among the thirteen original states, expanding to the west and adding new states, and gaining economic in addition to constitutional independence. Already before the Civil War, the great influx of European immigrants added cultural difficulties, which were always kept within manageable proportions for two main reasons: first, because of the wide agreement within the United States that European immigrants were needed in order to build up the country economically; and second, because most of these immigrants had left their homelands out of despair and with great expectations of the New World, so that they were eager to drop their old habits and connections and take on new ways of life.

For seventy years after the Civil War, economic problems were dominant once more. During that war, there began the intense industrialization whose completion made the United States the productive giant among the economies of the world. There are many parallels between this era and the even more rapid industrialization of the Soviet Union under Joseph Stalin. To be sure, Stalin by far outdid the "robber barons" in ruthlessness and violence, but he too harnessed a whole nation—and one much more backward economically—to the single purpose of building up vast new basic industries. With less violence and more competition, plus many other advantages, the Americans achieved a great deal more than the late-coming Russians did. They reduced the farming population to less than one-fifth of the total and mechanized agriculture along with much else. Only the South, defeated in the war, was left behind the general advance as an economic backwater. The South's discrimination against the former slaves and their descendants, and new waves of less easily assimilable immigrants elsewhere, were the two main cultural problems of these decades.

External problems continued to play a minor role, meanwhile. Even before the Civil War, there had been the War of 1812, which raised the constitutional problem of New England's half-hearted threat of secession; and the Mexican War. Both were chiefly fought on the home continent. The war against Spain in 1898 took American troops farther away and added "colonial" possessions, to which self-government was granted almost as soon as possible. There followed, before and after World War I, several minor involvements in Central America and the Caribbean. The "war to end all wars" brought the United States out into the great world of affairs, or the great affairs of the world, for the first time, and thereafter the trend toward the returning primacy of external problems became irreversible, no matter how much some isolationists opposed their recognition by insisting that nothing was more important than "business," or "America First." The Great Depression demonstrated that they had not been entirely wrong, for whatever reasons, and under the New Deal the organization of the American economy and of its component sectors, most noticeably labor, came to the forefront once more.

Since the beginning of World War II, the most important problems facing the United States have been of defense and foreign relations: the war in Europe and whether to enter it, later how to win it and for what goals; the reconstruction of world politics, this time irrevocably with United States participation; the threat of Soviet Communist expansion and subversion, in Europe, Asia, and the Americas—even in the United States itself; the Korean War; the race for weapons superiority and for allies; the work for disarmament under the threat of a mutually fatal nuclear war; the Near East and Outer Space; and all the other interlocking external problems in which, because of its new role of world leadership, the responsibilities of the United States are greater than those of any other of our eight countries.

At the same time, problems in the other fields continue to arise, many of them generated by international politics. The defense effort and American aid around the world have to be paid for, taking a bigger slice out of the United States budget than do similar items in the other countries. The descendants of immigrants have become "second-" and "third-generation," sometimes too well assimilated, and sometimes not well enough assimilated. In the first case, two-hundred-per-cent Americanism leads to equally strong isolationism and the rejection of all foreign involvements as un-American. In the second, foreign policy is seen in the light of its effects on the country of origin, as Ireland and Poland, or the country of identification, as Israel. Meanwhile, with ever-increasing urgency, the ancient cultural problems of the South are demanding a solution, for they too are entwined in the country's external problems. The issues arising out of this problem of the aftermath of slavery have been restated by each generation and resolved by none so far. In the late 1950's, as often before, they were being debated in constitutional terms, but their "resolution" by the Supreme Court was not acceptable to the white population involved, so that force was used by citizens, by state governments, and by the federal government. And ninety-six Southern Congressmen denounced the Supreme Court of the United States.

Issues and Politics

The problem of segregation is not the only one that has given rise to constitutional controversies in the United States. In fact, every type of problem has done so since the founding of the country. In none of the other six systems with written constitutions has there ever been as frequent reference to the much-vaunted "intentions of the Founding Fathers." One obvious reason for this is that the American Founding Fathers have long been dead, while at least in Italy, Germany, and France they are today still very much alive, so that they can tell people just what they did intend. On the other hand, the great religions and ideologies that motivate many participants in European politics often generate debates on "the true meaning of the Bible," or "what Marx really meant." In this sense, the Constitution of the United States and related documents, like the records of the Constitutional Convention and the Federalist Papers, perform a function similar to that of religious or ideological holy script.

All the great problems that have confronted the United States have at some time been converted into issues about the Constitution. Whether this means that Americans have often lacked constitutional consensus, or agreement on fundamentals, is a question to be dealt with later. These habits of debate may be connected with the first great debate, out of which the two great American parties grew. As in Switzerland and Canada, the first central issue was whether to establish the new federal system, and after its establishment, whether to strengthen or weaken it. The very name of the first of the parties, the Federalists, demonstrates this. Naturally, the Constitution was the ultimate focus of all discussions. Then, as the Constitution became widely accepted because it realized much of what its authors had promised themselves from it, new opportunities arose for constitutional argumentation about issues arising out of contemporary problems, then mainly economic. These opportunities are explained by Chief Justice Marshall's definition of the role of the Supreme Court. The role of the Court meant, in effect, that anyone who lost on an issue in the ordinary political process need not give up hope entirely, because there was always the possibility that the Court might void something that had happened in the course of that process. This is what actually happened in the Dred Scott case.

The Civil War itself was fought over the Constitution, and the founding of the Republican party as continuator of the Whig and Federalist tradition was in defense of a stronger federal system. The Democratic party, on the other hand, carried on with a looser interpretation of the Constitution and has retained the support of the states of the Confederacy ever since. No wonder then that any issue even remotely connected with the Civil War has been treated in constitutional terms. But so have many others: economic problems, like the income tax, the regulation of corporations, monopolies, the program of the New Deal to overcome the depression; cultural problems, like prohibition, state aid to parochial schools, and school children's refusals to salute the flag; and external problems, like membership in the League and the United Nations, and intervention in Korea.

Not all issues are given this kind of constitutional treatment, and those that do receive it do not get it all the time. The great issues arising out of sectional economic conflicts—like the tariff, "silver," and parity for farm prices—have more often been debated in terms of sectional interests and the general interest in the campaigns preceding presidential and congressional elections. Similarly, issues generated by the problem of the distribution of income among the various sectors of the economy—like labor law, taxes, social security—are usually discussed in terms of interest as much as in terms of the Constitution. This is also true of the issue of Communist infiltration and subversion.

Except for the period of the break-up of the major parties before the Civil War, the most important issues are usually stated by the two parties in the quadrennial presidential campaigns. However, the only issue normally resolved by these elections is that between the two contending presidential candidates. The two parties function as really national organizations only every four years, when each sets out to elect its nominee President of the United States. During the remaining three and one-half years, the losing party especially has little cohesion, because it lacks the central focus provided by the official leader of the parliamentary opposition in Great Britain and Canada. The winning party may have such a focus in the President, but this does not suffice to discipline the party, at either the level of Congress or that of the state organizations. Not even the dispensing of federal patronage, or the threat to withhold it, can do this job.

Within party organizations in the states, better discipline sometimes prevails. But many state party organizations perform unique functions, because they have been in an unchallenged majority position for many decades, as in the South. This casts the Democrats of the Deep South in a role similar to that of Social Credit in Alberta. In addition to resolving issues of internal, state, provincial, or sectional origin, they also formulate issues about the state in its relations with the federal government and/or other parts of the country.

Partly because the national party organizations put in such a haphazard performance between leap years, the formulation of issues and their deliberation and resolution is much more dispersed in the United States, and shared by many more organs and organizations, than in a system like the British. Public debate is often initiated, and a large part of the process of deliberation is carried on, by large, nationally organized interest groups—such as the United States Chamber of Commerce, the National Association of Manufacturers, the A.F.L.-C.I.O., the Farm Bureau Federation, the American Legion, the Air Force Association, the National Association for the Advancement of Colored People, the Committee for Economic Development, the American Civil Liberties Union, Daughters of the American Revolution, Americans for Democratic Action, the American Automobile Association, and hundreds of others. Direct affiliation between the interest organizations and a political party occurs less frequently in the United States than in the other countries studied. Individual citizens are more likely than in any of the Continental countries to belong to or support a great variety of these groups, some of which may have contradictory goals, and many of which are active in both the state and federal capitals.

Much of the business of the lobbyists who work for these organizations is taken care of in direct contacts with the bureaucracy and with members of Congress. Their public business is often performed before the specialized committees of the two houses of Congress. The members of these committees, by contrast with their Continental counterparts, are rarely officers of the organizations that are specially interested in the committee's activities. Nonetheless, much of the deliberation and resolution the Congress does perform, occurs in the committees of the two houses. The House of Representatives needs the committees even more for this purpose, because its larger size makes deliberation in its full meetings much more difficult than in the case of the smaller Senate. The Senate is more often used as a forum for deliberation on constitutional issues, including that of its own rules, which is a persistently recurring topic.

The President himself, assisted by his Cabinet, whose members are individually accountable to him, and by the federal bureaucracy, often states and resolves issues by proposing his solution of a problem to the Congress. The Congress deliberates upon these issues in a seemingly more meaningful way than the House of Commons, because it does share the function of resolution with the President. But, unlike Continental parliaments, the Congress itself never has to bring into being this organ, which is the major source of resolution in the system between general elections. The formal final resolution of issues takes place when the President signs congressional bills (unlike the Queen today, he is not obliged to approve all acts of the legislature). The actual solution of the problems is then taken care of by the various federal departments and their civil servants.

The honesty and efficiency of the United States bureaucracy compares unfavorably with those of all of our other countries, with the exception of Italy. The civil service of the United States is younger than all of the others (except for parts of the Canadian), and the spoils system remained in effect longer. The military services, on the other hand, have older traditions, dating back to the Independence period when external problems were paramount. Their traditions were largely taken over from the mother country, which may help to explain why, in the present, when external problems are once more becoming crucial, civil-military relations have given rise to few major issues. Among the exceptions to this was the dismissal of General Douglas MacArthur, and that issue was settled quickly.

Success

The Constitution of the United States has been stable. Its basic structure survived even the Civil War. It has been adapted to changes in the problems faced by the country in a manner that provided for the continuous achievement of the goals set forth in its Preamble: "to form a more perfect Union, establish justice, insure domestic tranquility, provide for the common defense, promote the general welfare, and secure the blessings of liberty. . . ." Only the Civil War was an exception to this adaptability. For the rest, it might be objected that the resources of the country, and its geographical location, were such that the United States could afford to adjust to changing circumstances much more slowly than most other countries. But since this no longer applies, we now have no cause for optimism concerning adaptation to the rapidly changing problems, especially of foreign relations, in the atomic age.

The efficiency of American politics has varied. Often its main organs have refused to recognize problems for fear of losing votes or generating avoidable controversy. Often, an issue is shunted back and forth between parties, Congress, President, and Supreme Court, before a widely acceptable resolution is arrived at. Meanwhile, groups especially concerned with the problem grow increasingly disaffected and bitter, and engage in recrimination. Again, the great resources of the United States have ameliorated the consequences of this kind of inefficiency. It has also been made tolerable by the relatively limited functions performed by the federal government until the 1920's. In those days, when something went wrong, the government was less likely to be blamed for it than is the case today. Even in the 1950's, however, Americans rely less on their government in the solution of some types of problems than probably any other nation; at any rate, they are more prone to add organized private efforts to those of the government: witness the recession of 1958 and the measures to fight it taken by large corporations and the Advertising Council. When this sort of thing happens, the issue of the relative importance of private and government action is immediately raised, but if the problem is solved, the issue resolves itself automatically. In more doctrinaire nations, this is rarely the case.

The Constitution itself is more effective than many policies produced according to its processes, as for example desegregation of schools. This is understandable, because every segment of the population is free to interpret the Constitution and the intentions of the Founding Fathers as it sees fit. Even policies that are not rejected outright by a defeated minority are frequently thwarted through evasion or circumvention. Corruption sometimes plays a role in this; so does private violence, of which there is a tradition dating back in part to the days of the frontier.

After all this has been said, however, it must be granted that individual citizens of the United States are today in a more favorable situation of responsibility than people anywhere in Europe. True, the political process in the United States is not as centralized as in the major European countries, because there are many more foci of decision-making, among them the states and the various organs of the federal government. Americans cannot as clearly contribute to one funnel in the policy flow as can the British in a general election. But Americans have a vastly greater range of alternatives to choose among at each of the many more phases through which policy develops. This means that the final outcome—in Britain the program of one of the two parties, and nothing else—is never as clear in United States politics. This detracts from the quality of their knowledge about the effects of their decisions. But because so many more problems than in Britain are decided at levels really close to the people immediately affected by the problems, they need not be as concerned about decisions made in Washington. Besides, the United States government does not reach the citizen in as many direct ways in as many of his activities as do European governments. The American still has more opportunities, and greater resources, to shape his private destiny without having to ask for government permission or support. "Private free enterprise" is not just a shibboleth but actually operative in many fields of American life.

This gives no cause for complacency about the success of United States politics. The system has not adequately adjusted to some of the most urgent contemporary problems it faces. Inefficiencies here are often due precisely to reluctance to focus the policy flow centrally, because of fear that this would reduce the opportunities of individuals, as such and as members of large organized groupings, to decide about their own future. This fear is not entirely warranted, as our study of Britain might indicate. There, the making of decisions about problems is highly centralized and operates in the open, according to stable procedures, allowing for responsible contributions by all. In totalitarian dictatorships, centralization is just as high, but decisions are made in the dark. In the Fourth French Republic, there were many foci for the making of national policy, although not as many as in the United States. The results are well known. The narrowness of the funnel through which policy flows is not as important as the brightness of the light of publicity that shines upon it. The more diffused that light has to be, the dimmer will it necessarily become. Decentralized policy-making by itself was not the greatest contribution made by the Founding Fathers to the success of the American political system, nor is it an important contribution that the United States can make to others who are building their constitutions today. They can benefit much more from lessons about the method by which the core of "the True Constitution" of the United States was first located and stated, and has since then been expanded and kept full of vitality.

PART III

Political Style

CHAPTER 12

Statement of Issues

If we were to tell eight different families that a notorious criminal was planning to burglarize their homes during the next few days, chances are that each would deal with this problem in its own peculiar way. One family might be so preoccupied with some ancient quarrel that its members would ignore the warning, that is, fail to recognize the problem, to the advantage of the burglar. In most of the families, however, someone would ask: What can we do about it? It might be the father or the mother, or both parents, or the children, or the whole family together. It makes a difference who asks this question, who formulates the issue. Thus, we could imagine that a very firm *pater familias* might not bother to state any alternatives to his family at all, preferring instead to decide on his own what to do. A family council, on the other hand, might come up with half a dozen alternatives, which will make for a great deal of discussion.

Once the alternatives have been given, the process of deliberation begins. In some of the families, this may be done in a very thorough, rational, "deliberate" fashion, in others very hastily and haphazardly. The kinds of arguments used by members in justifying their own approach to the problem, and in trying to persuade their relatives to go along with it, will also vary a great deal. In a very self-reliant family living out in the country, the whole discussion may be couched in terms of laying a trap for the expected burglar, and arming all the brothers with shotguns in order to get him. A more timid family of city folk, by contrast, might talk about it in legal terms, e.g., what it takes to be entitled to police protection, whether they have to accept police protection proffered by the district attorney, whether they are under obligation to inform their insurance company of the warning they have received, and so forth. Yet another family, whose members have for decades been opposed to the incumbent district attorney and to his party, would perhaps discuss the problem in an "I-told-you-so" way and worry more about discrediting the D.A. after the burglary had been committed than about preventing the crime. Or we could think of a wealthy family, whose home had been burglarized several times before, whose members did not particularly mind so long as their name would not be dragged through the newspapers and so long as the loss would be covered by insurance. In their case, the argument might be concerned with the question of who is on the best terms with the police sergeant.

All these families are facing the same problem, but each states the issue in its own fashion and deliberates about the issue with different types of argumentation. In other words, each has its own peculiar style of discussion. There are reasons for this peculiarity of style in the background of each family, and the style will have its effects upon the solution to the problem at which they will arrive. So it is with the political style of larger communities. We have seen that there is a great deal of similarity among many of the problems faced by some of the eight political systems just described. But these similar problems are often recognized, stated, and treated in radically different ways. Here, without attempting to "cover" the fields of labor relations, education and religion, and economic competition, we will draw some illustrations from them in order to describe differences in political style.

Labor Relations

In all these countries there are organized labor movements. The proportion of the total labor force that is organized in trade unions differs, as do the traditions and ages of the labor movements. Nevertheless, the problems they present for the politics of the countries today are very similar. They are problems of reconciling the goals of organized labor with the goals of other sectors of the economy—unorganized labor, different kinds of employers, agriculture, and so forth. Out of this similarity of problems, a great variety of issues has arisen in the different political systems.

In the United States, for example, there was until recently the issue of the type of organization, industrial or craft, that should provide the framework for the labor unions. This issue, internal to the labor movement itself, brought two large union federations into existence, the older

American Federation of Labor and the younger Congress of Industrial Organizations (along with some large independents). This resulted in many jurisdictional disputes between members of the two groups. Such disputes were fought over by a variety of means, among them jurisdictional strikes, violence and crime, decisions of the National Labor Relations Boards, and direct negotiations between the unions involved or their A.F.L. and C.I.O. leaders. Eventually, most aspects of this issue were resolved when the two organizations merged.

Many other matters continue to be at issue, meanwhile, between unions and employers. These are normally settled between union locals and the individual employer, by means of direct negotiations and, occasionally, by strikes. A running controversy usually goes on between the national organizations of the two sides. This is normally cast in terms of the general welfare. Labor leaders assert that the policies of the National Association of Manufacturers would impoverish the nation, while the N.A.M. claims that a new series of wage increases would ruin the country because of inflation. More often than not, individual disputes are settled and set the pattern for whole industries, as in the case of the escalator-wage agreement and the guaranteed annual wage. The latter innovation in labor-management relations called for changes in state laws, in order to make it possible for laid-off workers to receive both state unemployment compensation and employer's benefit payments. These changes were enacted by many state legislatures *after* the guaranteed annual wage contracts had been agreed to by the unions and large employing firms.

From time to time, the Congress engages in great debates on labor relations, which sometimes produce major legislation. In recent years, the main issues in these debates have been Communist and criminal influences within the unions. In the debates, the congressional organizations of the two parties cannot clearly be classified as prolabor or promanagement. The unions themselves are not affiliated with the parties, although many more labor leaders, especially of the C.I.O., have closer links with the Democratic than with the Republican party. At the state level, these ties are usually more evident, as in connection with right-to-work referenda in 1958.

In Canada, until the merger of the two great United States labor organizations, there were two labor federations affiliated with their larger counterparts south of the border. After the merger, they too combined, in the Canadian Labour Congress. We might therefore expect a great deal of similarity between labor issues in the two countries, which are otherwise so similar. But the differences go beyond the spelling of *labour*. The masthead of the official journal of the C.L.C. lists two Honorary Presidents: "Percy R. Bengough, C.B.E., LL.D.—A. R. Mosher, C.B.E., LL.D." [1] Many United States labor leaders also hold honorary degrees, but they do not display these. This difference may be considered superficial, although we will try later to show that it is not. In any case, there are more important differences. The C.L.C. has urged its member unions to support the Coöperative Commonwealth Federation (C.C.F.), Canada's socialist party. Some of the member unions of the former C.I.O. sister organization have been directly affiliated with this party for many years, and some of the leaders of this organization were among the principal founders of the C.C.F. The C.C.F., it must be remembered, advocates the socialization of basic industries in Canada. In the United States, by contrast, labor's official policy toward socialism is opposition, to put it mildly, and the most damaging accusation that its opponents can make is to call some labor leader a "socialist"—a charge he would promptly and indignantly deny.

The pattern of negotiations and strikes in Canada resembles that in the United States in many ways. It, too, is marked by occasional violence. The Canadian Cabinet established the custom of a regular annual meeting at which representatives of the several labor organizations wait upon the Prime Minister in order to discuss current issues. At these meetings, the Canadian Catholic Confederation of Labor (C.C.C.T.) is also represented. It is a French-Canadian union that was organized originally by some Catholic priests and only later became independent of clerical supervision. Confined to the Province of Quebec, the C.C.C.T. has so far refused to join the two larger national organizations in their merger, even though the first President of the Canadian Labour Congress is a French-Canadian. Before the merger, workers in Quebec therefore faced four alternatives: to stay unorganized, to join either the A.F.L. or the C.I.O. affiliates, or to join the C.C.C.T. In making this decision, religious and ethnic considerations played a role in addition to economic and partisan ones. Religious and ethnic issues have been infused into all labor debates at the provincial level in Quebec. The premier there has also accused various labor leaders of Communist sympathies, and has made this charge even against some of the Roman Catholic priests, professors at Laval University, who have given guidance to the C.C.C.T.

In the United Kingdom, denominational issues have been of no importance in the handling of the problems of organized labor. Instead,

[1] Commander of the British Empire, a decoration just short of knighthood, is conferred by the Crown on recommendation of the Cabinet. The Doctor of Laws degree is an honorary one in both cases.

partisan issues have been the significant ones. The Trades Union Congress (T.U.C.), which has no competitor as the national labor organization in Great Britain, was the numerically strongest participant in the founding of the Labour party, whose claim to be the party of the British working class is widely accepted by all levels of British society. Ever since 1918, the chief aims of the Labour party had been nationalization of basic industries, establishment of a comprehensive, free social security program, and electoral reform. After the party's overwhelming victory in the parliamentary election of 1945, its leader became Prime Minister, and it proceeded to put this program into effect. As a result, during the six years this Labour Cabinet spent in office, there were fewer strikes in the nationalized industries than before the war, and fewer than in parallel American industries in the same years. In other words, issues arising out of these problems in Britain were more often formulated by and resolved between the two great political parties. Because the T.U.C. is so close to the Labour party, employers' organizations have no alternative to working closely with the Conservative party, except for the Liberal party, whose chances for getting a majority have become negligible. More often than in the United States, the goals of the labor movement have been stated with reference to parliamentary action, as part of a comprehensive and integrated national program. As in the United States and Canada, these goals are usually couched in terms of material interests—shorter hours, better wages and working conditions—but with a more noticeable ideological overtone than in the United States. The groups mainly interested in these disputes, in the first instance employers and employees, were still willing to resolve their disagreements through a process of compromise, but the compromising has usually been carried out at a higher level than in the United States. In the last analysis, it involved the entire electorate, because it was the general election of 1945 that decided the principal issues arising out of this set of problems.

In the major Continental countries, problems of industrial relations have given rise to much more complicated issues than in the three English-speaking systems. France, Italy, and Germany have had trade-union organizations that were split by multiple cleavages, along partisan, ideological, and denominational lines. Under the Vichy, Fascist, and Nazi regimes, of course, they had no free unions at all. In France and Italy, after World War II, the split pattern of labor organization reëstablished itself. Communists, Socialists, and Christian Democrats each built up their own trade-union federation. In contrast with Britain, the parties tended to dominate the unions more than the unions the parties. Thus, the

Communists often called their union out on strike in order to back up some noneconomic move, which they were supporting simultaneously by means of parliamentary maneuvers. As a result, some issues that apparently arose out of problems of labor relations were actually generated by other problems, those of foreign policy among them. Some strikes called by the Communists were due to the dependence of the Communist parties on the Soviet Union and its current plans for subverting the government of the country in question or of undermining the United States' policy of building alliances through NATO or the European Defense Community. The relevant issues were formulated by political parties more than by unions and employers' organizations. Often they were stated in purely ideological terms, without overt reference to material interests. More often than in the United States or Canada or Britain, these issues were resolved through the use of violence—strikes, clashes between pickets and police, use of the army to operate struck industries, and the like. Once an issue was settled by the decision to use force, or by parliamentary action, or by compromise, the settlement was less likely to be accepted by those who felt themselves the losers than was the case in similar disputes in the English-speaking countries. In other words, these decisions to settle did not really resolve the issue, nor did they solve the problem that had given rise to it. The same problem continued to raise its head again and again, and to breed new issues of recrimination about an earlier unsatisfactory compromise. Where this happens, the problem-solving machinery that politics is supposed to provide operates less efficiently, and its policies are less widely accepted, than in the first three systems.

In West Germany, these problems of labor relations produced yet another type of issue, treated in another way. In the Weimar Republic, there were three trade-union organizations: Marxist, Christian, and Liberal, in descending order of strength. All three were suppressed by the Nazis. After the war, surviving leaders of the Weimar trade unions decided to form a single trade-union federation, which was to be neutral in politics. During the organizational years, which coincided with the Allied Occupation of the country, a completely novel scheme of labor-management relations grew up in the steel industry of the Ruhr area, Germany's industrial heartland. Known as codetermination, it involved the direct participation of employees and the trade unions in the actual management, including day-to-day direction, of great steel corporations. In most managerial functions, labor and management shared on a fifty-fifty basis. The new trade-union federation soon made the retention of codetermination, and its extension to other industries, its primary goal. When self-government was returned to the Germans, labor insisted that the scheme be firmly anchored in German legislation, and that it be applied to the coal industry as well as to steel. Until 1954, hardly any strikes on wages, hours, or working conditions took place in West Germany. But strikes were threatened, and one-day protest strikes actually carried out, in order to put pressure on Parliament to pass the legislation demanded by the unions, and with considerable success. In the years since 1954, there have been some strikes, but these have been less frequent and less disruptive than in France and Italy.

The problems of labor relations in Germany were converted into issues largely on the initiative of the single union federation. Goals were stated largely in legislative terms. The controversies were debated between unions and employers' organizations on the first level, but decisively in Parliament. In Parliament, and especially on its committees, officers of labor and employers' organizations bore the brunt of the battle. Labor members of the Christian Democratic Union even broke parliamentary party discipline in some votes on codetermination bills. Strikes have been rare, violence virtually unknown. The parties did not initiate most of the issues, although this did not keep the debates from having a strong ideological tint. During the debates many references were made to the Basic Law and other legal matters. Participants often justified their stand in terms of constitutional provisions and attacked their opponents for their alleged violations of these. But once anything—even an innovation previously considered obnoxious—had the stamp of legality placed upon it, it was universally accepted.

Basically similar economic problems thus produce in these different political systems issues that vary in many ways: the number of alternatives considered, the style of the debates, the method of resolution, and the degree of acceptance. The style of discussion in the English-speaking countries is marked by emphasis on the material interests of the groups concerned, while in the Continental systems ideological arguments are more often used. In the United States, criminal violence plays a role in labor relations, while this is almost wholly unknown in Great Britain. In Italy and France, on the other hand, another kind of violence, as in clashes between strikers and the police, is a common occurrence. West Germany had neither kind of violence nor much reference to the possibility of the use of force in labor-relations debates. These debates rather showed great preoccupation with questions of constitutionality and legality.

Education and Religion

The problem of the relation between church schools and the state has given rise to controversy in many countries. In recent years, this has been a much-debated issue in Germany, France, Canada, and the United States. Although the denominational composition of the population and the history of the issue differ in these countries, the problems are generally quite similar: What, if any, financial support should the government give to Catholic schools? The problem arises because of a conflict of goals. The Catholic Church and many of its adherents pursue the goal of religious education for children and claim that, since a substantial proportion of the population is Catholic, the government should use public revenues for the support of schools that cater to this segment, just as it uses them for the public schools. Those who oppose the Catholic Church on this issue may do so because they believe in the separation of church and state, or because they pursue the goal of offering equal and joint educational opportunities to everyone regardless of faith.

In West Germany, as already indicated, this issue has been most important at the level of the states. It has rarely been argued in terms of the relative costs of maintaining separate Catholic schools. Usually, the debaters try to support their arguments by elaborate reference to the historical background of the problem, including the *Kulturkampf* of Bismarck, and to constitutional law. This kind of discussion is based not only on the Basic Law and the state constitutions, but also on treaties concluded between Hitler's Reich and the Vatican, and between one of the states, Bavaria, and the Vatican. The issue has been referred to the Federal Constitutional Court, which had to consider in its opinion the question of the legal continuity of the Federal Republic with Hitler's regime and the Weimar Republic. Neither the legal profession nor the general public have unanimously accepted the Court's verdicts in such cases. In the states, Catholics have organized silent protest marches of thousands of people in order to demonstrate their opposition to a policy that withdrew state subsidies to Catholic schools and instead made available nondenominational public "Christian community schools." In Bavaria, the issue of religious teacher-training colleges has brought about the end of coalition cabinets. All over West Germany, people frequently urge that the schools be returned to federal control, either because they object to the lack of uniformity among the state school systems, or because they expect their point of view on the religious issue to win at the federal level, while it is losing in their state.

In France, church and state were separated fifty years ago, in the aftermath of the Dreyfus Affair. But after World War II, the problem came up in the course of the nationalization of mining companies, which put the government in possession of twenty-eight company-owned Catholic schools. The issue of subsidies to church schools was vigorously debated all over the country. The National Assembly bill providing for subsidies was opposed by a national committee formed especially for that purpose, made up of teachers' and parents' organizations. The proponents of the subsidy worked through the Catholic Popular Republican party and De Gaulle's *Rassemblement du Peuple Française*. They organized the Parliamentary Association for Educational Liberty and managed to split some normally anticlerical deputies off from their parties on the vote. The Communists denounced the whole thing as a Vatican plot. The Socialists, unwilling to retreat from their anticlerical traditions, actually withdrew their support of a Cabinet coalition of a type they had been supporting for four years, thus breaking up the coalition and causing the Cabinet's fall. And after the bill had gone through all its parliamentary stages, its opponents tried to have it reëxamined by the Constitutional Committee, consisting of the President of the Republic and a number of parliamentarians, whose function, according to the constitution, was to see "whether the laws voted by the National Assembly entail a revision of the Constitution." Their justification for this attempt was Article 1 of the constitution, which refers to the separation of church and state: "France is a Republic, indivisible, *laic,* democratic, and social." [2] The subsidy was passed, but the issue has not been settled.

In Canada, this issue is as old as the British conquest of New France. The British North America Act assigns control over related matters to the provinces. The result has been that in the city of Montreal, in Quebec, for example, three school boards operate their separate school systems: one Roman Catholic, the second Protestant, the third Jewish. This arrangement has worked out with relatively little friction. But the private universities in the province of Quebec—mainly French and Catholic Laval and Montreal, and English and Protestant McGill—have become dependent upon provincial government subsidies. Premier Duplessis, head of the Union Nationale, tried to use the subsidy control to put pressure upon Laval University to dismiss priests who were professors in the faculty of social sciences and had acted as advisers to the Canadian Catholic Labor Confederation. Later, when the federal government offered subsidies, with no strings attached, to all Canadian universities by way of the Provincial governments, Quebec was the only province to reject this offer,

[2] See Philip Williams, *Politics in Postwar France,* 1958, pp. 292, 330.

because Duplessis interpreted it as an attack on the cultural autonomy of the French-Canadian people. The controversy continues.

The Catholic population of the United States is a smaller percentage of the total than in the three countries just discussed. Schools have traditionally been controlled by local governments in coöperation with the state rather than the federal government. And the separation of church and state, though not explicitly stated in the Constitution, has been accepted as one of the "intentions of the Founding Fathers." The First Amendment's prohibition—"Congress shall make no law respecting the establishment of religion, or prohibiting the free exercise thereof"—has been interpreted by the Supreme Court as applicable to the states as a result of the Fourteenth Amendment. The problem of state support to Catholic and other parochial schools arose, therefore, when priests and other ministers were permitted to give religious instruction on the premises of public schools, when public schools released pupils from attendance so that they could get religious instruction in their churches, when children attending Catholic schools were allowed to ride on school buses operated at state expense, and on other occasions. These issues were always stated with reference to the Constitution and the Fathers' intentions, and they have always been resolved by the Supreme Court, usually in order to be restated in another form for further litigation. The political parties have been able to avoid taking a clear stand on it. On the other hand, it has given the Catholic Church some interest in the composition of the Supreme Court and is related to the unwritten custom that one of the justices be a Catholic.

This problem, then, has also generated a variety of issues. In Germany and in the United States, these have been debated mainly in constitutional terms. The constitutional standard in Germany was provided less by the Basic Law than by treaties with the Vatican. In the United States, despite its relative obscurity on the issue, the Constitution has given the standard. Because education was under state and not federal control in both countries, the national parties in neither have had to take a stand on the issue. But in Germany, a period of central control over education preceded the present arrangement, so that parties operating at the state level have divided on it, have been more reluctant to accept court decisions of it, and have debated it in a very ideological fashion. This doctrinaire attitude is also characteristic of the Union Nationale in Quebec, because there the religious issue is complicated by the question of French-Canadian "nationality," and most of the French-Canadian population of Canada is concentrated in the one large province of Quebec. In France, finally, as the only unitary, nonfederal system of these four, where the problem has been a serious one ever since the Revolution, it has been debated with reference to historical precedents and traditional ideological convictions at the level of the national Parliament. There, it has divided the clerical from the anticlerical parties, and has brought about splits within parties, resulting in the fall of coalition Cabinets.

Coca-Cola

The introduction on a large scale of Coca-Cola to almost all European countries after World War II provides another illustration of the wide range of issues to which very similar problems can give rise. The problem was how to receive this American soft drink whose advanced marketing techniques were likely to give keen competition to established native beverages. It was not a problem caused by the influx of a great number of foreign, i.e., American, personnel, since the Coca-Cola Export Corporation of New York grants a lease on its production process and trade mark to indigenous companies. At first glance, the problem would appear to be purely one of competing material interests. And that is how it was treated in Sweden. Those businessmen who felt themselves threatened by the new competitor simply tried to out-advertise and out-sell Coca-Cola. It never became either an issue in Swedish politics or a subject of litigation in Swedish courts.

The British experience was identical, except for one minor occurrence. While Britain was suffering from a severe dollar shortage, a member of Parliament, during the daily question period in the House of Commons, inquired of the appropriate Minister whether any dollar funds were being used up because of the consumption of Coca-Cola. The answer was negative. Thereupon, another M.P. asked in a supplementary question, whether the Minister was aware that the flavor of this beverage could be improved considerably by adding a dash of gin to it. The House laughed, and that closed the matter.

In West Germany, the problem was treated in a slightly more doctrinaire way. A Bundestag deputy from Bavaria, which boasts of a good and influential beer-brewing industry, proposed that a special beverage tax be imposed on Coca-Cola because, like alcoholic beverages, it was allegedly habit-forming. A Social Democratic deputy at once rose to the defense of Coca-Cola. He said that Germany's sports-loving, nonalcoholic youth needed this nonalcoholic beverage. He was followed by a member of the liberal Free Democratic party, who expressed shock at the fact that a deputy of the Socialists, who professed to represent the German proletariat, had risen to defend Coca-Cola, which, as everyone knew, was a product of an international capitalistic monopoly. Finally, a Christian Democratic deputy said that he had checked on Coca-Cola consumption in the restaurant of the Parliament building and found it to be very high. He hoped that members would not let that influence their vote on the question. As for himself, he personally preferred Pepsi-Cola, and therefore did not care one way or the other. (The tax was not passed, but if it had, Pepsi-Cola would have been affected, too, of course.)

In France, the problem of Coca-Cola competition was first injected into politics by winegrowers' organizations. They tried to have its sale banned by a court because of a fifty-year-old law regulating the kinds of acids that could be added to foodstuffs. When they failed in this, they mobilized parliamentary opinion and actually managed to get the National Assembly, but not the Council of the Republic, to pass a bill instructing the Ministry of Health to enforce the old regulation. Coca-Cola became a *cause célèbre*. The Communists tried to emerge as champions of the opposition to it, by claiming that it was one of the strings attached to Marshall Plan aid from the United States and part of a vast and nefarious scheme to "Coca-colonize" France. The issue was discussed with reference to foreign policy, to French culture ("French wine is older than the French language. We must protect our national beverage!"), to the chemical properties and medical merits or demerits of the drink, and to the economic consequences of this new competition. It even evoked a response from the United States. Billy Rose threatened to boycott French champagne until the French Parliament would quit discriminating against Coca-Cola. And a congressman from Georgia, the home of Coca-Cola, said on the floor of the House of Representatives that Coca-Cola made people belch, and if there was anything that the people of France needed in these days, it was a good belch.

In Italy, too, winegrowers' associations initiated the debate, and the Communists tried to make hay of it. But here, most of the arguments revolved around the ancient Italian issue of the Vatican. Anticlerical newspapers pointed out that the officers of the Rome bottling company were members of the Vatican nobility, and that its headquarters was in a villa owned by the Vatican. When the Cardinal Archbishop of Naples dedicated a new bottling plant in that city, they ridiculed the ceremony. A Communist newspaper, in a very scurrilous article, quoted the Soviet journalist Ilya Ehrenburg, who claimed that Coca-Cola advertised in the United States by telling people that if Our Lord had been given a bottle of Coca-Cola on the Cross, instead of a sponge soaked in vinegar, He would have died deeply satisfied. He also asserted that it was the ambition of the president of the Coca-Cola Export Corporation to substitute Coca-Cola for wine in the communion service of the Catholic Church. A winegrowers' publication finally came around to recognizing the superiority of Coca-Cola's sales methods; it urged the wine industry to copy these, for example, by standardizing its product, insuring their sanitary qualities, and perhaps using smaller bottles.

Once more, virtually the same problem gave rise to different types of issues. In Sweden and Great Britain, the question was treated as a business matter. In Germany, it provided an occasion for some good-natured parliamentary ribbing about the ideology of the Socialist party. In France, it became the subject of litigation, but was treated not only in legal terms, but also with reference to foreign policy and the high standards of French, and the low standards of American "culture." In Italy, finally, the main focus of the whole debate was the old and unresolved issue of relations between the Roman Church and the Italian state.

Goals, Issues, and Style

Differences in the treatment of similar problems become most evident in the deliberative phase of the political process. Within that phase, they are most marked when politicians justify the stand they are going to take on an issue. But the ramifications of these differences in political style reach back to the earlier phase, the statement of the issue, and even beyond that to the recognition of problems. For instance, the Frenchman who habitually rationalizes all his political actions by way of his commitment to the ideals of the Great Revolution was likely to formulate the alternative policies open to France after General de Gaulle's return to power in 1958 in terms of his interpretation of the General's relation to the revolutionary tradition. Beyond that, he might even consider as an urgent problem something that, to others, did not appear as a problem at all, perhaps the inclusion of the Rights of Man and the Citizen in the constitution of the Fifth Republic.

For anyone who looks upon problems as the material obstacles between communities and their goals, three rules comprise the best way of conducting the politics of a constitutional democracy: State your goals as concretely as possible, in their order of importance, starting with the most important and most general goals, and working your way down to the less important and more specific ones. Next, state your problems just as concretely, relating them to your goals. Finally, give your views about the best means for dealing with the problems in order to come closer toward your goals.

Disagreements—that is, issues for politics—may arise between people who follow all three of these rules. They may disagree about goals, or about the problems, or about policies. The most efficient and effective manner for handling any of these possible sources of disagreement is through mutual understanding, leading to compromise. This is the hardest for people who disagree about their most important goals. Thus, when there is disagreement about the proper unit of politics, as in India when the British granted her full self-government, the political system may break up. Similarly, in international politics, two systems of alliances may have wholly irreconcilable goals, such as the complete subjugation of one by the other. This was true of the Axis countries and the Allies during World War II. It suggests that not all goals should be considered negotiable. In the conflict between the Axis and the Western Allies, the fundamental goal of individual responsibility was at issue. Had the Western countries been willing to yield this in compromise, then constitutional democracy, and with it the conditions for practicing the procedures of compromise for the purpose of realizing individual responsibility, might have been permanently destroyed. But this was an extreme case. Within a constitutional system, sufficient agreement is usually given to make compromise both possible and desirable. Often, disagreement on goals can be compromised by bringing out differences in the order of priority that the parties to the dispute assign to their goals. Thus, on the issue of church schools in France, the Popular Republicans considered state support of Catholic schools more important than the continued support of their coalition cabinet by the Socialists. But both Socialists and Popular Republicans considered the maintenance of the Republic against threats from the left and right more important than any of the subordinate goals either was pursuing.

Compromises are much easier to arrive at on disagreements about the nature of the problems faced, and the means best suited for dealing with them. The reaching of compromises can be hindered by several phenomena, each of which is directly related to political style. Threats to take recourse to violence, or its actual employment, present the most obvious barrier to compromise. If the parties to a disagreement constantly think and argue in terms of their relative ability to impose their will by force on one another, then the stronger have little incentive for making concessions to their weaker opponents. Compromise is also made difficult by stating and debating issues in terms of rigid ideologies. Thus, adherents of Soviet Communism and of German National Socialism might look at the same concrete situation, as they did during the last years of the Weimar Republic, and recognize different problems—and both conceptions would be most unrealistic. A rabidly Empire-minded English-Canadian and an equally rabid French-Canadian nationalist, although they agreed that the attractions of United States mass media present one of the gravest problems for the survival of Canada, could still be persuaded by their antagonistic ideologies to promote antithetical policies for dealing with this threat. And even if they agreed on the proper policy, they might still be unwilling to admit this agreement, because it goes counter to their ideologically dictated belief that agreement with the racial opponent is evil.

The process of arriving at a compromise may also be hampered by constant argument in terms of the constitution, especially when the constitution is young, or when the motive for this argumentation is something that might be called a yearning for constitutional and legal consistency. Arguments of this type often lead to calling the constitution itself into question, and to advocating its revision. This in turn is likely to create mistrust among the disputants—both as to one another's ultimate goals and as to the chances for fulfillment of the terms of any compromise that might be reached.

Compromise for its own sake, without regard to the goals the political process is meant to serve, is also likely to interfere with maintaining the conditions under which purposive compromises will continue to be possible over the long run. The cited example of World War II illustrates this. So does the Italian practice of *trasformismo* and more obvious forms of corruption in other systems. When someone changes his stand on an issue merely in order to obtain very immediate benefits, he may be surrendering his most important goals forever.

The norm of individual responsibility demands a willingness to reach purposive compromise and calls for the creation of conditions under which this willingness can be encouraged. Some kinds of political style help purposive compromise; others hinder it. In order to find ways of avoiding deleterious political style, we will seek in the next chapter a classification of style, before going on to account for differences in this respect among our eight countries.

CHAPTER 13

The Style of Politics

Political style describes the types of arguments that are used in connection with the discussions of issues, mainly in the course of deliberation. This is a matter of emphasis, since nearly all kinds of arguments are used in all political systems. Accordingly, the types suggested here are not regarded as mutually exclusive. Nor is this classification necessarily exhaustive, although comparison suggests that it is adequate at least for the Western countries we are studying. We will distinguish five types of political style; they are characterized by the predominance of arguments based on purposive interests, violence, ideology, law, and immediate goals.

Purposive Interest

In business bargaining, issues are most commonly discussed in terms of purposive material interests. The parties to a bargain understand that each is out to make a profit for himself. They accept this as entirely proper and try to resolve differences between themselves on the basis of self-interest, although they sometimes identify their own interest with a more general interest. A normal prerequisite for this style is adequate resources: whatever is the subject of the bargaining must be available in sufficient quantity to go around and, more or less, to satisfy everyone involved. Another condition is that there be fairly general agreement among the bargainers about the procedures by means of which the bargaining is to be carried out. This agreement may be subconscious and implicit, as among children trading in a Tom-Sawyer-like fashion.

In United States politics, logrolling is a good illustration of this style. Its motto has been coined: "I'll scratch your back if you scratch mine." It is based on the assumption that there is enough back-scratching to go around—or that there is enough gravy in the pork barrel to please all concerned. This assumption is made from the beginning of the process, so that willingness to compromise, or to make concessions, is implied from the outset. But arguments in terms of purposive material interests are sometimes used in systems that do not have sufficient resources to satisfy everyone, or where for other reasons the willingness to compromise is lacking. This then often leads to the next main category of political style: argumentation in terms of force.

Violence

Where people rationalize their position on an issue by reference to the possibility of employing force, or to power relationships, the political style may be described as violent. This has often, but not always, been true of international politics. Style marked by violence is the antithesis of the style of material interest, because neither of the conditions for the latter style are given: There is not enough to go around for everyone, and there is insufficient agreement on the procedures of bargaining. However, some agreement on some such rules is always given, although it may be pitifully little. Even in wartime, most belligerents will observe the Rules of Land Warfare at least some of the time.

Fascists used this style in the motto, "Might makes right." Marxism similarly justifies the ultimate victory of the proletariat over the bourgeoisie because of the majority position of the proletariat. This will give it the force to take over control of the means of production and, once it has achieved this control, to eliminate the power of the capitalists. Violent style may also have been the forerunner of democratic theories of majority rule, if the basic justification of these theories is: "It's better to count heads than to break 'em." In stable constitutional democracies, violent style does not play a major role. But when resources have become insufficient to meet people's basic needs, as during the periods of great unemployment in the 1920's and 1930's, the incidence of violence increases. Criminal violence may be used on the fringes of politics, as by union racketeers in the United States even in times of prosperity. But this should be distinguished from the noncriminal (or, perhaps, less criminal) kind of violence that is used against the constitutional system itself. Thus, if gangsters hired by crooked union leaders threaten the lives of witnesses before a congressional committee, which is preparing

an antiracketeering bill, these men and their bosses are common criminals who have no broad program to change the system; they merely wish
to beat the system. On the other hand, when Fascists or Communists
assassinate each other or representatives of the constitutional order, they
are doing this in order to revolutionize the entire system. This does not
make one kind of violent style superior to the other, of course. But it
does point to the mobster's acceptance of the goals of the system, by
contrast with the rejection of these goals by the Fascist or Communist
who engages in violence in order to follow the dictates of his ideology.

Ideology

The term *ideology* is used here with a more definite meaning than that
usually assigned to it. An *ideo-logy* must have both *ideas* and *logic*. It is
a comprehensive, consistent, closed system of knowledge, to which its
adherents turn to get answers to all their questions, solutions to all their
problems. We may distinguish three major types of ideology, in terms of
their *emphasis:* of knowledge, of recrimination, and of goals. Marxism
provides a good illustration of an ideology of total knowledge. Good
Marxists believe that the writings of Karl Marx and Friedrich Engels
(and, for many of them, the latter-day additions of Nikolai Lenin)
contain a complete interpretation of all reality, that this interpretation
is wholly consistent internally, and that all criticisms of any of its parts
have been definitively refuted.

Ideological arguments with emphasis on historical recrimination
usually arise out of the failure of a political system to solve some of its
more ancient problems, or—and this is the same thing—out of the failure on the part of some of its members to accept a "solution" imposed
upon them by procedures, such as force, whose authority they did not
recognize. Recriminatory ideologism thus describes use of the issue of
the Revolution in French debates over colonial policy and the church-
school problem. In Germany, injection of the issue of Nazi persecution
of the churches into debates of the same problem is also recriminatory
and has little bearing on the contemporary situation. This is just as true
of Canadian arguments about this problem with reference to the British
conquest of New France—in 1760.

Ideologism with emphasis on historical goals switches the orientation in time from the past to the future. This style prevails when some
remote and unrealistic, or unrealistically stated, goal is elaborated into
a comprehensive, consistent, closed system as a guide to action. Establishment of the classless society in Communist arguments is a case in

point. Certain strands of the Free Trade movement of the last century, or Prohibitionism in the United States, are also illustrations of political arguments based on historical goals, through which their proponents promised themselves and the world the solution of a great many more ills than these schemes could possibly have helped to solve. This is also true of the conviction that only complete universal disarmament or only the elaboration of a system of international law can serve as the first step toward bringing about world peace.

Law

Total reliance on the efficacy of law may have the same effects as total reliance on an ideology. Indeed, a legal system performs for some people the function of an ideology, by giving them the illusion of certainty in a world of uncertainties. This is one form that legalistic political style often takes. It leads its adherents—or addicts—to let all their actions be determined by legal considerations and legal considerations only. For example, some people who live in an urban residential area frequently demand that the police enforce the city ordinance banning overnight automobile parking. When they do this, not because they have strong feelings about having strangers park in front of their homes, but rather out of a yearning to have all the statutes on the books enforced, then their political style is legalistic. This kind of legalism often manifests itself in political litigiousness, that is, a high incidence of court proceedings with partisan political origins, and a large proportion of partisan political controversies that are settled in the courts.

In many American states, highways under reconstruction are "legally closed to all traffic; you travel at your own risk," according to signs posted at both ends of the stretch under repair. American motorists nevertheless keep right on using the roads, and nobody expects them not to do so. Posting of these signs is the result of a preventive kind of legalism, because it keeps the state or the contractor from being held liable for accidents resulting from the building activities. People who, like many Continental Europeans, are imbued with another kind of legalism, would not dream of using a road that is officially closed. Legalistic style of this variety is reflected in the desire to preregulate the entire future by means of legislation, to foreordain all eventualities through detailed and comprehensive, preferably unalterable, regulation, and rigidly to obey the letter of the law.

Legalism may concern the constitution and related fundamental laws, or it may concern matters farther removed from this basic level of the stable rules of the political system. Legalism in the United States, as displayed in litigation before the Supreme Court, is not usually about the Constitution itself; rather, within the framework of the accepted Constitution, it usually concerns a less permanent act of the Congress, or a state legislature, the President, or inferior courts. In West Germany, by contrast, cases have been argued before the Federal Constitutional Court about the Basic Law itself, as when one of its articles was challenged as inconsistent with another article. The two different kinds of legalism emerge in the treatment in the two countries of the issue of religious schools.

Immediate Goals

People who constantly argue with reference to the law are at the opposite extreme from those who forever use or threaten to use violence. People who rationalize their stand in terms of an ideology are at the opposite extreme from those who talk only in terms of their immediate goals and who never look beyond these. The total pragmatist, in this sense, is not pursuing any long-run goals. His actions, or the policies of a wholly pragmatic group, do not follow any stable pattern. Argument in terms of immediate goals will countenance any kind of compromise. When those who use it come up against a resolute opponent, they are easily persuaded to concede. This was true, for example, of some Western politicians in their diplomatic dealings with Hitler during the period of "appeasement" preceding World War II. Another example of this style is afforded by people whose "mind is so open" that they are persuaded by every contradictory argument to which they are exposed. They will pursue the goals of the last person with whom they have talked. Politicians of this type constantly waver from one policy to the next, because of expediency, without keeping their sights on the goals they are pursuing.

A Case Study of Political Style

In order to give a more detailed illustration of this approach to the description of political style, we will return to the issue of codetermination in West German labor-management relations. In this controversy, labor and the employers had some very concrete material interests at stake. The unions wanted better information about the finances of the corporations. They wanted influence or control over their personnel policies, including hiring and firing and fringe benefits. They also wanted responsible and well-paying jobs for union officials, who would, under co-determination, represent labor on the boards of directors and in the management of the corporations. The employers, on the other hand, wanted to retain their managerial discretion, to make their enterprises profitable, and to avoid labor unrest. Since these were the concrete goals of the two main groups that initiated the controversy, we might expect that their stands would have been justified in terms of compromisable material interests. Instead, however, ideological and legalistic arguments dominated the field almost to the complete exclusion of this first type.

On the ideological side, there were to begin with historical recriminations by trade unionists about the role of their industrial employers. They believed that the industrialists had helped Hitler to come to power, and had then coöperated with him in suppressing the free trade unions. These recriminations were partly based on the Marxian interpretation of the rise of National Socialism as a final stage of monopoly capitalism, which thus automatically identified the industrialists with the Nazis. Related to this retrospective ideological slant was another that looked forward to the goal of "industrial democracy," parts of which had already been ideologically elaborated by a trade-union theoretician in the late 1920's. According to this theory, political democracy was not enough unless accompanied by economic democracy. Under economic democracy, individuals would have the same equal rights as "citizens of the economy" that they enjoy as "citizens of the state."

In the course of the evolution of codetermination, something approaching an ideology in its own right was elaborated around that institution by the Trade Union Federation and its philosophers. The beginnings of this were found in certain strands of both Marxism, as just indicated, and Roman Catholic social doctrine, with its corporatist leanings and demands for "partnership relations" between employers and employees. These two strands were combined by academic economists, sociologists, and lawyers, who were in the full-time service of the trade unions. In many cases, these academic intellectuals quickly reached positions of high leadership in the labor organizations and became quite influential in making policy for them. In this respect, the contrast between German and American labor unions was striking. In Germany, the intellectuals often actually told the working-class leaders of the organizations what course to follow. The old unionists deferred to the academicians in every way. In the United States, union leaders used economists and other social scientists, or lawyers, to do a job for them, but never relinquished leadership to these men.

The style of German politics, as it revolved around the issue of codetermination, was not only ideological, but also quite legalistic. The scheme was begun in a haphazard, unplanned, "British" fashion, under the auspices of the British Occupation. As soon as its control of the steel industry was about to expire, the cry went up for German legislation to fill the legal vacuum that was about to come into being. This was in part motivated by what might be described as a "horror of a legal vacuum," which Germans frequently express. The desire generally exists to have all social relations regulated by laws, and to have these laws be detailed, comprehensive, and anticipatory of all eventualities. To proceed without prior legal authority by a method of trial and error in evolving new institutions and procedures—the English and American method—is virtually unknown in Germany and, with slight differences, in France and Italy.

After the demanded legislation was on the statute books, all participants in codetermination meticulously and rigidly abided by its provisions. During meetings of the committees of employers' and employees' representatives, for which the law called, several copies of books containing the relevant laws and regulations are kept on the board table and frequently referred to. Many issues arising out of the operation of the scheme have not had conflicts over material interests as their source, but differences over interpretations of the law—differences which often have few or no practical consequences for anyone.

There was also a great deal of legalism of the constitutional or fundamental variety. The proposed legislation was defended and attacked in terms of its consistency with the Basic Law, and in terms of its own internal consistency. The right of the trade unions to agitate for legislation, or to apply pressure to Parliament by means of threats to strike, was questioned. Trade unions were labeled economic organizations, which should remain in their compartment of activity, the economy, just as churches, as cultural organizations, should stay in their compartment. Parties are political organizations; only they have any business in the compartment designated as "The State."

These then were the types of arguments used in the course of the debate over codetermination. Ideological and legalistic arguments predominated over those couched in terms of material interest, or immediate goals—or of violence, of which there was none. During the same period, as noted in the preceding chapter, force was used in strikes in the other two major Continental countries. In American labor controversies, meanwhile, arguments over purposive and pragmatic material interest predominated. And in British debates arising out of problems of industrial relations, legalism of the type just described played virtually no role at all. Even in France and Italy, legalism was not as marked as in West Germany. In France, when ideological arguments were used, they seemed to serve the purpose of window-dressing to a much greater extent than in the Federal Republic, where they were on the whole taken very seriously by those who pronounced them and by those who listened.

Style and Success

The West German debate on codetermination as an issue arising out of labor-relations problems was successfully concluded. The solution codetermination offered for these problems has been generally accepted, although the issue of its extension to other parts of the economy continues to play a role. The operation of the scheme has made major contributions to the unity of the Trade Union Federation, despite the German tradition of a disunified labor movement. Beyond that, it has helped to reduce the ideologism and the legalism of the people who make codetermination work: employers and employees and the officers of their respective organizations. Their ideologism has been reduced because they have learned that orthodox Marxism or liberalism is of little use in solving the problems of steel or coal companies or of modern labor relations. They have learned that the men about whom they used to hold recriminatory views were not as bad as their ideological image of them, and that some of their own ideological goals were quite unrealistic. From the regular face-to-face contacts that accompany the operation of the scheme, they have learned the advantages of informal procedures and of direct compromise between the parties to a dispute, without the interference of outsiders, such as judges, bureaucrats, or lawyers.

This success is paradoxical, because the reduction of ideologism and legalism was the last thing the initiators of the debate intended to bring about, since they had actually been motivated by ideological and legalistic considerations. Later, we shall try to explain the success of this particular policy and also deal with the more general question of the "unintended consequences of purposive social action." At this point, we are interested in the relation between political style and the success of political systems. Style itself is not something that is deliberately made, created, or engineered, but seems to be one of the given, determined factors, one of the raw materials whose nature constitutional architects have to take into account in building or rebuilding their edifice. At any rate, before we can discover explanations of differences in political style and determine whether it can be deliberately molded, we must be clear about the relation between political style and the stability, adaptability, efficiency, and effectiveness of political systems.

Critique of Violence

Violent style most obviously interferes with success. Even totalitarian regimes have found this out over periods of time longer than those covered by a revolution or one or two purges. Of course, totalitarian systems do not seek to establish stability. Nevertheless, they usually discover that their industrial, agricultural, and scientific personnel operate much more efficiently—that they find better solutions to the problems of the system—if they do not have to expect at any moment to hear the knock of the secret police at their door. Even Hitler and Stalin could not rely on force alone to stay in power. They had to engineer consent by other than violent means. This is the meaning of the old adage according to which one can do everything with bayonets but sit on them. Besides, there is always the danger that the dictator himself will fall victim to the violence of his disciples.

The obstacles that violent style places in the path of the success of constitutional democracy are even more obvious. Nevertheless, we should not condemn references to the possibility of the use of force as completely inimical to democratic politics. We have already made the distinction between criminal and other kinds of violence, and suggested that arguments from force led to the democratic theory of majority rule. The establishment of constitutionalism, and later of democracy, in each of our eight countries was accompanied by the use of force at some time. That is why the concept of power has been the focus of analytical political science. Moreover, along with the authors of the Constitution of the United States, we would have to make "the common defense" an important goal of any constitutional and democratic system. Normally, this defense of a constitutional democracy would be against attack from the outside, in the international political system, or non-system, in which violent style so often predominates. But frequently, the survival of a constitution is threatened from within the system by those who would replace it with totalitarianism. When that happens, the upholders of the constitutional order are justified in using threats of violent reaction in defense of the constitution. When violent political style becomes predominant in such circumstances, however, this is already a sign that the constitution is no longer effective. This confirms the conclusion that violent political style endangers the success of a political system. That it also interferes with the realization of sound situations of responsibility need hardly be mentioned, since threats of force are obviously designed to take away from those who are threatened the opportunity to choose among alternatives and thereby to contribute to the making of policy.

Critique of Legalism

Since faithful observance of the rule of law seems to be the very antithesis of violence, we might expect that deliberation in terms of the law and the constitution could only be helpful. But here we should make a distinction between lawfulness and legalism. The attitude of lawfulness looks upon the legal system as one instrument among several for the attainment of the goals of constitutionalism. Legalism, on the contrary, looks upon the legal system, its consistency and its elaboration, as the goal itself. All other phases of the political process are considered mere means for reaching this goal. Legalism, in this sense of the term, contributed as much as violence in bringing down the Weimar Republic, since many Germans refused to offer violent resistance to the Hitler government because they interpreted its rise to power as having followed the letter of the constitution. If the French had taken the same attitude toward the Vichy regime and the German occupation of their country during World War II, they would not have organized their violent resistance against both. Violent and legalistic political style thus stand in a peculiar, almost dialectical relation to each other.

Legalism can interfere with success in several ways. For example, the insistence on legislation before experimentation with new institutions, procedures, or policies often stifles such experimentation. People might be perfectly willing to try out something new but unwilling to agree on its exact definition beforehand in a new law, for the passage of which their explicit agreement is required. This interferes with adaptability. Excessive awareness on the part of a population of varying and contradictory interpretations of the "meaning" of their constitution can easily lower its acceptance. Demands for maintaining the absolute internal consistency of the constitutional and legal system tend to complicate the treatment of ordinary, nonconstitutional problems and to generate an unnecessary profusion of controversies about the constitution itself. Thereby they contribute to constitutional instability. And one purpose of the constitution, from the point of view of the norm of responsibility, is to give citizens fair foreknowledge of the consequences of their decisions; this an unstable constitution cannot give them.

Critique of Ideologism

The inefficiency to which ideologism can lead has been recognized even by totalitarian regimes whose very existence is founded upon complete acceptance of a total system of knowledge. If Soviet scientists had not ignored some of the central tenets of Marxism-Leninism (or Marxism-Leninism-Stalinism), which has always pretended to give a scientific interpretation of *all* reality, including nature and the universe, they would never have beaten the United States in the race into outer space. Indeed, the occasional changes that are made in Soviet ideology suggest that the manipulators are afraid that innovation would be stifled if too many people became captives of a rigid ideology. Along similar lines, the fact that Hitler and many of his lieutenants were the captives of his completely unrealistic ideology led them to make the decisions that brought about the total defeat of the Third Reich.

Recriminatory ideologism interferes with both efficiency and effectiveness by keeping alive issues about problems that are no longer of importance, thereby reducing the system's capacity to deal with the real and more urgent problems it is facing in the present. Both doctrinaire recrimination and ideologism with emphasis on goals detract from the capacity of opposing politicians to arrive at compromises. For instance, those who feel that they are riding the wave of the future—whether they are the vanguard of the proletariat or the chosen race whose thousand-year Reich will rule the world—have little cause for compromising with their present opponents. The same is true of ideologists who believe themselves in possession of total knowledge. They believe that they do know with certainty the consequences of human actions. They are likely to conclude that anyone who disagrees with them, or with this presumption of total knowledge in general, is either a fool or a knave. They tend to consider even problems of the slightest importance in the light of their ideology. This makes them unwilling to make concessions that appear desirable from the standpoint of their material interests, because this would cast doubt on the validity of their doctrine itself and, with that, on the very roots of their existence. In any political system in which there is competition among ideologies, or between an ideology and more realistic interpretations of reality, ideological style will also reduce the effectiveness of the constitution and of the policies made under it.

The assumption of perfect knowledge itself makes for irresponsible behavior in view of the persistent limitation to all human knowledge.

The attempt to impose one ideology upon an entire population also threatens to take away from people the opportunity to consider alternative courses of action. Ideological style thus both hinders success and creates poor situations of responsibility.

Critique of Pragmatism

Pragmatism, the style characterized by the pursuit of immediate goals only, produces similar results. A political system whose style is completely pragmatic is a contradiction in terms, since it could not last long enough to become a system. Everyone's willingness to compromise away whatever long-run goals he might have, in order to satisfy his immediate wants, would preclude the emergence of any stable patterns of conduct or of any goals, institutions, or procedures of sufficient permanence to earn the title of a constitution. Different groups would be forever pursuing their separate immediate interests, and no integrated program of policies for the whole system could, therefore, be sustained over any period of time.

This lack of efficiency, combined with the absence of any agreement on goals for the future, would lower effectiveness to the point of bringing about anarchy. Individual citizens could not relate their decisions to purposeful goals and would be in very poor situations of responsibility as a result. Just as violent and legalistic style are at opposite poles of a spectrum, so are ideological and pragmatic style at opposite poles of another—the ideologist rigidly pursuing his distant goal, the pragmatist flitting this way and that without any consistent goals at all. At the midpoint of both of these ranges lies the politics of purposive compromise about material interests.

The Politics of Purposive Interest

This critique of violent, legalistic, ideological, and pragmatic styles as contrary to the success and the purpose of constitutional democracy leaves as wholly acceptable only deliberation in terms of purposive, compromisable, material interests. This was already indicated at the close of the last chapter. It follows logically from our conception of politics as the process by which men deal with the common problems they have to face, and from our statement of the purpose of constitutional democracy. According to that statement, responsible action is based on decisions among alternatives, using the best available resources and knowledge, in awareness of the constant limits set to both resources and knowledge, and in willingness to accept the consequences of decisions to which one has contributed.   •

All of this implies the need for compromise among the participants in politics. All the participants will be exposed to the consequences; all of them should, therefore, have opportunities to contribute to the making of central decisions, to the extent that they will be exposed to their consequences. Now, although all the members of a political system may be pursuing the same ultimate goals, they will disagree about intermediate goals. Since none of them has perfect knowledge, either about the realizability of the goals or about the suitability of the policy he is advocating as the means toward reaching them, he must be willing to make concessions to the others, in the light of the information cast upon both ends and means in the course of efficient deliberation. This will not guarantee either the success of the system or the attainment of the goals of particular policies. But it will let everyone share in the responsibility for either success or failure.

There is another way for arriving at this conclusion, that the success of constitutional democracy is favored most by the style of purposive compromise: it is the predominant style in those systems that have in fact been the most successful ones. The interest style prevails in the three English-speaking countries and in Switzerland and Sweden. Arguments couched in terms of this style are most frequently heard in the United States and Canada. They become slightly less frequent in Sweden, Great Britain, and Switzerland, in that order. In France, Italy, and Germany, such arguments become still less frequent. Violent style is completely absent in Sweden and Switzerland, and almost completely in the United Kingdom. In contemporary West Germany, violence is of little significance, but it was of great significance before 1945, and even today is being projected or deflected from internal West German politics to the Federal Republic's external relations with Communist East Germany. Violent style is more frequent in the politics of Canada and the United States than in those of Great Britain, and more frequent in France and Italy than in any of the others. Legalism, finally, is the least marked in Great Britain and Sweden. It increases in the three successful federal systems, Canada, the United States, and Switzerland, and then becomes successively more important in France, Italy, and Germany, in that order.

In subsequent chapters, we will try to account for these differences in order to find out whether there are methods by which the deleterious styles can be prevented, or their effects curbed, and whether there are constitutional or procedural devices by means of which debate in terms of material interests can be encouraged. Before we proceed to that analysis, however, we should clearly distinguish between this political style and "materialism."

Material Interest and Materialism

The conduct of deliberation in terms of compromisable material interests should not be confused with a philosophy of materialism, as opposed to "idealism," in the Marxian or any other sense. To justify one's stand in terms of material interests is not the same as materialism, because ideals are statements of goals whose content consists of material conditions as yet unrealized. The norm of individual responsibility is such an ideal, for example. From it, one could derive the goals of full employment or social security for everyone. To the extent that these goals have not yet been fully realized, they, too, are ideals, although they are more concretely stated than the norm of individual responsibility, from which they were derived. All the great ideals that have motivated men throughout the ages took on meaning only after their content was filled out with reference to the material conditions under which men live in nature and society.

Men who state the material goals they are pursuing, and in the pursuit of which they are willing to make compromises with others who are pursuing different material goals, are not necessarily engaged in the pursuit of selfish interests. Thus, the Conservative party in Britain opposed the nationalization of the steel industry and, when it returned to power, reversed this particular policy of the Labour party. Both parties asserted that they were interested in the material welfare of the whole nation. But they disagreed on the best means for promoting this goal. Neither party asserted that it was in possession of total knowledge that would have enabled it to tell with certainty which policy would best promote the material interest of the entire country. That is one reason why both were willing to make compromises on these differences, and to accept a resolution of the issue—either nationalization or denationalization—so long as it had been made according to responsible procedures. Making it according to responsible procedures meant, among other things, that it was made in a constitutional way, that is, in observance of the unwritten customs according to which decisions of this importance are made in Great Britain—and both parties insisted upon this. But this insistence did not make their conduct of the relevant debates legalistic, since their primary motive was not concern with any constitutional problem. Both parties were also devoted to certain ideals, but this did not make their political style ideological, except to the extent that it did detract from their willingness to compromise.

Both parties also agreed that the general interest should be promoted. The Conservatives saw nationalization of steel as opposed to the general interest. The electorate knew this when it returned them to a majority position in the House of Commons in 1951. The industry was brought back under private ownership forthwith. When the Labour party forms another Cabinet at some time in the future, this policy may be reversed once more. But more recent statements by the Labour party indicate that nationalization in the 1960's will be quite different from what it was or would have been in the early 1950's. The party has changed its immediate goals, although not its ultimate ones, as a result of demands made by some of its own membership and in reaction to experience gained from the operation of industries that, like coal, have been nationalized for more than a decade. If the Labourites were as rigidly ideological as members of some Continental parties, they would not have been willing to make these concessions. On the other hand, had they been interested only in the immediate goals which nationalization might have attained, they would have completely chucked their program overboard after their first defeat at the polls.

Style and "National Character"

The willingness of even the British Socialists to compromise in this fashion is often explained in terms of British "national character." The British, it is said, have always "muddled through" in an unsystematic way. That is how they built up their great Empire "in a fit of absent-mindedness." This is simply an expression of their national character. Similarly, the absence of violence from Swedish politics is attributed to the Swedes' phlegmatic character. The French are rationalists and individualists, and this keeps them from arriving at agreement on anything; hence there are "as many parties as there are Frenchmen." The Italians are "hot-blooded," therefore naturally prone to violence. The Germans are methodical, which explains their legalism. They are also supposed to be ferocious and therefore become militaristic periodically. Americans are nice, open-minded, and pragmatic, and this explains everything worth explaining about the politics of the United States. And so forth.

National character as an explanation of differences in political style presents a number of difficulties. To begin with, if national character is conceived of in determined biological or racial terms, it could be applied among the nations here considered only to the Swedes, because the others are much too heterogeneous. Swiss national character is alleged to be frugal and industrious, but which Swiss is this supposed to describe: German-speaking, French-speaking, Italian-speaking, or Romansch-speaking? If national character is a matter of culture, then all the German-speaking people—Swiss, Austrian, and German—should share the same national character, which they clearly do not. The German-speaking Swiss, whose cultural outlook was dominated by Germany, especially before World War I, obviously have more in common, so far as their manner of conducting their national politics is concerned, with their fellow Swiss citizens who speak other languages. The same analysis can be applied to Canada.

A nation is commonly defined as a community whose members are aware of sharing together a common past and a common future. In our terms, this would be a community whose members have faced and are facing problems together and want to solve them together. But commonly faced problems by themselves do not generate a political style. Shared procedures by means of which their solution is being attempted, on the other hand, do bring into being a distinctive political style. Nationality itself does not "cause" style. The best proof of this can be found in the case of nations whose national aspirations have not yet been fulfilled, because of colonial domination by two different states, for instance. Where two segments of a nation-to-be learn self-government under the supervision of different colonial administrations, each segment develops its own style, as in the French and British sectors of Togoland. In a similar manner, the two parts of Germany have been evolving differences in political style since the division of the country after the war. Only after divided nations or nations-to-be begin to operate with the same institutions and procedures in one political system, does a common political style begin to develop. At that time, national character may perhaps be used to *describe,* but not to *explain* anything.

The same is true of the concept of political style. As we have defined and described style, it enables us to isolate certain relevant differences among the politics of our eight countries. Description of the style of a political system may cast some light on what is distinctive about it. But it does not explain these distinctive traits. Rather, it calls for an explanation.

CHAPTER 14

Ideologism

In the search for valid explanations for the differences in success of various political systems, we will be proceeding from the more determined to the more created factors. This seems a logical sequence since the creator of new institutions and procedures—the constitution-maker—has to design his innovations to fit the given raw material with which he is working. Accordingly, in the descriptive chapters of Part II we have emphasized the problems faced by each country, and—again moving from the more determined to the more created—political style has been selected for consideration before parliamentary procedure is discussed in Part IV. At this point, and for similar reasons, the ideological aspects of political style are given precedence over the legalistic ones (which will be the subject of the next chapter). Legalism is, after all, obviously related to the legal system itself, and the legal systems of most non-English-speaking countries are deliberate creations to a far greater degree than the ideologism that forms the subject of this chapter.

Ideologism and pragmatism are here regarded as opposites. The perfect ideologist would believe that his ideology provides him with answers to all questions, solutions to all problems. He would make no decision without first referring it back to his ideology. And his ideology, presenting him with artificial issues, would lead him to make many decisions even where no objective need for them existed. No such perfect ideologist can be found, of course, but there are many people active in politics whose behavior comes closer to this model than to that of the perfect pragmatist, who also does not exist in real life.

The perfect pragmatist would have no system of knowledge at all upon which to rely. Nor would he follow any consistent pattern of conduct: He would make his decisions in response to the momentarily felt practical needs. Midway between these two extremes lies the politics of compromisable purposive interests. Political responsibility, in this sense, requires the making of decisions based upon the best knowledge available about their consequences, and also involves an awareness of the limits that inevitably restrict the scope and certainty of that knowledge.

The style of some political systems, as we noted in the last chapter, is much more ideological than that of others. Here, the search for an explanation of these differences leads to the question whether there is any common relevant factor shared by the more ideological countries. One such common feature in their histories relates particularly to those groups within the systems that have been or are even more ideological than the rest. This common feature, in all of the less successful constitutional democracies on the Continent, is the exclusion of large segments of the politically conscious and ambitious population from participation in political responsibility during the "adolescence" of the system—the tone-setting period for the system's style. Such exclusion invariably led to bitterness and resentment, and eventually, to recrimination. It also encouraged a high degree of abstract thinking about politics, the corollary of which was neglect of concrete concern with the immediate practical problems confronting the country.

Ideological Style and "Functional Autonomy"

The more comprehensive and internally consistent an ideology becomes, and the less opportunity there is for testing it by practical application, the more unrealistic and irresponsible is it likely to be. Thus, even a doctrine that grew initially out of concern with some genuine problem will cease to be realistic as the passage of time changes or removes the problem. If a whole system of knowledge, meant to be valid for all time, is elaborated out of a policy that never had a chance of being put into effect, this ideology will give its adherents distorted ideas of the consequences of their later decisions. Nevertheless, people who are converted to such an ideology often become wholly attached to it and dependent upon it for explanations of all events, for interpretations of their entire existence.

One reason for this total commitment is the thwarted opposition of the converts to the incumbent regime that the ideology also attacks. Even after this regime has passed on into history and the ideologists have achieved influence on the making of policy—that is, even after they have gained political responsibility—this attitude, having hardened during the period of their exclusion, stays with them. Conversely, groups that formerly shared in political responsibility also construct ideologies with recriminatory emphasis.

When an ideology continues to influence political conduct long after the original condition that inspired it has ceased to be a problem, we may say that this ideology has become "functionally autonomous." Professor Gordon K. Allport uses this term to describe a psychological phenomenon: A man may encounter great frustrations, rather suddenly, in his relations with his wife. In an effort to forget these troubles, and perhaps for other reasons as well, he engages in butterfly collecting or some such hobby, of which he becomes very fond. After a while, he and his wife become reconciled once more and live happily, presumably ever after. His original reason for taking up butterfly collecting has therefore disappeared. Nevertheless, he continues to engage in the hobby, for its own sake. The "function" of collecting butterflies has become "autonomous." [1]

Ideological style is particularly prone to the phenomenon of functional autonomy. Since it is first born out of the frustrations produced by exclusion from political responsibility, it is synonymous with an attitude of irresponsibility: failure to consider alternatives, disregard for available resources, overconfident expectations of the capacities of knowledge. The mere opening of opportunities for the exercise of political responsibility, by itself, rarely suffices to improve these distortions in popular perceptions and interpretations of reality. Indeed, prolonged periods of exclusion sometimes result in the loss of the human ability to forget. If we, as individuals, did not have this faculty of selective forgetfulness—especially if the worst events in our lives were constantly "on our minds"—misery and "maladjustment" would be inevitable. Similarly, in political systems with strong ideologism, groups previously excluded from participation constantly keep alive memories of the past and permit themselves to be motivated by their ideologies, which are, as it were, petrified memories.

---

[1] Mr. J. A. Lukas has suggested to the author that many English legal procedures were originally devised in order to protect private property. Over the years, much private property in Great Britain has been nationalized or otherwise socialized. Yet the same ancient legal procedures are still in use, some of them to protect different and, in part, novel civil rights. These procedures, too, have become functionally autonomous.

Germany

The classical example of ideologism caused by exclusion from politics, and kept functionally autonomous even after admission to politics, is provided by Germany. Repeatedly in its modern history, newly aspiring groups were barred from the political process. During the period following the Napoleonic Wars, the repressive policies of the Holy Alliance in Austria, Prussia, and other German states stifled even the expression of political opinions by the urban middle classes, and especially by the intellectuals among them. It was during this time that Karl Marx, who gave currency to the term *ideology* and himself created the most influential ideology, was forced into exile from Prussia.

Exclusion from participation took place once more after the brief tenure of the liberal national Parliament convened in Frankfurt in 1848. The majority of its members were intellectuals of the middle classes, who sought to bring about the national unification of the German states under the same liberal principles for which men were fighting violently in many European capitals that year. (In Paris, the Revolution of 1848 resulted in the overthrow of the July Monarchy and the establishment of the Second Republic.) In Berlin, the King of Prussia, to whom the Frankfurt Parliament offered the crown of German Emperor, scornfully refused to accept from a popularly elected assembly what he believed only his fellow princes could bestow. His refusal, coupled with the rejection by the governments of both Prussia and Austria of local demands for liberal constitutions, brought on the collapse of the Frankfurt plan. Thereafter, the middle classes, despite their increasing economic importance, found no outlet for their political aspirations, especially in Prussia, which finally effected German national unification, "from above," in 1871.

Within Prussia, the exclusion was continued for all practical purposes until after World War I. The Prussian Diet was elected under a three-class franchise, which gave the poorest class of the population—the majority of the people—only one-third of the seats in the state parliament. In any case, the head of the Prussian government—who was also Reich Chancellor—was not accountable in either capacity to the Diet but only to the Kaiser—who was both King of Prussia and German Emperor. Thus, although the national Reichstag was elected by universal male suffrage, politicians who tried to use it as a channel for sharing in responsibility could do so only in support of, not in opposition to, the Imperial government.

The Weimar Republic opened politics to all who wished to participate, but by this time the ideological style of many Marxists and liberals had become functionally autonomous. Under Hitler's National Socialist regime, opponents of the Nazis were excluded once more, often through imprisonment in concentration camps, through expulsion or emigration, or through execution. During the early years of Allied occupation after World War II, former Nazis were in turn excluded. Other German politicians—including those who aspired to be politicians, but were not licensed by the Allies—could do little but concentrate upon building a following, by sharply defining their goals and the means for reaching them. This encouraged them to spin forth ideologies and to define doctrines with great clarity and with the kind of consistency that would make them salable to the public. More than a decade after the return of self-government to the West Germans, some of these habits still persist.

France

France, like Germany, has passed through periods in which various politically ambitious segments of the population were excluded from responsibility. The classic illustration of this phenomenon is furnished by the *philosophes* of the French Enlightenment, the decades of the eighteenth century that preceded, and contributed so much to, the Great Revolution. The political theories written during those years set the categories of Continental thinking about politics forever after—and influenced not only Europe, as may be seen, for example, in Madison's reference to Montesquieu. Jean Jacques Rousseau is more representative of the French Enlightenment than Montesquieu, since he avoided addressing himself explicitly to the concrete problems of France or the world, preferring instead to construct an abstract and consistent theory in his *Social Contract,* which later served as basis of an ideology for many of the makers of the Revolution. And it is at this point that we encounter the great difference between Germany and France: Revolutions in Germany failed to occur at all, or failed to achieve the goals of the revolutionaries; France, by contrast, has had at least three major revolutions since the great one, and in each at least some of the revolutionaries have achieved part of their goal of greater political responsibility.

The consequences of this difference make contemporary politics in France less ideological than in West Germany. Periods of exclusion in France never lasted as long as in Germany. At some point, every politically aspiring group was given opportunities to test its doctrine by practical application. Groups dislodged from the sole exercise of power by their newly ambitious competitors, no matter how much they might recriminate in literature and oratory, never became so bitter in practice that they boycotted the established political process. The difference on this score between the two countries is particularly marked since 1871 —the time of the founding of both the Third French Republic and the German national state. Since then, every group represented today in the French National Assembly has had some influence on policy, although no one of them has ever had full responsibility for it. For groups like the Socialists, whose parties came under prohibition in both countries for some years during the early part of this period, the exclusion from influence lasted longer in Germany. Even under the Vichy regime and the German occupation, the Free French abroad and other anti-Vichy groups inside France were responsible for conducting active resistance and were already discussing constitutional arrangements to be made after Liberation.

The fact that no single group ever bore sole responsibility for government—as in Great Britain—enabled all the groups to state their goals in exaggerated form. This has made for a vocabulary of politics that sounds quite ideological. But the actual sharing in policy-making, either through participation in cabinet coalitions, or through exercise of the negative functions of Parliament and the logrolling practiced there, has always led everybody to expect that, for practical purposes, these goals would be moderated.

Italy

The Italian story in this respect is closer to the German than the French. Large segments of the politically ambitious population were excluded for long periods—involuntarily, as in the case of the Socialists in the nineteenth century, or by their own choice, as in the case of Roman Catholics loyal to the Vatican until the first decade of the twentieth century. The practice of *trasformismo*—the purchase of parliamentary support with patronage and without reference to the interests supposedly represented by deputies—tended to cut Parliament off from the politically aspiring parts of the population. Under the two decades of Fascism, the anti-Fascist groups had little to do but elaborate their ideologies, and some of these habits have persisted on into the present Republic.

In Italy, as in France, ideologism is further increased by the existence of large Communist parties, whose very *raison d'être,* according to their own image of themselves, is to fight for the fulfillment of their ideology, which they believe to be the only true one. This forces all the opposing parties to do so, at least partly, in ideological terms—to oppose Communist ideology with their own "true" and, they hope, more attractive ideologies. Like increase of appetite, ideologism grows by what it feeds on. The Italian Christian Democrats may sincerely want to debate concrete goals and the means for achieving them. But since their main opposition in the debates comes from the very prototype of the ideological party, they are pushed into talking in ideological terms themselves. In some instances, they even become captives of their own ideologism and act on its basis, to which the Communists then react— and so on *ad infinitum.*

The impetus to ideologism always provided by a large Communist party is lacking in West Germany today, which is one reason why its style is less ideological than under previous German regimes. At the same time, it is more ideological than in France or Italy, probably because Germany did not experience the active, often violent, and more or less successful resistance to Fascism and earlier undemocratic regimes, that took place in both France and Italy. Even the Communists played a prominent part in para-military operations against German troops during the Nazi occupation. In both France and Italy, the Communists also were members of early postwar Cabinet coalitions. Participation in resistance and in coalition may have toned down ideologism somewhat. In Germany, little violent resistance to National Socialism developed, and postwar self-government was severely circumscribed by the Allied occupation for four years. Ideologism—and legalism, too, as we will see in the next chapter—gained as a result.

Switzerland

Among Swiss groups, one might expect at least the Roman Catholic conservative party to have ideological inclinations, since the Constitution of 1848 was forced upon the Catholics by the Protestant cantons after the brief civil war of the preceding year. Another reason would be the exclusion of this party for half a century thereafter from the Federal Council, which performs cabinet functions, it will be recalled. Moreover, such constitutional provisions as the ban against the Jesuits in Switzerland, which is still in effect, might have created a persistent recriminatory issue. The fact is, however, that the Swiss Catholics are not nearly as ideological as the Italian Christian Democrats and the Catholic Center party in the Weimar Republic. Since the Swiss Conservatives were barred from political responsibility during the tone-setting period of the Confederation, this would seem to challenge our explanation of the causes of ideologism. But the challenge is only an apparent one. For, while restriction at the level of the Federal Council was of some importance, exclusion did not extend to either house of Parliament—the National Council and the Council of Estates—and the Liberals and Radicals never took advantage of the Catholics' lack of representation in the Federal Council in order to ignore their wishes, as expressed in Parliament.

Much more important than this incomplete exclusion at the federal level is the continued responsibility for government carried by the Catholic Conservatives in those cantons in which they were a majority, and which had been defeated in the civil war of 1847. This meant that, whatever theories may have evolved as a result of their lack of direct political responsibility for decisions made in Bern, the seat of the Federal Council, they always had to keep these theories reasonably realistic because of the constant opportunity to apply them in their home cantons, where they were in control. This is one of the great contributions that effective federalism can make to the success of a constitutional system. Excluded parties and politicians, who might be tempted into ideologism by their inability to make meaningful contributions to decisions about the future of the whole, can be forced to keep their feet firmly on the ground by being placed in charge of decisions about the future of its parts, the member states.

Swiss federalism, achieved through the slow growth of the Confederation from the grass roots of the cantons, has always made such a contribution. The attachment of citizens to these small units of politics is very strong even today, when there remain but few important problems that can be handled below the federal plane. In this respect, Swiss federalism has become as much functionally autonomous as has ideologism elsewhere. It is performing a function for which it was not at all designed, while it is no longer serving the one for which it was brought into being. It tones down ideologism so effectively that Swiss Socialists and advocates of the federal franchise for women, the two strongest segments of the population recently excluded, are not nearly as ideological as their counterparts elsewhere. The Socialists, although represented on the Federal Council inadequately, if at all, have controlled cantonal governments. And women have the vote in some of the larger cities. Thus, the member units and local governments within a federal system may not only be used as "laboratories," in the sense mentioned in Chapter 1, but can also reduce irresponsible conduct in federal politics.

Sweden

Of the five Continental European countries considered in this book, the political style of Sweden is the least ideological. The main reason for this is that hardly any group which aspired to share in political responsibility was ever excluded from it. By contrast with the rest of Europe, even the peasants were represented as one of the four separate estates in the Riksdag since its beginnings in the early fifteenth century. The peasants, along with the other three estates—nobles, clergy, burghers— have had continuous opportunities for political participation through representation in the Riksdag since that time. When new groups, whose interests were not adequately taken care of by these estates, began to demand admission, this was usually granted after a relatively short period. For example, intellectuals of the type that dominated Germany's Frankfurt assembly of 1848 began to be vocal in the first quarter of the nineteenth century. Their demands were soon met (in 1823) by giving representation in the estate of the clergy to universities and learned socities. A little later (in 1828), newly important ironmasters were similarly admitted to the estate of the burghers.

Another test of our thesis is presented by the lengthy and sometimes bitter fight over extension of the suffrage, after the estates had been superseded by the bicameral Riksdag in 1865. Again, however, the exclusion was not as prolonged or as complete as elsewhere. For example, the Swedish Social Democratic party was organized in 1889, its first member of Parliament took his seat in 1897, and universal male suffrage came in 1907.

At least as important in toning down the ideological effects of exclusion, in Sweden as in Switzerland, were ancient traditions of self-government at levels lower than the national. Since Sweden's was never a federal system, one equivalent of the Swiss cantons must be sought— and found—in local government. The functions of local governments were clearly defined very early, and the procedures by which these functions were performed have deep roots. This is true of the procedures by which representatives of localities were selected to the estates of the Riksdag, and equally so for the governmental procedures of towns and rural districts and of various kinds of associations that existed within each. Sweden, like Switzerland, has an ancient and continuous tradition of a richly articulated, self-governing associational life. This has afforded opportunities for some political experience in the management of their own organizational affairs even to those groups otherwise wholly excluded from sharing responsibility for the future of the state. We will return to associational politics later, when we deal with procedure, corporatism, and consensus. At this point, it is important merely to note that the ability of nonstate organizations to deal with their own problems without outside help or interference tends to discourage ideologism just as much as similar opportunities afforded by the member units of a federal state.

Great Britain

The British "governing class" responded much more quickly than its counterparts in the larger Continental countries to demands from new groups for political participation. To be sure, it did not always respond as speedily as impatient aspirants desired. Nevertheless, exclusion never lasted so long that revolutionary means became the admission mechanism. Further, the circle of participants in politics was extended so gradually that those who were newly admitted to it never felt the desire to exclude the old incumbents, who had been excluding them. In other words, by contrast with French and German experience, the new "ins" did not attempt to make "outs" of the old ins, but were willing to share responsibility with them, even under tutelage-like arrangements.

On the other hand, and again unlike the experience in the major Continental countries, those who were in charge of making central policy never extended simulated opportunities for contributing to the policy flow. In Germany, for example, the Reichstag was elected by universal male suffrage from the beginning, but since the Chancellor was not accountable to it, voting in parliamentary elections fell short of being an exercise in responsibility. And parliamentary politicians were encouraged to "package" their unrealistic ideological systems in order to attract electoral support, secure in the knowledge that they would not be called upon to put their programs into effect. In Britain, the franchise was extended only in response to demands for its extension, to those who demanded it for themselves, and as a meaningful channel for sharing political responsibility. Universalization and equalization of the franchise was completed much later than in Germany and France, and in the course of its slow extension, its new possessors were assimilated to responsible procedures group by group, as it were.

Nevertheless, in Britain as on the Continent, there were groups from time to time, like the Chartists in the middle of the nineteenth century, who were dissatisfied with the slowness of the process. There were others, mainly the Irish Nationalists, who would not let themselves

204: : : GOVERNMENT BY CONSTITUTION

be assimilated to parliamentary processes. They obstructed the work of Parliament and caused much violence, with the eventual result that independence was achieved for the Irish Free State. Because of the availability of this solution—secession of a geographically distinct part of the system—Irish nationalism did not introduce ideologism to British politics. Nor did the more impatient of temporarily excluded groups become as ideological as their Continental parallels. The reason for this was the practice of associational self-government, which has as strong and as ancient traditions in Great Britain as in Sweden.

Students of British and American democracy have often found the roots of democratic practices in the small congregations of various Protestant sects, like the Puritans and the Quakers, which became important in the seventeenth century. Several congregations belonging to these sects emigrated to America, as in the case of the Pilgrim Fathers who founded the Massachusetts Bay Colony. The sects themselves continued to thrive in Great Britain and to give birth to new religious movements, like John Wesley's Methodism in the eighteenth century. These "nonconformists"—so called because they did not conform to the official religion of the Church of England—have few counterparts in Germany, Italy, or France. The overwhelming Catholicism of the two Latin countries prevented parallel developments there, and in Germany, the formula *cuius regio, eius religio* meant that the religion of the subjects was determined by that of their prince who, if Protestant, was normally the head of the church in his state. The British nonconformists, by contrast, governed their congregations themselves. In Sweden, starting in the 1870's, the Free Church Movement, which was influenced by Methodism and Baptism, provided a later parallel, although on a much smaller scale.

Religious associations were not alone in Britain in providing political experience for people before they could contribute to the making of central policy. But congregational self-government probably set the pattern for the internal politics of other kinds of organizations: trade unions, coöperative societies, temperance associations, and, last but not least, business corporations. It was in Britain that joint-stock companies were first organized on a significant scale. While they did not, of course, provide opportunities for organizational self-government for very many people, they nevertheless did give direct experience in the procedures of making decisions about group problems to those who did own stock. A comparison of British and Continental corporation law might suggest that the internal government of corporations on the Continent gives less responsibility to shareholders and thereby encourages a kind of ideologism even within self-governing business companies. This is of special significance for the United States, because many of the colonies were originally constituted as joint-stock companies, whose form of government was laid down for them in a charter granted by the Crown.

Canada

British Imperial policy toward her colonies was changed as a result of the American War of Independence. The Canadians were able to extract concessions of increasingly greater responsibility for their own affairs from the mother country, without having to resort to military violence. If this had not occurred, or if the grant of self-government had been as long delayed as it was in many colonies with predominantly nonwhite populations, a nationalist and anticolonialist ideology would probably have been injected into Canadian politics. Such an anti-British ideology has been observed in the United States, where some Midwestern politicians have debated problems of twentieth-century foreign policy as though independence from Great Britain were still the major issue of relations between the United States and the outside world. The external problems of most newly independent nations are likely to be treated in this ideological fashion for a long time after their colonial status has ended. And here may be perceived one reason why international politics is characterized by a style that is both violent and ideological: Many of the states participating in international affairs were excluded from responsibility and denied an effective role in world politics for so long that they continue to view its current problems through recriminatory glasses.

Canada as a whole thus has little cause for taking ideological attitudes in international politics. Inside the country, no group has been excluded from meaningful participation in the making of central policy, at least since confederation in 1867. There have, however, been segments of the population, usually confined to particular areas, who believed that their needs for special policies—not changes in the constitution— were being thwarted by the majority represented by the two large federal parties. As a result, they worked out their own regional ideologies; French-Canadianism in Quebec and Social Credit in Alberta are the notable illustrations. But Canadian federalism reduced the effect of these regional ideologies on Canadian political style. Thus, the Social Credit movement has controlled the government of the province of Alberta since 1935, and one result has been a very obvious toning down of the ideologism of the movement itself. Immediately upon assuming responsibility for the provincial government, the leaders of Social Credit had to give up some of the more unconventional aspects of their economic doctrine. Similarly, when the socialists of the Coöperative Commonwealth Federation assumed control of the government of the province of Saskatchewan, they toned down their socialism.

The situation in Quebec has been a little different from that in the English-speaking prairie provinces. French-Canadian nationalists can make the historically valid claim that they were excluded from political responsibility until the recommendations of Lord Durham were put into effect in 1840. And even then they had to operate under the unitary constitution, whose avowed purpose was the amalgamation of the two races. Many French-Canadian nationalist politicians have made it their business to keep alive memories of this long exclusion, and to debate literally all issues with reference to the ideology produced by it. The official motto of the province of Quebec is, "I remember."

There are, moreover, other peculiarities of French-Canadian politics that make it more ideological than politics in the rest of Canada. One of these is the role of the Roman Catholic Church in the province. Since its priests were the only members of the governing class of New France who stayed on after the British conquest, the Catholic hierarchy undertook many functions performed elsewhere by procedures of self-government. There was no opportunity, further, for congregational self-government to develop as it did in the English-speaking (Protestant) parts of Canada, and in Britain and the United States. The Catholic Church itself, of course, is governed hierarchically, from the top down. In Quebec, as in many other countries, it has often taken dogmatic positions on some political issues, and this has led its followers to debate such issues in an ideological manner.

More than once, to be sure, disagreements on matters relating to politics have occurred within the Catholic hierarchy—usually between the Bishop of Montreal and the Bishop of Quebec City—which could not be settled until a special papal delegate was dispatched from the Vatican for that purpose. Many of these internal French-Canadian controversies have been conducted in what adherents of the national-character school would describe as a rather "French" manner. This has rarely been due to the direct influence of French politics on Quebec politics, although after the Revolution of 1848, a Quebec group which appropriately called itself *Rouges* espoused openly anticlerical policies. Most French-Canadians have been unfriendly to the various French Republics ever since the Great Revolution, because of their loyalty to the Church and to the institutions of monarchy. But their educational system and their notions of knowledge and of its powers have remained prerevolutionary French—again largely because the Catholic Church runs the schools—and, therefore, quite different from the English educational system and the English notions of knowledge. A related factor is the retention by the province of Quebec of the codified Civil Law of France, based on Roman law. As will be shown in greater detail in the next chapter, these factors have combined to make Quebec politics both more ideological and more legalistic than politics in the neighboring provinces.

United States of America

Politics in the United States is the least ideological, the most pragmatic of all our countries. There is no single American ideology, although some people have recently been looking hard for one, in order to fight Soviet Communism with it. And there are no competing American ideologies: The major parties have none, the labor movement has none, nor do any of the other great organized interests. Few groups in American politics have ever permitted their decisions to be shaped by a comprehensive, consistent, closed system of knowledge. The only major movements in American history that came close to basing their actions on a single ideal were those of the abolitionists and their opponents before the Civil War, but the most influential ones among them never systematized their ideals in any logical fashion. After the Civil War, the winning side, obliged to assume concrete responsibility for rebuilding the nation, naturally lost what few ideological inclinations it may have developed earlier. And the potential ideologists on the losing side returned, after a few years, to running the state governments in the South, with the same effects similar federal situations produced in Switzerland and Canada.

That this lack of ideologism cannot be explained in terms of "agreement on fundamentals" in the United States, we will try to show in Chapter 22, "Consensus." We can anticipate that discussion by suggesting that there is as much disagreement on questions of policy in American politics as in Canadian and British politics, and the frequency of constitutional controversies and litigation indicates that there is less agreement on the Constitution in the United States than in these other English-speaking countries. Accordingly, other explanations for this lack of ideologism will have to be sought. The most plausible one is the fact that, with the exception of Southern Negroes, no politically ambitious group has ever been denied a share in responsibility for very long. When-ever any such group was excluded from participation, it could and usu-ally did seek admission via the road of constitutional litigation. The availability of this outlet has often transformed potential ideologism into constitutional legalism.

Constitutional legalism in the United States is, as already men-tioned, a substitute ideology for some Americans, especially when they argue in terms of the intentions of the Founding Fathers. This will be discussed further in the next chapter, on legalism. Here we should note that even this quasi-ideological constitutional legalism rarely generates new issues on its own. Rather, legalistic arguments are used to justify the stand on conflicts about material interests that one would have taken in any case. Constitutional arguments are useful in "public relations"—they may persuade someone. But no one who matters in American politics ever starts a controversy from constitutional considerations alone, nor does anyone ever refuse to arrive at a compromise solely because of principled disagreement over the interpretation of the Constitution. And what has just been said of legalism applies with even greater strength to ideologism.

Lack of ideologism can thus be explained in terms of the rapid response to demands for admission to politics from excluded groups. This would include the admission to positions of leadership of members of cultural minority groups in the present century—of ethnic groups like the Irish, Italians, Jews; and of religious groups like the Mormons. How-ever, this explanation by itself will not serve fully, because the English-speaking provinces of Canada, especially in the Middle West, have dis-played a considerable degree of ideologism, and there was no more ex-clusion from political responsibility in Alberta, Saskatchewan, or Mani-toba than there was south of the international boundary. There must be some other factor to explain this difference; it is likely to be related to the chief constitutional and historical differences between the United States and Canada.

Canada is a constitutional monarchy that still shares the same mon-arch with Great Britain; the United States is a republic that broke its ties with Great Britain and the Old World almost two hundred years ago. This break with Europe and with monarchy, a feudal institution whose roots reach into the dim past, gave Americans less to remember than the Canadians. Indeed, the motto of the United States, unlike that of Quebec, might well be, "I forget." The deliberate break with the past made in the War of Independence meant that arguments in terms of tradition

would never carry as much weight in the United States as in the other seven countries, each of which has a feudal past from which no radical break was ever successfully completed. But in these other countries, revolutionary ideologies have usually been constructed in order to attack conservative ideologies, or reactionary ones in order to fight successful revolutionary systems of knowledge. This was true even of Canada, and even on the same "frontier" it has shared with the United States. Arguments based on tradition carried more weight in Canada and could best be answered with similarly systematized arguments against tradition, as in the ideology of Social Credit. Besides, since Canada never made the break from Britain, British ideologies could be exported directly to Canada to carry on the same fight there in which they were engaged at home, as in the case of the Labour party's socialism and the Coöperative Commonwealth Federation.

There is yet another consequence of the break with the past executed by the fathers of American Independence, reflected in the comparatively low prestige and influence of academically trained intellectuals *as intellectuals* in American politics. In all the older countries, with their awareness of the long past and their wish to treasure memories of it, these men perform the special function of keeping these memories alive for the rest of society. Academic intellectuals are also best qualified for, and most prone to, the construction of ideologies. They are the makers and propagators par excellence of comprehensive, consistent, and closed systems of knowledge. They are looked upon as, and consider themselves to be, the guardians of all knowledge. In the United States, they have played a much less important role than in any of the other seven countries. Even in Canada, politicians are much more likely to mention their academic qualifications when running for office, and these usually help them with the voters. This is more marked in Quebec than elsewhere in the country, just as it is more marked on the European Continent than in Great Britain. But even in the Canadian prairie provinces, the intellectual claim to fame of schoolteachers, for example, is an asset, whereas that of university professors in United States politics is a handicap. We will return to this difference when we consider the personnel of politics. At this point, it has been mentioned only as another reason for the low ideological content of American politics: Knowledge of the past—at least the past before 1776—is not valued as much as it is elsewhere. Neither are those who are officially certified as possessors of this and other impractical knowledge and who, for reasons of their training and status, are the most frequent contributors to ideological style.

Guidelines for Constitution-Makers—I

If we are in agreement that ideologism is harmful to the success of constitutional democracy, we can now, having isolated some of its causes, formulate the first guidelines for the makers and reformers of political systems:

Do not exclude groups aspiring to a share in political responsibility for any longer than may be necessary for reasons such as protection of the constitutional system from totalitarian enemies.

Give opportunities for making meaningful contributions in the flow of policy to all those who are given formal opportunities for political participation.

Provide units of politics smaller than the whole system itself, either geographical (such as member states or local governments) or functional (such as congregations or unions), in which groups temporarily excluded at the center of policy-making can assume responsibility for self-government.

Even if it were possible to follow this advice in all respects, and even if its observance would eliminate ideologism, this might still have other undesirable side effects. Thus, the transmutation of potential ideologism into legalism might create great constitutional instability. And since we wish to avoid both ideologism and legalism, we must next search for the causes of legalism and find appropriate guidelines in connection with that problem.

CHAPTER 15

Legalism

Politics can compromise conflicts over material interests only if the parties to a dispute are agreed upon the procedures according to which settlement should be reached. Without agreement on rules of procedure, violence is likely to be used. This was our reason for distinguishing between lawfulness and legalism. The conduct of negotiations according to accepted procedures cannot be described as legalistic, unless observance of these procedures is treated as an end in itself.

Legalism can be especially harmful when it undermines the stability of the constitution itself by bringing about continuous demands for changes in those matters that, according to Chief Justice Marshall, "are designed to be permanent." Legalism about matters which are not constitutional, in this sense, also impedes the process of compromise; it can, for example, make people unwilling to negotiate face to face about their disagreements, because they prefer to let these be settled by the "impersonal machinery of justice." Political systems differ with respect not only to legalism in general, but also to these two major kinds of legalism: about the constitution, and about laws of lesser importance or permanence. In order to be able to explain variations in legalistic style, this distinction must be taken into account, and must first, of course, be clarified.

Fundamentals and Circumstantials

The first to make the distinction was Oliver Cromwell, and he made it when this problem arose for the first time in modern history, after he had "new-modelled" the British constitution by basing it on the Instrument of Government, his written constitution. In a speech to Parliament, on September 12, 1654, Cromwell said:

> It is true, as there are some things in the Establishment which are Fundamental, so there are others which are not, but are Circumstantial. Of these no question but I shall easily agree to vary, to leave out. . . . But some things are Fundamentals! About which I shall deal plainly with you: These may *not* be parted with; but will, I trust, be delivered over to Posterity, as the fruits of our blood and travail. The Government by a single Person and a Parliament is a Fundamental! It is the *esse*, it is constitutive.
>
> In every Government there must be Somewhat Fundamental, Somewhat like a Magna Charta, which should be standing, be unalterable. . . . That Parliaments should not make themselves perpetual is a Fundamental! Of what assurance is a *Law* to prevent so great an evil, if it lie in the same Legislature to *un*law it again? Is such a Law like to be lasting? . . . Again, is not Liberty of Conscience in Religion a Fundamental?
>
> As for that of Money—I told you some things were Circumstantials. . . . Of this sort there are many Circumstantial things, which are not like the Laws of the Medes and the Persians. But the things which shall be necessary to deliver over to Posterity, these should be unalterable. Else every succeeding Parliament will be disputing to alter the Government; and we shall be as often brought into confusion as we have Parliaments and so make our remedy our disease.

Cromwell was so tortuously groping for this novel distinction, because he was facing a novel constitutional problem. Having himself "new-modelled" the English constitution, he could no longer base its legitimacy on tradition. What was to keep others from rearranging things again in the face of a new set of novel circumstances? The problem was the same as that of giving stability and permanence to an artificially and rationally engineered social contract. Cromwell's contemporaries, Thomas Hobbes and John Locke, also raised it, and they also failed to solve it. Both of them thought that the legitimacy of a social contract, that is, a constitution, ended when a successful revolution supplanted it with a new one—Hobbes, because he considered a sovereign without power to enforce the terms of the contract no longer sovereign; and Locke, because success in a rebellion gave the "judgment of Heaven," to which the ultimate appeal lies. The solution had to await the generation of the American Founding Fathers, who provided it, in words remarkably reminiscent of Cromwell's, in the constitutional amending procedure and in the judicial review of congressional legislation. Cromwell, by being the first to recognize the problem, also gave us the most useful distinction between the constitution and ordinary law, between fundamentals and circumstantials. What distinguishes them in the first place is their intended duration. With this in mind, we can now compare the style of political systems in terms of legalism about fundamentals and legalism about circumstantials.

Fundamental Legalism

The degree of legalism in connection with fundamentals—constitutional matters—is lowest in British politics. Debates about the British constitution are rare, and so is reference to the constitution in debates on matters of everyday (or every-year) policy. Fundamental legalism is most frequent in German politics. In West Germany, the Basic Law itself is the subject of constant discussion. Politicians, students of government, journalists, jurists, and other public figures are forever keeping it in the forefront of debate, questioning its internal consistency, recommending its amendment or its replacement by another constitution, justifying with reference to the Basic Law the position they take on circumstantial issues, and carrying cases before the Federal Constitutional Court. In France, constitutional legalism is almost as high as in Germany. In Italy, its strength is of roughly the same order as in France. The United States ranks next. Constitutional legalism in Canada and Switzerland falls somewhere near the midpoint between the extremes of Great Britain and Germany. And in Sweden, it is almost as rare as in Britain.

This scale immediately suggests several explanations. One is the obvious relation between a written constitution and legalism about fundamentals. Britain has neither, and the more fundamental parts of the written Swedish constitution are sufficiently old to command such widespread agreement that they are called into question but rarely. This suggests a second explanation: the relation between fundamental legalism and the age of the constitution. The younger the constitution, the more likely is it to be itself a topic of discussion. Hence the high incidence of such debates in the three major Continental countries, each of which adopted its present constitution since World War II. But age should be considered also in connection with the continuity between the present and the previous regimes. This continuity was greater in France's Fourth Republic than in the Italian and German republics.

The midway position on the scale of the three federal systems suggests a third explanation: Federalism encourages constitutional legalism. This is more marked in countries with a federal court that acts as umpire of the federal system than in those lacking such a tribunal. Switzerland has none; Canada had the Judicial Committee of the Privy Council and still has the Canadian Supreme Court; the United States Supreme Court has been the model for most other federal tribunals. While the lack of a federal court works to reduce fundamental legalism in Switzerland, the provisions for initiative and referendum, which apply to the constitution alone and not to circumstantial legislation, push in the other direction.

These judicial bodies in Germany, Canada, and the United States perform the functions, not only of federal courts, but also of constitutional courts: they umpire disputes among states or between states and the federal government, and they also interpret the constitution by applying it to the actions of organs of the federal government itself. The availability of such forums for the challenge of constitutionality also encourages legalism about fundamentals. It has had this effect in the Italian Republic which, although not a federal system, has provided for a Constitutional Court. By contrast, the Committee on the Constitution in the French Fourth Republic was used hardly at all, probably for two main reasons: First, this was a committee, not a court, and therefore operated without the public pomp and drama usually surrounding the judiciary. Second, French constitutional procedures were much more firmly established than Italian ones, so that they did not require the kind of external support that a constitutional court can give.

A final explanation of variations in fundamental legalism is related to the procedure of constitutional courts. Of those considered here, only the Supreme Court of the United States does not give advisory opinions before a suit has actually been brought before it. All the others must render such opinions at the request of certain other organs of government. This practice also contributes to legalistic style by allowing politicians to keep the constitutional court busy and constitutional issues in the limelight. The fact that similar issues in the United States are not resolved until an actual controversy at law has arisen about them, and the Supreme Court has decided to resolve them, often delays settlement for several years. During such a period, the particular issues in dispute are usually debated in a very legalistic way, although the total number of issues discussed with reference to the constitution is lower than in Italy or Germany. If fundamental legalism nevertheless seems as strong in the United States as in Canada, whose Supreme Court does give advisory opinions, this may be related to the weakness of ideologism in the United States. This, as mentioned in the last chapter, leads to the expression in constitutional litigation of issues that, in Canada, could be debated in a more ideological fashion.

Circumstantial Legalism

These explanations of differences in political style leave a number of questions unanswered. The most perplexing is the very carelessness of the constitutional documents of the countries in which fundamental legalism is relatively weak—all of the nations under study, that is, except Germany, Italy, and France. If the French had a constitution that nowhere defined relations between President, Cabinet, and Parliament—as the Canadians do—they would promptly pass organic laws to take care of this constitutional gap. Indeed, if they had the chance, they would probably adopt a completely new constitution, in order to bring the old one up to date. If the Germans had a constitution that failed even to mention political parties—as Americans do—they would debate this lacuna at great length and possibily ostracize the authors of the constitution. If the Italians had no written constitution at all—as is the case with the British—there is no telling what they might do. That we are not exaggerating these attitudes is corroborated by the fact that none of these nations has missed any opportunity in the twentieth century to revise old or adopt elaborate new constitutions. Continental literature on government in the English-speaking countries conveys the same impression. It usually criticizes these constitutions for their vagueness, internal inconsistency, lack of comprehensiveness, and for failure to define the locus of sovereignty.

Why are the English-speaking countries satisfied with such "technically inferior" constitutions, and why do the major Continental systems believe in the merits of comprehensive and internally consistent constitutions that define very clearly relations among all the organs of government and politics? This question is doubly important; without an answer to it, our explanation of fundamental legalism in relation to the youth of a constitution would turn out to be no explanation at all, since in several instances youth could have been avoided by retaining the prevailing constitution and modifying it informally in practice without its complete replacement. Why do the Continental Europeans have this yearning for constitutional and legal comprehensiveness, consistency, and clarity? Why do the English-speaking peoples, and the Swedes and the Swiss to a lesser degree, lack this desire?

This same difference is even more noticeable on the level of circumstantials. Here, legalism is much stronger in Germany, Italy, and France, than in Britain, Canada, or the United States. Some illustrations of this have already been given; many more could be added. For example, pocket editions of the several law codes and of specialized laws are constant bestsellers in the Continental countries. General popular familiarity with the contents of the various codes is much greater than in the English-speaking countries. The incidence of private litigation is probably higher, although no reliable comparative figures are available. Suits between competing politicians occur much more frequently, often for oratorical insults that, in the United States, would merely draw the opponent's laughs. Private relations are much more often defined by formal contracts, as in the case of domestic servants and their employers. Public signs advertising official prohibitions more often cite the specific law on which they are based; thus, the familiar French inscriptions, warning that the posting of placards upon, or the urinating against, certain walls is forbidden, always includes the nineteenth-century date of the specified law as part of the notice. In France, such signs are usually honored in the breach. In Germany, they are usually obeyed. But whether observed or not, in both countries they reflect and contribute to a widespread popular awareness of detailed legal provisions. One final illustration: Someone who wants to refer to homosexuality in polite German society simply mentions "the seventeenth of May," in full confidence that everyone is aware that paragraph 175 of the criminal code deals with that subject.

Excessive legalism about circumstantials contributes to legalism about fundamentals. Both types interfere with the politics of compromisable interests. And both types appear to a far greater degree in France, Italy, and Germany than in the three English-speaking countries. Why?

Roman Law and English Law

There is one major difference between these two sets of countries: their legal systems. Those of the three Continental countries were decisively influenced by the Roman law, as it was first codified on orders of the Emperor Justinian in the sixth century A.D. Law in the three English-speaking countries is based on the English common law, which has never been codified but has grown "from precedent to precedent," mainly as formulated in the decisions of judges. Before Justinian's great codification, Roman law had evolved for a thousand years in a very similar way. Its impact upon Continental legal theory and practice, however, was made in codified form—through three books that literally covered the field and one that was intended as a textbook. In this form, the Roman law came to Europe through the Italian universities at the end of the Middle Ages. The circumstances of what has been called "the Reception" of the Roman law during the eleventh and twelfth centuries were such as to surround the Justinian Code with a kind of halo and to convey the impression that it "contained justice" in a very literal sense.

In later centuries, the Roman law was recodified in various Continental countries, in order to bring it up to date. The most famous of these recodifications was undertaken on orders of the Emperor Napoleon, who considered his Code Napoleon one of his greatest achievements and thereby revealed, incidentally, the Continental tendency to measure individual historical greatness by the "giving" of law to one's nation. All the recodifications were comprehensive, deliberate, and very much engineered. This again confirmed people in their belief that the Code contained all the law, that it covered all contingencies, and that anyone who mastered its contents and the technique of reasoning in its terms would be most capable of administering justice.

English law, by contrast, was never received and never codified. It evolved slowly by unplanned, unengineered accretion. It had no single source like the great Continental lawgivers or "sovereigns." Until the sixteenth century, it was generally assumed in England that law was not "made" at all, but found. In the finding of it, the King-in-Parliament played a role about equal to that of the King's judges—and the chief judges were and still are members of that Parliament (as Law Lords). A succession of great English lawyers compiled a succession of great casebooks—collections of judges' opinions and commentaries upon these opinions, as well as treatises on the law. Bracton, Coke, and Blackstone are the most prominent names in this list. These great protagonists of the common law have been opposed by a succession of equally great rationalist reformers who wanted to codify this weirdly grown non-system— Francis Bacon, Jeremy Bentham, and Thomas Jefferson, among them. But the reformers never had their way, either in Great Britain or in the United States. No wholesale codification ever took place, and even where parts of the law were codified in statutes, the basic ancient procedures of the common law are still in use. The Seventh Amendment to the Constitution of the United States states that "no fact tried by a jury shall be otherwise re-examined in any court of the United States than according to the rules of the common law." The process by which English law has grown, combined with the failure ever to codify it, means that today, although there are many precedents, there is no single book to which Englishmen or Americans can go in order to find "the law" to resolve some issue that has arisen.

In the Roman-law countries, the reverse is true. An excerpt from the German Civil Code illustrates this:

Book Three, Law of Goods
Section III, Property
Title 3, Property in Mobile Goods
V. Appropriation

#960

Wild animals are ownerless as long as they are at liberty. Wild animals in zoos and fishes in ponds or other closed private waters are not ownerless.

If a captured wild animal regains liberty, then it becomes ownerless, unless the owner pursues the animal forthwith, or when he gives up the pursuit.

A tamed animal becomes ownerless when it gives up the habit of returning to the place assigned to it.

#961

If a swarm of bees departs, then it becomes ownerless, unless the owner pursues it forthwith, or when the owner gives up the pursuit.

#962

The owner of the bee swarm may, in his pursuit, enter the property of others. If the swarm has moved into another unoccupied beehive, then the owner of the swarm may, for the purpose of its capture, open the hive and take out or break out the combs. He must restore the resulting damage.

#963

If the escaped swarms of bees of several owners unite, then those owners who have pursued their swarms become coöwners of the captured united swarm; the shares are determined according to the number of pursued swarms.

#964

If a swarm of bees has moved into another occupied beehive, then property and other rights to the bees, by which the hive was occupied, extend to the swarm newly moved in. Property and other rights to the swarm newly moved in expire.

This law on the pursuit of bees has its counterpart in the codes of other Roman-law countries. A multitude of other topics are treated in the same exhaustive and somewhat exhausting detail, including, for example, the right of a girl who has been jilted to recover damages in cash from her former fiancé, if she had permitted him sexual relations. The common law contains no equivalent of this; in order to find the law on escaped bees or escaped fiancés, one would do research in casebooks and would probably discover that there are precedents on both sides of the issue and the outcome of a suit would be uncertain.

This inaccessible and esoteric quality of the English law has the effect of reducing what might be called popular legal initiative. Citizens in the English-speaking countries are likely to become interested in the law only after they have come into conflict with it or with one another. In the Roman-law countries, citizens are more likely to be tempted into initiating a suit as a result of their prior knowledge of the gains litigation might bring them. To use the illustration given, it is probable that most German beekeepers are familiar with paragraphs 960 through 964 of the Civil Code and more willing to go to court about bee escapades than American beekeepers. It is also possible that courting in Germany is affected by people's familiarity with the relevant legal provisions. The very knowledge that all the eventualities that might arise in such intimate relations are anticipated by the Civil Code would encourage people to let themselves be governed by such regulations in all aspects of their lives and, conversely, to undertake nothing without prior legislation or regulation. The English-speaking peoples, by contrast, because no wholesale codifications have ever occurred, do not have this yearning for full anticipatory legislation prior to experimentation, whether it be personal, institutional, or procedural. Just as the law was built up by the "method" of trial and error, so are institutions and procedures. After they have proved themselves in practice, they may then be confirmed by explicit legislation, or they may not.

This major difference between the systematic Roman law and the unsystematic English law has been reflected in the training and careers of judges, bureaucrats, and lawyers, as will be seen in the discussion of the personnel of politics, in Chapter 18. The training of Continental jurists is more systematic, puts more emphasis on memory work, and offers less practical experience before the exercise of actual legal responsibility. This, together with the easy accessibility of the codes to the public and the relatively low cost of litigation, explains the difference under the two systems in popular conceptions of the nature of the judicial process.

The Machinery of Justice

In Roman-law countries, a judge's career normally begins with his passing of a state examination shortly after the completion of university studies. In the English-law countries, judges normally are not appointed to the bench until they have reached middle age and have behind them a career in the private practice of law or in politics. They need this background of experience more than their Continental colleagues, because they exercise more discretion in performing their judicial functions. Because their legal systems have never been codified, these judges have to take a more active hand in shaping the development of the law. In France, Germany, and Italy, the sovereign lawmaker who created the great codes largely precluded the need for shaping the law. And the codes themselves were intended to be so comprehensive that judges get much more specific and certain guidance from them than do British, American, and Canadian judges from collections of precedents.

These distinctive features of Continental judiciaries all contribute to a popular conception of the judicial process that differs from that prevailing in the English-speaking countries, and especially in the United States. Continental Europeans tend to think of the courts in much more impersonal terms than do the English-speaking peoples. The origin of their codes is partly the cause of this, because it excludes from identification great personalities, like Lord Coke and Lord Mansfield and Chief Justice Marshall and Associate Justice Oliver Wendell Holmes. Continental judges give much shorter opinions than their English-speaking colleagues, and the opinions are never signed. Courts consisting of several judges do not publish dissenting opinions.[1] To do so would be tantamount to admitting that "justice" could find more than one true position. As a result, Continental people think much more nearly in terms of the "machinery" of justice than do people in the English-speaking world. And even when they admit that judges do not and perhaps cannot behave like nonhuman automatons, they still adhere to this automatic conception of justice as the goal toward which the courts should strive. This is again related to the belief that "the law" contains absolute justice, sprung more or less full blown from the head of the code-giver. In the light of these notions, we can understand the Continental preference for adjudication over negotiation. Negotiation between the parties to a dispute would probably lead to compromise, and compromise on the Con-

[1] Arthur T. Von Mehren, "The Judicial Process: A Comparative Analysis," *American Journal of Comparative Law,* V (1956), pp. 197 ff.

tinent carries the invidious implication of the word more often than the constructive one. Settlement by the courts, on the other hand, will give something that comes much closer to true justice to the side "in the right." And Continental Europeans are much more prone to think that only one side can be right than are people in the English-speaking world, again for reasons related to the differences between the legal systems, as will be seen presently.

If these causes of circumstantial legalism were confined to private life, especially in business, they would be of only minor interest to us. However, they affect political style in a very significant way, by downgrading the prestige of the political process, while upgrading the judicial process and, most important, conceiving of the two as virtually watertight compartments, with no overflow from the one into the other. These effects are most marked in West Germany, where they have led to the widely prevailing conviction that politics is irregular, unpredictable, unclean, and corrupt, while adjudication is regular, predictable, clean, and honest. And this conviction, in turn, permits people to hope for the ever-greater reduction of the scope of politics, and perhaps for its eventual elimination in some utopia, which would resemble a perfectly bureaucratized state.

There is still another reason for the high degree of legalism about circumstantials in the larger Continental countries, and this is also connected with the differences between the two great legal systems, the Roman and the English. The great codifications and legal reforms on the Continent have been identified with progress. In spite of the fact that the great lawgivers themselves were not interested in promoting democracy, but only in establishing order, the promulgation of the comprehensive, consistent, and clear codes did bring about improvement in the lives of ordinary folk. They were now more secure against arbitrary interference from the state and had better foreknowledge of the consequences of their private decisions. Moreover, in several instances the codes were created during periods of great national power—the Code Napoleon while France dominated the Continent, the German Civil Code after national unification. This mental association of the law with progress has further helped to add prestige to knowledge of the law and recourse to the courts. It has also contributed to the generally strong Continental optimism concerning the feasibility of wholesale constitutional engineering, since the creation of the codes amounted to engineering of this kind, even if not, perhaps, on the level of fundamentals. The work of the great lawgivers has in many ways served as model for later constitution-makers, who hoped to create works as comprehensive, consistent, and as long lived as those of the codifiers of the law. In the English-speaking countries, such models were lacking. As a result, even the American Founding Fathers were as skeptical about their effort as Hamilton, when he quoted Hume, and quite restrained in their quantitative output.

Jurisprudence and Other Sciences

The Continental optimism about men's capacity to prearrange the future by means of legislation and the British and American opposite view are reflected in more general conceptions of knowledge and its powers, and in this indirect way also cast light on the differences in ideological style discussed in the preceding chapter. The law is one of the oldest academic disciplines in that part of the world that is heir to the traditions of ancient Rome. In Continental universities, the faculties of law are second in age only to the faculties of theology, and since the end of the Middle Ages, the law faculties have had more influence and prestige than those of theology. In England, the study of law has been at least as valued and influential as on the Continent. But it was not carried on in the universities, but by graduates of the universities in the Inns of Court, at the seat of the King's courts in London. There, would-be barristers "read" the law, that is, casebooks and commentaries, and listened in on proceedings before the King's courts. In the United States, through most of the nineteenth century, law clerks were apprenticed to lawyers, again in order to read the law. Not long after law schools were finally founded to provide formal instruction for future lawyers, the "case method" was developed at Harvard. Under the case method, students read series of cases dealing with similar issues. They learn to develop a critical attitude toward the way in which judges build the law from precedent to precedent. By contrast, in Continental law faculties, much greater emphasis is placed upon memorizing the codes and arguing about their internal coherence.

These methods of teaching under the Continental faculties of law have influenced pedagogy under other faculties, especially those concerned with the "social sciences," as they are called in the United States —sociology, economics, political science, and so on. This influence on teaching methods was only natural, in view of the greater age and higher prestige of jurisprudence as an academic discipline. Its effect was to produce a conception of knowledge—and not alone of legal knowledge— much like the mercantilist conception of wealth. It is looked upon as a substance of which there is just so much, which can be acquired through industry. In the English-speaking countries, the social sciences have also learned some of their methods from the law schools, but there knowledge tends to be looked upon as a dynamic relation rather than as a static substance, and as a relation that is somehow expanding and can never be fully apprehended. The difference between the two notions of knowledge is similar to that between mechanical and electrical power. The power stored in a wound clock spring is "all there" and is expended as the clock keeps running, until it comes to a stop. The power in an electricity network, on the other hand, must be constantly replenished at the source, since batteries cannot store much of it, and must be maintained at a level sufficiently high to offset consumption.

The English conception of knowledge is reflected in the extension of the case method beyond the law schools into other academic disciplines, such as sociology, public and business administration, military science, and human relations. In other words, the social sciences in the English-speaking world proceed more inductively, from the facts contained in series of cases or case studies, to more or less tentative generalized conclusions. In the Continental countries, the parallel disciplines use a more deductive method, starting from general "laws" contained in the "body of knowledge" on the subject, and going down from this high level of abstraction to concrete events that fit it.

This difference was noted by Josef Redlich, one of the keenest Continental students of the parliamentary and legal procedures of the English-speaking countries:

> Brief reflection shows clearly that it is only a step from [the "scientific" character of the case method] to a completely changed conception of the purpose of legal education as a whole; to the conception, namely, that the real purpose of scientific instruction in law is not to impart the content of the law, not to teach the law, but rather to arouse, to strengthen, to carry to the highest possible pitch of perfection a specially legal manner of thinking.[2]

Even the languages reflect these differences. The English language has grown just as the English law. As a result, English spelling and pronunciation contain the innumerable inconsistencies that have driven many a European to despair. English has never been codified, and every attempt to systematize spelling and to modernize it has failed. The French language has been codified, on orders of Napoleon, the great code-giver himself, who reorganized the French Academy partly for the purpose of systematizing the language and keeping it up to date. Neither French nor Italian nor German is permeated by inconsistencies like the

[2] *The Common Law and the Case Method in American University Law Schools: Report to the Carnegie Foundation for the Advancement of Teaching,* 1914.

different English pronunciations of *-ough*. On the Continent, they have long since eliminated superfluous letters, while in English it is still incorrect to write *lite* for *light,* or *thoro* for *thorough*. Similarly, the metric and decimal systems have never been popularly accepted in the English-speaking world. It still uses ancient measures—the foot and the mile, the pound and the gallon—while the Continental countries base all of their measures on the rationally engineered meter. The British have even retained their asymmetrical money—twelve pennies to the shilling, twenty shillings to the pound, twenty-one to the guinea, and two-and-a-half to the "half crown" (there is no full crown).

This difference in methods of teaching and learning, and in conceptions of knowledge, can offer us another explanation of the more strongly ideological style of the Continental systems. Just as all the law has been put together in a comprehensive, consistent, and closed fashion, so should all knowledge about other fields be ordered. Just as those who are learned in the law can dispense justice, so should those learned in the science of the state or of the economy or of society be able to dispense the fruits of their study. Just as progress was achieved by compiling the law in codes, so could progress be achieved by compiling knowledge in these other spheres into comprehensive, coherent, and closed systems. Such an attitude leads to excessive expectations of the capabilities of knowledge and of those who "possess" this knowledge; hence the crucial role played by the academic intelligentsia on the Continent, to which we will return.

At this point, it is appropriate to note how legalism and ideologism reënforce each other. Because of legalism, people believe that all knowledge should be susceptible to systematization and comprehensiveness, so that in the end it will present one symmetrical edifice, which covers all reality and eliminates all uncertainty. By transferring this notion to politics, they adopt ideologies, which are just such aesthetically beautiful constructs, no matter how much they may distort reality. Then, by acting in politics on the basis of their ideologies, they make compromise difficult. This both increases litigiousness and disparages the political process. It may also discredit the machinery of justice, which eventually finds itself unable to keep up the façade of impartiality in its efforts to resolve conflicts between rigidly implacable ideological antagonists. The final outcome can be civil war.

In the English-speaking countries, lower expectations are placed on legal knowledge and political science. The law has never been systematized and, as a consequence, there is little encouragement for attempts to systematize the social sciences in general, or political science in particular. They, too, may more safely grow from precedent to precedent. Just as British and American judges and lawyers have managed to adapt the law to novel problems that have arisen in the course of the centuries, so can their politicians and even the leaders of great political movements adapt their policies and programs. Neither they nor their followers feel the Continental need for a total ideology by which to justify their actions and from which to draw a false certainty about the future of the world. And when they experiment with a new institution or procedure, they are not nearly as worried as the Continentals about whether it will fit in consistently with everything that is already established. They are not so eager that the whole system of government should present one symmetrical whole. A cursory comparison of standard textbooks on the relevant constitutions clearly shows this.

The same relative disregard for symmetry is also noticeable at the level of circumstantials. A discrepancy between traffic or divorce laws in different states of the American Union causes few Americans any loss of sleep. And individual politicians in the English-speaking countries are not usually very much concerned over the consistency of their own stand on various issues over the years, while in the Continental systems one can often damage an opposing politician most effectively by demonstrating contradictions between his present and past positions—unless his was a radical conversion, from the espousal of one ideology to another. This yearning for consistency on the one hand, and the complacency with unevenness on the other, is related to the final major difference between the Roman and the English law.

The Adversary Method of the Common Law

Comparisons between the Roman and the English legal systems have often been made, usually by Englishmen who have set out to praise the merits of the common law—by Sir John Fortescue in the fifteenth century, for example, and by Sir Thomas Smith in the seventeenth. Sir Edward Coke joined the distinguished list when he opposed the plan of James I and Francis Bacon to bring the Roman law of James's Scotland down to England upon the union of the two realms. These comparisons have focused on what they considered advantages of the common law, which the Roman Law lacked: trial by jury, habeas corpus, the Crown's lack of full imperial *potestas,* which was a forerunner of theories of sovereignty. Our focus here has been somewhat different. In order to find explanations for differences in political style, we have been more interested in the methods by which the Roman codes have been made and by which the common law has evolved, and in the procedures used under these two legal systems.

One procedural peculiarity of the common law is the very ancient adversary method of pleading used in the courts. Under this procedure, the plaintiff and the defendant alternately state their claim and their defense.[3] Adversary pleading, as the term suggests, makes adversaries, antagonists, or opponents out of the parties to a lawsuit. These adversaries contend their case before a court, consisting of one or more judges, or judge and jury, which plays the role of a neutral umpire. This procedure leaves it squarely up to the adversaries—plaintiff or prosecution and defendant, and their respective counsel—to bring out just what is at issue between them.

> The law of pleading has for its foundation this proposition, that every dispute between man and man, no matter how complicated its nature is, may nevertheless be resolved into its elements and be shown to spring from a *single* point of fact or law as to which the parties are at variance. The object of a system of pleading is to unearth this disputed point from the mass of unimportant details which usually surround it, and to present it to the court for decision.[4]

If there is no real issue between them, the court will refuse the case. And the court itself will not take the initiative to isolate the matter under dispute.

There are variations in the use of the adversary method in different common-law jurisdictions. For example, English judges in criminal trials take a more active part in the proceedings than their brethren in the United States. But they all share in common the main features and—what is more important for our purposes—differ markedly on this score from court usage on the Continent. Under the common law, the parties to a suit must themselves take the initiative in clarifying what is at stake and in *trying* to persuade the court that their side ought to win the *trial*. Continental usage has no equivalent term for "trial." [5] The contrast with Continental courts is pronounced:

[3] "Pleading is the stating in a logical and legal form the facts which constitute the plaintiff's cause of action or the defendant's ground of defense; it is the formal mode of alleging that on the record which constitutes the support or the defense of the party in evidence. The *alternate* statements of claim and of defense are called the pleadings." George Wharton Pepper, *Pleading at Common Law and under the Codes*, 1891, p. 3. Italics supplied.
[4] *Ibid*. Italics supplied.
[5] Robert Wynness Millar, "The Mechanism of Fact Discovery: A Study in Comparative Civil Procedure," *Illinois Law Review*, XXXII (1937-38), pp. 261 ff., pp. 424 ff.

Under systems other than the English, the parties are allowed to make their statements at large [in narrative form, rather than through alternating cross-examination], and with no view to the extrication of the *precise* question in controversy. The different statements are then examined with care, in order that undisputed and irrelevant matter may be sifted out. This examination, in the case of some judicatures, is made privately by each of the parties for himself, as a necessary preliminary to the adjustment of his evidence. In others, the point for decision is selected by the court, or its officer, in advance of the trial. By the common law, however, the parties are obliged so to plead as to evolve some disputed question by the effect of their own alternate allegations, and to agree upon this question so evolved as the point for decision in the cause.[6]

This forces the parties to agree at least on what it is that they are in disagreement about, in order that this issue may then be resolved by the court. The "specific point or matter affirmed on the one side and denied on the other is called the issue—the *exitus,* or outcome of the pleadings." [7] On the Continent, this issue can often not be described as a "point," but is something much broader and vaguer. Because the parties do not bring it out, the court itself has to try to do so. As a result, Continental judges seem to conduct themselves in a much less umpire-like fashion.

The effects of this difference between the adversary method and its Continental counterpart can be brought out more clearly by way of an admitted exaggeration: We might say that British and American courts seem more interested in achieving a decision, in settling the controversy and removing it from the world, than in arriving at "the real truth" of the dispute. Continental courts, on the contrary, seem more interested in establishing this truth, no matter how many new disputes, which the parties themselves had not anticipated, may be generated as a result. If they cannot establish the real truth, they would rather forgo a decision than to make one that would involve injustice. A law-school anecdote may illustrate this: A student, upon being told by the professor of the verdict in a case under study, exclaimed indignantly, "But that's unjust!" Whereupon the professor replied, "Young man, we are studying the law; if you want to study justice, you will have to go across the street to the divinity school."

The origins of the adversary method go back to the very beginnings of English law. Because of the steady development of the law by the judges, this procedure was passed down from generation to genera-

[6] Pepper, *op. cit.,* pp. 3-4. Italics supplied.
[7] *Ibid.,* p. 4.

tion. The term "issue" occurs as part of the ordinary legal vocabulary in the very beginning of the Year Books, the verbatim reports of judicial proceedings, which were first recorded during the same period that saw the founding of the Inns of Court, that is, in the reigns of the first three Edwards, between 1272 and 1377. Pleading became highly formalized and very intricate. According to Littleton, one of the great commentators on the common law, it was "one of the most honorable, laudable and profitable things in the law to have the science of well-pleading in actions, real and personal." [8]

The purpose of pleading always was to produce a clear issue. This "science of pleading" according to the adversary method reached its fullest development during the same period in which "the High Court of Parliament" ceased to function mainly as a court to "find" the law, and began to operate in a more consciously creative way by "making" law.[9] This transformation of Parliament served to introduce the adversary method, or its echoes, into parliamentary politics and with that into the very matrix of British political procedure, as will be shown in more detail in Chapter 16.

While law and legal procedures were being developed by judges in England, they were being deliberately engineered by French Kings for their own purposes. In France, judges either served as royal instruments, or they were ineffective. Legal change was always geared to the substantive aims of the centralizing King, just as was Napoleon's great codification later. All these factors combined to give judges and lawyers on the Continent a role quite different from that of their English colleagues. It led them also to take a different attitude toward their work and their clients: It made them less committed to their clients' procedural rights. Perhaps partly as a side effect of the adversary procedure, one can still get the impression that trial lawyers in English-speaking countries habitually make exaggerated statements of their stand, but do so without necessarily being strongly committed to the position they take in court. The exaggeration and the relative lack of commitment are known to and accepted by both the lawyers themselves and everyone else involved. Lawyers in Roman-law courts are more likely to seem to be committed to their clients' cases. This difference has ramifications far beyond the courts of law, for one thing because of the high proportion of legally trained persons in the politics of each of the six countries with which we

[8] Quoted in *ibid.*, p. 9.
[9] See Charles Howard McIlwain, *The High Court of Parliament and Its Supremacy*, 1910.

are concerned at present (Sweden and Switzerland are separately discussed later in this chapter).

The political effects of the adversary method of pleading are perhaps too indirect to be demonstrable. Nevertheless, some of these may be suggested by the following illustration: In the keynote speech at the Democratic National Convention in 1956, the keynoter—Tennessee's Governor Clement—deliberately cast himself in the role of a prosecuting attorney, bringing a "ten-point indictment" against the incumbent Republican administration. The keynoter knew, of course, that he was overstating things vastly. His audience knew it, too. The accused Republicans knew it as well. And everybody loved the whole show. Foreign observers from beyond the English-speaking world were completely misled by the whole performance. They thought that the keynoter and his loyal party audience believed in, and were committed to, every word that was said. They are misled in this way every four years, during each American presidential election campaign. Sometimes they are similarly misled during British general election campaigns. The latter are shorter, it is true, and the British are supposed to be masters of the art of understatement. Nevertheless, party politicians tend to drive each other into extreme adversary positions, if not with regard to their programs then with regard to their views of each other. But since they are used to doing this in the House of Commons every day it is in session, only to mingle cheerfully and on good terms upon leaving the chamber, this neither involves the kind of commitment nor results in the kind of bitterness that similar debates always produce on the Continent.

Continental parliamentarians and other politicians, by contrast, generally take the stand they believe to be "true," rather than to dilute their vision of the truth to the point where they can take a stand designed to win a maximum of electoral advantage. Because they are more committed to their public statements than their English-speaking colleagues normally are, they tend to be less willing to compromise. Moreover, their public believes that they are so committed and would desert a political leader whom it suspected of behaving like a legal counsel. One illustration for this may be taken from an area lying somewhat outside politics proper: school debates. Continental Europeans usually express sheer horror at this common practice of American schools and colleges, especially upon being told that the contestants in a debating tournament may not know until just before its beginning whether they are to present the affirmative or the negative side. "But that is immoral," the Europeans say; "how can you take a position in which you do not believe—and in public at that?" They are, once again, more interested in the emergence of the truth out of this kind of dialectic, than in a decisive settlement of the issue under debate.

Use of the adversary method in the English-speaking systems thus contributes to lowering any conviction that only one side to an argument is in possession of all the truth. One must not assume, however, that the effect is achieved because lawyers, politicians, and the public are aware of their use of this method of conducting litigation and debate. On the contrary, it is largely because of their lack of any such awareness, which in turn is related to the antiquity of the procedure, that it produces these subtle results. For example, because lawyers and parliamentarians have been conducting their business according to its rules since time immemorial, men who are strongly opposed to each other in public debates find it easy to be on very friendly terms with one another in their private lives. The useful and ancient legal fiction that makes lawyers officers of the court in Britain and America undoubtedly contributes to toning down the private effects of public antagonisms, once more through its transference from the courts to parliamenatry politics. Such spectacles as the intimacy between the Speaker of the United States House of Representatives and the House Minority Leader, who becomes Speaker when his party is in control, have no parallels in the major Continental countries. The point here—and we will take it up again in dealing with consensus in Chapter 22—is that this is not only due to the relative mildness of political disagreements in the English-speaking countries, but that this relative mildness itself would not be as noticeable as it is without the support it receives from the political ramifications of the adversary method.

The British and American procedure encourages opposing sides to arrive at decisions that compromise their conflicts about material interests. Its absence on the Continent lets compromise appear as immoral. Other factors contributing to legalism and ideologism in Germany, France, and Italy lead politicians there to take stands that are more antagonistic to begin with, thereby making initially more difficult the task of finding compromises. Their parliamentary procedures, as we will see in the next chapter, are not as well designed as those of Great Britain, the United States, and Canada to help in the accomplishment of this task.

Legalism on the Continent

The style of all three major Continental systems is more legalistic than that of the English-speaking ones, but there are variations among them on this score. Each of these countries has a recently engineered constitution. Of these, that of the Fourth Republic presented the least break with past constitutional tradition, to the extent that scholars have been speaking of the "easy return from the Fourth to the Third Republic." Still, antiquity did not hallow that constitution to the same degree that it did those of the English-speaking countries, and proposals for its reform were therefore made with greater hope of success. Parliament by itself could amend it, so that constitutional controversies were more likely to be *about* the constitution than *within* the constitution, as in the United States. But France also has her tradition of "progress on the barricades" —reform through the use of violence—which has resulted in a generally lower respect for any kind of law, whether fundamental or circumstantial, than in Germany, for example. Finally, the constitution of the Fourth Republic did not provide for a supreme court with power of judicial review, as both the German and Italian constitutions do. It is probable that if such a court had been established in France, it would not have been as effective as the German one or its even more effective model in the United States. The French have not been legalistic to the extent that they observed the very letter of their constitution. If they had, so many practices of the Third Republic, which the constitution of the Fourth was designed to abolish or reform, could not have reappeared as they did. The same failure to observe the letter of the constitution has occurred in postwar Italy, which did not even establish for seven years the Supreme Court for which its republican constitution called. In Italy, as in France, a tradition of violence that is stronger than the German one, and related old habits of corruption, have also contributed to a lackadaisical attitude toward circumstantial law—in the field of taxation, for example.

Legalism is stronger in West Germany, for several reasons: First, it is the only federal system among these three. Second, it has less of a tradition of violence associated with democratic progress. Third, its Basic Law was explicitly intended as a provisional constitution. Fourth, its reaction to lawlessness had been stronger because of the experience of Nazi totalitarianism and, at present, Soviet totalitarianism in Communist East Germany. And finally, its present constitutional arrangements appear to have been very successful; people therefore associate their well-being with observance of fundamental and circumstantial legal provisions—since "nothing succeeds like success."

Legalism Under English Law

British politics is less legalistic than Canadian or American primarily because of the absence of a written constitution. Canada and the United States both have such documents and both are federal systems, yet there are differences in the degree of legalism in the two North American countries. To begin with, the United States federal system is more complicated than the Canadian, because there are more member units and because more functions were assigned to them constitutionally than to the Canadian provinces. Moreover, the United States fought a Civil War on a federal issue. Also, its Constitution, because of the break with Great Britain, is more comprehensive than the British North America Act. However, the retention of the common law obviated any need for the wholesale construction of circumstantial law and thereby worked against legalism at this level. At the fundamental level, nevertheless, there is more legalism in the United States than in Canada.

In one part of Canada, however, circumstantial legalism is more strongly developed than anywhere else in the English-speaking world— because it is not really a part of the English-speaking world. French-speaking Quebec was permitted soon after the British conquest to retain French civil law, and this grant was subsequently confirmed by successive constitutional documents. Under the British North America Act of 1867, only criminal law was to be uniform throughout the Dominion. Quebec's civil code was reformed in the 1840's, in order to bring it up to date with the reforms effected in France by the Code Napoleon. Civil courts in the province are still governed by this descendant of the Roman law. This gives Quebec an almost unique position in the British Commonwealth—almost, but not quite, because Scotland still has Roman law, and Dutch Roman law is in effect in parts of the Union of South Africa, whose problems present many parallels with those of Canada. In Scotland, legal procedure has been sufficiently assimilated to the common law to make the effects of this peculiarity negligible. This is not true of Quebec, where, for example, the more exalted role the Roman law assigns to the state and to the concept of sovereignty has interfered with giving civil rights the same protection they receive in the other Canadian provinces. This has led to demands that a bill of rights be added to the British North America Act. Under Quebec law, too, the legal status of women is inferior to that of men. But these substantive differences are not as important, for the purposes of our study, as the contribution made by the Roman law to legalism and ideologism in politics.

Ever since the French-Canadians were given the beginnings of self-government by the Constitutional Act of 1791, their lawyers have played a very prominent role in Quebec politics. These lawyers are trained in the Roman law, although nowadays they must, of course, be equally competent in English law. But the basis of their legal education shares the same characteristics that mark the making of Continental jurists. And legal pedagogy has had a similar influence on the teaching of the social sciences as on the Continent. The Church-controlled educational system has spread conceptions of legal and other knowledge that are more like those prevailing in the Continental countries than they are like the ones of the English-speaking peoples. One incidental reason for this is the canon law, which governs the Roman Catholic Church and is entirely based on the Roman law. As a result of all this, provincial politics in Quebec is both more legalistic and more ideological than in neighboring Ontario and the other provinces. The fact that it is not as legalistic as in France itself must be ascribed to the combined influence of the English environment and British parliamentary procedures. The latter have been used in Quebec ever since their first legislature met, because New France did not use any parliamentary procedures—even Old France before the British conquest had none in use.

Switzerland and Sweden

These two countries have so far been left out of the discussion, because neither of them has been influenced by Roman law as profoundly as their Continental neighbors. According to the Swiss constitution, the organization and procedure of the courts continued to be reserved to the cantons, in many of which the roots of present judicial practices go as far back as in England. While Swiss jurisprudence has undoubtedly learned much from its neighbor nations, with their legal systems based on Roman law, there is no association of legal codification with political progress in Switzerland. A federal civil code was put into effect only in 1912. The strength of legalism about fundamentals, which nevertheless exists in the country, has already been explained in terms of the provisions for constitutional initiative and referendum. Just how fundamental are such debates, which seem to be about the constitution, we will be able to judge in the course of discussing the content of the "true" constitution, in Chapter 23.

In Sweden, this question is not so important, since there is as little legalism about fundamentals in Sweden as in Great Britain, and for very similar reasons. On the other hand, according to some students of Swedish politics, legalism at the level of circumstantials is very strong. This is asserted, for example, by Dankwart A. Rustow, who concludes his excellent study of Swedish politics, *The Politics of Compromise,* with the ancient motto *"Land skall med lag byggas"*—"Country shall be built with law." [10] In our terms, the fine regard for legal and administrative rules that marks Swedish politics must be described as lawfulness rather than legalism. The law is not invoked for its own sake—for example, in order to maintain its internal consistency. This kind of attitude does not produce artificial issues. Few partisan issues are referred to the courts for resolution. And there is no hesitancy to experiment with new institutions without prior legislation. The evolution of Swedish law, which shows many parallels with that of English law, suggests the explanation for this lack of legalism. Like the common law, Swedish law has its roots in the Middle Ages. No wholesale codification along French lines has ever occurred, although Swedish medieval law was recompiled and brought up to date in 1734, during the so-called Age of Freedom, that is, under the auspices of a Riksdag that had asserted itself against royal absolutism. Moreover, even this reform did not affect procedure and was the fruit of more than a century of preparatory work, so that comprehensive legal engineering never occurred in Sweden any more than comprehensive constitutional engineering, and the most important single reform of the law was not handed down from above by a sovereign lawmaker, as in France, Germany, and Italy.

Guidelines for Constitution-Makers—II

Most of the explanations of legalism that we have found have been historical; they have come from given, determined factors. This should offer anything but comfort to optimists about the feasibility of constitutional engineering. After all, the age of a constitution is not normally subject to planned control, and whether a country has a Roman or an English legal system is only rarely a matter of deliberate choice. In fact, the deliberate transplanting of the common law without lawyers who have been brought up under it seems impossible: The common law is so complex and unsystematic that any such effort would be bound to fail. Former British colonies—among them the United States, Canada,

[10] P. 237.

and India—are simply fortunate that it was brought to them by Englishmen themselves.

The Roman law codes, on the other hand, can boast that systematic symmetry is their greatest virtue, which is the reason why they have been adopted by many political systems in need of legal reform, in Russia, South America, the Middle and Far East. Does this mean that the political style of these systems is therefore bound to be legalistic, and their politics doomed to failure? Certainly not. The differences in this respect among the three major Continental countries, each of which has codified Roman law, suggest that other factors also play a role, among them those connected with violent or ideological style. One must not condemn or underestimate the value of the Roman law or of its re-codification a century and a half ago—this was a great accomplishment, and its anniversary was justly celebrated in Europe and America only a few years ago.[11] For those in quick need of a complete legal system, some version of the Roman law is probably still the best solution. Nevertheless, by way of advice to the makers or reformers of political systems, one should still offer these *caveats:*

If possible, avoid making a complete break with the legal and constitutional traditions of the system.

Confine engineering, at the levels of both fundamentals and circumstantials, to the minimum compatible with the goals the reform is designed to serve.

Incorporate a maximum of prevailing legal and constitutional provisions into a newly constructed political system.

Encourage the negotiation of disputes outside the courts.

Discourage the belief that the courts are completely apart from the political process and that they can provide better, "juster" resolutions to public issues than the political process.

Above all, do not try to do too much too quickly. There is no reason for producing all at once a comprehensive legal system, which will then stand for all time to come. By leaving the task of developing the law to those who are most concerned with its operation—in various areas, functions, and periods of time—a nation is much more likely to achieve a system of law that will be stable, adaptable, efficient, and effective.

[11] See Bernard Schwartz, ed., *The Code Napoleon and the Common-Law World,* 1956.

Often it will be very difficult to follow these guidelines. All prevailing law may be so firmly identified with a hated regime that has just been overthrown, and the revolution itself may have been driven on by the ideological promise of radically changing everything, that no amount of cautious advice could slow down this impetus. When that occurs, the style of the new political system will probably be strongly ideological and legalistic. But this is no cause for despair, either. It is at such junctures in history that the inventive genius of constitutional architects can become most active and most beneficial. It must take style into account as part of the problems the new system is confronting, and it must build as best it can with this material.

One of the first things that will be needed in a situation such as has just been described is a set of procedures according to which deliberation about the new constitution is to be carried on. Parliamentary procedure has often been designed with success and is more susceptible to the influence of conscious planning than political style. It is for this reason that we turn next to procedure.

PART IV

Institutions and Procedures

CHAPTER 16

Deliberation

The peculiarities of the style of a political system are more often than not the product of historical accident. At least they have to be taken as such by the constitution-maker, who cannot undo the past, whatever else he may be able to do. But the procedures or rules according to which political deliberation is carried on are not predetermined to the same extent. Some such rules of debate are always used in any discussion, although the debaters may not be aware of them. The builders or reformers of political systems often retain procedures of long standing. Sometimes they transplant them from elsewhere. The constitution-makers themselves, in every case, need rules for their own deliberations. When they become aware of this constitutional problem, the function of procedure is highlighted with a brilliance otherwise rare. This happened in the course of the French Revolution, as we will see shortly.

Deliberative procedures are, of course, used in all phases of the policy flow. Different organs of politics employ different types of procedure, as was pointed out in the critique of the theory of the separation of powers, in Chapter 1. In the United States, the House of Representatives, the Senate, the President and his Cabinet, and the Supreme Court all have firmly established rules, according to which they deliberate, and which are set forth in various manuals composed for that purpose. Each uses a different set of rules, presumably because each makes its own distinctive type of decisions. The procedures of various political institutions in the same system, nevertheless, normally have much in common. We saw one illustration of this in the adversary method of the common law, which, according to our suggestion, has influenced parliamentary and partisan politics and even activities as nonpolitical or pre-political as school debates.

These common characteristics of specialized procedures in a single political system enable us to concentrate on parliamentary procedure in this chapter. In most countries, the procedures of parliamentary debate are the model for all other deliberative rules. But even where this is not true, parliamentary procedure provides the clearest example of, or the best case study in, methods of deliberation.

In turning now to procedure, we will be advancing one step in our study of the flow of policy. Political style colored this flow through three successive phases: the recognition of problems, the statement of issues, and the deliberation about them. Procedure shapes the political process during the statement of issues, during their deliberation, and during their resolution. We want to know what kinds of procedure are in use in our systems, how these procedures came into use, and what contributions they have made to success or failure. Finally, we will want to arrive at a judgment about the relative merits of different types of parliamentary procedure.

"Legislative Tactics"

The classic attempt to transplant a set of parliamentary rules occurred during the French Revolution. The revolutionaries had had little experience with parliamentary procedure, because the Estates General had not met for several generations and there had been very little self-government in France. When the Estates General was finally convoked, in 1789, this lack of experience began to be evident immediately. Because of this, Mirabeau, as the leading figure in the Constituent Assembly, wrote to Jeremy Bentham, the English Utilitarian philosopher, asking his advice on parliamentary rules. Bentham responded with an essay, later published under the title "Tactics of Legislative Assemblies." His proposals were not accepted immediately, but later French parliaments did adopt rules of procedure based on Bentham's recommendations. The fact that these rules subsequently served as the model for parliamentary procedure in other Continental countries, and spread from there to other parts of the world and to international assemblies, gives this case of procedural engineering unusual importance.

Bentham's diagnosis of the troubles of the Constituent Assembly was this: The two functions of voting and debating were combined; deputies rose in alphabetical order, each casting his vote and explaining it at the same time. Bentham criticized this as a bad arrangement. He thought that it was the function of the Assembly to deliberate, that is, to weigh alternative courses of action, to bring knowledge to bear on the issue at hand, and to do so in a manner that would give all participants fairly equal access to the knowledge needed for arriving at a rational resolution of the issue. Bentham believed that this sequence took place in British parliamentary debates and, for his time, this belief was on the whole correct. In the House of Commons, alternatives were stated first, then deliberated upon, and finally resolved by means of a vote. In view of this, Bentham thought that debate should be characterized by speed, wit, originality, argument without violence, and the emergence of new ideas in a dialectical fashion—these have in fact been the hallmarks of the House of Commons. Bentham systematized the rules of Commons in these terms; but despite his good intentions, the Continental parliaments that adopted them have consistently failed to emulate their model at Westminster. How can this be explained?

Deliberation and Legislation

The institutionalist school of comparative government would answer this question by saying that the French and other Continental parliaments failed to copy accurately and completely. According to this view, it would have been better if they had done as the Canadian and other British Colonial parliaments overseas did at their inception: take over as a whole the Standing Orders of the House of Commons. Since Canada first did this, her House of Commons has adapted these rules to certain peculiarly Canadian needs. Two large compendiums of these Canadian rules have been published. Nevertheless, even today, when a procedural dispute arises at Ottawa, such as the one about the role of the Speaker in 1956, the authority of the thick volume by Erskine May is often invoked. (Erskine May compiled a manual on the rules of the British House of Commons; heavy with precedents, it has gone through more than a dozen editions.)

Critics of the German Bundestag have also implied that better results could be obtained by copying as accurately as possible from the House of Commons. The rules of the Bundestag, some of which are contained in the Basic Law, while the main body is set forth in a separate set of 132 paragraphs, show several such efforts. For example, one rule limits the length of speeches, and another requires that speeches be delivered extemporaneously. Among more recent innovations, microphones are placed on the floor of the chamber, in order to speed up question periods. And the presiding officer of the Bundestag has been dressed up in white tie and tails, in order to endow his office with prestige similar to that of the Speaker at Westminster, who wears buckled shoes, gaiters, and a wig.

Some institutionalists have even argued that the superiority of the British House of Commons owes a great deal to the physical arrangements of its meeting place. It is small, without enough benches to accommodate all members. Members have neither permanently assigned seats nor desks. Government and Opposition parties face each other across the center aisle of the rectangular chamber, and this naturally pits them against each other. The French chamber, by contrast, is large, constructed like an amphitheater; deputies do have permanent seats with desks (which they can bang loudly during parliamentary riots); and speeches are usually made from an elevated rostrum. The other Continental parliaments resemble the French.

The determinist school would, of course, deny that any kind of copying—no matter how complete or accurate—would significantly affect the performance of a parliament or of the political system as a whole. The functional approach has criticized Bentham and his followers for overlooking factors like party struggle and government leadership in the British and other parliaments.[1] The method used in this book leads us to ask: What types of decisions do the various parliaments have to make? Which procedures are best suited to deal with these types of decisions? The answers suggest the conclusion that Continental parliaments—which do not make the same kinds of decisions—copied British procedure too closely to succeed.

Bentham and procedural engineers on the Continent, as in America, assumed that the main function of the British and any other parliament was legislation, that is, lawmaking. The title of Bentham's essay clearly indicates this. Lawmaking, they believed, amounted to an expression of the will of the electorate that is represented in parliament. In order to arrive at this will, prior deliberation is required. As a historical matter of fact, however, lawmaking was not a function of the English Parliament until the sixteenth century. Before that time, a "parley"—a talk— was carried on in Parliament between the King and representatives of the "Lords Spiritual and Temporal, and Commons," about money to be granted to the Crown to carry on the government, about petitions presented by members, and about conflicts between subjects of the Monarch. For a long time, this last-mentioned "judicial" function continued to be a very important one. It meant that those parts of Parliament that rendered judgments had to be able to come to decisions quickly, in order

[1] See Carl J. Friedrich, *Constitutional Government and Democracy*, 1950, pp. 306 ff.

to restore the quarreling subjects to a condition of "domestic tranquility." The quick resolution of such conflicts, whose general pattern did not differ very much from one case to the next, could best be achieved by means of stable and publicly known rules. These rules were provided by the common law. Their stability explains why parliamentarians and judges believed themselves to be "finding" existing law and applying it to new cases, rather than "making" new law.

Awareness of the possibility of creating new law grew only gradually in the sixteenth century. This awareness never reached the proportions in England it took on in Continental countries. There, not only law but whole constitutional systems repeatedly had to be brought into being as explicit acts of will. This was never the case in Great Britain because of the nearly unbroken continuity of the Crown. The Crown—and, later, Cabinets acting on behalf of the Crown—always performed the function of "carrying on the government," of proposing policy—that is, solutions to problems—and of integrating policies about all the problems confronting the realm. Students of the British constitution have sometimes let themselves be misled into assuming that Parliament created Cabinets, when actually there would always have been a Cabinet, even though Parliament might not have been able to agree on one—as French Parliaments often have been unable to agree. In point of fact, Parliament could confine its main activity to deliberation on policies proposed by the Crown-Cabinet. Parliament had neither to initiate nor to integrate. It did not have to build anew. It did not have to express a will, since the Cabinet did that; nor did it have to create Cabinets. All it had to do was to consent to, or dissent from, the will—that is, the resolution of issues—the Cabinet presented to it. This has been and still is the emphasis in the types of decisions the British Parliament makes. The rules, according to which these decisions are arrived at, fit functions that are primarily deliberative: they involve discussions of issues whose resolution is expressed by another organ in the political process, the Cabinet.

To transplant British procedure to the French and other Continental parliaments was a mistake, because these organs performed deliberative functions only secondarily. Primarily, Continental parliaments had to resolve issues themselves, first by creating a Cabinet that would propose policy and integrate policies; and then by resolving later issues between themselves and their Cabinets. In the act of creating a coalition Cabinet, Continental parliaments simultaneously also resolve the dominant current issues. Then, having done this, they deliberate upon the expressed will of the Cabinet created by themselves. For the French

Parliament, these resolving, will-creating, "voluntarist" decisions are more important than the deliberative ones; for the British Parliament, the order of importance is reversed.

The difference is one of emphasis. All parliaments engage in both deliberation and resolution. So do all individuals. We have to beware of repeating the mistake made by adherents of the most simple version of the separation of powers, and should continue to look on politics as the *flow* of policy. Different types of decisions are continuously being made in the course of this flow. Each "little" decision is a microscopic replica of the big decisions. For example, many little decisions are made in the course of deliberation, involving recognition of the problem, i.e., the need for deliberation, formulation of the issue, "deliberation about deliberation," resolution, and solution of the problem. In the course that a problem follows, from its initial recognition to its final solution, the emphasis in the type of decisions made about it constantly changes. Different procedures are suited for each emphasis, and this must be taken into account in attempts to copy procedures that have been useful in any particular context.

Resolution and Will

In transplanting British procedure to the Continent, an error was made that readers may duplicate by conducting a little experiment. Take a group of a dozen or so people and give them the opportunity to develop practice in deliberating critically about the policies of an independent-minded, strong-willed individual, who sits at the head of the table. Then remove this leader, and let the same group use the same procedures in trying to select a steering committee and, at the same time, to criticize the policies advanced by this subgroup. Chances are that the result will be confusion. But what makes the French case even worse is the compounding of copying that was too accurate to suit the different type of decisions, with copying that was negligently slovenly on one detail of unsuspected importance.

English procedure contains one device in particular that makes for great resoluteness and decisiveness and helps to structure the debate efficiently. This is the practice, followed in all debates, of stating the issue at the outset in such a way that members of Parliament can take only one of two positions, either for the proposed resolution or against it. This practice probably derives from the early function of Parliament as a court. In conflicts that come up for adjudication, it is often more important to make a decision, to settle the case and get what lawyers call *res judicata,* than to get an absolutely just decision. Settlement of the issue removes the disturbance and enables the suing subjects to return to a condition of peace. The practice of the two-alternative statement of issues, in a way facilitating settlement with dispatch, seems to be related to the adversary method of pleading under the common law. The adversary method reduces litigation at the outset, because it makes the courts refuse to consider any disputed facts but those brought out by the adversaries themselves. By discouraging the judge from adding a third position, which might be closer to absolute justice, to the two opposing positions taken by the contending parties, it removes delays in reaching the verdict. The two-way statement of issues in the House of Commons serves the same purpose. Indeed, because of the early judicial role of Parliament, this practice may be considered a direct procedural descendant of the adversary method itself.

This transference of the adversary method of parliamentary procedure is reflected in a number of ways. Members of Parliament tend to speak as advocates to a House—and beyond it, to the electorate—that in some respects conducts itself like a jury. The House of Commons is presided over by its Speaker, who behaves very much like the judge in a common-law court. He is the umpire. He upholds the rules of the House. He is surrounded by great pomp and circumstance. While the House is in session, members who leave or enter the chamber bow to his thronelike chair. But, unlike the presiding officers of Continental parliaments, he does not have to state what is at issue in the debate. He has much greater authority than the presidents of the National Assembly or the Bundestag. In part this undoubtedly stems from the greater antiquity of his office. But in part it is due to his known lack of partisanship: Normally, the Speaker, although the member of one of the major parties, is not opposed for reëlection. He is committed more to upholding the rules of the House of Commons than to the content of any of its debates.

Another instance of the decisiveness of the two-alternative statement of issues is provided by the annual debates on appropriations for various departments of the government. In these debates, the Opposition will move to reduce appropriations for, say, the Royal Air Force, by £100. It neither wants to bring about such a nominal reduction nor believes that this would make the slightest difference for defense policy. Further, there is no expectation that the motion will pass, for the Opposition knows that the appropriations proposed by the cabinet are invariably supported by the Cabinet's majority in the House, without which it would not be in office. Nevertheless, the practice of moving this infinitesimal reduction in an item of billions of pounds helps to structure the debate, to focus it and bring it to a point, to deliberate upon the resolution decided upon by the Cabinet, and to lead the debate to its conclusion—which invariably upholds the original proposal. Another case in point is the daily question period in the House of Commons, when members of the Cabinet reply in rapid succession to specific, concrete questions posed by Members of Parliament. The Speaker admits only bona-fide questions—a practice that structures the debate much more efficiently than would be the case if members of the Opposition were allowed to make long statements of their principled rejection of a policy pursued by the Cabinet.

These procedures making for decisiveness are no longer really required by the British Parliament, since it now exercises a predominantly deliberative function. Indeed, quite possibly parliamentary decisiveness may have become superfluous in Britain, precisely because it has always been there. This has not been true of the parliaments of the major Continental systems. They need decisiveness, not only because they have not had it, but also because their primary function is that of resolution. Accordingly, the procedural engineers of the nineteenth century would have done well to copy this particular device from their model at Westminster. Their failure to do so is shown by the Continental practice of debating some general question—whether "foreign policy," "labor unrest," or "Coca-Cola"—for several days, without first stating the issue. At the end of the debate, the issue may still not be formulated, or it may be formulated, as is often the practice, by the presiding officer rather than by a parliamentary party leader who is a participant in the debate. Finally, there may or may not be a vote meant to express the will of the assembly. Thus the debates tend to be poorly structured and inconclusive, despite the fact that the resolving function of Continental parliaments calls for a great deal more decisiveness than the deliberative function of the Mother of Parliaments.

The consequences of this negligence in procedural copying have been particularly unfortunate, because neither Cabinets nor any other organ in the Continental systems provide the continuity in resolving issues that the British Crown-Cabinet always gives. On the Continent, parliaments have a twofold task: they must deliberate upon policies, and they must also endeavor to create a resolving organ—usually the Cabinet—out of their own midst. The House of Commons does not have to do this. Nor does the American Congress, because the central resolving organ in the United States, the Presidency, is maintained independently, regardless of anything the Congress does or fails to do.

Law and Sovereignty

Bentham wrote a panegyric on the rules of the House of Commons:

> In this bye-corner, an observing eye may trace the original seed-plot of English liberty: it is in this hitherto neglected spot that the seeds of that invaluable production have germinated and grown up to their present maturity, scarce noticed by the husbandman, and unsuspected by the destroyer.

Coming from the mechanistically inclined Bentham, this metaphor sounds strangely organic, especially in view of his opposition to the common law and the close connection between it and the procedures of Parliament. He was right—but for the wrong reasons, since the making of laws was not the most important business of the House of Commons. This is illustrated by the prevailing conceptions of law and lawmaking. Note the ancient preamble to bills passed by the British Parliament: "Be it therefore *enacted* and *declared* by the Queen's most Excellent Majesty, by and with the *Advice* and *Consent* of the Lords Spiritual and Temporal, and Commons. . . ." The persistence of the old phrase suggests that the House is today still thought of as merely giving its advice and consent to what the Crown-Cabinet has resolved to enact. This is a much easier thing for a large group of men to do than to create a collective will of its own. Six hundred members of Parliament can advise and consent, that is, "see and think with" the Crown and what it intends to do. But it must remain doubtful whether two or more human beings can ever "will" together, except as a mob. The paradox of this situation lies in the fact that the House of Commons could exercise a will of wider scope and greater effect than its Continental counterparts. It is not restricted, as they are, by a written constitution; by a mere transitory majority of one vote, it could pass laws of the most fundamental nature. But it does not do this, partly perhaps because it has not usually been as aware as Continental parliaments of its capacity to "new-model" the constitution. This lack of awareness, in turn, is undoubtedly connected with the fact that Britain has never had to construct or reconstruct its constitutional system as a whole, as Continental countries and, on one occasion, the United States, have had to do. One result is that the British conception of law, including circumstantial law, is much less voluntarist than the Continental conception, even today. The notion still persists to some extent that laws are not really made, but somehow found in the laws of nature and the fundamental ancient laws of the Realm, or that these preëxisting laws are merely elaborated and brought up to date by Parliament. Hence bills passed by Parliament are not entitled "Laws," but "Acts," and they are "enacted and declared." The United States has this same tradition of natural and fundamental law, strengthened by the role of the Supreme Court. But the American conception of law is more voluntarist than the British, because of the engineered background of the Constitution of the United States. Englishmen are not as likely as Americans to say, "There ought to be a law. . . ."

On the Continent of Europe, by contrast, the conception of law is almost wholly voluntarist. Law is looked upon as the product of will—the will of the sovereign. This concept of the law-willing, law-making sovereign was originally derived from the Roman law and its notion of imperial *potestas*. It was first elaborated by Jean Bodin in the sixteenth century in order to buttress the position of the French King. The more powerful character of kingship under the Roman law was one of the differences noted by early English students of comparative government, like Fortescue and Smith. They denied that the phrase of the Roman law, *quod principi placuit, legis vigorem habet* ("what pleases the prince has the force of law"), was applicable under English law. Again, Sir Edward Coke, in his struggle against the Roman-law aspirations of James I, said that the common law "knows no such fellow as the sovereign." Thereafter, the notion that law is the product of the sovereign's will was never able to become established in the English-speaking countries, despite many attempts to that effect—one of them by Bentham's follower, John Austin. But this is the Continental concept of law. Jean Jacques Rousseau put this very clearly in his *Social Contract:* "Here too force and will are distinguished, will under the name of legislative power and force under that of executive power." This, incidentally, was his reason for denying the feasibility of lawmaking by representatives: "Will does not admit of representation: it is either the same, or other; there is no intermediate possibility." Rousseau's denial of the possibility of legislative representation was ignored by his followers in the French Revolution and thereafter. But his voluntarist conception of law, and his legislative conception of sovereignty were taken over, and they can still help us to understand differences between the types of decisions made by Continental and British parliaments.

The Declaration of the Rights of Man and the Citizen, proclaimed by the French Revolution, stated:

> The nation is essentially the source of all sovereignty; nor shall any body of men or any individual exercise authority which is not expressly derived from it.

The law is an expression of the common will. All citizens have the right to concur, either personally or by the representation, in its formation.

The Constitutions of the Fourth and Fifth Republics incorporated the Declaration of the French Revolution. In Germany, a similar facet of the voluntarist notion of legislation is reflected in an article of the Basic Law, according to which the political parties participate in the "formation of the political will [*politische Willensbildung*] of the people."

The theoretical influence of the Roman law and of Rousseau have thus contributed to assigning a will-forming function to Continental parliaments. Historical circumstances contributed as well. At the inception of each revolution in France, the established will-forming, issue-resolving, and policy-integrating organ was abolished. Something similar happened in the founding of other Continental democracies, thus leaving to parliament, in addition to its deliberative job, the task previously performed by the monarch. At the beginning of modern parliamentarism in these countries, the problem of devising procedures was, therefore, much more difficult than at any time in Great Britain. In the first place, parliamentary procedures had to be devised, whereas in England there was at worst a need for revising them. Secondly, they had to be devised to serve the purpose, not only of deliberating upon policies proposed by a continuous governing organ, but also of bringing such an organ into being.

Deliberation versus *Registration*

Parliaments whose functions are primarily voluntarist reflect this emphasis in both the form and content of their debates. It is particularly noticeable in the declaratory quality of their oratory. As an illustration of this, we may take debates in an international parliament like the United Nations. Especially in the General Assembly, but to some extent also in the Security Council, speakers are obviously not trying to deliberate or to persuade one another. They are acting as pure delegates without real discretion, there to register the wills of their governments. In some of the debates during the Hungarian crisis of 1956, voting preceded the explanation of votes when an urgent tally of governmental wills was needed. Hardly anyone was seriously trying to persuade other states to change their minds. The main effort was rather directed toward getting the several sovereign states to register their wills, so that a majority will might be discovered.

Most speeches in the French, German, and Italian parliaments are also delivered without the intention of persuading anyone who is not already convinced of the rightness of their content. This could also be said of the less oratorical debates of the House of Commons, since the Cabinet's victory is foreordained. But there is an important difference: Because the British cabinet is capable of carrying on the government with the support of its disciplined majority, there is no need for parliamentarians to compromise their stands beyond the point at which the two great opposing camps fight out the issues. Since Continental parliaments have the additional function of reconciling several highly differentiated programs, the need for persuasion and compromise among Continental parliamentarians is greater. But it is rarely met. Again, in the House of Commons, the relatively lower degree of commitment by the debaters to what they say—related to the adversary method—makes declarative speeches there less divisive than in Paris, Berlin and Bonn, or Rome. Moreover, British parliamentary debate could be considered a dialectical form of deliberation, because it includes the politically interested public over the longer run of time, even if not with regard to the immediate issues under discussion in the House of Commons.

The practice of delivering speeches from a rostrum further encourages declaratory, nondeliberative, and nonpersuasive speechmaking. The House of Commons does not provide its members with this kind of elevated platform from which to harangue or lecture their colleagues. Another factor contributes to the more formal and lecture-like oratory of Continental parliaments: Their members are more often aware than British parliamentarians of having to make decisions of really fundamental importance. Because of the nonvoluntarist conception of its functions, the House of Commons tends to think of itself as making circumstantial decisions, on policies proposed by the Cabinet, in terms of older standards, which are not of the making of the present House or any recent predecessor. The knowledge required for making decisions or engaging in deliberation of this type is knowledge about precedents —knowledge, that is, in which practitioners of the common law excel. It is a comparatively conservative kind of knowledge. In France, on the other hand, where a new constitution or other laws of fundamental nature have to be brought into being more often, new standards have to be created more frequently and old traditions may more safely be disregarded. The kind of knowledge needed for making this type of decision is of the rationalist Enlightenment variety, in which Roman-law jurists and their colleagues of related academic disciplines excel. These differences are also reflected in, and are reflections of, the professional composition of the different parliaments, a topic to which we will return in Chapter 18.

Another illustration of the French notion that Parliament serves the purpose of registering the people's will is found in the practice of voting by proxy. In the Fourth Republic's National Assembly, as in its Third Republic predecessor, the Chamber of Deputies, the votes of deputies were frequently cast in a package of little white or blue cards by the secretaries of the parliamentary party delegations. This means that the great majority of deputies was often not present in the chamber and neither participated in, nor listened to, the "discussion" going on there. How they would vote on various issues could be predicted by almost anyone. When a deputy's proxy vote was cast for him, he was letting his party secretary in the National Assembly register the will of the constituents represented by the deputy.

In the West German Bundestag, voting by proxy is not permitted. On the contrary, its deputies are subject to rules requiring their attendance at all sessions unless excused by the presiding officer—much as in some schools. Their leanings toward legalism have led many German students of politics, and some practitioners, to point out that party discipline contravenes a provision in their Basic Law making parliamentary deputies representatives of the entire nation, not bound by instructions, but subject only to their conscience. Despite these legalistic compunctions, party discipline has been enforced with much more success in the Bundestag than in the National Assembly. It is needed especially in primarily nondeliberative parliaments in order to weed out alternatives and push issues along their way toward resolution.

The compulsory attendance of deputies has so far not sufficed to give German parliamentary debates a more deliberative cast than French debates or earlier German ones. This should come as a surprise in one respect, at least, because the German Cabinet is nowadays in a position quite similar to that of the British Cabinet. The provisions of Article 67, for the constructive vote of no confidence, give it virtually guaranteed tenure for the duration of the four-year term of the Bundestag. The West German Chancellor and his Cabinet can therefore take care independently of the function of resolving issues and integrating policies. They do in fact initiate most policies, although not to the same degree as the British Cabinet, which has virtually excluded initiative on the part of private members of Parliament. German Cabinets are also more unified than French Cabinets under the Fourth Republic, and for constitutional reasons. The Basic Law provides that the Chancellor set the general guidelines of policy. For these reasons, it seems entirely conceivable that after the election of the Chancellor, the Bundestag should concentrate on deliberation of policies proposed by him and his Cabinet. And a trend in that direction seems in fact to be developing, although the debates of the full house itself do not convey this impression. Their tone seems still as declarative as ever, and efforts such as the placing of microphones and the limit on the duration of speeches have not brought much improvement. However, because of the Chancellor's security of tenure, this failure of the Bundestag to engage in deliberation in its full meetings has not been as harmful as under the Fourth Republic. There, neither the creation of a resolving organ, nor the resolution of issues, nor deliberation of policies was being adequately taken care of. French deputies were so busy with their twofold attempt—to form a governing will *and* to deliberate in terms of the interests of their constituents upon policies proposed by that will—that they produced neither resolution nor representative deliberation.

Italian parliamentary procedure has also been handicapped in this way. The division of popular and parliamentary opinion into supporters and opponents of the Republic, and the near-majority position of the Christian Democrats, has so far given tenuous assurance that Cabinets dominated by this party will be able to stay in office. But the Christian Democrats' lack of a clear majority has forced them to maneuver for the support of minor proconstitutional parties, so that the emphasis in Parliament is more on resolution than on deliberation, and neither is being performed any better than in the Fourth Republic.

In Great Britain, where the continued existence of the Cabinet is guaranteed, most of the energy of Parliament can go into deliberation about the merits of the two great alternative programs. The same has been true in Canada. In the United States, the Presidency assures that the government of the country will be carried on. But the difference between the United States and the other two English-speaking countries is the greater dispersal of the resolving function under the formal separation of powers. The Congress shares in this with the President and, for some issues, even with the Supreme Court. Still, the most important activity of the Congress, on the basis of time devoted and otherwise, consists of deliberation about, and interference with, policies proposed by the President, in terms of the interests of its constituents, without anything approaching British parliamentary party discipline.

Swiss parliamentary procedure is also based in part on Bentham's essay. This has not had the same confusing results as elsewhere, for two main reasons. In the first place, the National Council and the Council of Estates can actually confine themselves largely to deliberation, since there can be no threat to the continued capability of the Federal Council, Switzerland's equivalent of the cabinet, to carry on the government.

Secondly, the political process in Switzerland is so decentralized that its parliament is not as important a focus of either deliberation or resolution as it is in the other countries, and as it should be in France.

The Swedish Riksdag is not in quite as fortunate a position: it is the most important deliberative focus in the system and does from time to time also have to bring new coalition Cabinets into being. It has combined the two types of decisions very well, since the beginning of the period of Social-Democratic Cabinets in 1932, because Cabinet resignations have only in very extraordinary circumstances been brought about by parliamentary action. This has meant that the Riksdag can concentrate on its deliberative functions once a coalition has been formed after a general election. Nevertheless, since four major parties have been represented in the Riksdag during this period, we might expect that its debates would be as poorly structured as those of the French National Assembly. That this is not in fact the case is due largely to the great age and extreme efficiency of Swedish parliamentary procedure and to one of its devices in particular, the "counterproposition." Under this rule, the chamber always chooses between two and only two alternatives in any vote it takes. Rustow describes this procedure:

(1) On each vote the chamber chooses between two alternatives—called "proposition" and "counterproposition."

(2) The winning alternative in any one vote appears as the "counterproposition"—that is to say, is paired off against a new motion—on the following vote. Every motion thus enters the contest only once and stays in it until rejected in favor of another.

(3) All motions are taken up in reverse order of their support as ascertained by the speaker in a preliminary series of voice votes.[2]

This method has roughly the same effects as the British practice of stating the issue at the outset of any debate in terms of two alternatives. It structures the debate, brings relevant information to bear upon the issues, and forces it to a conclusion with "all deliberate speed." It is much older than the bicameral Riksdag; indeed, it dates back to the long period when the Swedish Parliament consisted of four estates.

Because of the repeated need for constructing parliamentary majorities out of shifting coalitions in support of resolutions to particular issues, deliberation in the Riksdag is more meaningful than in many other parliaments. In other words, parliamentary deliberation in Sweden actually precedes the resolution of issues under debate, whereas in Britain parliamentary debate actually follows resolution, which has

[2] Dankwart A. Rustow, *The Politics of Compromise,* 1955, p. 192.

previously been decided by the Cabinet or the voters. We are not suggesting that debates in the House of Commons are purposeless; they are deliberative over the longer run, helping to shape the major issue to be decided in the next general election: which party is to control the Cabinet with what kind of mandate. In Sweden, by contrast, parliamentary deliberation affects the resolution of issues of lower importance than those decided in elections.

This is also true of the United States, because of the lack of party discipline in the Congress. This, combined with the American conception of law, which is more voluntarist than the British, and the fact that President and Congress cannot get rid of each other, might lead us to expect that congressional procedure is inefficient. In the past, it has often been. Actual fist fights or riots among congressmen, on the French and Italian pattern, have not happened, although one senator was "caned into insensibility" on the floor of the Senate before the Civil War. But obstruction, especially through the filibuster, has not been uncommon, again in the Senate. The rules of both houses are as old as the Constitution—indeed, parts of them are really older, because they were carried forward from earlier colonial and British parliamentary practice. Some aspects of the rules have been changed from time to time, like those defining the functions of the Speaker of the House of Representatives or setting the number of committees. Others have been the subject of prolonged controversies, notably the rules affecting unlimited debate in the Senate. The Senate, partly because of its smaller size, has conducted more efficient deliberations on the whole, but both houses have recently been able to contribute adequately to deliberation and, secondarily, to resolution of issues.

Not so the Italian and French Parliaments. There, the need for building coalitions simultaneously for resolving current issues and for carrying on the government has resulted in making the performance of both functions inefficient. Neither parliament makes a worth-while contribution to either the short-run or the long-run deliberation of issues. In France especially, the resolution of issues is often postponed, and even when it is finally reached, policies in various special fields frequently turn out to be mutually contradictory. Nevertheless, in France and Italy, as in Germany and the United States, the parliaments do produce decisions at some point on those issues that the peculiar composition of each system leaves to parliamentary resolution. And even though the three Continental parliaments and the House of Representatives do not seem to engage in much deliberation in their meetings, their decisions are not reached without prior deliberation. Most of the real deliberation—

the weighing of alternatives in the light of relevant knowledge—goes on in the specialized committees. The House of Commons, on the other hand, does not have specialized committees, because it does not need them for this purpose. Its committees—named "A," "B," "C," and so on—are miniature replicas of the House itself, and merely give more thorough and detailed, but still unspecialized, scrutiny to bills about to be considered by the full House.

Parliamentary Committees

Parliamentary committees are usually compared with regard to their number, size, partisan composition, and method of operation, in order to explain differences in their "power" in different countries. The power of committees is often deemed to be lower in West Germany than in Italy and France. Both French and American committees are considered very strong, British and Canadian very weak. This approach yields some explanation of the greater influence of French than German committees. The German constitution-makers deliberately tried to keep committees of the Bundestag from becoming as strong as their French and American counterparts, in order to prevent them from competing with or challenging the Chancellor and his Cabinet. The Basic Law therefore circumscribes the powers of committees, by giving Cabinet ministers and members of the upper house, or their representatives, the right to attend and be heard in committee meetings. The committees, as a result of this constitutional provision, cannot secretly hatch bills opposed to government policies, and they have found it very difficult to initiate legislation in competition with the federal ministries.

But this institutional explanation is inadequate. One should also consider other factors. For example, each of these Continental parliaments has inferior procedures, ill suited for deliberation. To the extent that issues are to be deliberated upon and resolved, both France and Germany have to find some place outside of the full meetings of their parliaments to accomplish this. In France, the overt pursuit of material interests is not considered as improper or "unethical" as in Germany, whose ideologism is stronger in this respect. Hence France needs efficient committee work even more. This need is still further enhanced by the lack, under the Fourth Republic, of an equivalent of the resolving and integrating focus Article 67 of the Basic Law set up in the Chancellor's office. Differences in the locus of the resolving function thus exert their influence.

Comparisons in terms of operating procedure of committees do not yield adequate answers, either. For example, most of the most business-like and efficient deliberation in the three major Continental parliaments is done in the committees, as it is in the United States House of Representatives. Yet the Continental committees, in contrast to the American ones, usually operate behind closed doors and do not receive much publicity. They rarely follow the congressional practice of subpoenaing witnesses, nor do they normally publish their proceedings. All that the public generally knows about their activities is contained in the speech delivered by the committee's *rapporteur* to the chamber as a whole in reporting out the bill. All of this should make these Continental committees less efficient and effective than their counterparts in the United States. Actually, the reverse is closer to the truth. Why?

In looking for an answer to this question, we will again have to inquire into the type of decisions these committees have to make, and the kind of problems out of which the issues arise. We will return to this inquiry when we consider the subject of representation in Chapter 20. Meanwhile, we may summarize our findings about procedure.

Guidelines for Constitution-Makers—III

Procedures can be rationally designed. In fact, procedure seems to be one of the pipelines or faucets through which policy flows where new plumbing can be installed. But this is no excuse for taking a cold-water faucet from Britain and trying to make it serve as a steam valve in France. Until we get further along in the political process, we will have to confine ourselves to some more negative guidelines for constitutional engineers.

Do not transplant a complete set of procedures unless you can transplant along with it political personnel experienced in its operation.

Do not encourage unstructured debate. Or, to put it positively, force a clear statement of the issue under discussion at its outset.

Do not confuse deliberation with resolution. Determine beforehand whether you are dealing with an assembly that mainly deliberates, in terms of the interests its members represent, about the resolution of issues proposed by another organ, or whether it is one that mainly performs the resolution of issues itself.

Do not completely segregate deliberation from resolution, on the other hand. If deliberation cannot influence the resolution of issues even in the long run, it will become irresponsible, both inside and outside parliament.

These recommendations may not satisfy those who have been asking themselves what useful purpose is served by those parliaments that do not make significant contributions to the resolution of issues. Why have all the debate in the House of Commons, if the outcome is a foregone conclusion, and if everyone knows that it is? One answer is that actual and potential parliamentary criticism maintains the accountability of the bureaucracy to those it is supposed to be serving. Another, with which we will deal next, is that a parliament may—and the House of Commons does—serve as the model of political procedure for the entire system and, in particular, as the school for ministers.

CHAPTER 17

Resolution

Some men are called deliberate, others resolute, and a few are considered both deliberate and resolute. The deliberate man carefully weighs all possible alternative courses of action in the light of all available information about them. He may be so deliberate that he experiences terrible difficulty in making up his mind and postpones his final decision again and again. People who will be affected by his decision would call him irresolute or feckless. Another man may have no such difficulties at all. Whenever he recognizes a problem, he immediately makes up his mind what to do about it, without ever bothering to think of alternatives or the consequences of his action. Very resolute, people will say, but impulsive and careless. Their greatest respect will be accorded to the man who makes his decisions on time—and most issues have an optimum time for resolving them—but does so only after careful weighing of the alternatives and their likely consequences.

All human beings have to exercise both deliberation and resolution to deal with the problems with which life presents them, and so do all political systems. In the individual, the two activities are closely intertwined. Except for the "disintegrated personality," resolution is the normal goal and conclusion of deliberation, and deliberation is the normal preparation for resolution. Both are phases in the same flow of decisions, which goes on in each of us all the time.

Since political systems are not integrated units, but consist of millions of individuals, these two and other phases of the flow of policies can be more clearly distinguished in them. The organs and processes taking care of each are more easily identifiable and more highly differentiated or specialized. We have just seen how parliamentary procedure is often designed to facilitate the specialized function of deliberation for parliaments. We know that general elections and referenda resolve major long-term issues in all the successful constitutional democracies, and we will later return to this topic. Issues arising out of constitutional problems, or connected with the policies and personnel of the central government for the period until the next scheduled election, are resolved on these occasions. Political systems also need the means for resolving issues that are raised and have to be dealt with between elections, and issues of lesser importance than those that dominate the great campaigns during which the electorate is asked to resolve them. This kind of resolution is provided by the British Cabinet (and its Canadian copy), the President of the United States, and the Chancellor of the German Federal Republic. In this chapter, we will observe the way in which these institutions give resolution, and contrast them with the French Cabinet under the Fourth Republic, which was meant to be resolute but could not be.

Great Britain: The Cabinet

The Cabinet provides resolution in the day-to-day operation of British politics. It decides which alternative course of action to follow on all issues of national concern arising between elections of the House of Commons. Its decisions are almost always put into effect. They may be criticized in Parliament, and the Cabinet may make minor concessions to these criticisms, but in the end its policies will prevail.

The British Cabinet is unique in this respect among the eight systems we are studying. In the others, the resolving institution either cannot make definitive decisions, or does not consist of a committee, or lacks both of these attributes. The latter applies to American Presidency, whose resolution of issues can be overridden by the Congress or the Supreme Court or obstructed by its own subordinates, and which was deliberately established as a single rather than a "plural executive." In Number 70 of the Federalist Papers, Hamilton argued:

> That unity is conducive to energy will not be disputed. Decision, activity, secrecy, and despatch will generally characterize the proceedings of one man in a much more eminent degree than the proceedings of any great number; and in proportion as the number is increased, these qualities will be diminished.

Hamilton turned out to be wrong. The British Cabinet, which has recently consisted of about sixteen members, excels in all of these qualities. It has often been much more decisive, active, secret, and quick in its operations than contemporary Presidents of the United States dealing with the very same problems. Moreover, resolution by the British Cabinet usually occurs after more efficient internal deliberation than goes on within the Executive of the United States. How can we explain Hamilton's error in judgment?

He himself took up the example of the British Cabinet, but found it inapplicable to the American Constitution, because he considered the King the British chief executive. But since the British Monarch no longer performs this function, its superior performance by the Cabinet as a committee still seems like a "wonder" to many students of politics. This miraculous aspect has been enhanced by the paucity of information about the organization and procedures of the Cabinet. Compared with all that is known about the Cabinets of American Presidents, not much knowledge is available. The main reason for this was mentioned in Chapter 9: the rigidly enforced rule of secrecy for the Privy Council, of which the Cabinet is the active part. Even retired Cabinet members are still under oath not to reveal what was said at Cabinet meetings, unless they first obtain special permission to make such revelations. The collective accountability of the Cabinet to the House of Commons, which is ensured by the rule of secrecy, also reduces what is known about its proceedings by outsiders. Only when a Minister resigns because he no longer agrees with a major policy of the Cabinet does the public find out a little bit about alignments on issues inside the Cabinet. Even then, it is only the outcome of the dispute that is exposed. So far as is known, votes are never counted in the Cabinet, and the procedure by which it arrives at the resolution is therefore veiled in something of a haze.

Normally, the Cabinet consists of members of one party, although this was not true in wartime. Belonging to the same party naturally helps Cabinet ministers to arrive at decisions. The parliamentary leaders of the Opposition party are also accustomed to collaboration with each other, since they form the so-called "Shadow Cabinet," which faces the real Cabinet across the center well of the rectangular chamber of the House of Commons. In conducting its sessions efficiently, the Cabinet gets further aid from its secretariat, which was set up only as recently as World War I. Before that, no minutes were taken during Cabinet meetings, so that the secretary of a Minister could write to Prime Minister Gladstone's secretary:

Harcourt and Chamberlain have both been here this morning, and *at* my Chief about yesterday's Cabinet proceedings. They cannot agree about what occurred. There must have been some decision, as Bright's resignation shows. My Chief has told me to ask you what the devil *was* decided, for he be damned if he knows.

This was in 1882. Nowadays, the secretariat prepares the agenda, keeps records, and facilitates communication among members of the Cabinet, but even today nothing remotely approaching a stenographic transcript of meetings is kept, and when issues of partisan politics are discussed, no member of the secretariat sits in on Cabinet meetings.

In the last few decades, a number of committees, specializing in different areas of policy, have existed within the Cabinet, or on its fringes, where such committees consist of some Ministers who are members of the Cabinet and others who are not. The structure and interrelationship of these committees is frequently changed—and not only when a new Cabinet comes into office—and their composition itself is often kept secret. Below these top Cabinet committees, there is a vast and intricate network of ministerial and interministerial committees. This network is so pervasive and complex that American students of it have found that it defies attempts to reduce it to a chart. Continental students of committees under the British Cabinet have been driven close to despair by it. It seems to present no clearly definable chain of command or allocation of functions. Yet the Cabinet is accountable not only collectively for the acts of its individual members, but also for the actions of the whole bureaucracy that forms the base of the pyramid at the apex of which the Cabinet sits. The enviable efficiency of these unsystematic arrangements is beyond the comprehension of most non-British observers of the United Kingdom's government.

The success of the Cabinet as the focus of resolution in British politics cannot be explained in terms of the role of the Prime Minister. This has usually been described as first among equals, though it undoubtedly amounts to more than that. After all, the Prime Minister is appointed by the Queen and then presents to her the other Ministers, who are of his choice. Normally, the leader of the winning party in the last election campaign becomes Prime Minister, and the voters are, therefore, making just as much of a choice between national leaders as in American presidential elections. His colleagues in the Cabinet are, as a result, less than the Prime Minister's equals. But their deliberations are presumably conducted in a more egalitarian atmosphere than those of the United States or West German Cabinets, whose heads are less dependent upon the support of their Secretaries or Ministers than is the Prime Minister.

What, then, accounts for the superior combination of resolution and deliberation that characterizes the British Cabinet? Its continuous collective accountability to the House of Commons, where its policies are ever being debated and criticized in the physical presence of the Cabinet members themselves, must be placed high on any list of causes. The fact that the Cabinet is assured support of its policies by its majority in the House, combined with its constant collective accountability, means that it is encouraged—indeed, prodded—to be resolute and at the same time given the parliamentary wherewithal for resolution. But even if we grant this much, there is still no reason why the existence of factions within the majority party should not interfere with the true collegiality of the Cabinet, or why it should not find it difficult to resolve difficult issues intelligently and with speed. After all, French Ministers, according to the constitution of the Fourth Republic, were also "collectively responsible to the National Assembly for the general policy of the Cabinet." This is where the service rendered by the House of Commons as the school for Cabinet ministers should be considered.

Members of the Cabinet in Britain are always members of Parliament. This has usually been true in France and Germany, too, but never in the United States, of course, because of the constitutional separation of powers. For the British, this has meant that election to the House of Commons (or inheritance of a seat in the House of Lords) is the road to Cabinet membership. Cabinet ministers are, therefore, experienced parliamentarians. And their experience has invariably been with the procedures of Parliament. They are used to deliberation according to the methods governing debate in the House of Commons. They are accustomed to debates that are structured efficiently. Since they can carry on discussions in such a way in a House with more than six hundred members, how much easier it must be for them to do so around an oval table in a room containing only sixteen people. It has become second nature for them to state what is at issue before they begin their deliberations and to explore, for any policy, possible alternatives and their consequences. Although they do not vote in the Cabinet or in most other committees, they employ the same procedures making for conclusive resoluteness that Parliament has probably inherited from its days as a court and that Parliament no longer needs, precisely because the Cabinet has taken over the function of providing resolution for the British political system.

United States: The President

The heads of the great departments of the federal government, who are members of the President's Cabinet, do not share common backgrounds as do their British opposite numbers. Some of them are former members of Congress, others former governors of states, still others businessmen or party politicians who may have never before held any government office. They owe their appointment to the President—and to the consent of the Senate. The President, in turn, may be under obligation to some of them for helping him be elected. But he can dismiss them if he wishes to, and he is not obligated to consult them or to heed their advice, individual or collective, once it has been given. President Lincoln, according to a famous anecdote, once took a vote in his Cabinet and found everyone to be against a policy he had proposed. "Five nays, one aye," he said, "the ayes have it." The Cabinet is thus clearly subordinated to the President. Some Presidents have relied more upon advice from outsiders, like so-called "kitchen cabinets," than from the heads of the departments.

The procedures of the Cabinet were not regularized until after World War II. A Cabinet secretariat was set up only under the Eisenhower administration. In general, there can be no question that the deliberations of the American President's Cabinet are inferior to those of its British counterpart with regard to both deliberation and resolution. This is not because American Cabinet members necessarily have less information or poorer congressional contacts. They have all the information with which their departments can provide them, and the practice of letting them testify before congressional committees, combined with the application of pressure by congressmen on behalf of their constituents, puts them into close touch with relevant sectors of public opinion. Some members of the Cabinet, moreover, are appointed because they come from the very interest whose problems are handled by their department. This is hardly ever the case in Great Britain. For the United States, it means that conflicts between interests, as between labor and employers or between advocates of public and private power or between the different armed services, may be carried right into the President's Cabinet, for discussion and possibly even for resolution. In most cases when this happens, the disagreement is resolved in the Congress, or between the Congress and the President, or even later, by the Supreme Court. And this is why the Cabinet is not very useful for purposes of either deliberation or resolution. Its members know that they do not have the wherewithal for the definitive resolution of issues, that they can be overriden by several different institutions. Together with their dissimilar backgrounds, this factor leaves the resolving function with the President.

He has other agencies in addition to the Cabinet for helping him in the deliberative process that should precede resolution, especially the Executive Office of the President, which includes the important Bureau of the Budget. Since the end of World War II, the National Security Council has been set up, consisting of those Cabinet members whose departments are concerned with external problems, supplemented by certain other military and civilian officers. It acts as a sort of supplementary cabinet, between which and the real Cabinet there is an overlap. This undoubtedly helps the President in giving deliberation to external problems, while at the same time weakening the Cabinet. In any case, it is the President himself who has to make the final decisions on the resolution of all issues that are not resolved by, or in collaboration with, the other two branches of the federal government. This is the import of the classic statement of President Harry S. Truman, visibly displayed on his desk in the White House: "The buck stops here."

The President alone is responsible and finally accountable, and knowledge of this is likely to make the deliberative contributions of his subordinates inferior to those made in this process by their British counterparts, who know that they share in both responsibility and accountability. On the whole, it seems that the British Cabinet has put in a better performance over the decades of this century than the Presidency of the United States. It may well be that Alexander Hamilton was quite wrong in attributing so many qualities to "singular executives," and that his bad judgment has in our time been pointed up by the universal trend toward "teamwork," as it is called in the United States, "government by committee," as it operates in Great Britain, and "collective leadership," the post-Stalinist motto of the Soviet Union. If Hamilton was wrong, he need nevertheless not turn over in his grave, because the relative dispersal of the function of resolution in the American system makes the performance by the "chief executive" of his share of it less crucial than the performance of Her Majesty's Government in the United Kingdom.

Germany: The Chancellor

In the Weimar Republic, Cabinets could be as resolute as the parliamentary majority coalition behind them was united. Except for the five years between the end of the Great Inflation of 1924 and the begin-

ning of the Great Depression in 1929, this made Cabinets fairly irresolute. While the Reich Chancellor was given a preëminent position in the
Cabinet by the constitution, he had to be on good terms with the popularly elected Reich President and to face the constant threat of being
forced out of office by losing a vote of confidence in the Reichstag.

In the Federal Republic of Germany, all this has changed as a result
of the constructive vote of no confidence (Article 67) and related provisions of the Basic Law. It is the Federal Chancellor—and not his program or his Cabinet—who requires the support of a majority of the members of the Bundestag for election, and who cannot be voted out of office
unless a majority agrees on his successor. He sets the general guidelines
of policy, according to the constitution, which also states that "the Federal Government [Cabinet] decides about differences of opinion among
Federal Ministers. The Federal Chancellor guides its business according
to rules of procedure, which are adopted by it [the Cabinet] and approved by the Federal President." This provision is typical of the comprehensive legalism that pervades the Basic Law. Nothing similar is
found even in the constitution of the Fourth Republic. Most of the constitutions we are studying do provide that the houses of their parliaments
establish their own rules of procedure, but to make the same requirement for a Cabinet suggests either that its members would not know
how to conduct their business without such explicit rules, or that they
should be prodded into conducting their meetings properly through the
knowledge that improper conduct would amount to violating the rules.

Apparently, meetings of the West German Cabinet have been rather
stiff and formal, and the only Chancellor during the first decade, Dr.
Konrad Adenauer, on occasion took votes of the Cabinet, though probably not on issues on which he had previously made up his mind and
stood to lose. Although his own party, the Christian Democratic Union,
originally controlled only about one-third of the seats in the Bundestag
and he therefore had to rely on the support of the other parties in his
Cabinet coalition, he clearly dominated all of his Cabinets. He was able
to do this since defection from his coalition would not have been enough
to displace him as Chancellor, because of Article 67.

Far more often than business-organization leaders have served as
American Secretaries of Commerce, German Ministers fulfill a representative function in the Cabinet—a displaced person and sometime
head of the Refugee League, for example, as Federal Minister for Displaced Persons. Recent German Cabinets, like past ones, have contained
more experts as heads of various ministries than is the custom in Britain
and, usually, in the United States. In Great Britain, Ministers frequently

shift from one ministry to another, so that potential Prime Ministers especially have often had experience as heads of half a dozen different ministries before they reach the peak of their career. In Germany, on the contrary, Ministers tend to be professional specialists—a professor of economics as Federal Minister of Economics, for example—as opposed to the British tendency toward "generalists." German Cabinet members need not be members of Parliament, although most have been.

In West Germany, the presence of specialists has probably helped the Chancellor in learning something from the deliberations of his Cabinet. The function of resolving issues other than those up for decision in parliamentary elections is clearly his. And since West German parties have much better parliamentary voting discipline than the two national parties in the United States, the Chancellor can perform this function more satisfactorily than the American President.

The resolution the Federal Chancellor can give to West German politics today stands in sharp contrast with the irresolute pattern of politics under the Weimar Republic. It has enabled the Federal Republic to deal efficiently with its problems—certainly more efficiently than the French Fourth Republic dealt with its own set at the same time. The Chancellor has been able to resolve issues after presiding over very adequate deliberations within the Cabinet and the bureaucracy it directs. From our point of view, this situation has only one drawback, and that a serious one: Too little meaningful public deliberation precedes this resolution of issues coming up for decision between elections. We have already seen that the debates in the Bundestag are usually more declaratory than deliberative, and suggested that the best of the deliberation that does go on in the Bundestag is conducted at the meetings of its committees, from which the public and the press are excluded. Since the Chancellor can be almost as sure of majority support in the Bundestag as the British Cabinet in the House of Commons, his followers there need make no effort to persuade the Social Democratic opposition, which, in turn, is neither inclined to be persuaded nor so unaware of its minority position as to try to persuade the majority parties. Only issues requiring a two-thirds vote for resolution—that is, constitutional amendments—have truly been deliberated upon, and those are precisely the ones the Chancellor cannot resolve by himself.

None of this would, by itself, call for our criticism if it were true in France, Great Britain, or the United States. In each of these systems, procedures of compromise are more firmly established at all levels of politics, and beyond politics in private life, than they are in Germany. In Britain especially, the whole nation, without being aware of it, practices the methods of deliberation of which Parliament provides the prototype. People do not know precisely how the Cabinet operates, but they do know that it is a committee, that it deliberates informally, yet in a disciplined way, and that it always arrives at resolution. This fact itself lends tremendous prestige to deliberation by and in committees and goes far toward explaining the success of "government by committee" at all levels of British politics, despite the often chaotic appearance of any diagram to which students of British politics may try to reduce these arrangements.

In Germany, by contrast, past political systems have provided few opportunities for informal deliberation in groups. If the Bundestag were to conduct its debates in a more deliberative manner than it has so far, politics at all levels might learn from this. Since the Bundestag does not in fact engage in much public deliberation, it seems even more desirable that the Cabinet should set an example of resolution, preceded by meaningful deliberation among men who are operating in an atmosphere of relative equality. Naturally, the Cabinet could not do this in public. But it would not have to, because if the Cabinet did conduct its business in this way, that fact would sooner or later push the procedures used in the ministries and the rest of the political process in the same direction. As things have actually been, however, the process of federal politics has taught the German people very little about procedures of compromise. Other efforts that have been made in this direction have been of such a formal nature that they had effects either negligible or negative, as will be shown later. The West Germans have gotten their best lessons in democratic methods of deliberation from schemes like codetermination,[1] which were started for totally different purposes.

France: The Council of Ministers

Under the Third and Fourth Republics, there was great paucity of resolution, but a plethora of deliberation. The founders of the Fourth Republic, or at any rate some of them, wanted to provide more resolution by making Cabinets more stable than they had been in the Third Republic. With this in mind, they made the premier accountable only to the National Assembly, not to the Council of the Republic; they made his removal from office dependent upon the adverse vote of a majority of deputies, not merely a majority of those voting; and they installed other innovations, which were mentioned in Chapter 8. However, with the slow but firm "return to the Third Republic," most of these efforts were

[1] See pages 168-69 ff.

thwarted. The constitutional amendments of 1954 restored many former functions to the upper chamber, and premiers often resigned although defeated by less than an absolute majority in the National Assembly—constitutional provisions to the contrary notwithstanding.

Cabinets were invariably coalitions of several parties, dependent on the support of more than two parties in the Assembly, since no two parties capable of agreeing on any policy ever controlled a majority of the seats. While the constitution provided for the collective accountability of the Cabinet, this was a dead letter for all purposes except the frequent forcing of Cabinet resignations. What went on at Cabinet meetings usually became public knowledge, regardless of whether the Cabinet was meeting as such, or as the Council of Ministers, in which case the President of the Republic was in the chair, according to the constitution. These arrangements were intended to be somewhat similar to those that distinguish the British Monarch's Privy Council from the Cabinet, but this attempt at reproduction, like so many others, failed. Ministers often "leaked" information about Cabinet disagreements in order to put themselves or their party in a more favorable position at the formation of the next Cabinet.

Despite all the instability of Cabinets, there was considerable continuity of service by individual ministers—so much that scholars have spoken of "instability of ministries, but stability of Ministers." Even when there was change of personnel, some ministries remained in the hands of members of the same party for several years, with the ministries often regarded as "fiefs" of this or that party. This had results somewhat similar to those brought about by the presence of interest representatives in the Cabinet of the American President, for example, someone who could speak for the users of federal lands in the West as Secretary of Interior. It meant that conflicts among interest groups were carried all the way into the Cabinet. But whereas such issues in the United States can be resolved either by the President or in the Congress, they could not be resolved in France by either the Cabinet or the National Assembly. Nothing and no one provided resolution in the Fourth Republic. Deliberation within the Cabinet was undoubtedly carried on in an atmosphere of equality, because the Premier was, if anything, less than first among equals. It involved compromise, since no Cabinet coalition could have been brought together in the first place without considerable compromise: If parliamentarians practiced what they preached in their ideologies, no coalition could ever have been brought into being. But deliberation stopped short of resolving major issues. Members of the Cabinet conducted themselves as though they were representative of their special constituencies, rather than members of the resolving organ whose function was to propose general policies to Parliament for deliberation there in terms of the interests represented in it.

This was General de Gaulle's reason for adding to the constitution of the Fifth Republic one novel provision, designed to implement his other efforts to focus resolution clearly in the Presidency and the Cabinet. Under the Fifth Republic, members of Parliament who become Cabinet Ministers will have to resign their parliamentary seats. Thus, presumably, they will not be tempted as much as in the past by constituency, interest, and party pressures to neglect resolution in favor of interest representation. If this attempt at constitutional engineering succeeds, procedures of deliberation and resolution will no longer be confused in France. On the other hand, there is at least the possibility that this move may result in too much of a "separation of powers" to make policies acceptable to Frenchmen. However this may turn out, it recalls a similar practice observed in British and Canadian politics until thirty or forty years ago. Members of Parliament, if they became Ministers later than one month after their last election, would resign their seat in order to run for reëlection in a special by-election. The purpose of this, however, was obviously not to separate powers or functions, but to make sure that the new Minister still had the confidence of his constituents even though he was now to hold an office of profit under the Crown. This practice was a hangover from the eighteenth century, when the Crown would literally buy the support of members of Parliament by giving them patronage. In other words, the former practice concerning resignation of new Ministers in Great Britain and the newly proposed practice in France were meant to serve opposite ends: In Britain, the minister resigned in order to prevent his corruption at the hands of the Crown. In France, he is to resign in order to prevent the corruption of the Cabinet at the hands of special interests.

Resolution of Emergencies

In the lives of both individuals and political systems, occasions arise when the moderate combination of deliberation and resolution, recommended at the outset of this chapter, would not serve success because it would threaten survival. In an emergency, the delay entailed in thorough deliberation might prove disastrous. In such a situation, any action may be more useful than none at all. The emergent problems may change so rapidly that careful deliberation would be futile, because it would be based upon information that grows obsolescent while it is being taken into consideration. This should not be understood as advocacy of impulsive action; on the contrary, the deliberation that ought properly to precede any resolution, but cannot in an emergency be conducted then and there, should be taken care of earlier and, as it were, put on the shelf until needed. All political systems must anticipate emergencies and can have general ideas as to the probable nature of any specific problems calling for immediate action that they may have to confront in the future. Provision for emergencies, in this sense, has been a recurrent problem for constitution-makers.

The British, as always, did not have to deal with it as a constitutional problem. Command-in-chief of the armed forces had remained within the royal prerogative over the centuries, while much of its other content was whittled away. It was, of course, dependent upon parliamentary grants of money and was exercised by the Cabinet, which also controlled external relations, and with much less interference from Parliament than the American Senate can give to the President for constitutional reasons. In order to buttress this capacity for resolute action in emergencies, Parliament passed the Defence of the Realm Acts, which were meant to deal with problems arising out of World War I, but a revised version of them was later employed to handle the general strike of 1926 as well. The Acts provided that the King-in-Council, that is, the Cabinet, could "issue regulations . . . for securing the public welfare and defence of the Realm." Under the Emergency Powers (Defence) Acts of World War II, the King-in-Council could, subject to parliamentary control, "make such regulations as appear to him to be necessary or expedient for securing the public safety, the defence of the Realm, the maintenance of public order, and the efficient prosecution of any war in which His Majesty may be engaged. . . ." These acts proved entirely adequate for their purpose. Indeed, it seems doubtful whether the Cabinet would not have been just as resolute without them, so that their main effect was to remove legal obstacles the Cabinet would otherwise have faced in restricting or reducing the rights of British subjects while trying to win the war.

The framers of the Constitution of the United States, as the words of Alexander Hamilton on page 259 clearly show, anticipated emergencies in which resolute action would be required. The Presidency was designed by them to solve this constitutional problem. The President, according to the Constitution, "shall be commander-in-chief of the army and navy of the United States." And "he shall take care that the laws be faithfully executed." This latter provision, which on the face of it does not seem to have any connection with resolution in emergencies, has often been used to justify presidential actions for which no other constitutional or congressional justification was given. In the United States, unlike Great Britain, resolute presidential emergency action has often been widely criticized—even on the part of President Washington, partly because it smacked of monarchism in those days to many of his critics. President Lincoln, who provided resolution the Congress could never have given in the prosecution of the Civil War, encountered similar criticism for suspending the writ of habeas corpus and subjecting civilians to military tribunals. After the war was over, the Supreme Court again returned to the antimonarchist theme in this connection. In *Ex parte Milligan*, Mr. Justice Davis wrote:

> Martial law, established on such a basis, destroys every guarantee of the Constitution, and effectually renders the "military independent of, and superior to, the civil power,"—the attempt to do which by the King of Great Britain was deemed by our fathers such an offense, that they assigned it to the world as one of the causes which impelled them to declare their independence.

But the Court did this only after the Civil War was safely over. It has only rarely and recently taken a direct part in the resolution of emergency issues. The Court did so notably in 1952, when it struck down a Truman order to seize the steel industry because of a strike, and again in 1958, when it held a special session in connection with the dispute over integration in Little Rock, Arkansas. With some exaggeration, these two cases could be contrasted by saying that, in the first one, the Court did not think that the strike emergency was of sufficient gravity to call for the speedy resolution with which the President acted, while in the second, the Court thought that speedier resolution was demanded than either the state or the two other branches of the federal government were willing or able to provide.

This question—How quickly does the issue have to be resolved?—is crucial in providing for decisiveness in emergencies. If the emergency is of internal origin, as with anticonstitutional insurrections, there is likely to be disagreement about the answer in parliament. If the opportunity for deliberation about the issue of speed is given, the resultant delay may cause the insurrection to succeed and constitutionalism to come to an end. That is why Article 48 of the Weimar Constitution, which enabled the Reich President to use troops against member states and to suspend civil rights, was soundly conceived. The President could act decisively in defense of the constitution, but still in accountability to the Reichstag, to which the measures taken had to be submitted and at whose request they could be rescinded. In the 1920's, Article 48 was used with success on several occasions. But during the last years of the Weimar Republic, the emergency provisions were abused by circumvention of the requirement for parliamentary sanction of their use.

The constitution-makers at Bonn sought to prevent exploitation of emergency situations for the subversion of the constitutional order. Accordingly, they placed the function of resolving emergencies in the hands of the Chancellor. If he cannot get the support of the Bundestag for bills he designates as urgent, he can declare a state of legislative emergency and the bills can become law with the consent of the upper house, in which the state governments are represented. But within the tenure of one Chancellor, these procedures can be employed for no longer than six months. Whether they are adequate is a question that will have to await the occurrence of an emergency in the Federal Republic. It is probable that they will be, because German constitutional tradition leans more toward quick resolution than toward public deliberation—at least, the Imperial and Nazi regimes suggest this. It is also likely that resolute emergency action by a Federal Chancellor today would be received not nearly as critically in Germany as similar presidential action has always been in the United States.

In the Third French Republic, yet another device was used to handle emergencies: legislation by decree, promulgated by the Cabinet after prior parliamentary authorization. Under this practice, a Cabinet could, for a definite period of time, issue decrees that had the same force as if they had been passed by Parliament itself. But often the emergencies dealt with in this manner were of Parliament's own making. In order to evade being associated with necessary but unpopular measures, it would "pass the buck" to a Cabinet by empowering it to issue legislative decrees. Since Parliament had procrastinated resolution of the issue, time would finally become short and a quick decision would be needed—an emergency had arisen! Parliament would then wash its hands of the whole matter and let a Cabinet deal with the emergency. The Cabinet normally did not long outlast resolution of the issue.

The founders of the Fourth Republic wished to avoid repetition of this irresponsible practice. Hence Article 13 of its constitution read: "The National Assembly alone has the right to legislate. It cannot delegate this right." As so many other good intentions of the authors of this constitution, it was honored in the breach; practice returned to the bad habits of the last years of the Third Republic. But this practice did not provide real resolution of emergency issues. In the final analysis, popular agreement about the means of solving the emergency problems was insufficient to provide resolution—an illustration of the fact that any

kind of resolution is difficult for a government to arrive at in the face
of irresolute public opinion. In such a situation, the government must
be able to lead public opinion away from irresolution before it can itself
act resolutely and find acceptance for its decisions. In the Fourth Republic, neither the constitution nor the personnel of politics worked toward
that goal.

This explains the way in which the Fourth Republic faded away.
Resolution of the issues arising out of the Algerian problem had been
deferred time and again, until it seemed even to staunch republicans
that only General de Gaulle—by profession a man of resolution—might
be able to prevent civil war. The National Assembly therefore voted
him into the premiership and delegated to him the function of drafting
a new constitution, to be approved or rejected in a national referendum.
He immediately proceeded to reduce the issues to manageable proportions: mainly the two alternatives of accepting or rejecting him and his
program.

General de Gaulle's draft constitution for the Fifth Republic char-
acteristically provided that the President of the Republic would be able
to take all necessary decisions in the event of a serious crisis threaten-
ing the political system. This proposal of De Gaulle was one of the most
controversial and hotly debated elements in his constitutional draft. The
reason for this is clear. The French have had bad experience with earlier
military leaders—men like the two Napoleons, Marshal MacMahon,
General Boulanger, Marshal Pétain—who were so intent upon taking
care of the resolving function that they reduced public deliberation to a
minimum. The Third and Fourth Republics sought to protect themselves from this threat by concentrating both deliberation and resolution
in the Parliament. The result was the thwarting of the efficient performance of either function. Their legalistic political style made the French
constitution-makers want to define clearly the function of emergency
resolution when the need for constitutional engineering again came upon
them in 1958. Recriminatory ideologism impeded solution of this constitutional problem through compromise. It remains to be seen whether any
solution the Fifth Republic finds to this problem will produce the desired
results any more than did Article 13 of its predecessor's constitution.

Guidelines for Constitution-Makers—IV

Every political system requires resolution of its issues if it is to survive.
The adequacy with which resolution is performed reflects in large measure the will of the members of the system to be in one system. Many

major issues can be resolved in elections and referenda. Others have to be decided upon during the intervals between those great acts of collective resolution. The processes by which such intermediate issues are decided has to be more clearly focused. This is particularly true of issues arising out of problems calling for an urgent solution. Issues of this kind will arise with increasing frequency in modern political systems because of the rapidity with which problems change in the contemporary world. One emergency succeeds the other, and we are living in a time of continuous crisis, a time calling for decisions. The crucial importance of resolution for the success of political systems is, therefore, likely to grow constantly. What suggestions, designed to improve its performance, can we make to founders and reformers of constitutions?

Clearly give to some institution "the first word" to speak in an emergency. The "sovereign power" under a constitution has been described as that organ with "the last word" in any dispute. For the success of a political system, clear definition of the speaker of the first word seems more helpful, so that emergency issues can be resolved in time.

Do not let this central focus of resolution operate apart from the process of public deliberation. If its members participate in this process, its decisions will be based upon better information and more adequate weighing of their consequences.

Resolution of emergency issues and of other issues arising between elections or referenda should be performed by the same institution.

Steps to be taken in future possible emergencies should be given some deliberation in times of "normalcy," in order both to improve their quality and to ensure their acceptance.

The alternatives of having a "singular" or "plural" organ take care of resolution should be carefully weighed. Most newly self-governing political systems, and those that have to make great strides to develop their economies, have started out by placing resolution in a one-man institution, often because the will to be independent and to forge ahead was dramatized by one great leader. In later phases of political development, central resolution is frequently performed more efficiently by a group like the British Cabinet.

For membership in the resolving organ, experience in the procedures of deliberation should be considered a more important qualification than expertise in a special field. Responsible politics relates alternative poli-

cies to available resources in the light of sound knowledge. Such knowledge by itself, which experts possess, is insufficient for the purpose of making responsible central decisions on behalf of others.

A system that operates with inefficient procedures of deliberation would have to be exempted from the last guideline. This raises the serious problem of finding men who are up to the tasks of deliberation and resolution. There are vast differences in this respect among our eight countries. To these differences, explanations for them, and their effects on the success of political systems, we now turn.

CHAPTER 18

Personnel

The personnel officer of any large organization, public or private, classifies applicants for employment and candidates for promotion on the basis of their background, training, and experience. He does this for the obvious reason that different jobs in the organization call for different qualifications. A modern American business corporation, for example, might be interested in the representativeness of its salespeople, because it would not expect optimum results through having a Northern Negro try to sell its goods in the business community of Atlanta, Georgia, or a white Southerner in the Harlem district of New York City. If the corporation is running a scientific research program, it would want to assign graduate scientists to it, rather than lawyers, who would be sent to the legal department. In considering men to fill the top "executive" positions, the board of directors would give weight to representativeness and training, but perhaps even more to experience and past performance, inside the corporation or in some other organization.

We have seen that, depending upon their location in the flow of policies and upon the type of decisions they have to make, politicians need different qualifications, too. But in democracies, the recruitment and promotion of politicians—as distinguished from civil servants for the moment—is not as rationally organized as it can be in business corporations. This is so simply because politicians are not selected by personnel and classification officers, but by the political process. Party politicians on their way up must please not only their superiors but also the voters, who look upon the politician as their representative. In this chapter, the quality of representativeness will not concern us as much as the training and experience of politicians. The importance of this factor for the success of any political system is related to the distinction between deliberation and resolution that was made at the beginning of the last chapter. A person trained and experienced in deliberation—a scholar of Sanskrit, perhaps—would probably not do a very efficient job in a position calling mainly for resolution, like the French Ministry of Interior, which is in charge of maintaining domestic order. This is especially true in societies where the normal career moves directly upward from the bottom to the top of one specialized activity, rather than switching horizontally from one specialty to another.

The training and experience of politicians is also related to political style. Men and women who intend to enter politics naturally tend to get the kind of training and experience that seems likely, in their political system, to help them achieve this goal. Old-time politicians, in recruiting their aides and successors, look for younger politicians to whom they have some affinity of training and experience. Thus style shapes the personnel of politics. However, this relation works in both directions: When an event of revolutionary proportions eliminates previously influential groups, as the French Revolution eliminated most of the clergy and nobility, politicians who speak for new groups will enter the scene—in this case spokesmen for the bourgeoisie and the peasantry. The training and experience of these men is likely to reshape the style of the system. Our goal in this chapter is the determination of the kind of training and experience of the personnel who make different types of decisions, and the consequences for success of this preparation.

The Intelligentsia

Parliaments have often been compared in terms of the professional composition of their members. Such a comparison will show that, of our eight countries, the United States has the highest proportion of lawyers, that there is a higher proportion of trade-union officials in the House of Commons than in the other parliaments, that there are more civil servants among the deputies of the major Continental systems than in the English-speaking countries, and that there are other differences of this nature. This kind of comparison, taken by itself, reveals a good deal about the workings of parliaments—but not enough, unless it is linked with a comparison of these professional groups as they operate within their national contexts, and with their education and experience.

This suggestion applies with particular force to the political role of the intelligentsia. By this term, we understand a self-conscious class or estate of intellectuals, whose members identify themselves primarily as belonging to this group. We are stressing this element of self-consciousness or identification, because some comparisons overlook it, with distorting results. These studies may note, for instance, that more than a quarter of the deputies in the Bundestag hold doctorates—indeed, that several deputies hold two doctorates each. They may then remark that a doctorate is easier to obtain in Germany than in the United States —that the *Doctor juris* is the equivalent of the American LL.B. degree. Finally, they may throw in figures on the academic degrees held by members of Congress, and then leave the whole comparison as inconclusive. However, the strong feeling of belonging to the intelligentsia, which academic intellectuals in the Continental countries generally have, does make it possible to draw conclusions from this kind of comparison, if it is related to the context of political style.

As we saw in Chapter 14, Continental professional people with academic background are trained systematically rather than in the school of (partly simulated) experience. This is due largely to the nature of the university curriculum. It gives students practice more in dealing with abstractions than in handling concrete problems. In jurisprudence and the social sciences, more emphasis is placed on memory work and logical argument, within the framework of whichever system is being studied, than on the observation of reality, especially contemporary reality, and the use of knowledge in the solution of present problems. Many European academic careers are so organized as to reduce exposure to practical problems before attaining professional status and to avoid experience in fields other than one's specialty. In Canada and the United States, on the other hand, college students are usually less sheltered, partly because of the more contemporary orientation of their courses, partly as a result of summer jobs, and partly because of the greater horizontal mobility between occupations for which the two North American economies are noted.

Because of the peculiarities of their education, Continental intellectuals, when placed in political positions calling for resolute action, are often not very good at making responsible decisions on the basis of incomplete information. Businessmen and experienced politicians do have practice in making decisions of this kind. When the buyer for some company decides how large an inventory to stock of the raw materials needed for its product, he rarely has complete information about future price and demand trends. He nevertheless makes his decision, recognizing risks and willing to take the consequences. Intellectuals, by contrast, are accustomed to making a decision only after all the obtainable relevant information has been gathered, and without early exposure to its effects.

For this very reason—because they have better knowledge than other people, and because they are trained in bringing it to bear on the solution of problems—it has often been suggested, usually by intellectuals, that the intellectuals ought to run society. This kind of intellectual elitism had its prototype in Plato's *Republic*. In more recent times, it has also been advocated by prominent European intellectuals, among them Karl Mannheim, who turned the Marxian concept of ideology against Karl Marx himself. Marx had asserted that all knowledge and philosophy was but a determined reflection of the class position of its holders. Mannheim applied this to Marx and then went on to suggest that in modern societies, with their division into classes, only the "freefloating intelligentsia" might be able to arrive at a "total orientation and synthesis," that is, to see things the way they really are.[1] This critique of the Marxian concept of ideology can, however, be turned against Mannheim himself. The intelligentsia may also be considered a class in the Marxian sense—in terms of the relation of its members to the means of production. The property of the intelligentsia consists of the knowledge of certain techniques without which no modern system could operate. Its class interest lies in enhancing the value of this property. The intellectuals can best do this by trying to make themselves and their knowledge indispensable, by persuading the rest of the population that complete knowledge exists, that it can be obtained, that the intellectuals have access to this total knowledge, and that they should therefore run things.

The most promising way to persuade people to this effect is by "packaging" knowledge in salable form. Knowledge can best be sold by making it simple and consistent, that is, simplified and distorted. Continental intellectuals have often done just that by offering one-factor ideologies to their public. This kind of activity on the part of intellectuals has contributed heavily to making political style more ideological. In some instances, intellectual ideologists have started political movements themselves. Karl Marx, a doctor of philosophy of the University of Jena, is the classic example. Academic intellectuals have often entered politics on their own during the very periods when ideologism was already being encouraged for other reasons. In many more cases, this kind of ideologism has had the long-run effect of making experienced nonintellectual politicians turn to the intellectuals for help. Later, these

[1] *Ideology and Utopia,* Harvest ed., p. 161.

men and others like them stayed in politics, even after the evaporation of the original needs for which their services had been solicited. We have already seen one illustration of this in the influential role played by academicians in the German labor movement. Many other examples could be cited, notably that of the intellectuals who dominated the German National Assembly of 1848 and set much of the tone of German politics from that day to this.

Almost every debate in the Bundestag in some way reflects this dominance of intellectuals by the many references made to the ideological antecedents of the orators' present position. Opinion surveys, in which people are asked to rank the professions and vocations in order of prestige, always come up with university professors in first place. The result is that regardless of how many university teachers are actually in politics, many politicans do tend to model their behavior on that of the academician. Even criminals do this: In the old Imperial days, confidence men used to play the role of noblemen to impress unsuspecting victims; nowadays, they pretend to have one or two doctorates.

In the other Continental countries, different types of intellectuals play important roles in politics. In France, men of literary achievement frequently use that claim to fame in order to become politicians. And emphasis on literary elegance pervades the French educational system and, indeed, all of French society. Great value is placed on the "elegance" and logical consistency of any piece of political literature and oratory. In both Italy and Germany, economists carry considerable authority in politics. This has also been true in Sweden. But there the admission of representatives of the universities and learned societies to the estate of the clergy in the Riksdag, more than a century ago, gave opportunities for political responsibility to academic people, thereby toning down their potential ideologism and its influence on Swedish political style in general. In Switzerland, academic degrees carry just as much prestige as in the three neighboring nations whose languages the Swiss speak. But academic status by itself does not usually lend any authority in politics to its holder. Self-government is too ancient and politics too decentralized in Switzerland to let the political authority of the individual rest on anything but his known performance as citizen and holder of lower elective offices. Experts rarely if ever head the seven specialized federal departments whose chiefs comprise the Federal Council.

We have already noted that the British Minister is usually not a specialist in the field with which his ministry deals. The very frequency of the rotation of Ministers from one job to another indicates that they have to be generalists. But this does not tell us anything about the role of intellectuals in British politics. If we defined intellectuals as university-trained people who make a living by using their intellects, then intellectuals certainly play an important role in all of our countries, Great Britain included. But that is not the definition we are using, since we stressed primary self-identification of intellectuals with the intelligentsia. In this sense, they play much less of a role in British than in German, Italian, or French politics. True, many British intellectuals have participated in politics and even been prominent in it. But their primary identification has usually been with a class—upper, lower, or middle— a topic we will consider when we deal with representation, in Chapter 19. And in many cases, intellectual prominence came to individuals only after they had first achieved political prominence. In Britain, a budding politician who is the author of a treatise on economics would not be likely to succeed with either his constituents or his colleagues in Parliament, were he to make this authorship his main claim to political fame. On the Continent, he would. Even the most learned Britishers, inside and outside of politics, generally play down their knowledge with understatement. On the Continent, everybody tends to play up his academic knowledge with overstatement. It is more valued there than in any of the English-speaking countries, and carries more authority in politics.

We have already suggested, in Chapter 14, that men with academic background carry more authority in Canadian politics than in American —especially in Quebec, but not there alone. We suggested as one explanation the break with Great Britain and the prerevolutionary past made by the United States during the War of Independence. But the lack of any feeling of belonging to an intelligentsia seems so marked among the counterparts of European intellectuals in the United States that additional explanations are called for. Americans who would be considered intellectuals in Europe have generally identified themselves with the goods or services they produce. They think of themselves, and like to be thought of, as teachers, authors, journalists, composers, painters, business or government consultants, and so forth, rather than as intellectuals. A member of any one of these professions who intends to become a politician will certainly stress his concrete achievements and play down his qualifications as an "egghead." Indeed, it was not until the wave of so-called anti-intellectualism that followed World War II and accompanied the increasing military and ideological threat from the Soviet Union that most Americans—intellectuals and others—became aware of the existence of a group in their midst that might be described as the intelligentsia. More recently, the low prestige accorded to these people became a national problem when the Soviet Union beat the United States into outer space. The very fact that it did then become an issue underlines the earlier lack of self-consciousness of intellectuals as such, the low prestige enjoyed by them as a result of McCarthyism, and the negligible authority which academic learning gave to politicians.

The lack of group consciousness on the part of American intellectuals has been explained as a particular aspect of the relative absence of class consciousness in general. Since no aristocracy of birth was permitted to establish itself in the early days of the Republic, no equivalent of the European bourgeoisie ever became conscious of the common antiaristocratic interests of its members. Neither did the proletariat, nor the intelligentsia. (In the Soviet Union, in which antagonistic classes are supposed to have been eliminated, according to Communist ideology, the only remaining distinctive strata in society are addressed as "workers, peasants, and toiling intelligentsia.") Because of the lack of class distinctions and class consciousness, European students of American politics have sought to identify the equivalent of the governing classes, to which they have been accustomed at home, somewhere in the society of the United States.

Lawyers and Jurists

The most distinguished European student of American politics, Alexis de Tocqueville, located this counterpart of a governing class in the legal profession. At the same time, he suggested that lawyers in the United States also perform the functions of an intelligentsia. After distinguishing between practitioners of the Roman and the English law—that is, jurists and lawyers—he describes lawyers in England as "the younger branch of the English aristocracy [who] mingle the aristocratic tastes and ideas of the circles in which they move with the aristocratic interests of their profession." Then he compares them with their brethren in the United States:

> In America there are no nobles or *literary men,* and the people are apt to mistrust the wealthy; lawyers consequently form the highest political class and the most *cultivated* portion of society.[2]

He goes on to state "without hesitation" that the American aristocracy "is not among the rich, who are united by no common tie, but that it occupies the judicial bench and the bar." Tocqueville also asserted that

[2] *Democracy in America,* Vintage ed., vol. 1, p. 288. Italics supplied.

the training and experience of English and American lawyers makes them naturally conservative, just as we suggested earlier that the kind of law-finding in which the House of Commons pretends to be engaged makes most useful the backward-looking knowledge in which practitioners of the common law excel. We will return later to this label of conservatism, and at this point pursue the first suggestion—that the American legal profession is the equivalent of both a governing class and an intelligentsia.

In the major Continental countries in which nobility of birth was abolished, one gets the impression that many of the former functions of this class are today being performed by the aristocracy of intellect. The high proportion of academic intellectuals in their politics has already been mentioned. A more dramatic and amusing illustration is provided in the Weimar Constitution, which contains an article whose third paragraph abolished titles of nobility but goes on in its fourth to specifically exempt academic titles. The proportion of lawyers in American politics is, if anything, even higher. The Constitution itself assigns a crucial role to the legal profession, at least by indirection, by providing for the Supreme Court. And American lawyers have always had a strong sense of professional fellowship, expressed through the various bar associations. Like the Continental intellectuals, American lawyers are united by the bond of common knowledge of certain techniques. But the two conceptions of knowledge are as different as the consequences for politics that flow from them.

In comparing Roman and English law, in Chapter 15, we observed that each of these legal systems may serve as the basis for its own notions about knowledge and about the capacities of knowledge and of its possessors. This difference is noticeable not only in practitioners of the law, and in nonlegal academicians, but also in the relations between lawyers and other academic intellectuals. Continental jurists are usually classified as members of the so-called "free professions" and, therefore, as academic intellectuals. They tend to identify themselves with the intelligentsia. English and American lawyers do not, and it seems reasonable to hazard the guess that they would not identify themselves with the intelligentsia in the United States even if the existence of such a class were to be generally recognized.

One reason for the comparatively great gap between the legal and other academic professions in the English-speaking countries has already been mentioned, in Chapter 15—the traditional separation of legal training from the universities in England and even in the United States. Here, lawyers are now trained in graduate schools of the universities, but these law schools are seldom as fully integrated with the rest of the academic community as in Continental universities. The law schools seem to have the closest relations with those of the other academic disciplines in which adaptations of the legal methods of teaching and research are employed. We noted earlier that many of the social sciences have modeled their pedagogical methods on the case method, which was pioneered by law schools. The social sciences generally in the United States have a more inductive, less deductive coloration than their sisters in Continental Europe. They owe this orientation in large measure to the American law schools.

The majority of politicians who achieve positions where central deliberation and resolution take place are products of legal education. Training in the law gives those who are exposed to it practice in making decisions on concrete problems in a limited time, without complete information, but with awareness of the consequences of the decision for others. It develops a critical attitude toward professors, judges, and colleagues, and an unusually deep, almost subconscious commitment to the ancient procedures of the law, rather than to the specific contents and goals of individual laws. The difference in emphasis between this commitment on the part of the legal profession and many other professions should be emphasized, because we will find it of importance later on, when we deal with "the American consensus." Two other professions, business and the military, can provide the contrast. In the United States today, both offer an academic education for their future leaders. Schools of business administration instill in their graduates commitment mainly to the goals of increased productivity and financial success. Military academies instill in theirs commitment to the general defense of the United States and victory in any particular conflict in which the country may become engaged. This is not to deny that members of both of these professions are also committed to the rules governing their profession, that is, business ethics and the rather more ancient military code, or that lawyers do not want to win their cases, or their political campaigns, if they run for office. But the emphasis of commitment is on the substantive goal of their activity in the case of businessmen and the military, whereas in the case of lawyers, it is on the procedures of the common law as methods for resolving conflicts that arise in the community.

The sources from which individuals in these three professions derive professional authority differ accordingly. For the businessman, it is wealth, and for the military leader, victories. These are relatively specialized and substantive marks of success. The American lawyer draws his professional authority from more generalized and more procedural sources. In fact, he is the generalist par excellence, and his faculty for dealing with the most diverse types of problems derives precisely from the procedural orientation of the common law and of teaching methods in the law schools. That is one reason—and there are others—why lawyers are found in crucial positions, not only in American politics, but on the *inside* of every other sphere of American life—business, banking, education, religion. Their use of the adversary method makes them superb bargaining agents and negotiators. Use of this procedure enables them, as spokesmen for opposing clients, to explore all possible avenues of settlement, to do so in a rational and nonviolent manner, and to arrive on time at resolution of the issue under dispute. Practitioners of the English law are above all technicians of the procedures of compromise. That is why they are employed on the inside of nonpolitical activities, where their prominence is much more remarkable than it would be if lawyers were merely concerned with the relations between, say, business and government or the universities and the churches.

Very little of what has been said about lawyers in the English-speaking countries applies to Continental jurists—or to the other members of the intelligentsia who, together with the jurists, are as influential in the politics of Continental systems as lawyers are in America. We have already contrasted the two types of training and the different conceptions of knowledge they encourage. The old belief that the Roman law in its successive codified versions literally contained true justice tends to give those trained in it a much greater commitment to the substantive goals of whatever they are doing. This makes jurists poorer negotiators than American and British lawyers. Continental intellectuals, with their leanings toward ideologism, are even less effective as bargainers for compromise than their legalistic colleagues. The greatest drawback of the jurists as politicians comes from the limited experience their training gives them in the responsible making of decisions. This is once more related to the notion that the law code contained all justice, that it covered all contingencies, and that anyone who mastered its contents and could reason in its categories would be best able to administer justice and the state, the institution designed for realizing justice on earth.

The methods used on the Continent in training jurists, judges, and bureaucrats reflect these attitudes. In Germany, and with some variations in France and Italy as well, university preparation for these three careers has been the same. After passing a civil service examination administered by the state—not the university—students make the choice of which of these careers to follow. Those who choose a judicial career are often launched upon this in a lower court after serving a short apprenticeship as an "assessor." Unlike judges in the common-law countries, they do not first engage in the private or public practice of law or in partisan politics. Judges are unlikely to have had prior experience as counsel for private parties or as prosecuting attorneys. This has the double effect of making the popular conception of the courts more machine-like, and of giving the judges a more limited appreciation for the realities of life in general and of politics in particular. The young man who is most likely to succeed as a judge is the type who, in the United States, would be described as the "straight-A student." In the United States, by contrast, a politician or a potential judge who labors under that stigma would emphasize his nonacademic accomplishments rather than his academic ones, both inside and outside college.

The historical grandeur of the British and American judiciary, in contrast with the relative historical insignificance of Continental judges as individuals, must in large part be attributed to the varied experience with political responsibility that its members normally receive prior to elevation to the bench. The pre-bench political experience of Chief Justices John Marshall, William Howard Taft, Charles Evans Hughes, and Earl Warren may illustrate this point, the importance of which cannot be grasped by most Continental students of American politics. Some of them were horrified to learn that Governor Warren became Chief Justice of the United States after he led the large California delegation to the Republican presidential nominating convention into the camp of the winning candidate, General Eisenhower. "This is gross political patronage applied to the highest judgeship in the land," they said. Had they been told that the Chief Justice had earlier been California's attorney general, their incomprehension would probably only have risen.

This attitude also accounts for the lack of sympathy granted the work of the Federal Constitutional Court in West Germany and the Italian Constitutional Court. The inclusion on these courts of professors of jurisprudence has been of little help in this respect, since their experience with the responsibility of active politics is usually just as limited as that of professional judges. But the issues that the new constitutional courts have to resolve are even more likely to be part of the central flow of policy, especially fundamental policy, than the issues that the Supreme Court of the United States has had to resolve. The success of the Supreme Court, in turn, is partly due to the paradox that in the careers of politicans, when viewed under the aspect of time, there has been a disregard for the doctrine of the separation of powers under the one constitution most explicitly based upon that doctrine.

Bureaucrats and Deliberation

The separation of powers has been more meticulously observed in the United States with respect to the bureaucracy, but only since the end of the nineteenth century, when the federal civil service truly got its start and bureaucrats began to achieve tenure. Before that time, it was usual for recipients of federal job patronage to run for elective office later on. At no time since ratification of the Constitution could members of Congress also be civil servants or members of the President's Cabinet, since the Constitution provides that "no person holding any office under the United States, shall be a member of either house during his continuance in office." In the United States, as in Britain and Canada, politicians cannot serve simultaneously as bureaucrats and members of Congress or Parliament. But in Canada and Britain—where Cabinet members must also hold parliamentary seats, although their subordinates are forbidden the dual function—individual careers move more frequently from the top levels of the bureaucracy to parliamentary politics than in the United States, where this is very rare. Another thing that is unusual in the three English-speaking countries, although strictly speaking there is no constitutional prohibition of it, is the simultaneous occupation of a national office and a state or local one. Mayors of cities and towns do not at the same time serve as members of Congress or Parliament.

Every one of these phenomena, which occur seldom or never in the United States, Canada, and Great Britain, happens often in France, Germany, and Italy. Many bureaucrats are elected to Parliament. So are many elected officers of local governments. Mayors of large cities serve at the same time both in that capacity and as parliamentarians. Civil servants with tenure run for Parliament and, if elected, go on the inactive list, only to return to the bureaucracy after retiring from Parliament or failing of reëlection. On first impression, these practices might be considered salutary, because bureaucrats are at least likely to have had experience in making responsible decisions about concrete problems. By contributing from this experience to parliamentary debates, the tone of which is otherwise dominated by intellectuals and jurists, they could contribute to the realism of deliberation. Very valuable contributions based on experience in the civil and military services have in fact been made in the British House of Lords by men elevated to the peerage for distinguished service to the Crown. However, the effects of the membership of a high proportion of bureaucrats in Continental parliaments has often been quite otherwise.

The initial reason for the bureaucrat's failure as a parliamentarian is the Roman-law academic training he has received, with its great similarity to that of future jurists and judges. The bureaucrat's presumed experience in making decisions about the solution of problems turns out on examination to provide no genuine counterbalance to his early training. It is true that the finance inspector has to decide whether to accept or reject a tax report, and the official in the Ministry for Home Construction has to decide how to plan a new housing development for which Parliament has allocated funds. But this is precisely the problem: Bureaucrats are experienced in making decisions that differ from those made by the institutions in which deliberation and resolution are focused. The range of alternatives, among which the bureaucrat can choose, is narrower and more clearly defined than that faced by parliamentary politicians. He does not have as much opportunity for the use of imaginative initiative in thinking up new alternatives or even new issues. The issue has already been resolved for him, and he merely applies the policy contained in the resolution to the solution of the problem that first gave rise to the issue.

The distinction that has been drawn does not lead to the conclusion that the bureaucrat does not also have to make decisions; indeed, the contrary was shown in the critique of the separation of powers, in Chapter 1. Nor does it mean that the bureaucrat operates in a context that comes as close to being a social vacuum as that of Continental judges. As a matter of fact, he has frequent face-to-face contacts with the citizens who are being affected by his decisions. However, again because of the juristic training the bureaucrat shares in common with judges and lawyers, and because of the prevailing legalistic style, the contacts between Continental bureaucrats and citizens tend to be much more formal and less "human" than those between their counterparts in the English-law world. This formality is expressed through the more rigid conduct of Continental bureaucrats, their greater hesitancy to exercise discretion, the relative lack of give-and-take between them and private citizens, as well as in the inordinately high deference which is shown to public officials in the three large Continental countries.

Corruption

Their juristic education and consequent close identification with the law and justice, and with the universities, offers one explanation for the high prestige that bureaucrats enjoy in these countries. There is another reason for this, which carries great weight in Germany, in France, though not in Italy: the traditions of honesty and efficiency of these civil services. Brought into being by the so-called enlightened despots of the eighteenth century, these bureaucracies were designed as efficient instruments of the King in his efforts to centralize and stabilize his power. The bureaucrats were accountable to the King, and it served his purposes to have them be as honest as possible. As a result, such devices as the merit system and appointment by competitive examination were introduced much earlier in Prussia and France than in England.

England had earlier faced the problem of the centralization of royal power—a problem that was never as difficult there as on the Continent, largely because of her insular position. And it was solved by means other than an honest bureaucracy. In fact, the British bureaucracy was notoriously corrupt and inefficient all through the eighteenth century and, at least parts of it, on into the nineteenth. British corruption led Alexander Hamilton, at the Constitutional Convention, to oppose a provision designed to prevent parallel developments in the United States:

> Regarding the possible effects of such a reform in Great Britain, he cites a remark attributed to "one of the ablest politicians" (Hume) to the effect that "all that influence on the side of the Crown, which went under the name of *corruption*" was "an essential part of the weight which maintained the equilibrium of the Constitution." [3]

Reform of the British bureaucracy and creation of a modern civil service were not begun in earnest until the middle of the last century. Before that time, the Crown had a vast number of offices at its disposal, which it could and did distribute as pure patronage, partly in order to bribe members of Parliament for their votes.

In the United States, of course, the spoils system and other forms of patronage were practiced on a very wide scale. Reform of the bureaucracy came even later than in Great Britain, and the federal civil service even today is not as famous either for probity or for efficiency as Her Majesty's civil service has since become.

All of this might lead the reader to conclude once more that the role played by Continental civil servants in parliamentary politics must be entirely beneficial. In fact, however, it seems to be anything but that. The traditions of corruption in public office, on which the English-speaking countries can look back with something less than pride, have produced other traditions as their own antidotes—the tradition of parliamentary watchfulness over the bureaucracy and of lack of deference

[3] Richard B. Morris, ed., *Alexander Hamilton and the Founding of the Nation,* pp. 146-47.

to its members. In Great Britain, even though her civil service has now been honest for more than eighty years, the negligence or zeal of bureaucrats is still exposed with devastating clarity from time to time, often as the result of questions asked during the daily question period in the House of Commons. In the United States Congress, the suspicion of bureaucrats is so strong that it often seems congressional investigators consider bureaucrats under subpoena guilty of corruption until proved innocent. Especially during periods when congressional committees uncover particularly dramatic instances of corruption in public office, the general public tends to look down on, rather than up to, members of the federal civil service. In Canada and Great Britain, the average citizen usually thinks of himself as being on the same plane with bureaucrats. On the Continent, the citizen normally defers to these men who are supposed to be the servants of the public.

Popular prestige is one reason why a bureaucratic career can serve as a good stepping stone to elective office on the Continent. If this were not so, fewer civil servants would be parliamentary deputies. As things are in Germany, Italy, and France, many members of Parliament do have a bureaucratic past—and a bureaucratic future. They contribute to the legalistic style of parliamentary debate. As a professional group, they are not prepared to contribute to true deliberation. Moreover, their background is likely to promote the bureaucratization of more and more parts of the political system—and this not only or even mainly because they, on their return to their former posts, would presumably benefit from increased bureaucratization. Rather, as products of the huge and ancient organizations in which they have been working, they will tend to favor the more orderly and predictable routines employed by the bureaus to the freer and easier procedures that even the best disciplined of parliaments uses. But in contributing to the bureaucratization of a parliament they will reduce its capacity for deliberation.

This effect, which the presence of a high proportion of bureaucrats may have on a parliament, is reënforced by other factors that work in the same direction in the major Continental countries. One of these is the strong aversion to parliamentary politics, as just so much quibbling, on the part of segments of the population who feel that they have gained nothing from parliamentarism, or have indeed lost something as a result of its introduction. In France, this has been true of many adherents of the Old Regime—groups from which the top levels of the civil service have traditionally been recruited. In Germany, nationalist and conservative opponents of the Weimar Republic also preferred orderly administration from above, by efficient and incorruptible bureaucrats, to the indecisiveness which characterized that constitutional democracy. They overlooked the fact that one reason why parliamentarism did not work out more efficiently was the very scope of things attended to by the bureaucracy under the Imperial regime, which afforded little practice in self-government at lower levels. Similarly in France, even under the Fourth Republic, the centrally appointed bureaucracy attended to many problems, such as law enforcement and public schools, that are much more subject to decisions by locally elected officials in the English-speaking countries, especially in North America. If it were not for the relative insignificance of elective local office, there would not be as many mayors of large cities in the lower houses of the French and German Parliaments—they simply would not have the time for it.

The bureaucratic bias in politics in reënforced not only from the right, but also from the left. After all, socialist ideology posits the ultimate goal of the total bureaucratization of society, as Friedrich Engels' prediction suggests that the administration of things would replace the government of men. According to Marxism, parliamentary politics in the bourgeois state is only a manifestation of class conflicts, which finally become so irreconcilable that they can be resolved only by the violent revolution. The Social Democrats do not go quite that far, since they believe that socialism can be established by evolutionary means, without the violent overthrow of the bourgeoisie. But both Socialists and Communists do believe that the classes represented in Parliament do have conflicting interests and that these conflicts can be eliminated only by doing away with classes. What is more important is their common conviction that the conflicts *should* be eliminated, because they are opposed to social conflict as such. This opposition logically flows from their ideological belief in the rightness of only one position, their own; accordingly, they must consider political conflict irrational and evil. But this means, in the end, that they are opposed to politics; in their utopia of the classless society, everyone would follow the same ideology, agree on the solution to all problems. There would be no issues and therefore no need for politics. This ultimate goal of the Marxists colors their behavior in the Continental parliaments. As advocates of socialism, they are also advocates of bureaucratization, inside parliament as well as outside. Add to this the fact that these socialist parties are run by bureaucratic machines of their own, and that their parliamentarians are products of these party bureaucracies, and the massive proportions of the bias toward the bureaucratization of the parliaments of Germany, Italy, and France must become apparent.

Bureaucrats and the Solution of Problems

In the major Continental systems, we have seen that bureaucratic experience interferes with the efficiency of debate in the issue-deliberating phase of the policy flow. The opposite type of transfer has similarly been unsuccessful in the English-speaking countries in the past, when politicians with experience in deliberative procedures became bureaucrats, charged with the solution of problems. In this final phase, special rather than general qualifications are often required—the trained accountant can best catch tax evaders, and the highway engineer can best draft plans for a road or specifications for contractors' bids. Here those habits are useful that are gained from long experience in carefully observing and impartially applying instructions issued by others. Here specialized competence and honesty are required for making decisions responsibly.

Before the establishment of the merit system, parliamentary politicians were frequently given bureaucratic jobs as bribes or rewards. Then, as now, the results of this kind of transfer have usually been unfortunate for all concerned. The former politician is accustomed to making decisions of a more "freewheeling" kind than he can or should make as a bureaucrat. He is unaccustomed to accepting instructions from a determinate superior in the hierarchy of the civil service, since he was expected to make up his own mind—within certain limits and to varying degrees—in the give-and-take of parliamentary deliberation. Now, as a bureaucrat, his goals are set down for him over a much shorter run of time, the major alternative policies have already been eliminated by the resolving organ, and he is asked to use his judgment and specialized knowledge in the selection of the best technical means for realizing the goals. Moreover, the bureaucrat is expected to devote himself to his work regardless of his agreement or disagreement with the instructions that come down to him after the resolution of issues. Regardless of which party or coalition of parties is in office, or how he himself may feel about a particular policy he is implementing, the bureaucrat is supposed to apply himself with equal vigor. For anyone raised in partisan politics, this kind of disinterestedness will be hard to affect.

Even today, many high jobs in the federal bureaucracy are filled with men whose main experience has been in partisan politics, including the Congress. Some of these positions have been deliberately kept out of the merit system because, although they are below Cabinet level, they are said to involve policy-making and therefore to require men who are in sympathy with the administration's program. This argument is made necessary by the rigid distinction between legislation and execution upon which the American Constitution is based.

A businessman, unless he had previous experience in a heavily bureaucratized private corporation, would also be likely to put in an unsatisfactory performance in a bureaucratic position. Like the parliamentary politician, the businessman is experienced in using more imaginative initiative and greater discretion than is normally appropriate for bureaucrats. The businessman, especially if he is of the "executive" type, may also be used to exercising greater resolution, without having to refer back to the deliberations and decisions of others, than most bureaucrats should. On the other hand, if the business executive is brought into politics at the level at which resolution takes place, he will feel much more at home. The reason for these difficulties, which arise when men with experience in deliberation and resolution are transferred to bureaucratic jobs, are connected with the peculiarities of the pattern of accountability within which bureaucrats do their work.

Bureaucratic Accountability

When absolute rulers on the European Continent created the first modern bureaucracies, these state-builders were intent upon consolidating power in their own hands. Bureaucracy was designed as a means to this end. The resolute rulers of the eighteenth century could best assure conformance to their will on the part of their civil servants by making them accountable to their sovereign.

The ruler insured bureaucratic accountability in a systematic way. To begin with, a rationally arranged hierarchy was set up, defining everyone's tasks. To make sure that the bureaucrats would be able to perform as intended, they were admitted to, and moved within, this hierarchy on the basis of professional qualifications. These qualifications, and the training by which they were acquired, made up part of the individual bureaucrat's resources. The resources also included the authority of the sovereign, with which decisions by his servants were backed up, and material and human tools, that is, subordinates. Each civil servant was equipped not only with resources but also with foreknowledge of the probable consequences of his decisions and actions, both to himself and to others affected by them. This foreknowledge was provided by the system of administrative law, which was created just as deliberately as the bureaucratic apparatus, together with which it grew up. Hence the close entanglement we have earlier noted between the evolution of the legal and bureaucratic professions on the Continent. Finally, the bureaucrat was endowed with the need as well as the capacity to make decisions. He had to exercise his discretion when he applied to specific cases the general and particular instructions given to him.

The bureaucrat was thus provided, by delegation from the ruler, with the three components of responsibility: alternatives, resources, and knowledge. Through this act of delegation, the ruler increased his own capacity for shaping the fate of his state. By giving to bureaucrats the capacity for responsible action proportionate to their accountability, he found the best means for guaranteeing the accountability of the civil service to himself. This, incidentally, gives us an additional pragmatic justification for our earlier insistence on sound situations of responsibility: They encourage better performance.

The member of one of these early bureaucratic organizations presents an excellent case study in responsibility. His capacity for action was well balanced with his exposure to their consequences, that is, his accountability. He knew that he derived his capacity for responsibility from his sovereign and, therefore, had to render to the same sovereign an account of how he employed this capacity. But the rise of constitutional democracy has made the situation of the bureaucrat much more complicated. The unitary sovereign has disappeared, so that the source of the civil servant's delegated responsibility is no longer unitary, either. He derives his resources, knowledge, and discretionary capacity from a multiplicity of sources, among them the constitutional and legal framework within which he functions, taxpayers and voters, special groups with which his bureau works, the central organs of deliberation and resolution, his superiors in the hierarchy, and his specialized profession, as well as the civil service itself as a distinct entity. Is he accountable to all of these?

The literature of public administration contains many controversies on this question. Admirers of the British system tend to favor a clear chain of command with accountability only to the immediate superior. Partisans of practices prevailing in the United States tend to prefer a greater dispersal of accountability. Here we are not concerned with the merits of the argument, but with its existence, because it demonstrates the difference between the type of decisions made by bureaucrats, on the one hand, and by members of organs of deliberation and resolution, on the other. Most of the latter are elected politicians and they are men who can be gotten rid of when up for reëlection, if their constituents, to whom they are accountable—despite what a constitution may say about responsibility to the deputy's conscience alone—are dissatisfied with their performance. Civil servants cannot be that easily removed, nor can they get such clear indications of the public's feelings about their per-formance. Moreover, bureaucrats do not have the same opportunity as parliamentary politicians to adjust themselves to changes in the senti-ments of their public. When they go about the final phase in the solution of a problem, the resolution of the issue has already been made, that is, will has been exercised. True, in any constitutional democracy this is done by the central government just as much on behalf of the citizenry as lower bureaucrats make their decisions on behalf of the citizenry.

The civil servant's lot is made such a difficult one by this fact: He is farther removed from the source of his own authority than is the focus of decision-making from which his instructions come; but he is at the same time closer to the problems that generate issues for politics, and to the people who are bothered by these problems. These people are identical with the source of his authority, or at any rate a part of it. It follows from this that any bureaucrat who conducts himself as though he were at the halfway point between the recognition and the solution of problems— which is where parliamentary politicians in fact are—is not likely to con-tribute to the success of his political system.

The vast expansion of modern bureaucracies during the past half century, and their continuing rate of expansion, makes these questions more complicated all the time. This is almost as true of systems in which little socialization has taken place as of those in which large sectors of the economy have been socialized; it is almost as true, that is, of the United States as of Great Britain. One fact that should not be over-looked in this connection is the existence of huge private organizations that are bureaucratically organized: American Telephone and Telegraph Company, Pennsylvania Railroad, and Ford Motor Company have their bureaucracies just as much as the German Ministry of Postal and Tele-communications or the British National Railways and National Coal Board.

Guidelines for Constitution-Makers—V

This survey of the personnel of politics, if it does nothing else, indicates the dangers involved in making simple international comparisons in terms of professional categories, like "lawyers," "journalists," "businessmen," "civil servants." Back of these terms in each country lies a different com-bination of education and experience, uniquely related to the political style and to the nature of the flow of policy of the system. We may per-haps be hopeful that in another fifty or one hundred years, as the global community of mankind becomes more of a reality, many of these differences will no longer be as marked as they are today. This is of special significance for international political processes and institutions. Meanwhile, however, the unique characteristics of professional groups in each political system have to be taken into account as part of the facts of politics. What does our survey of these facts suggest as guidelines for constitution-makers?

Self-conscious intellectuals without experience in the exercise of practical responsibility should ideally be kept out of positions of leadership. But since no one, least of all this type of intellectual, can permanently be kept out of politics, our earlier advice bears repetition: Give political responsibility, preferably starting at low levels, to possible later participants in the political process.

Encourage development of a conception of political authority—the "additive" to decisions, which leads those who are affected by them to accept them—based on performance in politics rather than on some specialized activity, like engineering, making money, teaching, writing.

Since lawyers are going to play an important role in the politics of any system, encourage legal training that has a practical orientation.

If a constitutional court is established, at least some of its judges should have first-hand political experience.

Structure the careers of lawyers in such a way that individual practitioners are exposed to many different types of practice.

What was said for lawyers, applies to bureaucrats as well: They should be encouraged to circulate among different departments. Their training should have a practical orientation, without excessive legal emphasis.

Except for the top levels of the bureaucracy, which share in the resolution of issues, parliamentary politicians should be kept from appointment to bureaucratic jobs.

Corruption should be controlled, and exposed in the course of deliberation. But once it has occurred, its memory should not be allowed to be erased entirely, in order to encourage vigilance over, and discourage excessive deference to, the bureaucracy.

Members of the bureaucracy may not like this last recommendation, of course. And the supervision of the bureaucracy by other organs of politics can become a divisive issue, especially in countries in which the bureaucrats are just as conscious of belonging to the corporate entity of the civil service as Continental intellectuals are conscious of belonging to the intelligentsia. Where this is true, the bureaucracy will be represented in the deliberative process, along with other groups whose members are conscious of sharing common interests.

PART V

Representation

CHAPTER 19

Democracy

and Representation

If man were not a political being and did not live in political systems, he would be completely responsible for everything that happened to him, except for his birth and the effects of nature upon his life. But he is a political being, and much of what happens to him is caused by other men. We have assumed that individual human beings still want to become responsible for their own fate—in any case, that they should have this desire—and have been looking for means to make this possible for them, in the great and complicated modern political systems in which they live today.

The size and complexity of modern politics is not, however, the only factor that makes our search difficult, although some political theories do suggest this. Theorists who are preoccupied with the "mass" aspects of modern societies often betray a certain nostalgia for the smaller and simpler political units of an earlier age. In those days, they say, citizens could look after their government themselves, instead of having representatives do this for them. They could exercise their political responsibility directly and immediately, instead of having intermediaries dilute individual responsibility. It was this kind of reasoning that led Rousseau to advocate the establishment of small states, somewhat on the model of his native city-state of Geneva and the earlier Greek polis. The many small states would be federated into a nation-state (though Rousseau never elaborated this suggestion in his *Social Contract*). But in the state he describes, legislation, which was the expression of the "general will," would not require representation. We have

already noted his denial that the will of the individual could be represented. This position led him to assert that the "people of England regards itself as free; but it is grossly mistaken; it is free only during the
election of members of parliament. As soon as they are elected, slavery
overtakes it, and it is nothing."

Even Rousseau, however, in denying the feasibility of representative democracy, did not assume that the members of his "sovereign"—
the citizens of his small state—could become directly responsible for all
the functions of politics. He made allowance for what he called the government or the administration, which would apply to specific cases the
general laws made by the sovereign. Had he more closely observed the
realities of politics, he might have discovered that there are functions that
have to be performed by fewer people than the whole body of even his
small sovereign assembly of all the citizens, if they are to be taken care
of at all.

We saw this in our study of parliamentary procedure. And anyone
who watches a New England town meeting—which comes close to Rousseau's ideal—would notice the same thing. Someone has to state the
issues which are to be discussed. Someone has to "moderate" the discussion. Someone has to "put" the question, since questions do not
ask themselves. And someone has to state what if any decision the meeting has made, as even so small a group as the British Cabinet discovered
in Mr. Gladstone's time. In other words, a small political system also
faces the problem of realizing individual responsibility, since the specialized functions just described cannot be performed by all the members. How can those who do not perform them contribute to the decisions made by those who do state the issues, preside over the debate, and
formulate the resolution? Even in a small assembly, registration of the
individual wills of the participants cannot by itself give to the whole
resolution, and still less, deliberation.

Direct and Electronic Democracy

The need for representation, which undeniably exists in modern political
systems, is thus not the only obstacle in the path of the responsibility of
individual citizens. It may not be the major obstacle, as may be seen on
analysis of two somewhat extreme illustrations: Swiss democracy and the
suggestion that modern technology makes possible direct, nonrepresent-
ative democracy even for the large and complex systems with which we
are dealing.

Some of the Swiss cantons, as already mentioned, still practice direct democracy. The male citizens assemble in the open, as the *Landsgemeinde*—the community of the country—to make decisions about the government of their canton.[1] The meeting is moderated by an individual elected for that purpose. Not everyone speaks in the course of the meeting, because this would hardly be efficient, if possible. There are leaders of the various groups with different stands on the issues under discussion. This need for leadership in politics is even more evident in the procedures of initiative and referendum, which are used so frequently in Switzerland. Someone has to be enterprising enough to propose and organize the movement for an initiative, and someone has to give the voters information about the issue and to try to persuade them of its importance to themselves and of the desirability of voting for it. And someone else usually has to organize the opposition.

This would also be true if we were to return to direct democracy by means of modern electronics. It is at least conceivable today that a set of push buttons be installed in every American home. All the major problems the country is facing at any one time could be voted upon at regular intervals, say once a week. There would be one button for voting aye, one for voting nay, and perhaps one for abstaining. The results of these nationwide weekly referenda could be immediately tabulated by UNIVAC or a similar electronic calculator, located in Washington, with which all of the home push buttons would be connected. In many respects, such a scheme would do much more efficiently and reliably what surveys of public opinion, like the Gallup poll, have been attempting for years. With this system, all citizens could feel a personal share in making every central decision and, therefore, in responsibility for national policy. But this would still leave many other problems of responsibility. To begin with, someone would have to focus the electorate's attention on the problems the United States is facing. Someone would have to formulate the issues on which they could then vote by pushing their little buttons. Someone would have to elicit support for particular stands on the issues, and provide the voters with information about both problems and issues. After the issues had been resolved, someone would have to attend to their solution in keeping with the "people's mandate." The bureaucrats, who would presumably have this task, would have to be kept accountable. In addition, means would have

[1] The *Landsgemeinde* is a carry-over from ancient days that still prevails in three rural German-speaking cantons—actually, to be precise, four half-cantons and one full canton—comprising perhaps 3 per cent of the country's total population.

to be provided for selecting the men and women to manage all of the functions just enumerated, and for giving them the training and experience needed for doing their jobs.

Electronic democracy would have some grave disadvantages. It would threaten the stability of the Constitution, of the fundamentals, and with it the foreknowledge citizens need in order to be in sound situations of responsibility. Since the entire electorate would be perpetually in session, this "constituent power" could act at any time. The safeguards for constitutional stability, which the historic amending process has given the United States, would be eliminated. This week's majority, which might become next week's minority, could presumably change even the rules governing the electronic voting process. This would endanger the Constitution, but it would make the conduct of circumstantial policy even more unstable. Public opinion polls show how rapidly the voters' views sometimes change, so that their ability to express their wills on a weekly basis might make it impossible to sustain any policy long enough to let it solve the problem to which it is addressed. In addition to this, it would tend to remove the opportunities to make special contributions to central decisions that specially affected groups have under prevailing systems of representation.

Thus, even if all the citizens were to engage in no other activity but politics—and automation might someday make that as possible for modern man as slavery made it possible for the restricted citizenry of ancient Athens—they would still be unable to make direct contributions to this succession of decisions, which have to be centralized more or less in modern political systems. These decisions would, therefore, have to be made by representatives—that is, by persons who are there, who are "present"—on behalf of many others. The problem of representation cannot be circumvented. It can easily be exaggerated or misunderstood and is likely to be, unless the purpose of representation is made clear and kept in mind.

Representation and Responsibility

Individuals often give power of attorney to a relative, friend, or lawyer, so that he can do something for them which, for one reason or another, they are unable to do themselves. In such cases, the person who gives the power of attorney wants his representative, his deputy, to act in his interest—to do what he himself would do if he did not have to delegate or deputize another. There is no disagreement that political representatives should similarly act on behalf of the interests of their constituents.

This agreement, however, by no means tells the representatives exactly what they should do. Their constituents may not be of one mind, or the representatives may think that they know better what is in their constituents' interest than do the constituents themselves, and so forth. Still, the general agreement to the effect that representatives should act with their constituents' interests at heart makes it possible for us to relate the purpose of representation to the norm of individual responsibility.

The channels of representation—and there are many in each political system—are designed to give individual citizens opportunities to contribute to the making of those decisions that have to be made centrally. These opportunities for the exercise of responsibility should be proportionate to the individual's exposure to the consequences of central decisions. Citizens who are especially affected by agricultural policy, for example, should have special means through which to contribute to the making of such policy. In the United States, polls conducted by the Department of Agriculture are sometimes used to provide this means for a particular group of farmers who are directly, perhaps even vitally, concerned with an issue. But graingrowers should not be allowed complete domination of policy-making in connection with price supports for wheat, for example; everyone else in the system will also be affected by the wheat policy, and by its integration with other specialized policies. In this sense, representation mediates between citizens and the central flow of policy by giving them access to the institutions of deliberation, resolution, and solution. It does this by giving to individuals alternatives among which to choose, like several competing programs; resources with which to implement their choices, like the personnel of politics and the bureaucracy; and knowledge about the consequences of their choices, like that provided by the accountability of various representatives.

Representatives—we are not thinking of parliamentarians alone—should act in terms of the interests of others. But these interests have to be compressed into a manageable, that is, limited, number. Even in a town meeting of only one hundred persons, where everyone could participate in deliberation, there might be one hundred different interests to begin with. If the hundred people lived on that many square lots of equal size, symmetrically distributed over the square township, and the construction of the main road were at issue, with only enough resources to let it pass through town by the shortest route—the length of ten lots— each of the hundred might want to have it pass by his house. If the issue is to be resolved, the alternatives will have to be reduced. To some of the citizens, it will occur that the road can at most pass directly by twenty lots. Those of them who are so located that their properties would be adjacent to one of the eighteen—or is it twenty-two!—possible routes might then join together, having become aware of their common interest. Others might have an eye to the interest of the whole township in relation to the outside world and urge that it be constructed through the middle—some from east to west, others from north to south. In this way, even with direct deliberation, numerous antagonistic interests would come into being.

In a large political system, the potential interests demanding representation are obviously much more numerous. Interests may be due to many causes, among them affinities of geography, source of income, size of income, religion, race, national origin, age, sex, traditions, or goals. But in no case can an interest be said to exist unless the people who share it are aware of this affinity. Such consciousness of a common interest can be and often is stimulated. Usually, awareness of interests is fairly stable, and those who have it are bound together by organizational ties. Organized interests become active in politics with regard to decisions that are going to affect them—decisions in which they are interested. The composition of the organized and potential interests in any political system is naturally related to the problems the system is, or has been, facing. An economic problem like the Canadian need to improve communications gave birth to organized interests somewhat similar to those in the town meeting example above. The cultural problems of Germany after national unification contributed to the organization of the Catholic Center party. The subjugation of Poland by the Communists led Americans of Polish descent to exert influence on the makers of United States foreign policy.

Sometimes it is the other way around. A stably organized interest decides to recognize a problem that may not be troubling other citizens, and to formulate an issue about it. Perhaps this was more nearly what happened in the Polish-Americans' case. Clearer illustrations of it can be taken from the activities of veterans' organizations; these show the interplay, back and forth, between problems and the centers of resolution. When World War I ended, millions of veterans did present a problem to the United States and did face problems of their own that nonveterans were not confronting at the time. The result was the founding of the American Legion, which was organized as it was and which operated as it did because of the structure of the policy flow in the United States. The Legion's particular organization was designed to enable its members, as veterans, to make maximum contributions to decisions about relevant policy—not at the level of the Congress or the Veterans

Administration alone, but also in the earlier phases of the political process, i.e., recognition of problems, statement of issues, and deliberation. Twenty years after the war had ended, the Legion was, if anything, more active than at the beginning, although the distinctive content of problems faced by veterans had by then become at least blurred. Yet the organization continued to move by its own impetus, encouraged in this by institutions of the federal government, including specialized congressional or Veterans Administration committees that had been brought into being, or whose scope of action had been widened, as a result of demands voiced by the American Legion and other veterans' organizations. And veterans were conscious, or were encouraged to remain or become conscious, of their common special interests as veterans.

Interest Organizations and Political Parties

Another example of the interplay between problems and institutions, in which interests engage, is provided by the League of the Homeless and the Disenfranchised, called the Refugee League for short, in West Germany. It was organized by leaders of various groups of ethnic German refugees and expellees from eastern Europe and the Soviet zone of Germany, about ten million of whom were living in the Western zones of occupation at the time the Federal Republic of Germany was established. The Refugee League tried to put up candidates for election to the first Bundestag, in 1949, but was prevented from doing so by the Occupation Powers, who refused to license it as a political party. They claimed that it was nothing but an interest organization. Thus the British and United States military governments made practical use of the distinction between political parties and interest organizations, which is a commonplace of political science in these two English-speaking countries. Most definitions distinguish parties from interest groups, because parties are said to be concerned with capturing a share in or control of a government.

As soon as elimination of Occupation interference enabled it to do so the Refugee League entered candidates for the state diets. Some resounding electoral successes ensued, and the League became a partner in coalition cabinets at the state level. In the federal election of 1953, the Refugee League attained 5.9 per cent of the popular vote and placed 27 deputies in a Bundestag of 487. Its two top leaders became federal Ministers, one of them in charge of the Ministry for Displaced Persons. The latter retained this position after the next federal election, in 1957, even though the Refugee League failed to elect any deputy that year, and he had led some of its former members and parliamentary representatives into the fold of the majority Christian Democratic Union.

Thus, the problem these refugees posed for West Germany brought this interest organization into being, after consciousness of a community of interests had been stimulated among the refugees and expellees themselves. Policy about these problems was going to have to be made in both the state capitals and in Bonn, but because of their proportions, mainly in Bonn. The refugees, as the group mainly affected by the consequences of these decisions, wanted opportunities to contribute to them. In 1949 and 1953, many of them felt that the presence of their own leaders in the Bundestag and, as it turned out, in the federal Cabinet, was the best way to accomplish their goal. By 1957, their special problem had been largely solved—at least to the point where fewer of them felt a continuing need for distinct central representation as an avenue for the exercise of responsibility. Changes in the electoral law also contributed to reducing the degree of interest-consciousness, as will be shown in Chapter 21.

The case of the West German Refugee League suggests that the absolute distinction between political parties and interest organizations made by most studies of comparative government is not always tenable. Even in the English-speaking countries, it is often difficult to recognize when an interest organization begins to behave like a party, or vice versa. In the Continental countries, the line is often impossible to draw. All that can be said is that organizations referred to by both of these terms are representative institutions, affording citizens opportunities for contributing to a variety of types of decisions that have to be made centrally.

Our concern with constitution-making leads us to ask how these opportunities differ in our eight political systems, in order to find out in what kind of situations of responsibility their citizens find themselves. Once this has been done, we should be able to reach some conclusions about the channels of representation that could be created, and about means for their creation. Before we can do this, however, we will have to account for differences among the systems of representation in the eight countries. Here as elsewhere, a number of ready-made explanations are at hand, again offered by the two main schools of thought, the determinist and the institutional. Members of both schools usually make the rigid distinction between parties and interest groups criticized above. Most of those who offer explanations of differences concentrate on parties. They distinguish party systems in terms of the number of parties they contain. First, there are one-party systems, which we can ignore in the case of totalitarian regimes, but will refer to in member states of federal systems. Next come two-party systems, which may be either tightly disciplined, as in Britain, or loosely organized as in the United States. Finally, there are multiparty systems, which exist in our five Continental European countries, and may run the gamut from three to an infinite number of parties, and from rigidity to flux.

Most of the literature on party systems has been preoccupied with the differences between two-party systems on the British model and multiparty systems on the French model. The determinist school explains these differences with reference to historical data, the institutional school in terms of constitutional and legal devices. In the next chapter, we will examine some of these interpretations critically, while bearing in mind both our rejection of an absolute distinction between political parties and interest organizations, and our conception of what it is that organizations of this type do in the flow of policy.

CHAPTER 20

Social Structure and

Interest Identification

The determinist and the institutional schools of thought offer opposing interpretations of differences among party systems. In this chapter, we will be concerned with the determinist approach, which focuses on historical causes. According to the determinists, differences in the past problems of political systems account for differences in their present party systems. The main distinction in the present, on which such studies concentrate, is that between two-party systems and multiparty systems. Some of the determinists do not deal directly with party systems at all, because they view these as an irrelevant part of the "superstructure." But their explanation of social structure and of the cleavages existing in a society have been used by political scientists, for whom differences among party systems are of importance.

We need not be very definite about a scheme for classifying party systems in order to become aware of the major difference on this score between the Continental and the English-speaking countries. In all of the latter, national politics has usually been dominated by two—or at the most, for brief periods, by three—political parties. In all of the Continental ones, national politics has always been dominated by at least three parties, and often by half a dozen or more. Nor is the preoccupation of political science with this major difference surprising, since popular elections are the most dramatic events in democracies, and parties are the most active participants in election campaigns. Almost as dramatic as elections is the maneuvering that follows the resignation of a cabinet, and this maneuvering, at least as reported in the press, takes place mainly among party leaders. Moreover, the paralysis of democratic politics in coping with its problems has often been demonstrated most obviously and disastrously by the inability of the parties to get together on common policies. This happened before the demise of the Weimar Republic and toward the end of the Third and Fourth French Republics.

Explanations of the French Party System

Many students of politics have been led to the conclusion that the French type of multiparty system is incompatible with the maintenance of constitutional democracy. The relative success of the party systems of the English-speaking countries, by contrast, has suggested to them that two-party systems are best suited for this purpose. This conclusion overlooks the success of multiparty systems in Sweden and other Scandinavian countries, in the Low Countries, and in Switzerland, but it has nevertheless stimulated a great deal of inquiry into the causes of the French multiparty system. Four of these explanations, arrived at by scholars of more or less determinist outlooks, are sketched below.

1. Three Institutional Orders: The sociologist John E. Sawyer speaks of three different "institutional orders" into which French society has been divided.[1] He labels them traditionalist, bourgeois, and industrial. Each of them has its own economic and social base. The traditionalist order is represented by the Catholic Church, the army, and others who respect traditional authority, among them some peasants. The bourgeois order is based upon the Revolution and the Third Republic. Its economic leanings are toward commercial, as distinguished from industrial, capitalism. The main conflicts within the Third Republic were over issues between these two institutional orders, and the great cleavage between them was never effectively resolved. Then, superimposed upon this unresolved conflict, there came into being the industrial order. It was built up outside the other two, but was never absorbed by either of them nor fitted into the framework of French society.

The industrial order has, instead, existed outside or alongside of French society, and has been resisted by the two older institutional orders, mainly because of its large-scale proportions, which are almost

[1] John E. Sawyer, "Strains in the Social Structure of Modern France," in Edwin M. Earle, ed., *Modern France,* 1951, pp. 293 ff.

"American." The traditionalists in Church and army would naturally resent the antitraditional effects that industrialism had upon French society and upon their own interests. And the bourgeoisie, whose economic base consisted of small enterprises and emphasized commercial exchange, would feel threatened by large economic organizations that emphasize production. The traditionalist order finds political expression in parties like that of the monarchists—who helped to bring the Third Republic into being, and whose various offshoots continued to play a role throughout the life of the Third Republic—and in supporters of Marshal Pétain's Vichy regime during World War II. The bourgeois order is represented by the Radicals and Conservatives. And the industrial order, by the Communists and Socialists.

2. *Three Traditions:* Another interpretation, which was popular during the brief period of tripartism that followed Liberation in 1944, has been advanced by Charles A. Micaud, a political scientist.[2] He traces three "traditions" in French politics: authority, liberty, and equality. The authoritarian tradition is represented by the forces of the political right: "traditionalists," "Bonapartists," and "integral nationalists." The egalitarian tradition is represented by the forces of the political left: Marxist socialists, syndicalists, and Communists. The libertarian tradition, finally, is represented by the political center and more especially its progressive part, which is constantly torn between the socialist left and the conservative or reactionary right.

Times of crisis aggravate this tripartite grouping by producing polarization around the two extremes. This would seem to suggest a trend toward a kind of two-camp division in French politics, which would be even worse than a similar division that some students of Italian politics have been detecting in that country. There, the supporters of the constitution were divided from its opponents. In France, under these conditions, the polarization would pit against each other two camps of opponents of the constitution. There is considerable overlap evident between the three institutional orders and the three traditions, in terms of which these two students of French politics explain the divisions of French society reflected in the party system. The authoritarian tradition corresponds to the traditionalist order, the libertarian tradition to the bourgeois order, and the egalitarian tradition to the industrial order. The next explanation does not show as much overlapping with the first two.

---

[2] Charles A. Micaud, "The Third Force Today," in Earle, *op. cit.,* pp. 137 ff.

3. Order versus *Movement:* François Goguel interprets French politics on the basis of two antagonistic "forces"—the force of established order and the force of movement.[3] In the Third Republic, the former was represented by conservatism, Roman Catholicism, and antirepublicanism. The force of movement was represented by progressivism, anticlericalism, and democracy. But superimposed upon this one cleavage, and complicating it, there are a number of new issues that have been of importance in the Fourth Republic. Among these are conflicts between the Resistance during World War II and French collaborators with the Germans, and disputes over retention or liquidation of France's overseas empire and over European union or maintenance of full national "sovereignty." These newer issues complicate the old two-way conflict, because not all the partisans of movement agree on proposals for the resolution of the new issues, nor do all the partisans of established order.

4. Two "Geological Faults": A similar multiplicity of cleavages, which do not always coincide with one another, is the basis of David Thomson's interpretation of French politics.[4] The two main geological faults, which divide Frenchmen from one another, were caused by the earthquakes of the French Revolution and the Industrial Revolution. The first cleavage divides supporters of the Revolution from supporters of the Old Regime. The second, which does not coincide with the first but cuts across it, divides the supporters of social and economic progress from the upholders of the status quo in these respects. In Britain, by contrast, the existence of only one such cleavage presumably accounts for the existence of only two major political camps. In France, the two revolutions—constitutional and Industrial—occurred simultaneously, whereas in Britain the one preceded the other.

The presence of two nonidentical cleavages in the French political system makes possible at least four different combinations of attitudes on issues. One can be both for the Republic and for social progress, like the Socialists. One can be against the Republic and for social progress, like the Communists. One can support the constitution but oppose economic progress, like the Radicals and Conservatives. And one can oppose both the Republic and social progress, as did groups like the semifascist *Croix de Feu* under the Third Republic. According to the logic of this interpretation, France should have a four-party system. The fact that she has never had one, however, may be due to the shifting

[3] *France Under the Fourth Republic,* 1952.
[4] *Democracy in France,* 1958, p. 36 and *passim.*

alignment of alliances, as different issues become dominant for short periods.

These four explanations of the French party system do not exhaust all the available ones, but they are reasonably typical of those advanced by scholars who look beyond institutions. They are fairly similar in their approach, in that they search for some historical "cause," which is then reflected in the social and economic structure, or in the people's attitudes toward authority. There is much to be said for each of these interpretations, and just because each contains some truth, they do not mutually contradict each other. They are also helpful, because—*mutatis mutandis*—they can tell us something about the other Continental party systems in addition to that of France. For example, the transition from preconstitutionalism to constitutional democracy in Germany also co-incided with the main impact of the Industrial Revolution, and was further complicated by the problem of national unification. Germany could also be said to have authoritarian, libertarian, and egalitarian strands, although it has lacked an unabsorbed industrial order. The point is that the questions suggested by these four theories of French politics could easily be asked about other countries and would result in meaningful answers.

The main shortcoming of these determinist interpretations is their excessive preoccupation with the problems that gave rise to divisions, to the neglect, first, of the machinery—like parliamentary committees—by means of which these problems have been dealt with; and, second, of the degree of awareness of their common interests on the part of groups that had special problems. Unless there is some such awareness, there would not be any parties—parts of the whole, that is. And the institutions by means of which decisions about problems are made are bound to affect the ways in which interests are organized and operate. We will see in greater detail how this happens in our critique, in Chapter 21, of the institutionalists' explanations of differences among party systems. At this point, we will deal with one instance of the effect of the structure of the policy flow on the representation of interests.

Interest Groups and Self-Regulation

In Chapter 16, we suggested that the most efficient deliberation occurring in the German, French, and Italian parliaments goes on in their specialized committees. In the Bundestag, the committees usually deliberate upon issues formulated by the Chancellor, the resolution of which is often a foregone conclusion. In France and Italy, many issues that the lower houses cannot resolve are passed on to the committees. Many others are generated there in the first place. In the Third and Fourth Republics, the National Assembly followed the recommendations of its own committees more readily than those of Cabinet ministers. In effect, this meant that some types of issues were almost regularly decided in the parliamentary committees, which therefore functioned as more decentralized equivalents of the single focus of resolution in Great Britain or Canada.

The types of issues handled by the committees are those whose settlement affects special segments of the population coming under the purview of the specialized committees. For example, the agriculture committee is in charge of the regulation of trademarks for cheese, and the committee on fermented liquors has jurisdiction over matters of wine labeling. In Germany, to turn to something more serious, the labor committee deals with labor relations, including matters like codetermination. The deliberation and resolution of these issues require specialized knowledge. They can be finally resolved only if the people affected by the consequences of decisions will accept the resolution arrived at centrally. And this kind of acceptance can be elicited, among other means, by getting these exposed groups to contribute to making the decisions, and to contribute in a more direct and obvious way than that provided by plenary meetings of parliament. In the United States, this additional channel for contributing to central deliberation and resolution is provided by congressional committees, where representatives of specially exposed groups are literally given a "hearing," normally in public. On the Continent, as already mentioned, the practice of hearing public or private testimony from interested groups is virtually unknown. Why do the Continental committees nevertheless constitute such important funnels in the policy flow?

The interest groups concerned with a committee's work need not be represented before the committee because they are represented *on* the committee—overrepresented in many cases. The labor committee, for example, always has many officers of both trade unions and employers' associations among its members. The agriculture committee has a high proportion of agriculturists of varying backgrounds, many of them also officers of agricultural interest organizations. In the Bundestag, at least twelve of the twenty-seven members of the committee on nutrition, agriculture, and forestry were officers of interest groups; ten of twenty-one members of the labor committee were leading officials of the Trade Union Federation; at least sixteen of the twenty-one members of the committee on civil service law were civil servants. And this list could be extended, as well as duplicated for the French and Italian parliaments.

The availability of this channel for contributing to deliberation or resolution of issues in which they are interested leads special groups to want to place their representatives right on the committees. In some cases, it has led to the founding of new organizations, whose members were not previously conscious of their common interests. The existence of the specialized committees encourages interest organizations to initiate the regulation of their own affairs. This means that in many cases it is not the state that initiates regulation of economic or cultural organizations, but the "pressure groups" that ask the state, through the parliamentary committees on which they are directly represented, to regulate their activities. When the availability of parliamentary committees leads to the organization of a new interest, this is usually for the expressed purpose of obtaining special state regulation. These practices are connected with the fact that groups we would consider interest organizations in the United States, like the Refugee League, go directly into politics by putting up candidates for elective office. The decisions made by the committees and their composition, combined with the leanings toward legalism, have produced a vast and intricate network of legislation and regulation of all spheres of life in the Continental countries.

Since every interest group has the opportunity to participate in its own regulation, most of them completely lack the kind of antistatist sentiments frequently associated, in the United States, with advocacy of private free enterprise capitalism. Even avowedly liberal businessmen in America are much more antistatist than their Continental counterparts. The latter often display what can best be described as a yearning to be regulated by the state. Of course, there are variations in this respect from one country to the next; e.g., this yearning seems stronger in Germany than in France, probably because Germany never had its equivalent of the French Revolution and has a more markedly legalistic style. In France, the regulation solicited from the state more often affects relations among various interests, and between them and the state. In Germany, where this kind of regulation is also sought, there is a strong additional desire to have the state lay down rules governing the internal activities and procedures of individual interest groups.

The pervasiveness of the desire for regulation by the state and national differences in this respect can be illustrated with one French and one German example. Before the French parliamentary elections of January, 1956, Pierre Poujade converted an interest group, which he had organized as an outlet for the economic grievances of small shop-keepers and artisans, into a political party—in the sense that its leaders ran for office. It immediately gained more than 11 per cent of the popular vote and about forty seats in the National Assembly. Before this, his organization had exerted pressure for revision of the tax laws in favor of its constituents, and to discourage implementation of the tax laws. It had also been responsible for some taxpayers' strikes. When Poujade decided that it would be more expedient to try to enter Parliament directly, he presented a program to the public. The only positive plank contained in this platform called for the reconstitution of the old Estates General, whose meeting in 1789 had set off the Revolution. At that time, the Estates General consisted of three estates: nobility, clergy, and the "third estate," the equivalent of the burghers' estate of the Swedish Riksdag. Poujade now advocated that it be reëstablished with six estates: shopkeepers, peasants, professional people, civil servants, employers, and industrial workers. Although he did not spell this out, each estate would presumably have run its own affairs, while relations among them would have been settled in the Estates General. This French interest organization thus first attempted to get protection from the state against other economic groups, whose progress, in contrast with the stagnation of the shopkeepers' sector of the economy, threatened it, especially through taxation. Then it sought to achieve even better contributions to the making of central decisions by sending its own leaders into the National Assembly, and at the same time advanced a program for constitutional reform, which would have resulted in stronger state regulation of relations among presumably antagonistic interests, leaving to each interest the regulation of its own internal affairs with the use of the authority of the state.

In Germany, some measure of self-regulation by economic interests has traditionally been exercised by the chambers of commerce and industry. These are creatures of public law, that is, they wield some of the powers of the "sovereign." Their public-law character is shown most clearly by legislation making membership in the chambers compulsory for certain categories of business. It is as though the United States Chamber of Commerce were an agency of the federal government and all business firms whose annual volume exceeded a stated minimum were required to belong to its branches in the fifty states of the Union. In German practice, this has meant that these businessmen's organizations, in regulating their own internal affairs, exercise powers that formerly "belonged" to the state and were delegated by it to the chambers of commerce and industry. Before the state acquired these functions through centralization, they had been exercised by medieval corporations, estates, or guilds, all of them forerunners of modern interest organizations.

In 1955, the German Trade Union Federation claimed that the wielding of state authority gave business and industry a privileged position. This might have led the unions to urge that the chambers be stripped of these sovereign functions. But far from urging that, the Trade Union Federation demanded that legislation be passed making the unions compulsory members of the chambers, along with business and industry. This controversy had still not been settled four years later.

Economic Councils

Similar motives have led the West German trade unions to advocate reëstablishment of a Federal Economic Council, to replace the Reich Economic Council of the Weimar Republic. They envisage this Economic Council as the capstone of the codetermination scheme, through which the state has laid down the procedures governing relations between employees, employers, and unions at the level of individual business companies. The Reich Economic Council was designed as a common meeting place for representatives of economic interests, especially employers, trade unions, and the "free professions," whose members are usually identified with the academic intelligentsia. In the Weimar Republic, this "third house of Parliament" turned out to be of little practical usefulness and performed functions that were mainly advisory. The Fourth Republic also had its Economic Council. It contained representatives of the trade unions, commerce and industry, agriculture, coöperatives, economists and other scientists, "victims of war damage," and family associations.[5] The French Economic Council was no more effective than the late German one.

One reason for the failure of these third houses was the fact that the specialized parliamentary committees already performed the function for which the economic councils were brought into being. Representatives of employers and employees in the great sectors of the economy can reconcile their differences on the labor and economic committees of the Bundestag and the National Assembly. Only when issues arise affecting more than one of these major sectors, do these committees cease to be useful in resolving conflicts. When this happens, disagreements usually arise between two committees or among several of them. These controversies develop when the meeting of the full house has to decide to which committee or committees to send a bill

[5] See Philip Williams, *Politics in Postwar France*, 1958, p. 297.

for specialized deliberation. This sort of conflict arose, for example, in the course of the French debates over Coca-Cola.

When a parliament fulfills its resolving function—a relatively rare thing in the Fourth Republic—the committees take on the role of representatives of interests, who deliberate upon the resolutions of parliament. When the parliament fails to take care of its job of resolution, this task is parceled out to the committees, which are not qualified for it. Then the result consists of a series of policies in separate fields of problems, each of which may be perfectly sound taken by itself, but all of which may mutually contradict one another. The many specialized policies then do not fit into an over-all program designed to deal with all the problems of the system, using all of its resources, based upon "representations" made by all of the affected interests.

Representation of Interests in Great Britain

We have argued that the availability of specialized parliamentary committees in the major Continental systems encourages interests to contribute to the policy flow at this point; and that the failure of these parliaments to give resolution encourages them to devolve this function to their committees. In West Germany today, the committees attract interests less because of parliamentary failure to resolve issues—since that is the Chancellor's responsibility—than because of parliamentary failure to provide for efficient deliberation upon resolution by the Chancellor. The committees of the Bundestag can engage in more efficient deliberation than the full meeting of the chamber, since committee members consider themselves representatives of interests more than representatives of political parties during committee sessions. And the interests represented on any one committee often seem more concerned with the orderly internal regulation of their sector of the political system than with conflicts among the subsectors existing within it. In other words, there is more agreement on the need for regulation of agriculture or of industrial relations than there is disagreement among the various groups interested in agricultural policy or in industrial relations policy. Above all, there is the desire to obtain a quantum of the state's authority for the purpose of ordering the internal affairs of the major interests—a desire that we will presently discuss. First, however, it is necessary to establish the fact that there truly exists an essential difference between the representation of interests on the Continent, as just described, and that function as it operates in Great Britain and the United States.

For the British case, one would have to admit that the Committees of the House of Commons are indeed so unspecialized as to be designated by letters of the alphabet.[6] But the various special-interest groups are nonetheless represented in the House, and have been since the eighteenth century. From its very beginnings, the Labour party's contingent in Parliament has included many M.P.'s who were—and still are—openly subsidized by trade unions. In recent years, about one-fifth of the members of Parliament have been directors of commercial or industrial companies. The head of the British Legion, the largest veterans' organization, has been a Conservative member for many years. Naturally, all these representatives of interest groups always vote as disciplined members of one of the two great political parties (unless they happen to be among the few Liberals). Still, there are additional channels through which interest groups can contribute to the flow of policy, by means of direct contacts with the ministries and the nationalized industries. In several instances, these contacts have been institutionalized through the establishment of permanent consultative councils, membership on which is extended to representatives of groups especially interested in the activities of the ministry or the nationalized industry in question.

Nevertheless, there are great differences in practice and motivation between all of this and its parallels on the Continent. Groups in Britain that are conscious of having special interests do not approach the state in order to obtain from it authority for the regulation of their internal affairs. The interest organizations know how to handle their own business and want to be left alone in its conduct. They approach Parliament, Cabinet, or bureaucracy in order to promote their interests in a concrete way—greater farm subsidies, higher social security benefits, a more advantageous tax structure, and so forth. These interests are thought of largely in economic terms. Whereas in the Continental countries the recipients of extremes of low and high income in the same sector of the economy are often more conscious of their common interests as, say, agriculturists, interest-consciousness in Britain is horizontally stratified. In other words, the owners of large estates recognize that their interests are different from those of small farmers. And workers in the steel industry are aware of having interests largely opposed to their employers', while on the Continent one sometimes gets the impression that most people in the steel industry, regardless of their status, are conscious of their common interests as opposed to those of, say, agriculture.

There is a further difference between British and Continental interest representation. Trade-union officials who are also members of Par-

[6] See page 255.

liament occasionally make speeches in the House giving the attitudes of their unions on the issue under deliberation. These views may be opposed to the resolution that has been proposed by the Cabinet. This happened from time to time even while the Labour party was in office. Nevertheless, these trade-union critics of Cabinet policy always voted with the Labour party, that is, in support of the Cabinet, when the debate had ended. In France, by contrast, representatives of winegrowers' interests voted against the policy on Coca-Cola of a Cabinet in which their political party was participating. In Germany, trade-union officers who were deputies of the Christian Democratic Union broke parliamentary party discipline in both the labor committee and meetings of the full Bundestag, when they disagreed with the Chancellor's resolution of the issue of codetermination. In both cases, these parliamentarians were motivated more by the special problems in which they were interested than by the general problem the leaders of their political parties were trying to solve by means of integrated over-all programs.

Finally, another peculiarity of interest participation in politics differentiates the British from the Continental cases. When the Labour Cabinet that came into office in 1945 put into effect its program for nationalizing many industries, their management was put into the hands of boards, such as the National Coal Board, whose members were appointed by a Cabinet minister. A number of trade-union officers were appointed to these boards in charge of great industries. These men immediately severed their connections with their unions, and board members of managerial background severed their connections with management. In this case, the background of personnel entrusted with making decisions about a special problem area pointed unmistakably to their previous position as representatives of interests specially affected. Nevertheless, the bias against self-regulation with public authority was still so strong that every effort was made to deny that this was an instance of self-regulation. The National Coal Board was set up to manage the coal industry for the government, not to enable the coal industry to manage its own affairs with added authority delegated to it by the government. For Continental schemes of regulation and nationalization, the latter statement gives a better description of both motives and practice.

Representation of Interests in the United States

The specialized committees of the Senate and the House of Representatives often do seem to make important decisions not unlike those made by parliamentary committees in France and Germany. Both inside and outside of the committees, congressional voting is characterized by lack of party discipline, at least as compared with Great Britain. But unlike Continental committees, the membership of the congressional committees very rarely contains officers of interest organizations whose activities are affected by the scope of a committee's work. Officers of economic-interest organizations hardly ever become candidates for congressional office. The banking committee is not controlled by men of financial background, or the civil service committee by former civil servants. The agriculture committee contains active members from such unagricultural districts as Brooklyn, New York. Whenever the suspicion is raised that a committee is unduly influenced by groups affected by its work, the cry of "vested interests" is immediately raised.

American like British interest organizations approach the Congress not for the regulation of their internal affairs, but in pursuit of concrete goals. It is only when some organization is suspected of grave internal crime or corruption that the Congress approaches it in order to clean its house, or—more often—help the organization clean its own house. And whenever that happens, it is usually on instigation of an opposing interest group. Even then, the Congress is frequently accused of undue meddling in the internal affairs of a "great American organization, consisting of law-abiding citizens. . . ."

United States regulatory commissions, like the Federal Communications Commission and the Federal Trade Commission, perform some functions similar to those of the national boards in Great Britain. They have to make decisions about internal conflicts, for example, between two applicants for a television channel. When a commissioner acts so as to cause suspicion that he has the interest of the regulated industry or some of its members more at heart than the "public interest," chances are that a congressional investigation will result in his dismissal or resignation from the commission. In order to keep the regulatory commissions from becoming instruments of industrial self-regulation with public authority, the Congress enacted laws that forbid commissioners or bureaucrats working for the commissions to accept private employment in the regulated industry for a specified period of time after leaving the commission.

At the top level, representatives of the great interests regulated by the executive departments of the federal government are frequently appointed to the President's Cabinet. A prominent businessman may become Secretary of Commerce, a labor-union official Secretary of Labor, and an industrialist or even a general Secretary of Defense. When this happens, these men are expected to divest themselves of their more direct connections with the interest in question. The case of the president of the General Motors Corporation, who had to sell millions of dollars' worth of stock in the company before the Senate would confirm his appointment as Secretary of Defense, illustrates this kind of effort, aimed at denying to special interests a share of public authority.

In the case of a general, the traditional American separation of civilian and military functions carries even further the effort to divorce interests. When General George C. Marshall was nominated Secretary of Defense, the normal senatorial consent to this appointment had to be supplemented by a special act of Congress before he could legally occupy the position. And General Dwight D. Eisenhower severed the connections normally retained for life by five-star generals before he became a candidate for the Republican nomination for President of the United States.

Continental interests thus obtain the regulation of their internal affairs, while British and American interests pursue material, mainly economic, goals through their representatives. These work on Congress and Parliament, and the bureaucracy, rather than through the direct presence of their officers in parliamentary committees. The English-speaking countries' bias against delegating public authority to private-interest organizations is lacking on the Continent. As a final difference, the British are conscious of, and organized in, horizontal interest groups, motivated by common economic problems, while the Continentals are more conscious of, and organized in, vertical interest groups, motivated by common functional or occupational problems. Most American interests follow the horizontal British pattern; e.g., employees are conscious of their common problems as such, as are employers, and individuals join or support organizations serving people of their economic status. But this pattern is somewhat confused by two factors: first, the geographical concentration of some economic interests, which is also reflected in congressional voting patterns; and second, the existence of great cultural interests, both ethnic and religious, which cut vertically across the horizontal lines dividing economic interests from one another. Despite these two factors, however, the consciousness and organization of economic interests in Britain and the United States are alike in their relation to levels of income. Economic-interest groups on the Continent, by contrast, often combine the many different levels of income of people connected with the same industry or sector of the economy.

Corporatism

We began this inquiry into the representation of interests, because we had found the determinist explanation of differences among party systems inadequate, since it dealt only with the problems that had given rise to political groupings, and neglected the institutional channels through which these groupings could seek to contribute to the making of policy. The existence of many specialized committees in the Continental parliaments provides one such channel, and the relative multiplicity of political groupings in these countries is likely to have some connection with this. Especially in the Third and Fourth Republics, where no other organ provided integrated resolution, the committees were in a position to do the next best thing to that, to resolve issues in their special fields. In Britain, the continuous capacity of the Cabinet to resolve issues makes committees superfluous. In the United States, the capacity of the President to carry on the government—a capacity lower than that of the British Cabinet, but higher than that of any French organ—leads congressional committees to spend much time on the deliberation of resolutions proposed by the President. In West Germany, where the tenure of the Chancellor is almost as secure as that of the President of the United States, but the deliberative functions of the Bundestag are performed much less efficiently than in the English-speaking countries, committees of the Bundestag offer interest organizations good opportunities to contribute to deliberation.

However, having said this much, we still have not explained the tendency of Continental interest organizations to form separate groupings inside parliament, either as new "parties," or within and cutting across existing parties. Nor have we explained why voters in the English-speaking countries have usually been content to let parliamentary deliberation take place between two major parties, each of which either combines many affiliated interest organizations among its followers, or tries to attract the support of interest organizations not affiliated with it. That the capacity for resolution of Cabinet or President cannot be the sole cause of these major differences between the English-speaking and the Continental systems is indicated by the Swedish case. The Crown-Cabinet has provided just as much resolution for Swedish politics as it has in Great Britain. As a result, the Riksdag has normally confined itself to deliberating upon decisions of the Cabinet. Yet five parties have been represented in the Riksdag during recent decades. And self-regulation of interest organizations with delegated public authority is frowned upon no more in Sweden than in the other Continental countries. This similarity in the politics of all the Continental countries must be due to something they share in common, something that is lacking in the English-speaking world.

Sweden presents the clearest illustration of this differentiating feature, which is the persistence of ancient corporatist institutions and habits of thought and action. By *corporatism* we mean a vertically, functionally, hierarchically structured conception of society, after the medieval model, in which the various estates of the realm were represented vis-à-vis the monarch in parliament. In order to avoid misunderstanding, the popular identification of corporatism with either Roman Catholicism or fascism should be ruled out from the beginning. It is true that Roman Catholic social doctrine is explicitly corporatist, partly because of its medieval source. But corporatist habits of thought and action are at least as strong in Sweden as in most Catholic countries, even though 99 per cent of the Swedes are Protestants. The stability of constitutional democracy in Sweden, and the failure of fascists to get a toehold there in the 1930's, should demonstrate that the espousal of corporatism by men like Benito Mussolini does not make it a fascist program. Nor are we including under our use of the term what has sometimes been called American "neocorporatism," that is, the alleged domination of politics by a few great interest organizations, like business, labor, or farmers. The main differences between this American phenomenon and Continental corporatism is the engineered and untraditionalist character of the American interest organizations and their horizontal stratification according to level of income. The lack of any corporatist tradition in the United States makes it very difficult indeed to defend the reform of society along these lines and to justify the self-regulation of interest organizations with public authority. The failure of attempts by the New Deal to legislate corporatism, as in the National Industrial Recovery Act, is a case in point.

Traditionalist corporatism is completely absent in the United States, but not in Canada, because the United States never passed through a feudal phase in its history, whereas Canada did. This explains, among other things, the existence of the separate Catholic trade union in Quebec. Corporate institutions in Great Britain are, of course, even stronger than in Canada and, at first glance, appear to be as important as on the Continent. The British Crown itself is even older than the Swedish and dates from a time when it was the apex of the whole corporate pyramid. Then there are ancient corporations like the City of London and the Fishmongers' Company—and the great universities, which even had their own special representatives in the House of Commons until the parliamentary reforms of the postwar Labour Cabinet. However, these institutions today perform only "dignified," as distinguished from "efficient" functions, in Walter Bagehot's terms, i.e., they do not affect policy. For example, the annual Guildhall dinner is the occasion for speeches by distinguished personalities, somewhat like American college commencements. The forms of corporatism have survived in the United Kingdom, but only to provide occasions for the display of pomp and circumstance. The best illustration of this is the survival of monarchy itself, the aloofness of the Queen from politics, and the tremendous popularity of the royal family with all classes of the population, in both Britain and the Commonwealth countries abroad.

The weakness of corporatism in Great Britain is shown by other events besides the abolition of the university constituencies. In the 1920's, a small group of socialist intellectuals, under the leadership of G. D. H. Cole, started a very vocal movement on behalf of what they called "guild socialism." Its goal was the reorganization of the economy on corporatist lines, that is, so that all the people connected with one industry, whether owners, managers, white-collar workers, or manual laborers, would be organized in and represented through one corporation or guild. At one time, even Winston Churchill, a staunch "House of Commons man" as he was later to call himself, suggested establishment of a third, economic house of Parliament. But, whether or not he ment this seriously, such proposals never got anywhere in Great Britain, and guild socialism turned out to be a total failure.

After the nationalization of industries, some of the earlier guild socialists in the Labour party wanted to introduce workers' control in these industries—a scheme which also smacks of corporatism—only to have the proposal rejected summarily by the overwhelming majority of the Labour party and the Trade Union Congress affiliated with it. Indeed, the British outlook is so uncorporatist that a study of German codetermination, conducted by the Fabian Society and the trade unions, roundly condemned this experiment, largely because its authors were unable to put themselves into the Germans' corporatist state of mind.

On the Continent, by contrast, codetermination evoked sympathetic understanding on the part of the French, who unsuccessfully tried out a similar scheme, and of the Italians, whose politics is still permeated by carry-overs of fascist corporate institutions. But there are many other, more dramatic examples of the persistence of corporatism in the Continental systems. The German Social Democratic Party, which originally came into existence in order to represent the working *class,* has repeatedly throughout the century of its existence referred to the "workers' *estate*" (*Arbeiterstand*) in its official programs. Many German workers today think of themselves as members of the workers' estate, which they and others distinguish from the artisans' estate, the peasants' estate, the middle estate (not class), and others. When the National Socialists under Hitler proclaimed their intention of doing away with all social distinctions in Germany, they attacked not merely classes, but *Klassen und Stände*—classes and estates. The public relations work of German interest organizations and parties alike nowadays almost always seeks to identify the particular public they happen to be addressing with some allegedly ancient and honorable guild or estate. This is true even of those interest organizations that cannot really make any such claim, like the automotive industry and its affiliates. Officers of these organizations, especially of the more modern and—temporally speaking—rootless ones, believe that this attempted identification with corporatist forerunners gives them status and prestige and feigned or real public authority which they would otherwise lack.

This is also true of members of Continental civil services, a point often missed by political scientists comparing the social and economic composition of Continental socialist parties with that of the Labour party. These comparisons are usually made in terms of the British categories of upper, middle, and lower class. The majority of British civil servants probably consider themselves members of the middle class. When a survey discloses that relatively fewer bureaucrats belong to the British Labour party than to the French Socialist party, the conclusion easily suggests itself that British bureaucrats are more "class-conscious" than their French counterparts and therefore avoid affiliation with the party of the working class. However, if the French civil servants are indeed less class-conscious, this may be due to their being more "estate-conscious." They do not consider themselves middle class; they consider themselves civil servants, that is, members of an ancient and honorable estate of the Realm and the regimes that followed it. West Germany's government personnel have the same attitude, although they further divide themselves up into two categories: "civil servants" (*Beamte*) and, enjoying less prestige, "public employees" (*öffentliche Angestellte*).

Poujade's desire to reconstitute the Estates General, already described, is another instance of the contemporary vitality of Continental corporatism. The attempt to initiate the complete revision of the Swiss constitution along corporatist lines, in 1935, is still another; it was defeated, to be sure, yet 196,000 voters supported this corporatist scheme, as did three cantons, while 511,000 voted against it.

Images of Social Structure

We can describe graphically the meaning of corporatist social-consciousness on the Continent with two diagrams (page 329). If we showed these two diagrams to a representative sample of Continentals and British and asked them which came closer to giving an accurate portrait of social structure, chances are that the British would pick the horizontally stratified diagram on the left, while at least a good many Continentals would pick the vertically stratified one on the right. It is difficult to assess accurately the degree of this difference between the two images of society; exaggeration is quite possible. Nevertheless, it is abundantly clear that even a difference of much lesser degree would still be of tremendous importance for a proper understanding of the politics of Continental countries, and especially of their party systems.

Most historians and social scientists who have studied these countries have been looking for classes and class-consciousness in them. Of course, "objectively" speaking, all of them do have classes, if classes are defined in terms of the relation of their members to the means of production, in the Marxian sense, or if they are defined with respect to levels of income. Even the United States, where there is very little of the British type of class-consciousness, has classes in both these senses. The Continental countries, however, in addition to classes and class-consciousness, also have institutional carry-overs of the old estates and subjective "hangovers" of corporate-consciousness. We cannot understand their politics unless we keep this corporate-consciousness in mind, although this may be just as difficult as it is for Americans to look at foreign governments without asking questions about the separation of powers into legislative, executive, and judicial branches—questions that make very little sense in very many countries.

This difficulty in looking for anything but classes and class-consciousness is largely due to the impact of the dictum of Karl Marx and Friedrich Engels, proclaimed in 1848 in *The Communist Manifesto,* that all history has been the history of class struggles. The challenge of this assertion has led most historians and social scientists, Marxists and anti-Marxists alike, to look for classes, that is, horizontal layers in society. As a result, they have sometimes seen things that were not really there, and overlooked others that were. They have done this because Marx's categories of thought have impressed themselves upon the mind in a much simpler way than even Marx himself intended. After all, he emphasized that

SIMPLIFIED DIAGRAMS
of
SOCIAL-CONSCIOUSNESS

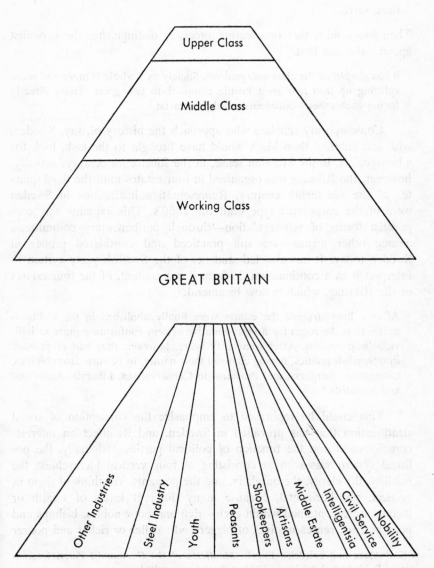

Upper Class

Middle Class

Working Class

GREAT BRITAIN

Other Industries · Steel Industry · Youth · Peasants · Shopkeepers · Artisans · Middle Estate · Intelligentsia · Civil Service · Nobility

CONTINENTAL COUNTRIES

in earlier epochs of history, we find almost everywhere a *complicated* arrangement of society into various orders, a manifold gradation of social rank. In ancient Rome we have patricians, knights, plebeians, slaves; in the Middle Ages, feudal lords, vassals, guild-masters, journeymen, apprentices, serfs. . . .

Then Marx adds that one feature precisely distinguishes the capitalist epoch—the fact that

it has *simplified* the class antagonisms. Society as a whole is more and more splitting up into *two* great hostile camps, into two great classes directly facing each other—bourgeoisie and proletariat.[7]

Contemporary scholars who approach the history of, say, Sweden, with less subtlety than Marx would have brought to the task, look for a bourgeoisie, in the Marxian sense, in the fourteenth century; actually, however, the Riksdag was organized in four estates until the third quarter of the nineteenth century. Representative institutions in Sweden were of the corporatist type until the 1860's. This explains why corporatist forms of self-regulation—through parliamentary committees, among other means—are still practiced and considered proper in Sweden today. It has also led students of the Swedish party system to interpret it as a continuation, in form if not content, of the four estates of the Riksdag, which is now bicameral:

After a long struggle the estates were finally abolished in the eighteen-sixties to make room for a representative system conforming more to individualistic notions. After some fifty years, however, they had crept back into Swedish politics, having changed their names, to be sure, from Nobles, Clergymen, Burghers, and Peasants, to Conservatives, Liberals, Agrarians, and Socialists.[8]

This could be rephrased to emphasize the conception of social stratification that has prevailed in Sweden, and its effect on interest-consciousness and the function of political parties. Originally, the political system was seen as consisting of four vertical hierarchies: the nobility, the clergy, the burghers, and the peasants. We think of them as vertical, not horizontal, because many different levels of wealth or income were contained within each—rich and poor nobles, bishops and poor pastors, representatives of bigger and smaller or richer and poorer

[7] Karl Marx and Friedrich Engels, *Manifesto of the Communist Party,* International Publishers, New York, 1932, p. 9. Italics supplied.
[8] Dankwart A. Rustow, *The Politics of Compromise,* 1955, p. 157.

towns, wealthy and poor peasants. The representatives of these estates were supposed to deliberate upon policies proposed to them by the Crown, not to bring forth comprehensive programs on their own for the future of Sweden.

Then, superimposed upon this corporatist consciousness, came the ideas about classes and class conflict in economic terms. Before the Social Democratic party was founded, the old estates were abolished. If all estate-consciousness had been wiped away by this constitutional reform, then the new Marxist party might have considered its function to be the presentation and implementation of a comprehensive program for Sweden. It did work out such a program, but once its leaders came into the Cabinet, the Social Democrats continued to conduct the business of the Cabinet in the same way that the business of the Crown had been conducted before abolition of the estates. More important, non-socialist Swedes never recognized this as the function of political parties, whereas in Britain both Labourites and their opponents did think that a party should both present and implement a comprehensive program. The Swedes continued to think of parties as channels for the representation of interests, and they were conscious of their own interests in both the old corporatist and the new class forms. In Britain, primary interest identification was and is with one of the three great classes, which are represented by the political parties, and only secondarily with narrower economic groups, which are affiliated with, or operate upon, the parties. Thus Swedish farmers prefer to be represented in the Riksdag by their own party, which is closely identified with their occupational organization. Even though this Peasant party has often formed coalitions with the Social Democrats, it has not wanted to merge with the Social Democratic party. If it did, farmers might find themselves in poorer situations of responsibility as a result. In any case, their corporatist social-consciousness militates against any such merger.

The continuity of resolution provided by the Crown-Cabinet makes it constitutionally unnecessary for the parliamentary parties to be considered agents of resolution and integration. Since the British Crown-Cabinet gives as much resolution as its Swedish counterpart, however, this constitutional factor operating against the formation of a two-party system cannot be the crucial one. This must rather be the difference in interest-consciousness. Swedes are conscious of a greater number of interests, with one of which they primarily identify themselves. The British are conscious of only two such interests, the working class and the middle class—the upper class having more or less merged with the middle class. Since, by general agreement, parties are channels of representation, they should be expected to reflect popular understanding of what there is to be represented, that is, the prevailing image of social structure and consciousness of interests. In Sweden, where corporatist representative institutions survived longer than in the other four Continental countries, this survival goes far toward explaining the multiparty system.

The Impact of Revolutions

The Swedish explanation does not seem to offer much help in explaining the survival of corporatism and the existence of multiparty systems in the other Continental countries, especially France. After all, the French Revolution was directed specifically against monarchy and any carry-overs from feudalism still attached to it. The Estates General had not been an operative institution when it was reconvened in 1789, and the equal representation it gave to the three estates, which stood for parts of the population very unequal in numbers, was condemned from the very beginning. In its course, the Revolution formally abolished feudal institutions, like estates, guilds, and other traditional and restrictive organizations, which could not be justified by arguments acceptable to the rationalist mind of the French Enlightenment. The *loi le Chapelier* was explicitly designed to wipe out corporatist organizations; it forbade their revival or the establishment of anything resembling them, and it remained on the statute books for a century. Since Great Britain never passed through an antifeudal revolution of this type, and still retains monarchy and other feudal forms, corporatist institutions and interest-consciousness should be stronger there than in France. Why is the reverse nevertheless closer to the truth?

The answer is connected with the single and uncomplicated impact of the Industrial Revolution on the British system, contrasted with its diluted and complex impact on France and the other Continental countries. In Great Britain, the Industrial Revolution took place after the great religious and constitutional problems had been largely solved. Its impact in France, on the contrary, was complicated by the failure to solve either the constitutional or the religious problems, which arose during the same period that brought industrialization to the country on a smaller scale than in the British case. The Industrial Revolution in Britain wiped out the efficient functions of corporate institutions in the flow of policy, leaving only their dignified functions. It was in Britain that Marx analyzed capitalism. His famous lament about the effects of capitalism was based on British experience:

The bourgeoisie, wherever it has got the upper hand has put an end to all feudal, patriarchal, idyllic relations. It has pitilessly torn asunder the motley *feudal ties* that bound man to his "natural superiors," and has left no other bond between man and man than naked self-interest, than callous "cash payment." [9]

This never happened in France, where several great problems struck the system at the same time, so that no one of them had the full impact it would have had alone, uncomplicated by the others. Not even all the deliberate constitutional engineering of the French Revolution, designed to wipe out feudal corporatism, was capable of bringing about the engineers' intentions. Old corporate institutions or new substitutes for them continued to function throughout the existence of the antiassociation law. And corporatist interest-consciousness has never been wiped from the minds of people in the Continental countries to the extent that it has been obliterated in Great Britain.

Guidelines for Constitution-Makers—VI

The determinist approach to the interpretation of differences among party systems contributes its focus on the divisions existing within a political system. That this focus is much needed, if only as an antidote to exclusive preoccupation with institutional devices, will become clear in the next chapter. But the determinists give only one side of the picture, because they neglect institutions. Most of them also make the mistake of rigidly distinguishing between political parties and interest groups. This error is due to failure to look behind the labels of these institutions to their roles in the flow of policy. If both are viewed as channels through which groups that are conscious of facing special problems can contribute to the making of central decisions, the distinction fades away. This becomes especially evident when we acknowledge the fact that parliaments are by no means the only kind of representative institution; many cabinets, courts, and bureaucracies are also deliberately constituted in a representative way, in that their personnel is composed of members of various groups in the system, each of which is aware of its own interests. For example, the Canadian Cabinet contains a fairly stable proportion of French-Canadians and of representatives of the prairie provinces. The United States Supreme Court will probably continue to have one associate justice of the Roman Catholic faith. The Swiss and Canadian federal bureaucracies are supposed to give repre-

[9] Marx and Engels, *op. cit.,* p. 11. Italics supplied.

sentation to various cultural groups in proportion to their share of the total population.

The first guideline for constitution-makers who are concerned with questions of representation is to get a clear picture of interest-conscious-ness in their political system. What are the problems that weigh most heavily on people's minds? What kind of cleavages do the issues arising out of these problems produce? What are the groupings with which people identify themselves?

Next, one should locate the points at which are made the central deci-sions of special interest to the various groupings. Where are issues about the different types of problems formulated, deliberated, and resolved?

Then, the constitution-makers should create channels through which the interest groups will be able to contribute to such decisions. In every case, there will be several points, and there can be a variety of channels.

New channels should, where possible, be constructed so as to facilitate in their operation the use of accepted procedures of associational and local self-government.

Not every form of interest-consciousness should be viewed as "given," since inherited forms, like those connected with ideologism, can be re-duced, and new forms can be created. Awareness of a new interest can be created, for example, through the establishment of a geographic elec-tion district, or of a new parliamentary committee. The effects of consti-tutional changes on interest-consciousness should be gauged in connec-tion with existing disagreements in the system and the new agreements that are sought.

In a political system that has an efficient organ of resolution, there need be no worry about the parties as institutions that integrate policies in special fields and therefore present the electorate with comprehensive and practicable alternative programs. This is generally said to be the chief advantage of two-party systems, but it is not required where sus-tained resolution comes from another source.

In political systems that do not have an efficient organ for the cen-tral resolution of issues, decisions of this type are likely to be pre-empted by the representatives of interest groups, which regulate them-selves with the aid of public authority. This kind of dispersed resolution, however inefficient its operation, may be better than none at all. In any case, its inefficiency in dealing with problems is not caused by the mere presence of the dispersed focuses of resolution—as in the case of French parliamentary committees—but by the absence of an accepted organ of resolution. And this, in turn, cannot be blamed in the first place on the multiparty system, but on the interest-consciousness the party system reflects. Where several interests seem irreconcilably opposed to one another, it may be impossible for them to agree on either the proper locus of resolution or the personnel that should be entrusted with resolution. We will turn to the causes of this kind of antagonism among interests when we take up "consensus," in Chapter 22. In the meantime, we may conclude that efforts to impose a two-party system upon a country with several strongly opposed interest groupings are likely to fail or, at any rate, to produce unintended results. Yet just such efforts have often been made, mainly through the manipulation of election laws. These attempts are based on assumptions arising out of institutional explanations of differences among party systems.

CHAPTER 21

Party Systems

The literature on comparative politics reveals a very strong bias in favor of the two-party system. This bias has often led political scientists to find the "cause" of the two-party system in the method of electing parliamentary representatives that has been in use in the English-speaking countries. By the same token, they have condemned various forms of proportional representation, or other deviations from the English method, that have been in use in the Continental systems and are said, by these political scientists of the institutionalist school, to be the cause of multiparty systems there. Later in this chapter, we will examine such institutional explanations of differences among party systems. Initially, however, we should determine what kind of decisions are made by or through party systems, and an analysis of the predilection in favor of two-party systems will serve this end. Why do so many students and practitioners of politics, especially in the English-speaking world, share this predilection? What functions do they think party systems perform? What do party systems actually do, in and for different political systems?

The Model of the Two-Party System

Three principal arguments, which are mutually related, are usually advanced in favor of "the two-party system." Their content, incidentally, will cast light on which of many actual or possible types of two-party systems the protagonists of these arguments have in mind. First, they say, representative democracy has been most successful in the English-speaking countries, and they have in fact had two-party systems most of the time. Second, only the two-party system satisfies the norms of constitutional democracy, by giving voters a real choice between realizable alternative programs. And third, only the two-party system affords opportunities for stable, efficient, and effective government, since the electorate is forced to make up its mind to give a mandate to one of the two parties.

The shortcomings of the first argument become at once apparent. To begin with, there are the successful democracies of Sweden and Switzerland, as well as other admittedly small systems, which have been quite successful with multiparty systems. Then, there are the great variations on the two-party theme that have been played in the English-speaking countries. Throughout the 1920's, three major parties were competing in Great Britain. Since then, it has been the only one of the three English-speaking countries under consideration here in which two disciplined parties have alone dominated the national parliament. In Canada, third and fourth parties have been able to elect sizable groups to the Dominion Parliament since the earlier 1920's. And the Republican and Democratic parties in the United States are so loosely organized and so undisciplined in their congressional voting that the American party "system" does not really seem to deserve that name, at least when compared with the British. This comparison has been at the bottom of many efforts to reform the party system of the United States along British lines. One such proposal, made in 1950 by a special committee of the American Political Science Association, was entitled "Toward a More Responsible Two-Party System." It leads us to the second argument.

Only a system in which two disciplined parties of roughly equal strength compete for the electorate's favors can offer meaningful choices to the voters. There is general agreement that the availability of meaningful choices is a requirement of constitutional democracy. This is why it was included as one of the three elements in sound situations of responsibility. In Britain, the decision in favor of either the Conservative or the Labour party, made by all but the 3 per cent of the electorate who have in recent general elections preferred the Liberal party, appears to offer such a meaningful choice. But this argument must lead to an outright condemnation of the American party system. In the United States, the two major parties are so undisciplined, and their platforms so much resemble each other, that they present the voters with a choice that is not meaningful at all. Hence the proposals for reforming the American parties: They should be as disciplined as the British, and their programs as strongly differentiated as are those of Labour and the Conservatives, in order to present true alternatives rather than artificial ones. But holding up the British system for emulation in this way raises a new question. Many problems with which British government has to deal cannot be anticipated at the time of the general election. Consequently, no plank about solutions to these problems can be included in the campaign platform. This restricts the voters' choice to one between leaders or teams of leaders, and the relative confidence they inspire. That, in turn, implies a conception of democracy like the one the sociologist Max Weber explained to the skeptical and antidemocratic General Ludendorff, during the founding time of the Weimar Republic:

WEBER: In a democracy the people choose a leader in whom they trust. Then the chosen leader says, "Now shut up and obey me." People and party are then no longer free to interfere in his business.

LUDENDORFF: I could like such a democracy.

WEBER: Later the people can sit in judgment. If the leader has made mistakes—to the gallows with him.[1]

The third argument on behalf of the two-party system insists that only one of two great parties can be capable of governing. Since the electorate is forced to make up its mind between only two alternatives, the winning party is bound to receive a true mandate in the election, and to be guaranteed reasonably safe tenure for the life of that parliament. As a matter of fact, however, this does not always happen, even in the United Kingdom. When one of the two parties wins only a slim parliamentary majority, as did the Labour party in 1950, it has neither mandate nor safe tenure. By contrast, multiparty systems often are accompanied by both the equivalent of a mandate and safe tenure; e.g., in Switzerland and Sweden. In West Germany, too, where the election of 1949 produced a clear multiparty system, the Christian Democratic Union was able to put its campaign program into effect, and its leader remained Chancellor for the full term of the Bundestag and beyond. These examples suggest that the ability of a party to govern—to provide resolution, in our terms—is due less to the make-up of the party system than to the constitutional distinction between deliberation and resolution.
    These three arguments in favor of the two-party system indicate the nature of the model its proponents have in mind. It is not the American model, and while the British comes closer to the ideal, it too suffers from the cited "deviations." *The* two-party system would consist of two

[1] *From Max Weber: Essays in Sociology,* translated and edited by H. H. Gerth and C. Wright Mills, 1946, pp. 41-42.

disciplined parties with clearly differentiated programs, which compete for control of the resolving organs of the political system, and which regularly alternate in safe control, based on a sound majority. No such party system exists anywhere in fact. Nevertheless, this mythical model implicitly underlies most discussions of party systems. It lies at the bottom of practically all attacks on multiparty systems and efforts to reform them. The influence of this model has been so pervasive that a more destructive criticism seems called for than that just given in refuting the three arguments.

Critique of the Model

We will criticize the model of the two-party system from the point of view of the norm of individual responsibility, on four main grounds: First, it excludes up to more than half the electorate from contributing to central decisions for periods up to five years. Second, this exclusion occurs while irreversible decisions, affecting everyone, may have to be made. Third, the two-party system creates artificial issues and unnecessary cleavages among the population. And fourth, it introduces an avoidable element of chance or gambling into the political process.

1. Exclusion from Participation: In Great Britain, whose party system comes closest to the model, one of the two great parties can come into control of the Cabinet, and stay there for the five years of the life of a House of Commons, even if fewer than half the voters supported it in a general election. This happens because of the distorting effects of the election law and the existence of the third (Liberal) party. The number of voters in each election district differs. The winning party may have "safe" seats in relatively underpopulated districts. It may win seats by slim majorities, and lose others by large ones. The returns may give 40 per cent to the winning candidate, and 30 per cent each to the candidates of the other major party and the Liberal party. Since the candidate with the highest number of votes is elected, 60 per cent of the voters would, in this case, be beaten by only 40 per cent. The margins are not normally that wide. Nevertheless, in the election of 1951, the national results were as follows:

Party	Per Cent of Vote	Seats in House
Conservative	48	321
Labour	49	295
Liberal	3	6

Having received fewer popular votes than the Labour party, the Conservatives won and stayed in office until 1955. In that year, with 50 per cent of the vote against 46 for the Labour party, the Conservatives took 345 seats in Commons as against 277 for Labour.

While a minority Cabinet, like that of 1951, is in office, it and it alone provides resolution. It does this subject to criticisms voiced in the House of Commons and the press, but it need not heed these. That the British are aware of the violations of democratic norms implied by these facts is shown by the practice of having coalition Cabinets in times of war or other crises. Another phenomenon also betrays their desire to give opportunities to participate by other means in the making of policy to people whose party is excluded from contributing to central resolution. This is the tendency toward a nontraditional kind of engineered neocorporatism, which has recently become evident. The function of resolving the most important issues has been steadily devolved, or pushed downward, to be performed by an increasingly expanding combination of institutions. Originally, it was performed by the Crown alone; then by the Crown combined with the Cabinet; later still by the Crown-Cabinet combined with the House of Commons; and today by the Crown-Cabinet-Commons complex combined with the parties, at least in a sense. This is suggested by the fact that all three parties present programs, which are comprehensive and integrated.

Parallel with the devolution of the resolving function from the Crown to the parties, there has occurred a similar devolution of the representation of interests, and of deliberation upon resolved issues in terms of interests, to each of the next lower levels. Originally, even some officers who are now members of the Cabinet represented interests vis-à-vis the Crown in Parliament. Next, interests were represented vis-à-vis the Cabinet by the House of Commons, which deliberated upon the resolution of issues offered by the Cabinet. Still later, interests were represented vis-à-vis the whole King-in-Parliament complex by the parliamentary delegations of the parties. Today, they are represented vis-à-vis the King-in-Parliament-*cum*-parties by the new, rationally constructed interest organizations. This kind of representation, and representative deliberation, takes place when trade unions criticize or try to change policies of the National Executive Committee of the Labour party at its annual congress; or when representatives of the workers or consumers, who are interested in the decisions made by the board of a nationalized industry, discuss these decisions at meetings of the board's consultative council, established for that purpose. These arrangements permit at least some degree of participation on the part of the people who would otherwise be excluded from the making of central decisions of lesser importance than the ones resolved in the last general election.

In the United States, the exclusion question is not as serious as in Great Britain. The potential distortion of the electoral-college system and occasional third-party movements have sometimes produced minority Presidents. The candidate elected President received a minority of the total popular vote in five successive elections from 1876 to 1892. In the twentieth century, however, there have been few instances: In both 1912 and 1916, Wilson's vote was less than that of his combined opposition, and the 1948 election, complicated by the Dixiecrat and Wallace Progressive candidacies, resulted in Truman's victory with only 49.4 per cent of the popular vote against 43.2 for Dewey.

Even more important than the relative rarity of a minority victory, the loose organization and low congressional discipline of the two major parties in America tend to minimize the exclusion question. Since the Congress has a greater share in resolution than the House of Commons, the channels of participation are more varied in the United States than in Great Britain. Even someone who voted for Republican presidential candidates during the height of the New Deal had other means for contributing to central resolution. Moreover, the federal government is often split between the two parties, with one controlling the Presidency while the other has a majority in one or both houses of the Congress. Federalism has the effect of leaving in a majority position in many of the states, usually about half of them, the party that has been excluded at the national level. And finally, central resolution in the United States is not—or has not become until recently—as important as in the United Kingdom. The resolution of issues arrived at in Washington has not affected citizens in San Antonio, Texas, as much as similar decisions made in London have affected subjects in Edinburgh, Scotland. But it is precisely all the factors usually cited as shortcomings of the American party system that save it from being as undemocratically exclusive as the model of the two-party system.

2. Irreversible Decisions: This exclusion takes place while irreversible issues have to be resolved in ways that will affect all the members of the political system. Two British examples may be cited, one involving an economic problem, the other an external one. Nationalization of the steel industry was a fairly fundamental issue, on which public opinion was split just about equally. The Labour party could not claim a mandate in its favor, yet it went ahead with nationalization of the industry in the face of Conservative declarations to the effect that a Tory Cabinet would immediately denationalize upon again winning a majority. The Conservatives did win in the 1951 election. Their Cabinet was able to unscramble this particular omelette—the cooking process had barely begun—but often, with policies of this type, reversals are impossible or enormously costly. In the field of foreign relations, especially, the resolution of issues is often both irreversible and irremediable, as is shown by war-or-peace issues. This would be particularly true of a nuclear world war, after the start of which there would probably be nothing left for anyone to reverse or remedy.

In order to avoid rigid exclusion from decisions of this type, British Prime Ministers occasionally call in the Leader of the Opposition for consultations. This was done by both Labour and Conservatives in connection with issues of nuclear armament. But the Opposition may decline to coöperate on such occasions, because it does not want to assume any responsibility for the consequences of the decision. Its job is to oppose, to disagree, and this leads to the third criticism of the model of the two-party system.

3. Artificial Issues: Many artificial issues are created by forcing all debate into the strait jacket of the two-party system. Neither party will feel that it can afford to agree with its opponent. Politicians, who are products of the system and want to advance in their careers, will want to keep the system going and, therefore, differentiate their respective stands as strongly as possible. When the two-party system first got started, meaningful two-way divisions on important problems may actually have existed. Eventually, however, this style of politics becomes functionally autonomous. In a disciplined two-party system, the generation of artificial issues may create unnecessary bitterness among the followers of the parties, and may result in the erosion of a firm previous agreement on policy.

It seems more desirable to postpone the resolution of deferable issues until broader agreement is available, not merely that of the supporters of the party in office—that is, until there exists a "concurrent majority," in the contemporary meaning of John Calhoun's term. This is exactly what usually happens when irreversible policies are being prepared in the politics of the United States. An issue that is considered so fundamental that it will evoke strong opposition, even from a small minority, often cannot be finally resolved until after the Supreme Court has rendered a decision on it. And sometimes even that does not suffice to make the policy definitive, lacking the explicit or implicit concurrence of all interests that will be affected by it—witness integration. In Great

Britain, too, something resembling a concurrent majority is sought, when advocates of the mandate theory have their way and also as a result of the devolutionary neocorporatism described above.[2] On this count again, existing two-party systems do not make for as much irresponsibility as the model of political science because, fortunately, they fall short of its requirements.

4. Chance: The operation of the two-party system involves a large element of chance. When the voter goes to the polls, he may indeed have two alternative programs to choose between, along with the certainty that one of these—whichever gets a majority—will be put into effect. But he does not know which of the two programs will win. This works to aggravate the divisiveness of the electoral struggle, because so very much may be at stake. In multiparty systems, on the other hand, "landslides" seldom occur, because changes in the popular vote are not exaggerated so much. Voters therefore do not run such great risks of wasting their votes, or of ending up on the losing side. From the point of view of constitutional and democratic values, it seems hardly justifiable to let the fate of the whole nation depend upon which party gains one more parliamentary seat than the other. It reduces people's foreknowledge of the consequences of their decisions and provides them with uncertain expectations of the future, as the British nationalization case also illustrated. If it is one of the purposes of constitutionalism and of the rule of law to give men reasonable expectations of the future, then again situations are undesirable in which fundamental issues are resolved by a few unpredictable chance votes. In a way, this reproduces at the level of the individual voter the confusion between the functions of resolution and deliberation that we earlier observed on the parliamentary level. Originally, the voter deliberated on who should represent his interests vis-à-vis the resolving organ. In the Swedish multiparty system, this is still done in general elections. Under the ideal two-party system, the voter tries to choose personnel for the resolving organ at the same time. As a result of this confusion between two different types of decisions, he is kept from performing either of them in a meaningful way and is reduced to the posture of a gambler.

Not much can be said on behalf of such a party system. The British party system has been successful—to the extent that it has—because it deviates substantially from the mythical model some political scientists have conjured up in their imagination. The British two-party system is

[2] For a discussion of the mandate theory, see page 116.

not as thoroughly contrary to the demands of the norm of responsibility, because of the existence of channels through which the otherwise excluded can contribute to central decisions. These channels circumvent the two-party system. The two-party "system" of the United States fares even better in the face of this critique, because it is so far removed from the mythical model. Neither system generates as much bitterness as the constant confrontation of two great opposing camps would be likely to create elsewhere, partly because of the effects of the adversary method: exaggeration of position without excessive commitment.

The adversary method may also go some way toward explaining the peculiar preference the English-speaking peoples show for the two-party system, whether or not they have it in their own countries at any given time, and whenever they can influence other nations to remodel their party systems, as in Germany and Japan under military government. The English method of electing members of Parliament cannot account for this phenomenon, as will be shown below. But it seems at least conceivable that this method of deliberation, which in courts leads so efficiently to resolution, set off the two-alternative pattern of parliamentary politics, when Parliament ceased to have mainly judicial functions. The adversary method is particularly likely to have had this effect because popular politics in the English-speaking countries started as parliamentary politics, through the gradual extension of participation to an ever-widening circle from the same center of authority. In the three major Continental systems, by contrast, participation was not extended gradually from one center, but popular politics was initiated beyond the parliamentary pale, as it were, in its own style, shaped by factors other than parliamentary procedure.

Electoral Choices

Uncritical adulation of the two-party system and unrestrained condemnation of multiparty systems both have a common source in failure to distinguish among the choices that voters make, or think they are making, in elections in different countries. They may all be voting for candidates whom they identify with specific political parties, but from one system to the next, they do not expect their candidates or their parties to do the same things for them. For example, Swedish and Swiss voters, when they go to the polls, believe that they are primarily making a decision on who, or which party, is to represent them in the Riksdag or the Federal Assembly for the purpose of deliberating about the resolution of issues as proposed by the Cabinet and its Swiss equivalent. They are not primarily choosing personnel for this resolving, integrating organ itself. That will be created in any case, although with less trouble in Switzerland than in Sweden.

In the United States, voters make both choices, but they make them separately. That American voters are aware of this distinction is shown by the frequent practice of splitting the ticket between Presidential and congressional candidates. They choose a President to perform the resolving and integrating function. They choose senators and representatives mainly to represent their interests as residents of states and congressional districts, geographically defined, vis-à-vis this President and to deliberate about the proposed resolution of issues from the viewpoint of their interests.

In Great Britain, the voters' choice is primarily one of who will run the Cabinet for the next few years. Representation of interests vis-à-vis Cabinet-Commons-*cum*-party has to be taken care of at lower levels by interest organizations. Representation of geographically defined interests vis-à-vis the resolving organs becomes an important choice only in by-elections to seats vacated between general elections. In Britain, however, by contrast with Continental countries, the availability of only two alternatives through which to contribute to the decision about the organ of resolution, and the lower importance of the choice of interest representation, does not produce dissatisfaction. People do not consider representation the main purpose of general elections. They see them more in the light of a combination of several Swiss referenda, in which major issues are resolved, but in the British case through the selection of the personnel of the majority in Commons. However, even if the British did consider interest representation as a major election choice, the availability of only two—really three—channels for its expression would not appear as limited to them as it would to their neighbors on the Continent. There, a more complicated and more highly differentiated interest-consciousness demands more channels of representation.

Election Law

These differences in the choices that voters in different countries believe themselves to be making are often overlooked by political scientists who focus on election law in studies of party systems. They usually assert that the best way to reform a party system is by manipulating the election law. How valid are such assertions? We will next try to answer that question by examining three different types of electoral systems: proportional representation, the single-member district, and a mixed system that has been in use in West Germany.

1. Proportional Representation: Citizens of countries that achieved representative democracy relatively late tend to place greater emphasis on "representative justice" than the British and especially the Americans usually do. This often happens because they were denied political participation commensurate with their popular strength for so long that they developed an ideology around this goal. Some such denial of participation in political responsibility to groups seeking it occurred in each of the three larger Continental countries. In Italy, property qualifications remained high for several decades after unification, and elections usually involved a good deal of corruption. In Germany, parliamentary strength gained the Social Democrats no influence on the making of policy by the Imperial Chancellor; and in Prussia, the three-class franchise obviously discriminated against the poorer parts of the population. In France, universal male suffrage as maintained by Louis Napoleon was accompanied by no more responsibility than as instituted by Bismarck in Germany. This denial of representative justice suggests why none of these countries today uses the electoral methods with which most English-speaking people have been satisfied for such a long time. We just saw how the election of a single candidate by a simple plurality from one district can result in getting a representative, for whom far less than a majority of the voters cast their ballots.

Two main paths can be followed in order to avoid this kind of distortion of the "will of the voters." The first of these is to retain single-member districts, but to hold a run-off election if no candidate receives a majority of the votes cast the first time around. This system was in use for the Reichstag under the Empire, for the French Chamber of Deputies during most of the Third Republic, and for the National Assembly in the Fifth. The run-off election in France is known as *ballotage*. The second way of keeping electoral distortion down to a minimum is proportional representation, under which several deputies are elected from larger districts. A fairly extreme form of proportional representation was used in the Weimar Republic. The whole country was divided into more than thirty large election districts. For each of these, the different parties nominated a list of candidates. Voters balloted for a party list of candidates, not for an individual. For every 60,000 votes received by the party's list, one of its candidates would be elected to the Reichstag. The candidates were taken in the order in which their names appeared on the list, and this order was determined by the party leadership. Remainders of more than 30,000 votes, left over after the division by 60,000, were then pooled in a district union and, finally, in a national pool, where additional candidates were declared elected for every additional 60,000 votes and for each final remainder in excess of 30,000. This meant that the Reichstag provided an almost exact mirror of political opinion among the electorate. It meant also that the number of deputies in the Reichstag varied from one election to the next, depending upon the number of votes cast—491 members in 1928; 647 in 1933, the last Reichstag elected.

This form of proportional representation has often been blamed for the failure of the Weimar Republic.[3] It is supposed to have contributed to the splintering or other deterioration of existing parties and the entry into parliamentary politics of "interest organizations." The standard example for this is the Party of the German Middle Estate. It got its start in a local election in a Berlin district, then spread to the metropolitan area. It allied with another corporatist group, the Bavarian Peasants League, and in May, 1924, obtained ten seats in the Reichstag. In the election of December, 1924, this went up to seventeen. In 1928, its candidates stood alone, unallied, and got more than 1,300,000 votes, or 4.5 per cent of the total, and twenty-three seats in Parliament. This was its peak of strength. Yet, even in 1928, the Party of the Middle Estate had no local strongholds. From this, the conclusion is drawn that it could not have won any seats under a law providing for the election of one deputy per district by plurality.

While proportional representation was in effect, some of the existing parties not only had splinters break off from them but also became more ideological and more bureaucratic. For example, the Social Democrats lost their left, Communist wing, which got four-fifths as many seats as the Social Democrats did in the election of November, 1932. The Social Democratic party organization and the trade-union federation allied with it became more bureaucratized. Critics of the electoral system also claim that they became more doctrinaire because they knew that they could not win a majority of the seats in the Reichstag, and therefore were not encouraged to make any effort to appeal to the lowest denominator of public opinion, as British and American parties supposedly do. Similar arguments have been advanced to explain the rise of the National Socialist party from obscurity to the position of strongest single party, which it reached with the election of July, 1932, and maintained until Hitler was appointed Chancellor in January, 1933.

[3] See Ferdinand A. Hermens, *Democracy or Anarchy?*, 1941.

Most of these arguments can be refuted. The number of parties represented in the Reichstag did not increase significantly as compared with Imperial days, when single-member districts and run-offs were in use. But at that time, the problem of forming Cabinets with parliamentary majority backing did not arise, since the Chancellor provided resolution, and he was more dependent upon the Emperor than on the Reichstag. Minor interests, like the Bavarian Peasants League, were represented in the Imperial Reichstag, and they did no more harm there than the Party of the Middle Estate did in the Weimar Republic, with less than one-twentieth of the seats in the Reichstag at its zenith. Moreover, interest groups can get directly into parliaments without proportional representation, as they have done repeatedly in Canada, under the English electoral system. Even in the United States, the two major parties sometimes splinter during presidential campaigns, as in 1948, when the Dixiecrats and the Progressives left their fold. And the voting behavior of senators and congressmen is quite splintery most of the time. The growth of Communist parties all over the Continent during the life of the Weimar Republic suggests that the German Communists would have left the Social Democratic party no matter what kind of election law had been in effect. The Labour party in Britain, during this period, was just as bureaucratized as the German Socialists, judging from appearances—and such things can hardly be compared after the fact. The final strength of the Nazis suggests that there were no lowest common denominators to which two great parties could have appealed, unless it be support of the Republic as against its overthrow. But even this would have called for three lowest common denominators, since the Communists and Nazis did not agree on their reasons for wanting to destroy the Weimar system.

One great difficulty in attributing to a single institutional cause the whole development of the party system is that this ignores what Professor Carl J. Friedrich has called the "rule of anticipated reaction." This suggests that politicians adjust their behavior to changed institutions and laws, and that those who are able to bring about legal changes are influenced in this by the anticipated reactions to the changes by others. In the case of the rise of Hitler's party, for example, it seems likely that he would have used other methods for coming to power if another election law had been in effect. The leanings toward legalism, even of the Nazis, might have led him to try to exploit almost any law for his own purposes. And there is no telling how the voters might have reacted to a less violent appeal from the National Socialists. On the other hand, had a less representative electoral system been in force, they might have employed more violence and obtained more support from another part of the population to whom this system appeared "unjust" and who would therefore have felt excluded and cheated.

This same difficulty also arises in connection with proportional representation, as it has been used and changed in France and Italy since World War II. During most of the Third Republic's life, as has been mentioned, France used single-member districts and *ballotage*. This was believed to have made for lack of parliamentary party discipline—the very opposite of bureaucratization. The Fourth Republic started off with its own form of proportional representation, under which from five to nine deputies were elected for larger districts, from lists supplied by the parties. This did not change the pattern of French parliamentary politics very much. But before the election of 1951, the election law was specifically amended so as to discriminate against the two extreme parties, the Communists on the left, and De Gaulle's Rally of the French People on (what the center parties alleged to be) the right. This discrimination went so far as to retain the old election system in some departments, in which it was feared that the new setup would favor these two parties. The result in 1951 did not justify this manipulation of election law on the part of the proconstitutional parties. All of them lost votes compared with 1946, and so did the Communists. How the Gaullists were affected cannot be determined, since they participated neither in the previous general election nor in the next one. In any case, the fact of deliberate discrimination through manipulation of the electoral system probably contributed heavily to general disillusionment with the Fourth Republic.

In Italy, discriminatory electoral legislation resulted in an even worse debacle. Before the parliamentary election of 1953, Parliament changed the prevailing form of proportional representation so that any party or alliance of parties receiving 50 per cent or more of the popular vote would get 65 per cent of the seats in Parliament. This was intended to operate in favor of the Christian Democrats and their allies of the center, and against the Communists and left-wing Socialists on the left, and the Monarchists and neo-Fascists on the right. But the Christian Democrats and their allies did not achieve the required 50 per cent. And who is to say that one reason for this was not the disillusionment with this kind of electoral discrimination on the part of voters, who might otherwise have supported the parties that claimed to be upholders of the democratic constitution? Many attempts to reform party systems through constitutional engineering have been self-defeating in this way, because they have disregarded the purposes of representation and failed to take into account prevailing forms of interest-consciousness in the political system.

2. *Single-Member Districts:* It is often argued that election districts from which only one representative can be elected will produce two parties or at any rate two opposing camps. This thesis is unsupported by logic, and there are many historical cases that contradict it. Logically, there is no reason why the issue of the representation of a district should be fought out as a two-way contest. If there are three or more eager candidates or traditionally antagonistic groups in the district, there will be three or more alternatives. If the antagonisms are not very strong, the alternatives might be reduced to two. If there are no issues at all— for instance, because the population is very homogeneous and aware of its common interests as opposed to those of another part of the country —then there will probably be only one party. This has been true in many of the American states and, for long periods, some of the Canadian provinces. Nevertheless, this argument has also been used to explain the American two-party system at the federal level. There, the whole country may be considered one constituency for the purpose of electing one President (if we ignore the electoral college). In order to capture this prize, it is argued, two great opposing parties necessarily had to come into being, each of them appealing to the lowest common denominator of political opinion in order to attract the fence-sitting voters in the middle, who would be repelled by anything extremist.

Whether or not this explanation of the American two-party system sounds convincing, it has often appeared persuasive to some people in Continental countries. A popularly elected President was proposed from time to time as a cure for the ills of the Third and Fourth Republics and as the means for getting rid of the multiparty system there. Such proposals have usually run into a good deal of spirited, usually ideological opposition in France, and the President of the Fifth Republic will continue to be elected indirectly. But the Weimar Republic in Germany actually had a popularly elected President, and if the above thesis about the American Presidency has much merit, this should have led to a two-camp alignment, if not a two-party system, before the establishment of Hitler's one-party system in 1933.

The Reich Presidency, in the constitutional design of which prominent social scientists like Max Weber played an important role, was meant as a substitute for the former throne. The President was nationally elected, in a separate election, for a term of seven years. When the first President died in 1925, seven candidates contested the election, of whom none got the required majority on the first ballot. Thereupon, the parties of the right persuaded Field Marshal von Hindenburg, hero of World War I, to become a candidate. In the run-off, he received 43 per cent of the votes cast, the candidate on whom the center and left-of-center parties agreed polled 41 per cent, and the Communist candidate 6 per cent. When Hindenburg's first term expired, in 1932, four candidates appeared against him on the first ballot; as a result, he fell short of the necessary 50 per cent majority by four-tenths of one per cent. In the run-off, Hitler received 38.6 per cent, the Communist candidate 10.2 per cent, and Hindenburg won with 53 per cent. By then, the political importance of the office as the only remaining center of resolution in a deeply divided nation had become obvious to everyone. The whole country formed a single constituency, yet nothing approaching a two-camp alignment was brought into being. At best, there were three great camps, with the Nazis and Communists at the extremes, and the pro-Republicans united in the center for only brief periods of time.

It could be argued that the importance of the Presidency of the Weimar Republic by itself was not great enough to counteract a trend that had been too strongly established through twelve years of proportional representation. In reply to this, the question must be raised whether some form of proportional representation did not have to be introduced at the time of the founding of the Republic, because of the strong ideological commitment to "representative justice" on the part of the Social Democrats. If their demands in this respect had not then been met, they might not have supported the Republic as long and as loyally as they did. A political system in which ideologies and interest-consciousness are as highly differentiated as was true in the Weimar Republic, and as has been the case elsewhere on the European Continent, needs the kind of representative articulation which a multiparty system provides. If forced into the strait jacket of something approaching a two-party system, the dividing line between the two major parties is likely to be also the dividing line between the supporters and the opponents of the constitutional order itself.

3. The Mixed Election System: When the Allies occupied Germany after World War II, many Germans, officials of United States and British military government, and consulted political scientists agreed that proportional representation had made a heavy contribution to the failure of the Weimar Republic. Despite this near unanimity, they were unable to wipe "P.R." from the German constitutional map, again because of the Social Democrats' strong ideological commitment to it. This commitment persisted even after some of the Socialist leaders arrived at the conclusion that their party might stand to gain from the introduction of the English single-member plurality system. The outcome of this conflict was introduction of a hybrid system. Under it, three-fifths of the deputies to the first Bundestag of 1949 were elected in single-member districts by pluralities, while the remaining two-fifths were elected from lists of candidates furnished by each of the parties in the several states—not for the Federal Republic as a whole. The outcome of the election of 1949 showed that both the Christian Democratic and the Social Democratic parties had been right in advocating the English system and P.R. respectively, since most of the former's candidates were elected from single-member districts, while most of the latter's candidates who moved into the Bundestag came from state lists under the provisions for proportional representation. But the Free Democratic Party, the strongest partner in Adenauer's first coalition Cabinet, elected four-fifths of their successful candidates under proportional representation—so that the Christian Democratic Union might have been unable to govern had it not been for the fruits of proportional representation, which it opposed in the debates on the election law. We say "might," because one cannot tell what the results would have been under some other law. People presumably would have voted differently, again following the rule of anticipated reaction. Politicians would have formulated their appeals in a different way.

For the Bundestag election of 1953, the election law was changed to elect half the deputies from single-member districts, and half from state party lists. Each voter cast two votes for this purpose—one for an individual district candidate, the other for a state party list. Life was made more difficult for small parties by requiring that they either receive 5 per cent of the total popular vote cast in the entire Federal Republic (it had been 5 per cent in one state), or elect a candidate in at least one district anywhere in the Republic, before they could benefit from the provisions for proportional representation. This excluded several of the minor parties represented in the first Bundestag, but resulted in the arrival of the previously unrepresented Refugee League. Before the election of 1957, the Christian Democrats threatened to change the electoral law even more drastically than in 1953, so as to reduce even further the probable representation of minor parties. Actually, the only change this time upped the requirements for benefiting from P.R. to three individual constituencies, from the previous minimum of one. Since the Refugee League got only 4.6 per cent of the popular vote and not a single individual district, it disappeared from the Bundestag. In contrast, the German Party, which received 3.4 per cent but elected six constituency candidates, because of its geographically concentrated electoral support, placed seventeen candidates, or two more than in 1953.

In 1957, the Christian Democratic Union (50.2 per cent) and the Social Democratic Party (31.8 per cent) attracted more than four-fifths of the popular vote to themselves, although half of the deputies to the Bundestag were still elected by proportional representation. Of 497 seats, these two parties controlled 439. Whether the West German party system will continue to evolve toward something resembling one of those in the English-speaking countries cannot be foreseen. For example, it is quite possible that the Christian Democratic Union will fall apart after Dr. Adenauer's retirement. The two-way pattern of politics, however, may outlive such eventualities. But this pattern, which pits *the* government against *the* opposition, became well established during the first Bundestag, when the two largest parties together controlled only 270 of 400 deputies. The two-way pattern, therefore, must be attributed not to changes in the election law, but to the constitutional provision for the constructive vote of no confidence, contained in Article 67 of the Basic Law. The only changes in election law that seem to have had the intended results were the increases in the requirements for benefiting from P.R., and their effects are very hard to gauge, because of many other factors involved, including the rule of anticipated reaction.

Election Law and Constitutional Stability

The "improvements" brought about by manipulation of election law seem to be far outweighed by its less fortunate side effects. We would say that the worst offense of the theorists who link election law with party systems, and party systems with the success of constitutional democracy, is the popularity of their theories in the major Continental countries. This popularity has led to great instability in their election laws. As we have seen, these are changed before most elections, in a manner designed to help the incumbent parliamentary majority. This quite naturally makes the incumbent minority unhappy and tends to disillusion its members and followers with representative democracy as such. A part of the rules of politics, which at least comes close to being fundamental, is thus being treated as merely circumstantial. It is like a football game in which the winning team can change the rules halfway through the game, so that it will roll up an even greater margin of victory. The losing side would hardly appreciate this sort of thing and would probably walk off the field. The instability of election laws in the three major Continental countries is a direct result of the excessive awareness of politicians, and even of the general public, of the benefits they might derive from manipulating election laws. Americans are familiar with a somewhat similar though less harmful practice, gerry-mandering—changing the boundaries of an election district in favor of the current majority, usually in a state legislature. But gerrymandering does not involve a change in the basic rules according to which representatives are elected, as in the Continental cases. Moreover, this very stability of election rules in the United States reflects widespread agreement on some fundamental procedures—an agreement that is lacking in Germany, France, and Italy. In this respect, the excessive preoccupation of many political scientists with election law—the study of which is sometimes conducted on obscure levels of higher mathematics—may be a real disservice to the goals of constitutional democracy.

Resolution: The Merits of Two Alternatives

If the advantages usually attributed to various types of two-party systems are illusory, does the two-alternative pattern of politics still possess merits? We have come across this pattern in the procedure of the English-speaking systems, in Swedish parliamentary procedure, in the formulation of issues in Swiss referenda, and now in parliamentary politics in the German Federal Republic. In each of these cases, the two-alternative pattern facilitates resolution and gears deliberation to resolution. The issues that are resolved by being formulated in double alternatives differ from one system to the next: to accept or reject a proposed policy, to have action or inaction, to elect or to replace a leader. In every case where resolution is needed, however, it seems to be achieved most easily when the issue is stated in terms of "either, or." And this seems quite logical, at least to Western minds that are heirs to Greek dialectical logic, because resolution is the transition from deliberation to action and, therefore, synonymous with will. In the last instance before resolving an issue, the question is always: Do I will to do this? And the answer can be only *Yes* or *No*.

On the other hand, when citizens are offered choices on the issue of who, or which organization, is to participate in central deliberation on their behalf, only one reason could justify the restriction of alternatives to two—that citizens were conscious of only two primary interests with which they could identify themselves. Wherever there are more than two, there should also be more than two alternative routes of representation, whether these are called parties, interest organizations, or something else. The more successful political systems confirm this distinction between the alternative patterns fitted, respectively, for resolution and deliberation.

In the United States, the two-alternative pattern is used effectively only in presidential campaigns, when the electorate is called upon to resolve the issue of who is to provide central resolution for the next four years. In Great Britain, the same issue is resolved in parliamentary elections. The lack of opportunities for making choices about representation, comparable to those made in American congressional elections, does not result in dissatisfaction among the British, because of their primary interest identification with one of two classes, each represented by one of the two great parties, and because of the opportunities to contribute to deliberation at lower levels through the neocorporatist interest organizations. In Canada, dissatisfaction with the two alternatives presented by the Liberal and Conservative parties led to the entry of other groups into the Dominion Parliament, and to attempts to handle geographically restricted problems through provincial politics. At this level, near unanimity on solutions has resulted in one-party dominance, if not in one-party systems.

The survival of the resolving organ, in Sweden and Switzerland, is not dependent on decisions by voters or members of parliament. In these two countries, the decision to maintain resolution in the Crown-Cabinet and the Federal Council was made once and for all. Voters are therefore confronted with either-or alternatives only in referenda, which are more frequent in Switzerland than in Sweden. Sweden, where the possibility of Cabinet resignation is stronger than in Switzerland, employs one parliamentary procedure, the counterproposition device, which does call for only two alternatives to be decided at one time and thereby provides a reservoir of parliamentary resoluteness, to be used when needed.

In West Germany, since the federal election of 1953, voters have actually been given two votes each—one for the single member who would represent their district in the Bundestag, the other for the party list from which deputies of their state would be elected to the Bundestag. Thus, they could feel that they were deciding on resolution in the second ballot, representative deliberation in the first. The election law permits multiple candidacies, with the result that federal party leaders often head several of their party's P.R. lists in the states. The first act of a newly elected Bundestag is the election of the Chancellor. The voters therefore know that, having provided at the outset for the organ of resolution for the next four years, their deputies can then deliberate as the representatives of interests, during the remainder of their term, about the resolution of issues proposed to them by the Chancellor.

In these six systems, the creation and maintenance of the organ that provides sustained central resolution presents few problems. In Italy and France, on the other hand, this has been the major problem. Every parliamentary election in Italy has presented voters with the major issue of whether or not to continue the Republic. This issue was resolved through the election of representatives of interests, who then faced the task of bringing a Cabinet into being and keeping it in office. Interest-consciousness in Italy is such that interest representatives could only with difficulty agree on integrated and sustained sets of policies in different fields, the more so because no procedures making for resoluteness have been available to them. French parliamentary elections have similarly confused the voters' choice of organs of resolution and of representative deliberation. Had it been possible to keep the two choices separate under the Third and Fourth Republics, then a two-way formulation of the decision on resolution might have been helpful. But they could not be kept distinct at the electoral level, because of the fear of Bonapartism, which has resulted in retaining an indirect method of electing the President of the Fifth Republic. The only hope for distinguishing between the two functions, resolution and deliberation, lies at the level of Parliament, where it could be achieved by reducing the frequency with which the National Assembly can go through the "great exertion" of producing political will.

Individuals who have lost their will power, their capacity to make decisions, are sometimes cured by shock treatment. Political systems with the same malady can sometimes also be shocked into making up their mind by being confronted with two clear and basic alternatives. This is what General de Gaulle did to his compatriots in the summer of 1958. The result was adoption of the constitution of the Fifth Republic in a referendum that offered only two alternatives—accept or reject—with one of them foreshadowing civil war and the end of republican government. The new constitution, by restricting Parliament to deliberation, and by enhancing the capacity for resolute action of both President and Premier, may be crowned with success. But whether it is or not, and regardless of the type of election law that will be used, France will continue to have a multiplicity of channels of representation, both political parties and interest groups. A political system whose population is aware of the existence of many competing interests is likely to have many competing channels through which those who identify themselves with these interests can contribute to the flow of policy.

Where there is lacking such channels for contributing to central decisions, and for insuring the accountability of those who make these decisions, policy is not likely to be accepted. Without acceptance, efficiency is likely to be reduced. In any case, multiparty systems do not interfere with the efficiency of a political system in solving its problem, but confusing resolution with deliberation does. Efforts to reduce the number of competing interests operating as political parties are, at best, superfluous. At worst, they lead to constant manipulation of election laws and thereby lower both stability and acceptance.

Guidelines for Constitution-Makers—VII

Montesquieu once said that the election law in a democracy is of just as fundamental importance as the law of succession in a monarchy. These laws of succession were usually simple and clear. In order to be effective, they had to remain the same for many generations. This is true of election laws as well. Monarchs occasionally tried to change the law of succession to their own advantage. Modern politicians similarly sometimes try to change the law of election to their own advantage. But at least in the days of hereditary monarchy, political scientists did not preach the need for this kind of reform as a matter of principle, as they are doing today. These preachments are based on the assumption that political parties and party systems perform the same functions in different political systems. In fact, they do this no more than did all hereditary kings.

The two-party system has no inherent merit. A two-way pattern of politics can be helpful for the resolution of issues. Where a fairly tight two-party system exists, the articulation of interest organizations at lower levels, including inside the two parties, seems advisable. (In the German Social Democratic party and Christian Democratic Union, this has actually happened.)

The system of representation should be fitted to the interest-consciousness of the electorate and to prevailing notions of representative justice. In every constitutional democracy, these notions will call for opportunities to assume some responsibility for central decisions on the part of those citizens who believe that they will be affected by the consequences of these decisions.

In many cases, a new sense of unity may be created, where previous interest-consciousness had been the cause of antagonism. Where interest-

consciousness overlaps with geographical areas, this purpose can be served by setting up election districts that correspond to interest-consciousness.

When the electorate living in one geographically defined constituency is in sufficient agreement not to start a civil war because they can send only one representative into parliament, setting up a single-member district may in fact generate a new sense of unity.

Where antagonisms within potential territorial constituencies are too strong to be contained in this manner, other forms of representation, including corporatist ones, will reflect interest-consciousness more accurately and keep disagreements from erupting into violence.

Finally, there are political systems in which any form of representation might reveal such strong disagreement on the goals of the system, and on the means by which these should be reached and by which disagreements about ends and means should be resolved, that the survival of the system is threatened. In such a situation, mere manipulation of representative institutions will not be enough to solve the problem, which rather raises questions about people's will to remain under one constitution. How can one gauge the strength of that wlil and, where it is weak, how can one encourage agreement on the proper unit of politics? Part VI deals with these crucial questions.

The Conditions of Constitutional Success

CHAPTER 22

Consensus

The members of any political system must clearly be in some agreement if the system is to continue to produce decisions. If there is wide disagreement among citizens about the size and scope of the existing or proposed system, the methods by which common problems should be handled, and the authority that policies require in order to be accepted, then the likelihood is that the established system will cease to function or that the new one will fail to come into being. This truism accounts for the fact that the concept of consensus, or agreement, has been used frequently in order to explain differences in success among constitutional democracies. Lord Balfour, for example, said that the British people were so fundamentally at one that they could safely afford to bicker. This fundamental agreement in Great Britain has even been pointed to as the cause of the two-party system—although it seems curious that this alleged "oneness" on fundamentals should bring into being *two* parties, unless, of course, disagreements between them are merely feigned, which would not speak well for the choices available to British voters. We saw, too, that the determinist explanations of the French party system focused on disagreements, which cause cleavages to appear in French political opinion.

Few theories of consensus would insist that complete agreement is a prerequisite for the success of a political system. We noticed on our earlier detours to Paradise, in Chapter 2, that it was ruled by perfect consensus, which is why it could not be considered a political system. The classless society of Marxism would, so far as we can tell from the prophecies of Marx and Engels, also bring total agreement, and therefore have no need for politics. But few other *political* theorists—those who believe in the primacy of politics—would go that far. Most of them consider it essential for the success of a constitutional system that its members be in agreement on the most important matters. Our problem, however, is that many of the theorists do not go on to tell us just what these most important matters are; and among those who do offer suggestions, there is disagreement as to just what they are. This can be illustrated by two current interpretations of American and British politics.

Professor Louis Hartz claims that American politics and political thought have been dominated by an "irrational Lockean consensus" on the three values espoused by John Locke: life, liberty, and property.[1] Unlike European countries, the United States never passed through the historical stage of feudalism. Hence, neither classes nor class-consciousness ever took hold, and it never became necessary to forge ideas into the weapons of the class struggle. There was no need for the construction of ideologies, in the Marxian sense, because capitalism never had to oppose feudalism. As a result, consensus was built up on the values of what was later to become American capitalism. This explains, according to Hartz, why American politics has always been relatively "tame," nonviolent, and unideological.

Explanations of the stability and peaceful character of British politics naturally differ from this, since they also rely upon historical and sociological features. One of these is monarchy and the institution of the Crown as a unifying symbol. The Crown is said to unify the British people, by "siphoning off" their need to display emotions, which might otherwise be expressed in a more violent political style, like that of France, which lacks similar symbolism. The "natural deference" of ordinary Englishmen to their "betters" of the governing class has already been mentioned in connection with "national character." This deference is supposed to be reflected in their willingness to let their superiors—as selected by birth and the proper "public," that is, private, schools—do the governing, so long as there is a choice between the two segments of this elite, the leaders of the two major political parties.

Neither of these concepts of consensus seems adequate for our purposes. They do not tell us just what it is that there is agreement about. In Britain, we know that there has been disagreement of varying degrees of intensity on all sort of issues—the constitutional role of the House of Lords, representation in the House of Commons, nationalization of industries, social services, foreign policy, educational oppor-

[1] *The Liberal Tradition in America,* 1955.

tunities, and many more. Similarly, Americans may be at one on some matters, but they are and have been in sometimes violent disagreement on many others—slavery and then segregation, national security needs versus civil rights, isolationism versus interventionism, the functions of the Supreme Court, and the like. Besides, even if there had originally been consensus on the value of life, liberty, and property—and the substitution for Locke's third value of the phrase "pursuit of happiness" in the Declaration of Independence suggests that early disagreement existed—the meaning of these values has certainly been changing since 1776, so that there has been less consensus over the generations.

Types of Consensus

We have been looking for the conditions of successful constitution-making. We know that some kind of agreement is required for the success of any constitution. In order to find out what kind of agreement has existed in the more successful constitutional democracies, we will have to use a more refined concept of consensus than those in the preceding illustrations. For this purpose, we propose two main distinctions: Consensus may be about *procedure* or about *substance;* and it may involve *fundamentals* or *circumstantials*.

The difference between fundamentals and circumstantials has already been defined.[2] Since time is the main criterion for distinguishing between the two, the difference is not an absolute one. Rather, we may think of a spectrum that runs from the extremity marked "fundamentals" —things meant to last eternally—to the opposite end marked "circumstantials"—things meant to last not at all. This is also true of the distinction between agreement on procedural and substantive matters. In the chapter on procedure, we saw how the same procedures can be used over the years and the centuries, as means toward attaining radically different substantive goals—in the case of British parliamentary rules, for example. Sometimes an old procedure is changed or a new one devised for the specific purpose of achieving an immediate substantive policy, as when election law is altered in order to help the incumbent parliamentary majority.

This effect of procedures on the substantive solution of problems indicates that we should think of the difference between procedural and substantive consensus again along the line of a spectrum. For example, three boys may agree that each of them should receive one-third of an apple pie that has been given them; this is substantive consensus. They

[2] See pages 211-213.

may also agree that the size of their pieces should be determined by lot; this would be procedural agreement. The fact that this distinction is not an absolute one becomes apparent when the boys act on their substantive agreement to share the pie equally. Having decided this, they may next agree on the procedure for distribution: to have a fourth person cut up the pie into equal pieces. This calls for a substantive decision: Who is going to be the fourth person? They may still be in agreement on this issue, until it is discovered that the pie came out of the oven uneven, or that most of the apples are concentrated in one piece. Each of the boys will want the best slice, and they may go so far as to try to manipulate the lighting in the room in which the distribution is to take place. If they do reach agreement on the question of lighting, is this a matter of substance of procedure? This difficulty is as obvious as that about determining the fundamental or circumstantial character of their agreement. The principle of equal division seems closest to fundamentals, the issue of lighting closest to circumstantials, but the issue of which person is to be in charge of distribution is somewhere in the middle. He may do the job so much to the satisfaction of all three boys that they will continue to return to him on similar subsequent occasions. If this happens, circumstantial agreement is transformed into fundamental agreement. This will not occur if the boys state explicitly on the first pie-cutting occasion that they will not let themselves be bound by it as precedent.

Which values—that is, matters of substance—command the widest consensus among men? There are some goals on which universal agreement is virtually dictated by the common humanity of human beings: man's superiority over animate and inanimate nature, the perpetuation of mankind (in some form), the prevention of the extermination of all humanity. Similarly, there are fundamental procedures commanding universal agreement, again dictated by "human nature" or, better, "the human situation." The workings of the human mind and body make it inescapable for men to agree about some basic forms of communication among themselves. But as we move away from this rock bottom of procedures, on the use of which all human beings have to agree, we encounter differences, like those between Orientals and men who are heirs to Greek dialectical logic. The latter approach problems in an analytical way, and distinguish opposites. Orientals are less analytical, tend to view things as blending into one another, and think in terms of the "undifferentiated aesthetic continuum."[3] And while the

[3] See F. S. C. Northrop, *The Meeting of East and West*, 1946.

improvement in communications may be erasing this procedural disagreement, another point of disagreement may be in the making, between people trained to think in terms of dialectical materialism and those who use pre-Marxian logic. However, on the substantive plane that parallels this lack of procedural agreement, there is still strong consensus between these two parts of mankind on the value of the individual human personality, on the ultimate goal of individual responsibility. Neither Chinese nor Russian Communists, nor an absolute Arab monarch, would deny this—at least publicly.

From this very fundamental level of substantive values and of procedures, less fundamental values and procedures can be derived. Two people who agree on the value of the individual personality can deduce from this two quite different sets of derived values—for example, individual responsibility or paternalistic absolutism—because they disagree about the best means for realizing the more fundamental goal on which they do agree. As we move still farther away from the most fundamental plane of substantive values, but before we get to the level of circumstantial policies, we find still less consensus. For example, from the value of individual responsibility, the substantive value of private property may be derived—or the value of social property. In the case of the United States, there has always been strong consensus on the value of individual responsibility, derived from the more fundamental values of liberty, reason, and individualism. From it, such goals as private property and freedom of speech were derived.

In order to protect these fundamental values, in terms of their content as of 1787, the fundamental procedures of the Constitution were laid down. But neither at the time of the founding nor since then, has consensus on the procedures of the Constitution been as strong as was the consensus on the procedures by which deliberation was carried on in the Constitutional Convention. These procedures were closer to the rock-bottom level, and because they were older and less artificial than the Constitution itself, were objects of stronger agreement. To a large extent, they were the procedures in which practitioners of the common law had been trained and experienced. The procedures of the Constitutional Convention were also shaped by the peculiarities of both the English language and English parliamentary rules. Americans and British still share consensus on many of these fundamental procedures, although there is no agreement on one constitution between them. This illustrates the possibility of deriving more than one set of procedures from the same set of more fundamental procedures. It also suggests that one factor that contributes to the weakening of consensus is increasing awareness of its objects—of the matters on which people are agreed.

Those matters that are given by nature or otherwise taken for granted are much less likely to become subjects of controversy than those that have been deliberately created by men. Increasing awareness also leads to more interplay between the substantive and procedural sides. People are more aware of their derived goals than of their fundamental goals; they are more conscious of wanting full employment this year than of wanting individual responsibility all the time. They are therefore more willing to change circumstantial procedures, like the composition of a congressional committee, in order to achieve this year's goal, than they would be willing to amend the Constitution for the purpose of realizing the more fundamental substantive value. In other words, consensus is everywhere weakest at the level of substantive circumstantials, that is, day-to-day policies. The illustration of the pie-eating boys showed this, as did the earlier suggestion of installing direct electronic democracy. When men are concerned only with their own immediate wants, each of them is likely to want something different from every other one, and if only very few can be wholly satisfied, at the expense of many others, very little agreement will result. In such situations, there is also the greatest probability of tampering with circumstantial procedures. What happened to some civil liberties in the United States during periods of external threats to the survival of the system illustrates this, as does gerrymandering. But here we can notice that some political systems maintain a sharper distinction than others between matters of substance and matters of procedure. Sometimes they do this because procedural consensus is stronger than substantive consensus. For example, even in war in the international political "system," some belligerent states will observe the Rules of Land Warfare, even though complete absence of agreement on substantive issues has led to the outbreak of open violence between them.

That the distinction between matters of procedure and substance becomes stronger as one moves away from fundamentals and toward circumstantials, can be shown by analogy to the individual human being. The wants of a baby, so far as the baby is conscious of them, are undifferentiated. It needs food and reaches for it without deliberation. The adult, by contrast, has many different kinds of needs, is aware of this differentiation of his wants, and knows that many of his desires cannot be satisfied at all and some only at the cost of sacrificing others. At some time during the process of growing up, he develops procedures for reconciling his different needs and desires. For example, as a boy he may want to eat both regular food and candy, to watch television and to do well in school, to have fun playing and to please his parents. Gradually he develops certain methods of deliberation for selecting from among these needs and desires. He does this both automatically and in response to training. Gradually, too, he will become conscious of the procedures he uses for reconciling his conflicting wishes. In most cases, procedures that are first developed in response to the simple need for resolving conflicts between other substantive needs will persist into adulthood. When a person of whom this is true is conscious of making his decisions on the basis of such procedures of deliberation, his behavior is called rational. The more rational he is, the better will he be able to deal with new substantive problems that confront him, regardless of their content or their novelty. The best illustration of this is the managerial "generalist," who has learned certain methods in some special field, like the law or engineering, and later applies them to problems of management, finance, or politics.

Young, primitive societies, just like babies, are relatively undifferentiated, both in fact and in the view of their members. According to some anthropologists, primitive people see nature as a part of society, without making any distinction between the two. Individuals are more conscious of belonging to the group than of belonging to themselves, more aware of group identity than of self-identity. There is little awareness of differentiated needs, and all needs are seen as closely interrelated —food, shelter, procreation, propitiation of the gods, and so forth. As the society becomes more differentiated, and smaller groups as well as individuals more self-conscious of their separate identities, they begin to be aware also of their separate substantive needs, apart from those of the society as a whole. Individuals and groups increasingly pursue their own "selfish" interests. But the demands of the society's natural and human environment—that is, of our four problem areas—create the need for reconciling these internal conflicts. Slowly, procedures for this reconciliation are evolved. Eventually, these procedures become functionally autonomous and remain in use for the conciliation of conflicts of substantive interest, which may be quite different in content from those that originally gave rise to the procedures. A society in which such procedures are highly developed and cultivated for their own sake is likely to be a successful constitutional system.

Modern political systems cannot look back on the kind of slow and regular evolution that has just been described for societies not far removed from primitive conditions. Many of them were literally "founded" as political systems at a time when their societies were already highly differentiated. At the founding of a system, some procedural consensus must be in existence. The founders are usually aware of their agreement on fundamental procedures, although their awareness grows dimmer the more fundamental the procedures are on which they agree. The founding itself, however, is usually due to concern with consensus, or the lack of it, on fundamental values, on matters of substance. Often, one problem of overriding importance forces the founders to subordinate their disagreements on other issues. A typical single problem of this type is the threat of extermination from the outside, by another system based on hostile fundamental values. In the face of the problem presented by such a threat, a constitution may then be created, that is, a set of fundamental procedures, designed to insure realization of the substantive goals of the newly founded system. One of these goals must always be the reconciliation of internal conflicts, especially at the level of circumstantial policies.

Political systems founded in response to such needs often live on, once they have been safely launched, although the original problem giving rise to the desire for the new unity has been solved. They continue to use the same fundamental procedures that were at first devised in order to deal with the new problem, since disappeared. What happens to these political systems is similar to what happens to the individual human being and his rationality, developed in the course of maturing childhood. But the case of the individual is simpler, because he is one integrated unit to begin with and will remain a unit until death, at least physically. If he becomes at all aware of the possibility of giving up the procedures by which he reconciles his conflicting substantive needs, it is only in the course of a radical conversion, or in terms of the alternatives, sanity or insanity. For political systems, on the contrary, there are many more alternatives that could replace the prevailing constitution. The same political unit could be given a new constitution, or a new constitution could be provided for a changed political system, that is, for an altered "body," covering an enlarged or reduced territory or population.

Issues of Substance and Procedure

Agreement on the national state as the proper unit of politics seems to be about equally strong in the United States, Great Britain, and France, in all three of which this has not presented an important substantive issue for the last century or more. On other fundamental values, consensus in France seems to have been weaker during most periods of her modern history than in the other two countries. On the level of circumstantial policies, however, instances have occurred when there was greater agreement in France than in the other two—during the Suez crisis in 1956, for example, at least in comparison with Britain. On issues arising out of cultural problems, like the anticlerical controversy in France and the segregation fight in the United States, these two countries have had stronger disagreement than Great Britain. In any case, anyone who attempts this kind of comparison must be impressed by the frequency with which substantive issues are transformed into procedural ones in France, and in Italy and Germany. In some cases, it is lack of agreement on procedure that creates substantive issues in the first place, despite the prior existence of a high degree of substantive consensus. The hesitancy to tamper with fundamental constitutional procedure, which is so marked in Great Britain, seems completely absent in France. Lack of general consensus on the electoral system, for example, is not taken as a bar for any transient majority to change it radically. Similarly, the constitution is amended from time to time, and proposals for amendment have been the subjects of continuous discussion.

The German case resembles the French, although it is even more complicated. Because of Germany's late national unification and the present division of the country, consensus on the value of national survival is weaker than in the other systems discussed. In West Germany today, agreement on other substantive questions generally seems at least as strong, if not stronger, than in France, Great Britain, and the United States, partly as a reaction to the artificially created unanimity in Communist East Germany. On the procedural side, however, consensus has been weak. As in France, election laws are changed frequently. The rules of the Bundestag have been amended; for example, the requirements for the minimum parliamentary membership with which a party can obtain representation on committees, in order to discriminate against particular parties. Other instances of the weakness of procedural consensus have already been discussed in the chapter on legalism.

In Britain and the United States, there is usually as much disagreement on questions of policy as in these two Continental countries. Because of the difference between party systems, this disagreement is usually formulated in fewer alternatives in the English-speaking countries than on the Continent, but that need not affect the intensity of feelings behind the disagreement. In any case, comparison shows considerable differences of consensus between Britain and the United States. In Britain, procedural consensus appears stronger than in the United

States, at least at a level closer to circumstantials. Electoral and parliamentary procedures have enjoyed greater stability in Britain. On the other hand, at the level of fundamentals—that is, of the formal constitution—more changes have been brought about deliberately in Great Britain than in the United States, and this despite strong opposition. The reverse has been true only in the American Civil War, and we are still witnessing the consequences of this violent imposition of changes in fundamentals in the absence of consensus. A comparison of the controversies over the Parliament Bill of 1911 and Franklin D. Roosevelt's "court-packing" plan of 1936 supports the proposition that procedural consensus on fundamentals has been stronger in the United States than in Great Britain. Lloyd George created the substantive issue of passage of his budget by the House of Lords, in order to be able to reduce its powers—to reform the constitution. Despite strong opposition, which was on the verge of breaking out into violence at times, he won the fight. Roosevelt devised the court-packing scheme only in order to push through the substance of his New Deal program of economic reforms. But his opposition, which expressed an almost universal procedural agreement, was so effective that he had to withdraw his plan. Nevertheless, the policies of the New Deal were soon thereafter accepted. This suggests the conclusion that at the level of fundamentals, American consensus on procedure is stronger than on substance, so that old procedures are adapted to be used for "processing" new substantive problems. This occurs even though the fundamental values, for whose protection the fundamental procedures were originally devised by the Founding Fathers, no longer command anywhere near as much consensus as do the procedures that have survived them.

In general, those matters command the strongest consensus of whose rationale or even existence people are the least aware. That is why consensus is the weakest on issues of policy, which arise out of immediate problems, about which a decision must be made speedily. This also explains why consensus on procedures, at all levels, is normally stronger than on substance. The need for the reconciliation of conflicts over issues of values or policies is a constant need. The methods by which this need is met become more or less matters of habit. Besides, the same procedures can be adapted to solve all sorts of diverse substantive problems. Procedural consensus is weaker when people are more conscious of the constitutional and circumstantial rules they are using. This awareness, in turn, is usually the result of the youth of these rules. When they have been engineered into existence only recently, as is true especially in Germany, this awareness of procedures is usually at its peak. It is at a minimum when the rules are as ancient as those that English parliamentary practice originally inherited from the common law.

We may now arrive at some tentative answers to the questions asked earlier in this chapter. The degree of substantive consensus is a function of the problems facing the political system. The degree of procedural consensus is a function of public consciousness of the procedures in use and of the rationale behind them. Legalism, especially about fundamentals, may be considered an effect of incomplete procedural consensus; ideologism, of weak consensus on substantive values. These conclusions raise difficult problems for the founders of new constitutional systems. Often, the need for creating a new constitution arises in the face of agreement on substantive issues—that is, fundamental values or circumstantial policies. Communists, Liberals, and Christian Democrats in a country may be in disagreement on such fundamental values as property, educational rights, and the goals of foreign policy. They are in agreement on the more fundamental goal of national survival, at least for the time being. A constitution is needed, capable of reconciling these conflicting interests and at the same time dealing with the day-to-day problems the system will be facing. It may be impossible to devise such a constitution. But even if it can be engineered and the procedures for which it provides can command fairly widespread agreement, it will then be completely new. All participants in politics will be aware of its novelty and of the rationale that brought it into being. This will lower consensus on the constitution and on the more circumstantial rules derived from it. In the end, the need for rules, which arose out of conflicting values, may exacerbate the original conflict.

Something along these lines happened in several West German mining towns, in which company-owned miners' houses needed new toilets. All the interest groups in each town generally agreed upon this substantive need for new flush toilets: the company management, the trade union, the municipal government, Christian Democrats, Liberals, and Social Democrats—even the Communists. However, for ideological reasons, they mistrusted each other's motives for agreeing. Management thought that the unions were trying to get a stronger hold over their membership, while the unions thought the managers were preparing to turn down their next demand for wage increases. The Christian Democrats suspected the Social Democrats of using the toilets to stimulate the workers' class-consciousness, while the Socialists had a hunch that the Christian Democrats were supporting the new installations in order to attract the workers to their corporatist doctrines of partnership between employees and employers. In some of the towns, existing procedures were found inadequate for resolving this conflict at the more fundamental level, which precluded implementation of the agreement existing at the more circumstantial level. As a result, new procedures were devised, suited to the novelty of the issue. But the parties to the dispute did not really trust the new procedures, so that replacement of the toilets sometimes had to await developments completely external to the situation in the town concerned.

Substantive and Procedural Authority

Political systems also differ with respect to prevailing conceptions of authority, and the consensus that authority commands. If we understand authority as a kind of additive to decisions, which leads those who will be affected by their consequences to accept them,[4] then the sources of authority may be either substantive or procedural. A child accepts his parents' decisions, because the parents are older, and later, because he knows that they have his best interest at heart. Stockholders accept decisions of their company's president, because he has made money for them in the past. We accept the decisions of a traffic policeman because he wears a uniform. President Washington had authority, among other reasons, because he had been associated with the founding of the country and the winning of a war. President Eisenhower had nothing to do with the founding, but came into office in accordance with procedures that were laid down at the time of the founding, and this fact enhanced the authority of his policies. A physician's decisions about his patient's illness are accepted because of the doctor's past training, experience, and demonstrated capacity to heal.

The substantive sources of authority are like qualities attached to, or possessed by, a policy or its maker. Procedural sources of authority are connected with the method that produced the policy or selected its makers. Some substantive sources of authority are age, experience, training, study, foundation, wealth, beauty, inherited titles, symbols, strength, religion. Some procedural sources of authority are methods of election or appointment, systems of accountability, participation in the making of policy, information about the policy flow, publicity for policy. Again, these two sources of authority are not mutually exclusive. Mr. Dulles had authority as Secretary of State because of both his personal and family background and the methods by which he was appointed and according to which he operated. But for his job as Secretary

See Chapter 3.

of State, the procedural sources of his authority were more important than the substantive ones, as became evident whenever his policies ran into domestic difficulties.

Political systems may be classified according to the emphasis on prevailing sources of authority. In the systems considered by us, a shift of emphasis from substantive to procedural sources seems to have occurred in the course of time. Changing American concepts of authority illustrate this shift. When the colonies declared their independence from Great Britain, they eliminated tradition as a useful source of authority. The founders of the Massachusetts Bay Colony had, with the name of "our dread Sovereign Lord King James," invoked all the traditions of monarchy, in an act whose religious motivation is well known. The Founding Fathers of the Republic, by contrast, were rejecting not only the tradition of the monarchy of George III, but a great many other traditions as well. They had to seek some substitute for these lost sources of authority in order to build a new authority of their own. They found this substitute in reason, and in the consent—the word is related to consensus—of the governed. The whole system of government that they created, almost from scratch, was a construct of self-conscious and relatively self-confident reason. The Constitution may be viewed as a device designed to facilitate rational participation, by those capable of it, in the selection of the personnel and policies of government. In this sense, reason gave authority to the Constitution itself and continues to give authority to the governments that operate under the Constitution today.

Reason also gives authority in the universal community of scholars. Men and women are admitted to this community, not because they have made an invention, but because they have given evidence of mastery of the methods—that is, the procedures—of their particular scientific discipline. When American and Russian mathematicians or chemists or biologists assemble at international scholarly conferences, understanding between them depends upon the extent to which they agree on the methods by which their sciences solve problems—not on the actual solutions that may be advanced. Indeed, the very basis of all scientific activity is agreement on methods rather than on solutions.

All over the Western world, substantive sources of authority are becoming less important than procedural sources. In the Soviet countries, by contrast, substantive sources still seem to be relatively more important —control of the secret police, the party bureaucracy, or the army; participation in the Revolution; and the like. But there are still wide variations on this count in the West. The authority of a leader who makes central decisions as a result of a rational procedure of selection and within a constitutional framework of accountability may be enhanced from several different sources: founding associations (Adenauer, De Gasperi); traditional associations (Churchill) or their exact opposite (election to the United States House of Representatives of an immigrant from India); possession of academic degrees (Germany) or literary distinction (France); military achievement (De Gaulle, Eisenhower); parentage (Chamberlain, Robert Taft) or ascent from lowly beginnings (Al Smith, Bevan).

Authority and Time

The age of a political system affects the role of time, or association with the passage of time, as a source of authority. This was already suggested in comparing the role of intellectuals in American and Canadian politics. Since some of its members are always viewed as guardians of knowledge about the past, an older system with stronger ties to a deeper past is likely to accord the intelligentsia greater prestige than a newer one. A brand-new system often displays an antihistorical, antitraditional orientation, and therefore one that is "antitemporal"—opposed to time— especially when its founders want to bring about a clean break with what went before. In that case, association with the founding of the new system supersedes as a source of authority either traditional association or learnedness in the lore of the past. Still, as we just saw from the instance of the United States, the founders of a new constitution usually agree strongly on the goal of maintaining the constitutional system they have established. They are not just building it for themselves, but for their posterity as well. It is their agreement on this goal that creates for them the constitutional problem of stability, of preserving what Cromwell called the fundamentals.

This means that the founders of a new constitution must ask themselves two principal questions: First, the "horizontal" question, with which we have been dealing so far in this chapter: What kind of popular consensus do we need for the success of our constitution? And second, the "vertical," temporal question: How can we maintain consensus among various generations of citizens? This is the question for which neither Cromwell, nor Hobbes, nor Locke were able to find satisfactory answers. Another Englishman, Edmund Burke, tried to solve it in the other direction, by denying the possibility or legitimacy of devising a new political system through the mere exercise of human reason. In

CONSENSUS : : : 375

his *Reflections on the Revolution in France* (which he vehemently opposed), Burke wrote:

Society is indeed a contract. Subordinate contracts for objects of mere occasional interest may be dissolved at pleasure—but the state ought not to be considered as nothing better than a partnership agreement in trade of pepper and coffee, callico or tobacco, or some other such low concern, to be taken up for a little temporary interest, and to be dissolved by the fancy of the parties. It is to be looked on with other reverence; because it is not a partnership in things subservient only to the gross animal existence of a temporary and perishable nature. It is a partnership in all science; a partnership in all art; a partnership in every virtue and in all perfection. As the ends of such a partnership cannot be obtained in many generations, it becomes a partnership not only between those who are living, but between those who are living, those who are dead, and those who are to be born. Each contract of each particular state is but a clause in the great primæval contract of eternal society, linking the lower with the higher natures, connecting the visible and invisible world, according to the fixed compact sanctioned by the inviolable oath which holds all physical and all moral natures each in their appointed place.[5]

Many devices have been used in order to maintain agreement among generations. In effect, most of them give representation to the interests of "those who are dead, and those who are to be born." This is true of hereditary monarchy as it exists in Great Britain and Sweden. In the United Kingdom, the King and the hereditary nobility represented these past and future temporal interests, and this function of the Crown is probably much more important, though less easy to detect or isolate, than the "siphoning off" of political emotions. Revolutionists and anti-monarchists have always said that monarchy and a hereditary nobility represent—if, indeed, anyone but themselves—only the "dead hand of the past." That is why Thomas Jefferson, who authored the Declaration of Independence but did not participate in the Constitutional Convention, urged that each new generation have a revolution of its own. It was Jefferson, too, who encouraged the Virginia legislature to abolish primogeniture and entail, the feudal institutions under which the eldest son inherited his father's entire estate. He also led the movement for the abolition of the common law in the United States, thereby attacking another ancient institution of feudal origins, but in this instance in vain. Again, it was Jefferson who substituted "the pursuit of happiness" for John Locke's last item in the trinity of "life, liberty, and property." (And

[5] London, 1790, pp. 143-44.

Locke had hoped that the stability of his social contract could be insured by impressing the heirs of property with the theory that by accepting the property, they also accepted the social contract entered into by their forefathers, since without it they would not be secure in its enjoyment.)

Ever since the generation of the Founding Fathers passed away, it has been more difficult in the United States to arrive at agreement on the content of the "general welfare," the "general interest," or the "public interest," than in other countries whose uncut roots reach deeper into the past. The only agreement that could usually be obtained was arrived at arithmetically through the mutual canceling out and balancing of conflicting interests, as voiced by the living for the living. This difficulty in finding agreement on the general interest has been much greater in the United States than elsewhere, particularly in such fields as the conservation of natural resources—soil, water, lumber, oil. This must be understood in light of the relative brevity of United States history and the shallow perspective of Americans on their own past. True, the Constitution of the United States is the oldest one still operating in the world today, but because of the radical break with the past that was made at the time of its adoption, the American perspective on the past is shorter even than the Canadian, whose constitution is eighty years younger than that of the United States. Children, who are not aware of having lived very long, do not plan for a long future. Their perspective on the future is as shallow as their perspective on the past. In many ways, the same is true of nations, and it may help to explain why the United States appears to be so much in a hurry to settle its problems, especially the external ones, all at once. Europeans, in contrast, are perfectly willing to let their children and children's children solve their own problems or settle their feuds (a word of obviously feudal origins), which are in any case likely to be older than any living generation that so bequeaths them to its heirs.

Except for the Supreme Court, there is no institution in the United States that can represent the interests of the dead and the unborn in the deliberation of policy. The Court can perform this function fairly well, because it is an institution of the common law and interprets a Constitution that explicitly proclaims that one of its goals is to "secure the blessings of liberty to . . . our posterity." But since it is the only organ that does perform it—and despite the fact that it is aided by the entire legal profession—the interests of the future often get short shrift. In any case, they get shorter shrift than in neighboring Canada, and not just because the Canadian Senate consists of "elder statesmen" appointed for life, while the United States Senate consists of politicians who seek to please their constituents in the here and now in order to be reëlected. (Around the time of the American Revolution, there was some discussion of establishing a Canadian peerage and House of Lords, but in this respect feudalism lost out in the face of the exigencies of the frontier.) Canada's unborn get better consideration of their interests, because Canada is a constitutional monarchy. Even though the Queen resides in the United Kingdom, the fact of monarchy gives reality to the country's ties with even the pre-Canadian, European past. It gives Canadians a deeper perspective on their past, and therefore a farther view into the future of their country. What are known as "public lands" in the United States are called "Crown lands" in Canada, and government corporations are "Crown corporations." The difference is more than symbolic, for its effects on the Canadian concept of authority are likely to persist, even if Canada should break her connections with the Crown and Commonwealth at some time in the future. The ties with the Middle Ages of the Roman Catholic French-Canadians have a similar effect.

This difference is, of course, even more clearly evident in Great Britain itself. The Queen participates very little in the making of central decisions, except on those rare occasions when she can exercise discretion in the appointment of a new Prime Minister. But when race riots broke out in London and Nottingham, in 1958, the Home Secretary could say that the police "will brook no interference with the maintenance of the Queen's peace." This statement is likely to be much more effective than a similar one about the "law of the land," issued in connection with integration riots in Little Rock, Arkansas. The British statement is based on a different concept of authority, from which one can derive greater agreement about the content of the general interest— as opposed to interests less than the general, discussed in Part V, "Representation."

Nor is this British concept of authority likely to produce an ideological statement of the general interest, as is frequently true in Continental countries, where the intelligentsia has partly replaced those organs that, in prerevolutionary periods looked to both the past and the future. In France, Germany, and Italy, ideologists often formulate the general interest in comprehensive, consistent, closed, and substantive terms, derived from their total systems of knowledge. There is always present the competition of a body of diametrically opposed statements, formulated just as ideologically, with results that have already been described. The British time-laden conception of authority, on the other hand, is less likely to arrive at statements of the general interest alleged to be based on complete substantive knowledge. It is more likely to insist that the specific additive, leading to the acceptance of decisions issuing in such statements, be mature deliberation, conducted in accordance with definite procedures, giving consideration to both the experience of the past and the consequences for the future.

Consensus on fundamentals in the three major Continental countries is generally weaker than in the English-speaking systems, and the objects of consensus are more substantive than procedural. The dominant conceptions of authority in France, Italy, and Germany also lean more toward the side of substance. This will emerge more clearly in the case studies of constitution-making, in Chapter 24.

There remain the cases of Switzerland and Sweden. For Switzerland, we might expect that the initiative and the referendum would have led, when important issues are about to be resolved, to disregard for any interests but those of the living generation. Actually, the voters have been less inclined to accept constitutional changes than their elected representatives. Nor should this come as a surprise. The electorate considers both past and future in the making of policy, and not only because most of its members live where their forefathers have been living for generations. Many French, Germans, and Italians have these deep family roots, too; but different generations of these three nations have been resolving their disagreements by means of different sets of rules, none of which was very efficient or popular. Fundamental rules in Switzerland and Sweden, by contrast, have not changed very much over the centuries, and have proven their efficiency and effectiveness. In both countries, mature consideration of the interests of time beyond present life is secured through the procedures of deliberation. Observance of these procedures lends authority to decisions. Beyond this, in Sweden the prevailing notion of authority is very similar to that in Great Britain, for the obvious reason of other similarities between the two systems. In all three countries—Britain, Sweden, and Switzerland—procedural authority commands the widest consensus.

Once more, consensus on procedure turns out to be the most enduring, even where it was not intended to last much beyond the solution of the problem for which the procedure was originally devised. This is due to the greater adaptability of procedural consensus. Agreement on the substance of a problem has little cause for surviving the removal of the problem. In fact, solution of the problem often has the result of radically changing the parties' conception of their interests—as in the case of Soviet-Allied pursuit of the goal of victory over the Axis powers during World War II. But in dealing with the substance of the problem, certain procedures are employed that may later be used in dealing with novel problems. This applies particularly to procedures of communication, but to others as well.

The main question that the makers of new constitutions will be asking is how to create enough consensus to ensure the success of their handiwork. We may come closer to an answer by summarizing next the factors that contributed to giving each of our eight systems its own combination, qualitative and quantitative, of agreement.

Timing of Problems and Extension of Participation

The thickness of the "cake of consensus" built up in a political system is closely related to the timing of the major problems with which it had to deal and to the order in which they arose. We have had two occasions to compare Britain with France with respect to the timing of problems —in connection with ideologism and with deterministic explanations of party systems. In France, the constitutional and religious problems arose simultaneously, and the economic problem of industrialization came up before the other two sets had been resolved. In Great Britain, these problems not only arose one at a time, but in a certain order: first the religious, then the constitutional, and finally the economic problem. Settlement of the first set of problems was accompanied by the growth of procedures of nonviolent compromise, which were later to be utilized for the constitutional settlements of the seventeenth century. Solution of the constitutional problem—that is, the basic procedural conflict— at that time facilitated the processing of all problems that have arisen since. Moreover, this success gained great prestige for these successful procedures and for those experienced in their application, thus leading to a conception of authority that has been weighted heavily on the pro- cedural side. This emphasis was given further underpinning by the way in which participation in political responsibility has been extended in Great Britain—from one constantly accepted center of authority, the Crown, outward in widening, concentric circles, to newly aspiring groups. This reduced the seeds of ideologism. But more than that, it made the employment of the procedures of parliamentary politics the principal sign and symbol of the admission of newly enfranchised groups. The result of the extension of political responsibility to labor, for example, was not so much the achievement of their traditional substantive goals —mainly improvement in the status of the trade unions—as it was their admission to the center of authority.

In the United States and Canada, sets of major problems also arose one at a time. In the United States, independence was the first main problem, but after the obstacles to this substantive goal had been removed, the Constitution itself became the great goal and source of the major issues. By the end of the Civil War, sufficient procedural consensus had been built up to be capable of containing all subsequent substantive conflicts, after secession had been suppressed by force. Participation was extended gradually from the center of Presidency and Congress. Federal politicians mobilized support in the country in order to defeat one another, while in less fortunate lands, men who were not politicians at all, from a legal point of view, mobilized the support, usually of nonvoters, against the established constitutional or unconstitutional system.

In Canada, too, the first major problem for the embryo Dominion was the fundamental procedural one of the British North America Act. The agreement built upon these fundamental procedures has been strong enough to help in the solution of almost all problems that have arisen since 1867. Authority has had the same procedural emphasis as in the Mother Country, and for the same reasons. But on at least one occasion, a concerted effort was made to challenge this procedural conception of authority and the procedural consensus underlying it. This occurred after World War I, when agrarian Progressives from the prairie provinces elected enough members to the federal Parliament to become the second strongest group there, next to the governing Liberal party. The Progressives were openly opposed to party politics and the other "rules of the game." They particularly refused to enforce parliamentary party discipline, because they considered it immoral for members to vote otherwise than in conformity with direct instructions from their constituents. Because of this attitude, they refused to play the role of the official Opposition, and let this be performed by the smaller Conservative party. The result was that the parliamentary strength of the Progressives was decimated in the next federal election, although they continued to dominate provincial governments. The failure of this major attempt to challenge Canada's consensus on fundamental procedure demonstrates the pervasiveness of this agreement.

In France, the simultaneous incidence of, and failure to solve, several major problems generated ideologism. Agreement on the method for resolving future issues was, therefore, not built up. Worse than this, because of the irregular course of the extension of political responsibility, the authority of leaders of aspiring but excluded groups was derived, not from their role as constitutional politicians, but from their identification with the specific substantive goal they espoused: economic equality, overthrow of monarchy or Empire, separation of church and state, defeat of the Germans, and so on. The same has been true of other systems that have had, like the French, traumatic experience with the failure of one or more engineered constitutions. Their failure to solve the problem of how to solve other problems—that is, their inability to cope with the constitutional problem—precluded the accretion of layers of fundamental procedural consensus. This meant that if they were able to handle other problems more successfully—industrialization in Germany, for example—then the need for, or the utility of, constitutional consensus remained unappreciated. Because of the simultaneous incidence of sets of major problems, and the ideologism resulting from this, Germany and Italy not only ended up with weaker consensus in general than the English-speaking countries, but whatever consensus they did have was more substantive than procedural, and for that very reason less likely to endure.

All of this is reflected in the personnel of politics. In the English-speaking countries, the individual can rarely claim political authority because of his accomplishments in some special substantive field. We noted earlier that specialists or experts are rare in their politics, while they are frequent in those of the major Continental countries. Dr. Paul Dudley White's authority in making decisions about the health of President Eisenhower was unquestioningly accepted by the President and most others. But had the doctor tried to use his medical fame in order to run for political office, or even only to drop pearls of wisdom about United States policy in the field of public health, he would not have gotten very far. In fact, the opposite is often true and someone who is known to be a good citizen is considered an authority in relatively specialized fields, because of his general attainments as a citizen. Perhaps Mrs. Eleanor Roosevelt can illustrate this point. This same transfer of general political authority into special nonpolitical fields may also be found in Switzerland and Sweden. In the major Continental countries, however, many famous politicians achieved political authority because of their prior fame as experts in another field.

This emphasis on substantive over procedural sources of authority, and the precedence and greater stability and adaptability of procedural consensus, offer real obstacles to the building up of additional layers of agreement in the major Continental systems. We can illustrate this by analogy between these states and two pairs of businessmen—and the analogy is not as far-fetched as it may first seem, since Edmund Burke considered contracts in pepper and coffee alongside the social contract. The first two businessmen are dishonest; they are in agreement on the substantive goal of taking over control of a legitimate corporation by means of dishonest stock manipulation. Each of them has previously succeeded in similar enterprises and therefore each considers the other an authority in the field. The two of them succeed in their plot and take over the corporation. They may even divide up the profits equally but then, the substantive goal on which they had been in agreement having been achieved, discord is likely to arise between them, they may end up in the courts, "squeal" on each other's previous dishonesty, and finally land in prison.

Two honest corporation presidents, by contrast, engage in a battle royal for control of their respective companies. They are pursuing apparently irreconcilable substantive goals. But they fight their battle honestly and observe the prevailing code of business ethics and relevant laws. In the end, the victor may be so favorably impressed by the scrupulous integrity of his opponent, and vice versa, that the beginnings for a fruitful and lasting partnership will have been laid. Or, if the defeated man continues independently in business and another conflict arises between the two, they will be able to resolve it even more quickly and fairly than the first. Whatever the outcome of the first fight, these two businessmen will be able to adapt the initial procedural consensus, of whose bottom layer they first became aware during this fight, to all the substantively varied problems they may later encounter together.

Guidelines for Constitution-Makers—VIII

This advice to stock-market speculators indicates how difficult it is to give advice to constitution-makers, especially on questions of consensus. Often a new constitution is needed immediately after an outburst of revolutionary passion has overthrown the old regime. The only agreement among the revolutionaries seems to be the evils of the past. Can a new constitution be built upon this limited and negative substantive consensus? Yet it may have to be built, no matter how dim the prospects for the future. In that case, the builders will ask: Where do we find those matters on which agreement does exist and which should be included in our constitution?

This question is hard to answer—harder than the simpler notions of consensus cited at the beginning of this chapter would have indicated. The constitution must certainly reflect some consensus on the scope of the new political system. Beyond this, it seems that things can get exceedingly complicated. History may have been unkind to the country and not permitted anything but disagreement to develop. Nor can an answer be given in terms of common distinctions between ends and means, along lines of this argument: "Of course people are agreed on the end of living in one system, so that all you have to do is furnish them with the means. . . ." What kind of ends—substantive ones, long-run, intermediate-run, short-run? How many of them agree, and on how much? And what kind of means—prosperity, economic assistance, large-scale birth control, instruction in civics, or an honest bureaucracy?

We do know that total consensus is neither necessary nor desirable, even if it were possible. Only those ideologists who believe in the existence of complete knowledge could advocate total agreement. The members of a political system pursue different goals, not only because they identify themselves with different interests, but also because their interpretations of reality lead them to various estimates of the consequences of proposed policies. The norm of individual responsibility demands that different interpretations be aired in the course of deliberation. But both deliberation and resolution will be hampered unless there is agreement on the methods of compromise. There should also be consensus on the scope of the unit of politics—the nation-state, in our eight countries. But there need not be any but the vaguest notion of the long-range goals the system is supposed to serve. Constitutional goals like "the general welfare" and "domestic tranquility" are least likely to provoke controversy and, therefore, most likely to be stable and adaptable. For practical purposes, such vague goals only bespeak a willingness to find ways for compromising differences on more specific interests.

The only guideline for constitution-makers, then, that this chapter yields, is a tentative addition to a dictum attributed to Napoleon: A constitution should be short and vague—but above all it should be procedural.

At best, this advice is debatable, as anyone familiar with the successful Swedish and Swiss constitutions would at once suggest. That is our reason for testing this guideline by applying it to these constitutions in the next chapter. This time, our search will be for the content of the true constitution, the real fundamentals of the political system.

CHAPTER 23

The True Constitution

"In every Government there must be Somewhat Fundamental, Somewhat like a Magna Charta, which should be standing, be unalterable. . . ." Oliver Cromwell's assertion, as a statement of fact, is not true. Not every government has something fundamental and unalterable in it. Totalitarianism gets along without any institutions so fundamental that citizens can rely on the same rules from one day to the next. Indeed, this is one of the most distinctive features of totalitarianism. As a statement of goals, however, and a groping for his own goals, Cromwell's dictum is still as valid now as it was when made. Constitutional government does need fundamentals. Without them, there would be flux, political institutions could not be used as means to reach common goals, and individuals would not be provided with foreknowledge of the consequences of their decisions. Without fundamentals, the makers of central decisions could not be held accountable by those who are exposed to the consequences of policy.

Great Britain has never had a written constitution, and has not needed one as badly as the United States and France, among others, because of the almost uninterrupted gradual evolution of British institutions and procedures. Cromwell's own attempt to interrupt this slow growth, documented with his Instrument of Government, failed. The fundamentals he was trying to lay down in the Instrument turned out not to be fundamental enough. Whatever it was that made up the true fundamentals of British politics reasserted itself and survived, while the written Instrument of Government proved to be very circumstantial.

Cromwell's made constitution did not command sufficient consensus to endure. The old and unmade British constitution commanded too much consensus to be replaced. In this sense, every constitution must contain some fundamentals that are the object of widespread popular and deep generational consensus. But how can we isolate these fundamentals, since they are likely to be embedded in the midst of other matters that are also considered part of the constitution?

In Great Britain, this kind of isolation of the true constitution is virtually impossible, since there is no written constitution at all. In the Canadian case, the difficulties are almost as great, because the British North America Act is only a part—and probably not the core—of the Canadian constitution. The stability of the French, Italian, and German constitutions is so much in doubt that they are more useful as case studies in constitution-making than as guinea pigs for biopsy in search of the nerve center of fundamentals. For this purpose, Sweden and Switzerland, as stable constitutional systems, are best suited. There, we know the content of the formal constitution, and we can arrive at a fair idea of the content of those fundamentals about which consensus has been the strongest. Having discovered what kind of overlap exists between the formal and the true constitution, we may arrive at conclusions that will help to explain the relative failure of constitutional engineering in the three major Continental countries.

Sweden

At first glance, the Swedish constitution seems to refute our expansion of Napoleon's advice. It is long, specific, and full of substantive provisions. The four documents together run to about thirty-three pages—more than twice as long as that of the United States—in the standard collection of constitutions.[1] Their provisions are very detailed. For example, the Swedish Instrument of Government states that "The King alone shall govern the realm in accordance with the provisions of this Instrument of Government; he shall, however, in the instances hereafter specified, seek the information and advice of a Council of State [Cabinet], to which the King shall call and appoint capable, experienced, honorable and generally respected native Swedish subjects." The procedures of the Council of State and relations between it and the King are then specified. Another article states that "The judicial power of the King shall be vested in twelve experienced and honorable persons, learned in the law. . . ." Much of this would seem to be rather wordy and superfluous. Much of it is substantive, as well. There are, for in-

[1] Amos J. Peaslee, *Constitutions of Nations,* 3 vols., 2nd ed., The Hague, 1956.

stance, several articles about the government of the Church of Sweden, including a prohibition of the appointment of women to clerical office. Another article forbids princes of the royal house to marry without the King's permission. The Instrument also lays down detailed rules for some aspects of the work of the Riksdag, including a list of the committees it has to form, and some of the procedures to be used by the Committee on Foreign Affairs. Detailed provisions concerning the National Debt Office and the Bank of Sweden are also contained in the formal constitution.

The Riksdag Act lays down general rules about the election of members of Parliament. It provides for proportional representation, but is supplemented by a nonfundamental election law. It specifies the functions and the number of members of each committee, and the method by which individual members are to be selected. Even the voting procedures of the committees is laid down in this constitutional document. The same is true of procedure to be used in the two houses of the Riksdag. For example, "No one shall have the right to speak without his remarks being recorded in the minutes. No one shall indulge in personally insulting remarks or otherwise conduct himself in a manner inconsistent with good order. . . ." The rules for voting by proposition and counterproposition, described in Chapter 16, are also a part of the constitution; e.g., "A question shall always be answered only by 'yes' or 'no.' . . ."

Of the four constitutional documents, the Act of Succession is the shortest. Its Article 4 reads:

> In accordance with the express provision of Article 2 of the Instrument of Government that the King shall always profess the pure evangelical faith, as adopted and explained in the unaltered Augsburg Confession and in the Resolution of the Uppsala Meeting of the year 1593, princes of the royal family shall be brought up in that same faith and within the realm. Any member of the royal family not professing this faith shall be excluded from all rights of succession.

The Freedom of the Press Act, at present the version of 1949, runs to about ten pages. It provides for the public character of official documents, granting every Swedish citizen "free access to official documents," except where considerations of security or external relations call for restrictions of this right. It contains one chapter "On the Right to Anonymity," and others about the legal status of printing establishments, the circulation of printed matter, liability for violations, trial procedure in such cases, and so on.

Thus, the Swedish constitution is long, specific, and includes some substantive matter. Moreover, we know that parts of it are not very old and have given rise to hotly controverted issues, as in the case of proportional representation, in the first decade of this century, and the royal prerogative, in the second. Yet the resolution of some of these controversies, including the one last mentioned, has not yet become part of the formal written constitution. This fact suggests that the more enduring consensus has concerned, among others, many matters that lie at a more fundamental level than the constitution. The same conclusion could be based on a reading of the Preamble to the Instrument of Government of 1809:

We, Carl, by the Grace of God King of Sweden, the Goths and the Wends, &c., &c., &c., Heir to Norway, Duke of Slesvig-Holstein, Stormarn, and Ditmarsen, Count of Oldenburg and Delmenhorst, &c., &c., hereby make known that we, having with unlimited confidence unconditionally entrusted the Estates of the Realm with the provision of a new Instrument of Government, to form *in perpetuity* the basis of the happiness and independence of a common fatherland, do carry out a duty coveted and dear to our heart when we hereby publicly promulgate the *fundamental law* which has, after the most *careful consideration,* been *unanimously* enacted and accepted by the Estates of the Realm now assembled and delivered to us in the Hall of State this day, in conjunction with their voluntary and *unanimous* offer of Sweden's *crown and government.* As we, with deepest emotion and loving participation in the fortunes of the people who have given us such an unforgettable proof of confidence and affection, have acceded to this their desire, we have attached a much more certain hope for the success of our unremitting endeavors to serve the welfare of the fatherland, inasmuch as our and our subjects' mutual rights and obligations are so *clearly* laid down in the new Instrument of Government that they incorporate the liberty of the people of Sweden as by law established while maintaining the sanctity of the crown and its *capacity of action.* We are, consequently, pleased to adopt, accept and confirm this Instrument of Government, approved by the Estates of the Realm, exactly word for word:

We, the undersigned Estates of the Realm of Sweden, counts, barons, bishops, nobles, clergy, burghers, and peasants who are now, on our own behalf, and *on behalf of our brethren at home,* convened at a general national assembly, hereby make known that, in consequence of the recent change of rule, to which we have given our unanimous ratification, we, delegates of the Swedish people, have acquired the right, by drawing up an amended State constitution, ourselves to ameliorate the condition of the fatherland in the future; we have, therefore, in *repealing* the fundamental laws more or less in operation prior to the present, namely, The Instrument of Government of the 21st of August, *1772,* the Act of Union and Security of the 21st of February and the 3rd of April, *1789,* the Riksdag Act of the 24th of January, *1617,* as well as such other *ancient* and modern *laws,* acts, decrees, enactments and *decisions* as have been comprised under the name of *fundamental laws,* agreed and confirmed that there be enacted for the realm of Sweden and lands subject thereto the following Instrument of Government, which shall be in operation from this day onwards as the *principal fundamental law of the realm.* . . .

The Instrument of Government ends as follows:

Everything as herein provided we not only accept for ourselves as the established fundamental law, but also direct and graciously command all who are united in loyalty, fealty, and obedience to us, our successors and the realm, to acknowledge, observe, follow and obey this Instrument of Government. In witness whereof we have with our own hand signed and confirmed it, and duly affixed our royal seal below, in Stockholm, our city of residence, on the sixth day of June in the year of our Lord and Saviour Jesus Christ 1809.

CARL[2]

The true constitution of Sweden is contained only in part in the four documents, of which the Instrument of Government is the oldest. Those documents do contain some procedures that are much older than the parchment on which they are written. This is true of the rules governing voting, the committees of the Riksdag, and relations between the two houses. Some of these rules go back to the very beginnings of the Riksdag itself. Others are procedures that were transferred from early local or corporate *self*-government.

We have previously suggested that politics at lower levels, both public and private, gives people useful experience in the practices of carrying on common discussions for the purpose of arriving at decisions about a common problem. In the United States today, local government is neither the only nor the best training ground in these procedures. Children, from the time that they first start going to school, get experience in responsible decision-making. When they elect their class officers, for example, or decide when and where to hold a picnic, or discuss which band to hire for their school dance, they get practice in solving

[2] From *The Constitution of Sweden,* translated by Sarah V. Thørelli. Italics supplied, in order to emphasize the relation between time and fundamentals, the careful deliberation that preceded adoption of the constitution, the unanimity with which it was accepted by the Estates, the capacity for resolution with which the Crown was endowed, the theory of representation, and the listing of laws as decisions.

common problems by means of peaceful discussion. It may be that practically everybody reads Robert's *Rules of Order* somewhere along his way through school. But the widespread understanding of the nature and purpose of common deliberation is much less conscious than that, and therefore it goes much deeper. That is the reason why it can be so easily transferred—automatically, as it were—to "real" politics, once adulthood or citizenship is reached.

In the Roman-law countries, by contrast, this kind of early practice is lacking almost entirely. This is particularly true of a country as inexperienced in various forms of self-government as West Germany was after World War II. When the Occupation Powers made special efforts to give training in "democratic civics" to school children, this was done in a very formal and legalistic way. For instance, students were made to memorize the federal and state constitutions; but decisions about picnics and the like were made by the teacher. This helps to explain why adult Germans, when they are faced with the need for common deliberation for the purpose of resolving some issue, rely so stiffly on formal, legislated rules, and often seem more concerned with the strict observance of these rules than with accomplishing their task. On the other hand, where law, and especially procedural law, has evolved slowly from the grass roots, it is likely to contain important parts of the true constitution.

Where a new constitution has to be created formally, its authors would do well to make use of whatever fundamental procedural consensus, especially of the less than conscious variety, they can find in their political system. This utilization of existing procedural consensus was handled skillfully when the Swedish constitutional documents were brought into being. But the constitutional problems confronting the Swedes at the time of the adoption or amendment of any of these four documents were not as serious as those facing the three larger Continental countries at similar moments in their history. Rather, Sweden's constitutional problems are comparable to those of Great Britain during the nineteenth and early twentieth century. In both countries, the existing procedural consensus was capable of containing the struggle over issues arising out of these problems. The explanations of the strength of procedural consensus are also similar in the two cases. Sweden reached a tentative constitutional settlement during the "Age of Freedom" of the eighteenth century, after protracted struggles against royal absolutism and a religious settlement resembling that effected by Henry VIII in England. As in Great Britain, sets of major problems arose and were solved one at a time: first, the religious problem in the sixteenth century; next, the constitutional problem; and finally, the problems connected with the Industrial Revolution. Unlike most other Continental systems, Sweden never faced the problem of national unification. Feudalism came to Sweden much later than to the rest of Europe, and then in a different and milder form. Swedish peasants never lost their freedom, that is, they never became serfs. The nobility was put in the service of the king, or bureaucratized, quite early.

The formal changes in the constitution, which are reflected in the four documents, were brought about as the result of compromises among groups pursuing conflicting substantive goals. That, for example, was the cause of reform of the franchise in the early 1900's, when the left wanted manhood suffrage, while the right wanted to protect its interests by means of proportional representation. The fact that reform of the franchise was not an issue in the United States at the same time does not mean that constitutional consensus in Sweden was necessarily weaker, but that the franchise was somewhat farther removed from the plane of fundamentals than in the United States. The procedure for electing United States senators was at about the same level as the franchise in Sweden, and it, too, could be contained within the consensus on the true constitution.

This raises the question of how to locate the real fundamentals of any political system. Application of the dimension of time was suggested earlier, that is, to ask how stable institutions and procedures have been in the past and how difficult their change is meant to be in the future. Constitutional amendments in Sweden require passage by two different Parliaments, with a general election intervening. There are many provisions in the Instrument of Government that have been left unchanged since 1809. But that does not mean that all of them belong to the true constitution, since many of them have long since lapsed into innocuous desuetude. There are other procedures that are not contained in any document at all, but that are much older than the Instrument.

In the United States, formal amendment of the Constitution is even more difficult than in Sweden, which is why informal amendment has so often occurred. But again, there are many fundamental procedures which are older than the written Constitution, some of them as old as the common law itself. This is true of Great Britain, too, where the unwritten constitution could be amended by a passing majority of the House of Commons. This suggests that truly constitutional rules need not be included in the formal constitution, but for the system to be stable and to elicit acceptance, some procedures commanding consensus must be fundamental. Only then will participants in politics feel sure that the rules of the game will not be switched on them by a group that happens to have the upper hand at any particular point in time. What Chief Justice Marshall said in *Marbury* v. *Madison* need not be true of the formal constitution itself, but it must be true of something; and where the constitution is engineered to the extent of those of France, Germany, and Italy, it must be true largely of the constitution itself: "The principles, therefore, so established, are deemed fundamental. And as the authority from which they proceed is supreme, and can seldom act, they are designed to be fundamental." Where, on the other hand, these procedural principles were never really established at all, but taken over more or less subconsciously from the dim past, their permanence is assured in any case. As a result, those matters that the written constitution does establish need not be treated with quite the same reverence.

To sum up: There "must be Somewhat Fundamental" commanding consensus. This "Somewhat" should consist of procedures that are fundamental in the sense that they have lasted over long periods of time and are difficult to change. A successful constitution should contain such procedural fundamentals. This hypothesis we will now test with the case of Switzerland.

Switzerland

The federal constitution of Switzerland, which consists of only one document, is roughly two-thirds as long as that of Sweden. Nevertheless, many of its provisions are quite specific and detailed, especially on the substantive side. It contains no provisions concerning the rules of procedure of the Federal Assembly. Readers will recall, from Chapter 5, that the Swiss constitution of 1874 has been amended many times, because of the relative ease with which amendments may be submitted to the referendum by presenting a popular initiative. Initiative also lies at the bottom of the high substantive content of the constitution, since it applies only to constitutional amendments. This means that a group favoring a measure they cannot hope to have passed through the usual parliamentary channels can always resort to the initiative; if the measure is accepted in the referendum, it becomes a part of the constitution itself.

The Preamble to the federal constitution is quite brief:

> In the Name of God the Almighty!
> The Swiss Association of the Oath
> with the intention to confirm the Union of the Associates of the Oath, to maintain and promote the unity, strength, and honor of the Swiss Nation, has accepted the following Constitution.

"Association of the Oath" is a translation of the German term, *Eidgenossenschaft*. *Eid* means "oath," and the remainder of the term could be translated as "fellowship" or "coöperative." This concept goes back to the Rütli Oath, sworn by the members of the three founding cantons in 1307, and commemorated in the story of William Tell. Its full meaning can perhaps be conveyed by the fact that Max Weber, in analyzing the political system of the ancient Jews, used the term *Eidgenossenschaft* to describe the Jewish "league of the Covenant," which was based on the mutual covenant between Abraham and the God of the Old Testament. We shall return to its significance below, and note only the religious basis this concept gives to the Swiss political system. We already know of another substantive religious provision that the constitution contains: exclusion of the Order of Jesuits from the territory of the Confederation.

The detailed substantive provisions cover a wide range of problems. For example, one article instructs the federal government to stock sufficient bread grains for the supply of the country. For this purpose, it can require that millers maintain stores of grain. Customs revenue is retained by the federal government, but the constitution provides that four of the cantons, which have to keep up international Alpine highways, are to be given annual federal subsidies, in amounts specified constitutionally. Freedom of trades and crafts is to be guaranteed by the Confederation, but the federal government can interfere with it for a number of purposes, among them the "maintenance of a healthy peasant estate." Several lengthy articles deal with the production and distribution of alcoholic beverages. Another assigns to the federal government the function of fighting unemployment. Social security provisions are spelled out by amendments resulting from the initiative and referendum. It also regulates gambling casinos. The constitution prohibits the slaughter of animals without rendering them unconscious prior to bloodletting—a provision adopted in the belief that ritual (kosher) slaughter of cattle and other animals for food is less humane than alternative methods. This last item of constitutional coverage indicates, in effect, that animals, as well as men, have basic rights under the Swiss constitution. (It will be recalled, however, that *women* do not have the franchise in Switzerland.)

How can we reconcile this high substantive content and the relative instability of the Swiss constitution with the success of constitutional democracy in the country? What is it that is truly fundamental in the Swiss political system? Instability has already been explained by reference to the provisions for initiative and referendum, which also account for many of the substantive articles. Another reason for the high substantive content is the federal character of the Swiss constitution. Federalism always calls for many provisions, dealing with relations between the central government and member units, that are unnecessary in unitary systems like the French or Swedish. Moreover, the present Swiss constitution was adopted in 1874—at a time, that is, when industrialization had proceeded further than in the United States of 1788. As a result, many matters, such as those covered by the brief commerce clause of the American Constitution, had to be spelled out in much greater detail, simply because there were by then more details to spell out. Also, Switzerland does not have the institution of judicial review and has had, therefore, to forgo the easy flexibility this has given to the United States Constitution in the face of its complicated amending procedure.

All this still leaves the question: What is the basis of fundamental agreement in the Swiss League of the Covenant? To begin with, there are the ninety-five unchanged articles of the 1874 constitution. These deal mainly with federal matters and relations among the major organs of government. These articles contain, in a sense, a partial definition of the Swiss concept of authority. Most of them deal with procedure, although not in much detail. The Swiss did not have to write such procedural provisions into their constitution because they had had centuries of experience with the procedures of deliberating about and resolving issues arising out of commonly faced problems.

A reading of the early "constitutional" documents of, and treaties between, the communities that were eventually to make up the Confederation, shows great preoccupation with problems of procedures.[3] Excerpts from the "First Eternal League" of the three founding cantons, concluded in 1291, may illustrate this:

> In the name of God, amen. It is an honorable work and serves the public welfare, when treaties serving tranquillity and peace are secured in correct form. . . . With common council and unanimous agreement, we have assured, resolved, and laid down, that we in the forenamed valleys will accept no one as judge, who has attained his office through any kind of service or through payment of a sum of money. . . . When, however, discord shall arise between individual covenanters, then the most judicious amongst the covenanters shall settle the quarrel between the two parties in a manner appearing good to them, and if one of the parties shall refuse this settlement of the quarrel, then the remaining covenanters shall take the side against it. . . .
>
> The above agreements, made with the solemn intention to serve the common welfare, shall, God willing, last eternally.

[3] See *Quellenbuch zur Verfassungsgeschichte der Schweizerischen Eidgenossenschaft und der Kantone,* Hans Nabholz and Paul Kläui, editors.

Later treaties reveal this same desire to establish enduring leagues. Often, their first paragraph bemoans the stupid and transitory character of the human mind, which easily and soon forgets things that were meant to endure. Later treaties usually refer to earlier ones, of which they are supposed to be continuations or extensions. One peace treaty, of the year 1712, provides that when meetings of the diet are considering religious disputes, the minutes be taken by one Catholic and one Protestant secretary. Similar provisions are frequent throughout—how to keep records, how to count votes, how to arbitrate disputes, and so forth.

In most cases, these procedures were originally devised in order to enable the groups involved to reach specific substantive goals—mutual defense against outside oppressors or aggressors, prevention of religious conflicts, and the like. But after decades and centuries of experience with these rules, the procedures became firmly established in their own right and were practiced for their own sake. This explains why the procedural emphasis of the earlier constitutional documents diminishes as one comes closer to the modern period of Swiss constitution-writing, which starts with the French Revolution. This relative silence of the later constitutions suggests that the Swiss had by then built up a deep, firm, and therefore less than conscious consensus on fundamental procedures. This agreement was so firm that they did not have to mention these matters in their constitutions. The adoption by the federal parliament of parliamentary rules inspired by Bentham does not contradict this, since the decentralization of the deliberative and resolving processes in Switzerland lowers the importance of the role of parliament in this respect. And the divisive substantive issues that have dominated Swiss politics for the last century serve to confirm the supple firmness of the procedures that have been capable of containing struggles over them. The true constitution of Switzerland has indeed been "engraved in the hearts of the citizens," as the Swiss-born Rousseau put it, but in a less substantive sense than he implied. The Swiss could, therefore, afford to devote their formal, written constitutions to matters less than fundamental and, in many instances, quite circumstantial.

The Priority of Procedural Agreement

The cases of Sweden and Switzerland suggest that the true constitution is made up of the procedures people use, both inside and outside of politics proper, in dealing with issues or disagreements among themselves. In systems whose true constitution, in this sense, is ancient, awareness of its existence is correspondingly low. Their formal constitution may contain expressions of substantive consensus on matters that actually command less agreement than the rules that governed the process by which these constitutional provisions were arrived at. The true constitution must also contain some substantive consensus, at least on the survival of the system, that is, on the state as the proper unit of politics. However, substantive agreement is not a prerequisite for fundamental procedural consensus. The history of the growth of national states suggests that agreement on procedures was reached before consensus on goals, values, or policies. Warfare in the Middle Ages was conducted according to very definite rules. These rules could be effectively enforced because they were backed up by the powerful religious sanctions of the Church. In a sense, therefore, it could be said that men obeyed these rules in the pursuit of substantive, though otherworldly, goals—mainly the salvation of their souls. But for their conduct in this world, consensus on these rules of warfare preceded consensus on dynastic or national substantive goals. When princes formed voluntary alliances, they first had to have some common language and common procedures, simply to conduct negotiations. Next, they needed some consensus on rules of conduct, to warrant the expectation that agreements among themselves would be kept.

Here can be seen why, especially in the less religious era that followed the Middle Ages, political theorists devoted so much concentrated attention to problems raised by promises and contracts. It explains refusal by many English political thinkers and actors of the seventeenth century to extend religious toleration to atheists: They could not be relied upon to keep their promises, their oaths. It sheds light also on the Swiss conception of their Confederation as a league of the covenant.

To be sure, both during and after the Middle Ages, contracts were often broken and rules violated, when substantive interests seemed to call for this. But unless some consensus on procedure had existed beforehand, the treaties and contracts could never have been concluded in the first place. Some sociologies of law suggest that in the evolution of legal systems, a first, primitive, Draconic, substantive stage is followed by increasingly procedural phases of development. If this is the normal sequence, the reason for it may be the inability of primitive people to distinguish between their substantive and their procedural needs. And since substantive needs change over periods of time, while procedural needs do not, methods for meeting the latter can more easily be adapted to serving the purpose of reconciling disagreements about the solution of novel substantive problems. In any case, there is no way for men to arrive at or to formulate their substantive agreements or disagreements if they do not have common procedures and means of communication for doing this. The Biblical story of the Tower of Babel perhaps conveys this lesson better than anything else.

When the Swedes and the Swiss wrote and amended their formal written constitutions, they were not obliged to address themselves to the problem of creating fundamental procedural consensus, because that had already been built up over the centuries. Hence the making of their constitutions did not involve the "very great exertion" of which John Marshall spoke in the Marbury case. They needed only to engineer new consensus at a level relatively far removed from that of Cromwell's true fundamentals. Even when issues arose that divided people sufficiently to cause recourse to civil war—as in Switzerland in 1847—procedural agreement at more basic levels was strong enough to repair this crack in the cake of consensus, and to do so with reasonable ease. The high degree of common experience with unconsciously accepted and efficient methods of discussion made any attempt to create a new constitution much less of an effort than elsewhere. This was as true in Sweden and Switzerland as in the English-speaking countries. It is illustrated by the facility with which the Constitutional Convention, when it first gathered at Philadelphia in 1787, was able to agree on the procedures that were to govern its deliberations. And it was not only the fact of agreement that helped them, but also the efficiency of the procedures on which they agreed. This point can be backed up by the contention that people in the major Continental systems may also have had strong consensus on certain procedures—but these were the procedures of legalism, which are inefficient.

The firmness of agreement on fundamental procedures may be attributed, not only to the length of experience with self-government at lower levels, but also to the variety of such experiences that political and associational life in the successful constitutional democracies offers to its people. Almost every citizen belongs to a number of organized groups, all of which use stable and similar procedures for dealing with their problems. In one of these clubs or unions or fraternal groups or societies, the citizen may be a member of the majority at a given time; in others, at the very same time, he may find himself part of the outvoted minority. Some of his organizations will be minorities at the national level, other majorities. This will tend to give him a commitment to the rules by which his occasional minority position is protected—a greater commitment than to the means his occasional majority position gives him for riding roughshod over the interests of a minority that may then be at his mercy. Most Americans are in this position with respect to traffic rules. At different times of the same day, we are pedestrians, motorists, bus passengers, possibly even cyclists. This makes us more considerate toward pedestrians, when we are at the wheel, than we would be if we were never pedestrians ourselves. In some Continental countries with little economic mobility and underdeveloped associational life, some people are perpetual motorists, and nothing but that; they behave accordingly in traffic. Others have never been members of anything but majorities in what little experience with self-government they have had. As a result, their commitment to procedures is virtually nil.

Systems with strong consensus on fundamental procedures could afford to give their formal constitutions a less fundamental and more circumstantial content, than the French, the Italians, and the Germans in their recent experiments in constitution-making. When these peoples made their constitutions, they had to create true constitutions, which not only reflected existing consensus, but had to generate more consensus at a deeper level. This last statement could be criticized as a circular argument, leading to very pessimistic conclusions about the feasibility of constitutional engineering. Since we defined consensus as agreement of both contemporary width and temporal depth, its objects logically cannot be anything but fundamentals. It is precisely the absence of such consensus that brings about the need for writing new constitutions. Its presence relegates apparently new constitutions to the more nearly circumstantial level. This has been our main explanation for the success of the Swedish and Swiss constitutions, and those of the English-speaking countries, and for the failure of constitutional engineering in the three major Continental systems. However, before we jump to these pessimistic conclusions, we should compare the French, Italian, and German cases in terms of the gravity of the constitutional problems involved, and their relative success in solving them. For this purpose, we need first to define standards of gravity.

Constitutional Needs

The need for a new constitution or for constitutional reform arises out of difficulties in the handling of substantive problems—economic, cultural, or external. That is why constitutional problems are the most important ones, and the issues arising out of them potentially the most divisive.

Constitutional problems can arise for different reasons. Those hardest to solve are the ones that occur when an entirely new, wider political system is about to be created out of existing systems whose constitutions have little in common with one another. The dim prospects for European Union and the dimmer ones for a global political system are cases in point. Next in difficulty is the "new-modeling" of an older constitution, undertaken when new substantive values have won out over old ones and are to be realized by means of a new constitution—as in the case of the French Revolution. The gravity of the constitutional problem under this heading will vary from instance to instance, depending in part on the given consensus on the new goals—for example, on whether opponents have been liquidated, bought off, or otherwise silenced. Least difficult of all is the streamlining of a functioning and accepted constitution simply for the purpose of increased efficiency, which itself may be a new value. Greater efficiency may be desired in order to achieve substantive circumstantials, about which agreement prevails. The Swedish and Swiss experiences with constitution-making, in the 1860's and 1870's, fall somewhere between these last two categories of difficulty.

Since the constitution provides the procedures for recognizing problems; stating, deliberating, and resolving issues; and solving the problems, the analogy between the political system and the individual human being, as a maker of decisions, should be recalled once more. For the individual, the equivalent of a constitutional breakdown is a nervous breakdown of the "integrated personality." The person has needs—food, shelter, clothing, information about and adjustment to his environment, relations with other people and defense against them. In seeking to meet these substantive needs, he encounters obstacles that create problems for him. One of these problems is the reconciliation of his different needs with one another, according to some fairly stable pattern. When he has trouble making up his mind or facing up to the realities of his substantive problems, people will say that he has had a nervous breakdown, that he is psychotic, that he is crazy, that he has a split personality, or something similar. Different methods may be used for trying to solve the individual's "constitutional" problems. He may become aware of them himself and try to "pull himself up by his psychological bootstraps"—a rare Munchausian feat. Or he may seek the help of an outsider. Sometimes, a person in this kind of trouble turns to his minister, who will try to save him by providing strengthened or clarified or new goals for his parishioner. Sometimes, this type of patient seeks the help of a psychiatrist or psychoanalyst, who may try to "reconstruct" his personality. There are many parallels between all of this and what happens when a political system has constitutional problems and tries to overcome them on its own or seeks remedies from the outside.

The way in which issues arising out of constitutional problems are formulated depends in part on the difficulty of the problem, and especially on the extent to which the constitutional problem is complicated by economic, cultural, and external ones. If the constitutional problem arises alone, then issues about it may be formulated most clearly and deliberated most efficiently. To this latter possibility, the objection might be raised that constitutional reform is never advocated for its own sake, but always as a means to some substantive end. However, instances of relatively uncomplicated constitutional problems are on the historical record—the Swiss *Totalrevision* of 1874, for example, which amounted to streamlining as much as to substantive controversy. The West German Basic Law, too, was drafted by an assembly whose debates were confined mainly to procedural issues, because its influence on substantive policy was severely restricted.

Now that we have a clearer notion about the content of the true constitution, we can turn to the three systems that have several times during the past century confronted constitutional problems of such gravity that it was decided to solve them by means of explicit constitutional engineering.

CHAPTER 24

Constitution-Making

This chapter includes seven case studies in constitution-making: the Third, Fourth, and Fifth French Republics; the Kingdom of Italy and the Republic of Italy; and the Weimar Republic and the German Federal Republic. The considerations about the true constitution will shape the three sets of questions to be asked about each case: *First,* what was the constitutional problem? Was it complicated by other problems? How close did it come to amounting to a need for a true constitution? What kind of consensus was given at the time? *Second,* what solution did the constitution-makers offer? How was the new constitution produced—by the regular parliament, a constituent assembly, or a "great legislator," like the one proposed by Rousseau for this purpose? Was it popularly ratified and, if so, how? What was the content of the constitution? Was its emphasis procedural or substantive? Did it create consensus on new procedures or values? And *third,* did it succeed? Under this question, we will make more detailed inquiries into five points: stability, adaptability, efficiency, effectiveness, and achievement of the authors' intentions.

The Third Republic

In 1870, France was defeated by Prussia and her German allies, for whom this was the occasion for national unification. The Second Empire of Louis Napoleon ended with rather less of a bang than the First Empire of his uncle, the great Napoleon I. France lost two of her richest provinces, and heavy reparations were imposed upon her. In the course of military defeat, the revolutionary Paris Commune was crushed in a bloody intramural civil war. The constitutional problem was, therefore, complicated by many others; indeed, it was not even uppermost in the minds of politicians. There was little constitutional consensus and, largely for that reason, no attempt at wholesale constitutional engineering. Agreement existed neither against monarchy, nor for a republic. There was no consensus on universal male suffrage or, among those who did support it, on the age at which the franchise should begin—twenty-five or twenty-one. Consensus on a few substantive problems, like policy toward Germany, was stronger than constitutional consensus. This can be illustrated by the passage of several laws, by barest minimum majorities, that later turned out to be "organic," that is, constitutional. These laws, which later became the constitution of the Third Republic, were not ratified by the electorate, except in the sense that pro-Republicans won parliamentary by-elections until 1875. The only matter on which agreement could be said to have existed was that France needed some kind of a constitution with which to keep things running.

The nature of the constitutional problem explains the way in which it was solved. With so little consensus at hand, the "constitution" had to be brief and purely procedural. And even the procedural provisions that the Organic Laws did contain were quite limited. Many other procedural matters, often included in constitutional documents because they are considered fundamental, were omitted. Both kinds of procedures—those that were and those that were not mentioned in the Organic Laws —were devised by falling back upon a variety of older rules, taken over from previous French regimes. The admixture was hard to make up, since each type of procedure was identified with the advocates of some particular set of substantive goals, as Bonapartist, Orleanist, Conservative, or Republican. As a result, the constitution of the Third Republic created new procedural consensus to a greater degree than it drew on old procedural consensus. The persistence of constitutional practices of the Third Republic under the constitution of the Fourth clearly demonstrated this.

How successful was this solution to the French constitutional problem of the 1870's? In terms of stability, quite successful. The Third Republic lasted until the third modern German invasion of French territory, having been born out of the first one. The Fourth Republic used a constitution that did not differ very much from that of the Third, at least in its spirit if not in its letters—which were by far more numerous. Its adaptability, however, could not be rated so highly, especially in view of the failure to provide resolution during the period between the two

World Wars, a failure that led to the repeated advocacy of constitutional reforms. Efficiency in solving problems should be judged with reference to the problem input, not just the policy output as evaluated by a very "rational" efficiency expert. But no matter how the Third Republic is judged, it does not rank very well when compared with its contemporaries.

Economic problems were digested less satisfactorily and less promptly in France than in Germany or Britain, although more satisfactorily than in Italy. If we examine the period after World War I, we must take into account that France faced a graver economic modernization problem than Germany or Great Britain. In another sense, however —in resources relative to the economic aspirations of a nation's own people—one could say that France was richer than the other two countries. Moreover, government as a machine for processing economic problems was not so important in France. This still was not considered a primary function of government, and not recognized as such until it was too late. Observers have pointed out that politics was not very relevant to what happened to ordinary Frenchmen in their everyday lives. Therefore, the French were perhaps able to afford the luxury of this inefficient machinery. If this is true, then politics in France may also have been performing a function that, in Great Britain, is supposed to be performed by the symbolism of monarchy—to provide an outlet for certain kinds of emotional drives. Instead of deflecting these emotions on a symbol on which there is strong consensus, they were in France deflected to politics as a sort of sport. There was strong agreement on the merits of being concerned with this sport, although people cheered for different individual athletes—politics is not a team sport in France. Meanwhile, they were able to look after their private lives in a responsible manner, without politicizing them excessively. Under the Weimar Republic, the reverse may have been the case. Politics received as much attention as in France, with a similar lack of consensus. But politics was more relevant to the everyday lives of German citizens, which meant that many spheres of life were subjected to central decisions to an excessive extent.

On many other problems, the Third Republic turned in a poor performance. The issue of relations between church and state was not resolved as satisfactorily as in Germany. But there, this issue was settled largely in the course of Bismarck's *Kulturkampf* under the Empire, so that the Weimar Republic was not much bothered by it. The French solution was superior to the handling of this problem in Italy, where Vatican-loyal Catholics did not participate in parliamentary politics until the turn of the century. This meant that Italy lacked agreement concerning the proper arena for thrashing out issues. Partly because the Italian problem of late national unification did not arise, France at least had no important group that withdrew from the political arena the Republic provided.

The Third Republic was more effective than it was efficient, because it did gain widespread acceptance for both its constitution and solutions of those problems that its politics did solve. It had to contain a number of very divisive substantive controversies, in the course of which a near breaking point was reached more than once—the Boulanger and Dreyfus affairs, and antirepublicanism in the 1930's, among others. Each of these crises culminated in the conversion of substantive into constitutional issues. Each was resolved, and its resolution was accepted once it had been made. Where such issues were resolved in a clear and unequivocal way, solution of the problem normally followed, thanks largely to the bureaucracy. However, some problem areas have to be exempted from this generalization, among them taxation, although it must remain doubtful whether decisions to collect taxes were ever really meant seriously.

Were the intentions of the authors of the Third Republic's constitution realized? This question is hard to answer, because there was so little consensus among "the authors" on their intentions. The only thing on which they were agreed was the desirability of compromising their conflicting intentions, perhaps by way of instituting a permanent stalemate. In this they succeeded until the German victory of 1940.

The Fourth Republic

In 1945, the drafters of a new French constitution, like their predecessors in the 1870's, were facing a series of very urgent substantive problems. Half of France had just been liberated from German occupation. The antirepublican regime of Marshal Pétain had been liquidated. Recriminatory issues over collaboration with the enemy had arisen out of these twin problems. Two million Frenchmen, who had been prisoners of war, had returned home. The economy was in need of physical and organizational reconstruction and modernization. Demands for the introduction of a comprehensive system of social security were raised and soon met. The overseas empire, and especially those parts of it where French control had lapsed during the war, was beginning to cause trouble. And all of these cross-cutting substantive problems were complicated by a question, which had already been raised by the Free French and the Resistance fighters during the war: Was the Third Republic still in existence? In other words, was there a constitutional problem, too?

How did the French deal with their constitutional problem? First, they decided in a referendum that it existed. In October, 1945, the electorate overwhelmingly voted in favor of convening a Constituent Assembly to draft a new constitution, and against a Parliament that would merely have revised the Organic Laws of the Third Republic. 18,585,000 voters favored a Constituent Assembly, 699,000 opposed it. This led to the election of a Constituent Assembly, which also had to perform normal parliamentary functions while preparing a new constitution. It completed the latter task so that the constitution could be submitted to a referendum in May, 1946, to be rejected by 10,583,000 votes against 9,453,000. A second Constituent Assembly was thereupon elected, which produced a second constitutional draft; this was accepted in a referendum held in October, 1946. This time, out of 26,312,000 eligible voters, 9,297,000 voted in favor, and 8,165,000 against. Thus, slightly more than a third of the eligible voters, and just half the number that had demanded a new constitution to replace that of the Third Republic, ratified the constitution of the Fourth.

The constitution of the Fourth Republic was about twice as long as that of its predecessor, and half again as long as that of the United States. As its length suggests, it contained more circumstantial provisions. Had there been more procedural consensus among its authors, the constitution would have been even longer. The likelihood of General de Gaulle's candidacy for the Presidency may serve as an illustration of this. It raised a major controversy about the method for electing the President—whether by open or secret ballot of the Parliament. This was settled by a compromise, according to which the constitution remained silent on the point, while a gentleman's agreement provided that the first President should be elected by secret ballot.[1]

Many other provisions that were actually included in the constitution, even though they seem to be of a purely procedural nature, were really the product of similar compromises among the groups who clashed in the Constituent Assembly in the pursuit of their material interests. These disagreements also are manifest in the preamble to the constitution itself:

> On the morrow of the victory gained by the free peoples over the regimes which have attempted to subjugate and degrade the human person, the French people proclaims anew that every human being, without dis-

[1] See Gordon Wright, *The Reshaping of French Democracy,* 1948, pp. 215-16.

tinction of race, religion or creed, possesses inalienable and sacred rights. It solemnly reaffirms the rights and freedoms of man and citizen as set forth in the Declaration of Rights of 1789, and the fundamental principles recognized by the laws of the Republic.

In addition, it proclaims as particularly necessary in our time, the following political, economic and social principles:

The law guarantees to women, in all spheres, rights equal to those of men. . . .

It is the duty of all to work, and the right of all to obtain employment. . . .

The right to strike is recognized within the framework of the laws which govern it.

Each worker participates, through his delegates, in the collective settlement of working conditions as well as in the management of enterprises.

Any property, and undertaking, which possesses or acquires the character of a public service or of a monopoly must come under collective ownership. . . .

The nation guarantees . . . to all, especially to children, mothers, and elderly workers, the safeguarding of their health, material security, rest, and leisure. . . .

It is the duty of the State to organize free and secular public education at all levels.

The beginning of the preamble reflects the strong substantive consensus, partly directed against the recent German occupation of France, that had been generated by the experience of the Resistance movement. It had given the French people an outside foe in opposition to which they could bridge their internal disagreements. Substantive consensus from this field of external relations was carried forward to a new spirit of reform in economic, cultural, and constitutional policy. But the agreement often seemed to be more on reform as such, rather than on the direction it was to take. Hence the inclusion of mutually contradictory statements of substantive goals in the preamble, such as the reaffirmation of the French Revolution's Declaration of the Rights of Man, which proclaimed the right of private property, while the preamble goes on to make provision for collective ownership. Yet agreement on the need for restricting private property rights was sufficiently wide to make possible the early nationalization of some basic industries without much bitter controversy.

The positive statement of substantive rights is a peculiarity this constitution shared with many other Continental constitutions. It presents an aspect sharply different from constitutional documents in the English-speaking world. Magna Charta and the English and American Bills of Rights contain limitations—*prohibitions* of certain actions by the King or the Congress. For example, "Congress shall make no law respecting the establishment of religion. . . . The right of the people to keep and bear arms shall not be infringed. . . . No soldier shall . . . be quartered in any house. . . . No person shall be held to answer for a capital or otherwise infamous crime, unless . . . Excessive bail shall not be required. . . ."

Such negative wording is connected with the way in which the English-speaking peoples, and especially the English themselves, gradually obtained concessions from government, particularly from the Crown. It is related, also, to the methods of the English law, requiring clear statements of issues or grievances, and looking back to the last concrete conflict to have been settled. In this way, the English Bill of Rights of 1689 listed various offenses of the newly deposed King James II, concluding each item by condemning the action as "illegal," "against the law," or "illegal and pernicious." Then it goes on to provide for the future by prohibiting similar violations of the liberties of Englishmen thereafter.

Rights stated in this way are understandable, and their violation easily recognizable. They can, therefore, be enforced more easily than rights stated in positive and universalist terms. As a result, a constitution containing negative statements of rights is likely to elicit greater popular acceptance than one containing positively stated rights, many of which must remain dead letters. Many of the rights listed in the preamble to the constitution of the Fourth Republic did remain dead letters. Other provisions of the constitution, like Article 1, proclaiming the "laic" character of the Republic, were so substantive as to generate later ideological issues.

The Fourth Republic was a failure, certainly by comparison with its predecessor, since it lasted for only twelve years. Its failure was so blatant that we need not describe it in any detail that goes beyond the discussion in Chapter 8. In 1958, only the delegation by an irresolute National Assembly of virtually all of its functions to General de Gaulle saved France from having the military uprising in Algeria spread to Paris itself. How can we account for this difference in the success of the constitution-makers of the 1870's and the 1940's? The dissimilarities under which the two constitutions were drafted must be taken into account. The Organic Laws of the Third Republic were not created by a

Constituent Assembly but by the ordinary Parliament. There were no referenda, few people faced up to the reality of the constitutional problem, and no time limit had to be met, as in 1946. Moreover, the men of the 1940's had the experience of the Third Republic to look back upon. In the 1870's, awareness of being engaged in constitutional engineering was much lower than in 1945. Public opinion did not concern the authors nearly as much, since it was not to be called upon to give its verdict on their efforts. Also, there was much less consensus among the founding grandfathers of the 1870's, than among their grandsons in the Constituent Assemblies. That is why the founders of the Third Republic included in their Organic Laws only a minimum of procedures, while the founders of the Fourth went far beyond this to include substantive values as well.

The fact that the authors of the constitution of the Fourth Republic were self-consciously trying to correct what they believed to have been the shortcomings of the Third Republic may have had even more important consequences. Different political persuasions led to different interpretations of its failures. There was not even general agreement among politicians that the Third Republic had failed and should be replaced, although there seemed little doubt among the electorate. The founders of the Fourth Republic behaved very much like diplomats or strategists, who are often "fighting the last war" or trying to prevent it. Just as American neutrality legislation of the 1930's may have been admirably designed to keep the United States out of World War I, but had little to do with the problems that brought the country into World War II, so some of the efforts of the constitution drafters of 1946 seemed to be directed more toward prevention of the unrest and the inefficiencies of the 1920's and 1930's than toward the problems that France was likely to be facing in the 1950's. This tendency was further exaggerated by the predominance of academic intellectuals on the committee of the Constituent Assembly that was entrusted with preparing the constitutional draft. Of its forty-two members, twenty-six were lawyers or professors, and an additional eight were journalists, who would also be likely to have an ideological orientation. The French constitution writers, unlike their German counterparts, had not passed through a hiatus of nonpolitical life. On the contrary, many of these Frenchmen had participated in Resistance fighting, an experience designed to tone down their intellectualism. At the same time, this Resistance experience was also likely to make them more interested in substantive constitutional provisions and give them a recriminatory ideological orientation.

Our comparison of the making of the Constitutions of the Third and Fourth Republics suggests this tentative conclusion: The success of a constitution cannot be ensured merely by efforts to fill it with declarations of agreement. Awareness of disagreements, accompanied by attempts to provide means for resolving them in the future, seems to have been more helpful. It seems that, in 1958, the Father of the Fifth Republic set about his work on the basis of somewhat similar assumptions.

The Fifth Republic

The failure of the Fourth Republic to provide for the efficient handling of France's substantive problems led to the threat from the military, the French colonials in Algeria, and other disaffected groups within Metropolitan France to abolish the Republic altogether and to substitute for it a less representative regime. That is what most of these groups had in mind when they called for General Charles de Gaulle's return to power. He insisted upon assuming office as Premier according to constitutional procedures, but only if he could be sure of no obstruction from Parliament. Both chambers of parliament gave him authority to draft a new republican constitution, but the parliamentary regime had by then been so discredited that De Gaulle did not really need this authority. Parliament went on vacation. Premier de Gaulle took into his Cabinet members of all major political groups, except the Communists and the Poujadistes. He became the sole source of resolution for the interim between the expiration of the Fourth Republic and the beginning of the Fifth. He was also able to define the nature of the constitutional problem the country was facing. Since the antirepublicans had no other leader, and the supporters of the Republic saw De Gaulle as the only shield between themselves and a military coup and/or civil war, his statement of the issue was likely to be accepted by both sides.

De Gaulle's conception of the problem was revealed by the constitutional draft, which was produced in three months and submitted to a referendum a little more than four months after he became Premier. The draft differed from the previous constitution by changing the relations between France and her overseas possessions. Much more important than this, however, was a clear distinction between resolution and representative deliberation. Article 5 states this most dramatically:

> The President of the Republic sees to the respect of the Constitution. He assures, by his arbitration, the regular functioning of public powers, as well as the continuity of the state.

He is the guarantor of national independence, of the integrity of the territory, and of the respect for Community accords and for treaties.[2]

Largely because of continued fears of Bonapartism, the President is now chosen not by direct popular vote but by an electoral college consisting of about seventy thousand persons, including the members of Parliament. He is given the unhedged capacity to dissolve the National Assembly, and emergency powers limited only by the prohibition of dissolution during their exercise. The Premier and his Cabinet—whose members must resign their parliamentary seats upon assuming office—can be overthrown only by an absolute majority of the members of the National Assembly. The Cabinet can stake its existence on passage of specific policies by the National Assembly. If it does this, the bill in question is considered adopted unless an absolute majority supports a motion of censure, in which case the Cabinet has to resign.

This means that on occasions when resoluteness is demanded, issues will be stated as two-way alternatives. Parliamentary deputies may become accustomed to their new role of deliberating, in terms of the interests they represent, upon the resolution of issues proposed to them by the Cabinet. Even if they do not, the deputies can be circumvented in constitutional controversies, since the President of the Republic can "submit to a referendum any bill dealing with the organization of public powers," with agreements within the French Community, or with treaties of constitutional consequences.

The constitution of the Fifth Republic is about as long as that of the Fourth. In the Preamble,

> The French people solemnly proclaims its attachment to the rights of man and to the principles of national sovereignty as defined by the Declaration of 1789, confirmed and perfected by the Preamble of the Constitution of 1946.

This simple incorporation, without repetition, of the substantive content of the preceding constitution, gives the present document a more procedural emphasis. This is further strengthened by omission of such recriminatory substantive provisions as the one in its predecessor according to which "Members of families which have reigned over France are ineligible for the Presidency of the Republic." Nevertheless, in order to

[2] "Community" is the concept that replaced the French Union of the Fourth Republic, used to describe relations between Metropolitan France and her overseas territories.

demonstrate his republicanism, General de Gaulle resorted to ideological symbolism, like opening the referendum campaign on the anniversary of the proclamation of the Third Republic, in the Place de la République. The referendum brought him and his constitution an overwhelming 4-to-1 victory. This victory must be attributed mainly to the simple two-way choice that his formulation of the issue gave to the French electorate: This constitution and De Gaulle as the presumptive first President of the Fifth Republic—or no constitution and the probable end of constitutionalism in France.

That the simplicity of the two-way alternative accounts for the proportions of the victory was also suggested by the distribution of the popular vote in the first parliamentary election held under the new constitution, and in the first municipal elections held a few months later. The first Senate of the Fifth Republic turned out to be virtually an exact replica of the last Council of the Republic in the Fourth. The distribution of the popular vote among the parties in these three elections indicated that French political opinion would continue as fragmented under the Fifth Republic as under the Fourth, even though the new election law reduced the degree to which this fragmentation is reflected in the National Assembly. Still, when Frenchmen choose a representative who is to participate in deliberation rather than resolution, they identify themselves with a great variety of interests. Only when they were asked to resolve the most crucial issue of the decade were they able to transcend identification with these special interests and to choose in terms of the interest of France.

It is of course difficult to judge the success of a constitution that has been in operation only for such a short time. However, in terms of the guidelines for constitution-making that have so far emerged from our study, prospects for the Fifth Republic in 1959 looked brighter than for the Fourth in 1946. It was likely to operate more efficiently, mainly because of the clearer definition of resolution and deliberation. It was also likely to elicit greater acceptance from the electorate, partly because of improved efficiency, partly because of a reduction in the obscurity of channels of representation, and partly because of the dramatic way in which De Gaulle staged the renaissance of French constitutionalism.

But none of this can guarantee success. It is possible, for example, that the new Presidency was too much tailored for the tailor himself, and that after De Gaulle leaves the scene, no other man will be capable of filling his clothes. Or the effects of the law under which the first National Assembly of the new Republic was elected may be considered too discriminatory. This law returned to the system used in the Third Republic—small single-member constituencies and election by a majority on the first ballot or a plurality on the run-off. It resulted in decimating the number of Communist deputies in the National Assembly, although the Communists continued to be the strongest single party in terms of electoral support.

Similarly, the tentative rules of procedure of the National Assembly were designed to have a discriminatory effect, once more against the Communists. The number of committees was reduced to six, most of which are much larger than their nineteen predecessors. The parliamentary delegation of a party, in order to qualify for representation on the committees, must number at least thirty. This meant that the Communist deputies, who represent more than one-fifth of the electorate, are excluded from the committees. This instance of discrimination is not likely to be taken as seriously as the electoral system, since the committees will probably play a much less important role than in the Fourth Republic, because of the concentration of capacity for resolution in President and Premier. Nevertheless, any kind of too blatant discrimination that appears to violate standards of electoral justice may result in more or less general disillusionment with representative democracy.

Also, there can be no guarantee that—the constitution to the contrary notwithstanding—politicians will not return to their bad old habits. The Fourth Republic, for example, was also meant to prevent the overthrow of Cabinets by less than an absolute majority of the National Assembly. Nevertheless, many Cabinets resigned when they lost a vote of confidence by a simple majority. Consensus on the procedures of the Third Republic was so strong in the Fourth that its constitution was frequently circumvented in similar ways.

To paraphrase Justice Holmes: "If the people of France want to go to hell, there is nothing in the constitution of the Fifth Republic to keep them from it." But there is the hope that constitution-maker De Gaulle has inspired his compatriots with enough resolution to keep them from wanting to go to hell, and that the improved machinery he gave them for dealing with their problems will gain sufficient initial impetus to realize his intentions. Whether or not the Fifth Republic turns out to be more successful than its predecessor, its founder showed that he believed in the truth of Article 16 of the Declaration of the Rights of Man and the Citizen: "Every community in which a security of rights and a separation of powers is not provided for needs a constitution."

The Statuto of 1848

The Piedmontese Constitution of 1848 was promulgated by King Charles Albert in response to the revolutionary uprisings of that year. Other Italian princes made similar concessions, but revoked them as soon as they had restored their control of the situation. The *Statuto,* however, remained in effect to serve as the constitution of the Kingdom of Italy until the referendum of 1946 opted in favor of the Republic. The preamble sounds even more monarchical than that of the Swedish Instrument of Government. The reason for this is that King Charles Albert, "with the affection of a father," granted his constitution as a royal gift to his people, who had given proof of their "faith, obedience, and love," while King Carl of Sweden accepted the Instrument that had been prepared for his signature by the firmly established Estates of the Realm. Charles Albert could have remained a monarch who ruled without parliamentary participation. He chose not to, but the recognition of the constitutional problem was up to him, and he provided the solution.

The *Statuto* consisted of eighty-four articles, most of them quite brief. A perusal conveys the impression that its content was almost wholly procedural. And in fact, its only important substantive provision appears in Article 1, according to which Roman Catholicism is the only state religion. Two other substantive items were derived from Article 1: qualification of bishops and archbishops as eligible for appointment to the Senate; and a limitation of freedom of the press, under which "Bibles, catechisms, and liturgical and prayer books may be printed only with the prior consent of the bishop." This brief, fairly vague, largely procedural constitution, while it gave Italy the fundamental framework for national unification and formally remained in effect for almost one hundred years, was not otherwise a great success.

Any analysis of its shortcomings must involve the failure of this central substantive provision of the *Statuto* to reconcile the Papacy to the Italian national state, with its capital in the Holy City. The Pope declared himself a prisoner in the Vatican and refused to renounce his secular sovereignty over the former papal states. Even when the Italian government passed a law in 1871 that declared the person of the Pope "holy and inviolable" and gave him full sovereignty within the Vatican, he still refused to recognize the Kingdom of Italy. (Nor did he ever accept the annual subsidy of 3,225,000 lire granted by the 1871 law.) As a result, the political institutions for which the *Statuto* provided were not accepted as the proper arena for negotiation of conflicts of interest by Italian Catholics loyal to the Papacy.

This was not the only reason for the relative failure of this brief and procedural constitution. Another was the imported character of the procedures for which it provided, and which Charles Albert imposed from above. They were copied from France and England and involved no effort to make use of familiar procedures on which there was an existing consensus. In any case, given the lack of self-government in most of Italy during most of the preceding centuries, it would have been hard to find any such domestic procedures. Moreover, even after a half-century of operation, the *Statuto* procedures still had not filtered down to all those levels of the population below that of the professional politicians. The practices of *trasformismo*, of electoral corruption, and of the highly centralized local administration saw to that. Italy's economic problems during this period were much more difficult than those of any of our other countries, but its political processes were less efficient in dealing with them. Two major factors—the exclusion from responsibility of the poorer parts of the population, and the refusal of the Catholic loyalists to participate in politics until after the turn of the century—combined with the simultaneous high substantive problems facing the system to give this constitution little chance of success. On the other hand, the intentions of the author of the *Statuto* were realized to a large extent. National unification was, after all, achieved. The Pope did eventually accede, and the descendants of Charles Albert were Kings of Italy until 1946—a considerable achievement.

The Republic of Italy

The nature of the constitutional problem confronting the Italians after World War II was determined by the referendum of 1946, in which the electorate was asked to resolve the issue between Monarchy and Republic. Their decision was in favor of the Republic, but by a majority of only 54 per cent. Far from revealing constitutional consensus, therefore, the referendum showed a deep cleavage of opinion. The same lack of consensus on substantive issues was exposed by the parliamentary elections that took place at the same time as the referendum. Together, the Socialists and Communists elected a few more deputies than the Christian Democrats, and various minor parties also won enough seats to enable them to make the claim to be heard in the deliberations of the Constituent Assembly. The aftermath of the war, and of more than two decades of Fascism, added to Italy's chronic and unequally distributed poverty, gave at least as much urgency to substantive problems as to the constitutional one.

It was the task of the Constituent Assembly to solve the problem of the constitution, but just as in France at the same time, the Assembly had to look after normal parliamentary functions as well. And as in France, this had the effect of converting circumstantial into fundamental issues, so that many provisions of the constitution reflected partisan and personal considerations. Unlike its French counterparts, however, the Italian Constituent Assembly did not have to meet a deadline and did not submit the fruits of its labor to another popular referendum. This meant that it could take its time, which led to rather more abstruse and legalistic deliberations than in the case of the founders of the Fourth Republic. Among other models, the three Baltic republics of Estonia, Latvia, and Lithuania were mentioned during the debates on the new constitution, although their experience was neither particularly successful nor relevant to the work at hand. The long exclusion from political responsibility under the Fascist regime, which had no parallel in France, contributed to this theoretical and ideological bent. H. Stuart Hughes mentions an island concentration camp, in which the "elite of anti-Fascism spent years . . . endlessly chewing their ideological cud." [3] They were unable to drop these habits when they finally returned to real politics.

The constitution thus created greatly resembled that of the Fourth Republic. It was slightly longer and if anything even more substantive in content. Its first article proclaims that "Italy is a democratic republic based on labor." It asserts that "All citizens have equal social rank. . . ." The seventh article returns to the perennial issue of relations between church and state:

> The State and the Catholic Church are, each in its own sphere, independent and sovereign.
> Their relations are regulated by the Lateran Pacts. Any amendments to the Pacts, if bilaterally agreed upon, do not require a process of constitutional revision.

The Lateran Pacts, it will be recalled, had been concluded between Benito Mussolini and the Vatican in 1929. Now they were included, without alteration, in the republican constitution. Their inclusion was supported by the votes of the Communist deputies in the Constituent Assembly, not because they agreed with their substance, but as a parlia-

[3] *The United States and Italy*, 1953, p. 110.

mentary maneuver intended to keep the Communists in the coalition Cabinet with the Christian Democrats and the Socialists. In this way, the appearance of substantive consensus given by many constitutional provisions barely obscures profound disagreements that have crisscrossed the Italian political system in the past and continue to do so today.

Another article asserts that "The Republic . . . protects the landscape and the historical and artistic patrimony of the Nation." This provision is not only substantive, but also meaningless, as anyone knows who has driven on Italian highways, where advertising signs completely hide the landscape. In the unlikely event that constitutional reformers in an English-speaking country should ever be motivated by a similar substantive goal, they would probably word the corresponding constitutional provision negatively: "Advertisers may not deface the scenery." Such efforts would be more likely to be crowned with success than the pious statement of the Italian constitution.

The preamble contains a number of similar statements. It is followed by Part I, "Rights and Duties of Citizens," which is divided into four titles, which deal, respectively, with "Civil Relations," "Ethical and Social Relations," "Economic Relations," and finally, "Political Relations." The title about ethical and social relations deals at some length with the family. Among other provisions, it contains one according to which "The law regulates and limits the investigation of paternity." Another gives gifted students without means of their own the right to university scholarships from the state. According to an article under the title about economic relations, the worker has the "right to weekly rest and annual vacations with pay, which he cannot renounce." Trade unions have the right to strike. "Private economic initiative is unrestricted."

The Italian constitution is thus not only heavily substantive in its content, but various substantive provisions contradict each other. Some amount to little more than pious declarations of good intentions that cannot possibly be enforced. Most of the substantive content of the constitution was included in order to assuage the various antagonistic groups in the Constituent Assembly. Each was allowed to register the will of its constituents by way of inserting a declaration of its goals in the fundamental document. But the Assembly was never able to resolve conflicts among the different declarations, so that no integrated constitutional policy emerged.

In Chapter 6, we saw the new fundamental procedures that the constitution brought into being. After the end of the Fascist regime, Italy needed a true constitution more than France did at the beginning of any of her last three Republics. But the work of the Constituent Assembly met this need only to a very limited extent. Where success in solving some of Italy's economic problems was achieved despite the inefficiency of her political machinery, this was often due to outside help, especially from the United States. The church-state issue is still as divisive as ever. On the right, the proportion of monarchists has undoubtedly been reduced considerably, but on the left, the anticonstitutional Communists and left-wing Socialists have maintained their electoral support. Far from having created any new consensus, the new Italian constitution has helped to harden disagreements that divided the Constituent Assembly and that it permanently anchored in the system's fundamental charter.

Have the intentions of the founders of the Republic been realized? The answer depends on which of the founders one has in mind. This same question about the Third and Fourth Republics in France was also hard to answer. The members of the Constituent Assembly were, if anything, even more divided than the electorate at the time. Their ideologism led them to exaggerate existing popular disagreements, especially as to their goals and constitutional intentions. For example, the Communists certainly did not want constitutional democracy along the Western model to succeed in Italy. They participated in early postwar Cabinets in order to exploit the creditable role they had played in the resistance against the Germans and Fascists for their own interests and those of international Communism. Inefficient government under the new republican constitution, they must have believed, would redound to their own benefit. Most of those Italians who would be disillusioned by the performance of the constitutional regime that had replaced Fascism would probably turn to the Communists—although some might turn to neo-Fascism. The Communist members of the Constituent Assembly, therefore, may have been eager to include in the constitution mutually contradictory substantive provisions and inefficient procedural ones. This would later enable them to point to the constitution as a divisive symbol—as, in fact, they later used the Lateran Pacts to denounce the Christian Democrats as "lackeys of the Vatican."

Similarly cynical intentions cannot be attributed to the Christian Democrats and the other proconstitutional groups participating in the Constituent Assembly. They truly sought to solve Italy's constitutional problem as the indispensable first step toward solving her other substantive problems. These intentions were realized to an only limited extent.

The three French and two Italian experiences with constitution-making have shown how much more difficult it is to give a political system a set of new true fundamentals than to streamline an existing constitution based on so deep a procedural agreement that it can safely contain relatively circumstantial material. They also confirm our earlier tentative conclusion that the success of a made constitution is directly related to its brevity, vagueness, and procedural emphasis. The case of the Third Republic particularly backs up the suggestion that agreement on the goals of a political system is no prerequisite for developing consensus on fundamental procedures.

We can now expand the injunction against length and substantive content in engineered constitutions. Both are likely to be motivated by the desire to create more consensus within the system than exists at the time of the writing of the constitution. And both are likely to be self-defeating. Putting a great many substantive "principles" into a constitution is not by itself going to lead people initially opposed to these goals to accept them. On the contrary, the meaningless character of these provisions may result in the disillusionment of even the supporters of the constitution and of some of its substantive goals. But this does not mean that any constitution that is brief and procedural is bound to succeed— otherwise Fascism would not have won in Italy after World War I. The fundamental procedures for which a new constitution provides should also be related to—and preferably derived from—practices with which both politicians and other citizens are familiar. And they should be adapted to the different types of decisions for which they are used in the policy flow. The Organic Laws of the Third Republic came closer to these standards than did the Italian *Statuto,* and this fact goes far toward explaining the relative success of the constitution of the Third Republic.

Finally, the French and Italian experience with constitution-writing suggests that a divided constituent assembly, which simultaneously exercises resolution on current issues, is likely to produce an inferior document. There are two other major alternatives to letting a constitution be written by an assembly that at the same time also performs normal parliamentary functions. One is to let a single individual act as the constitutional legislator, as the King in Italy and Charles de Gaulle in France. This alternative is unattractive, and for fairly obvious reasons. The other assigns the constitution-making to an assembly, much smaller than modern parliaments, which has no tasks other than the constitutional one. The Constitutional Convention at Philadelphia operated in this fashion, and the work wrought by it has not been equaled in success anywhere. The British North America Act, too, was drafted by an assembly that had no other function but to deliberate about confederation, and its draft was then polished by British politicians. More recently, the Basic Law of the Federal Republic of Germany was composed in a similar manner. We next turn to it and its predecessor, the Weimar Constitution.

The Weimar Republic

The German Reich, which Bismarck founded in 1871, had a federal constitution. To be sure, many scholars have not considered it a constitutional state, because the Chancellor was accountable not to the Reichstag, its national parliament, but to the Emperor. Yet, the Reichstag was elected by universal male suffrage, and the rule of law prevailed. It would therefore be wrong to call the Weimar Constitution Germany's first experiment with constitution-making, the more so in view of the vain efforts of the National Assembly at Frankfurt in 1848, and the various constitutions of German states prior to unification. But Weimar was Germany's first experiment with constitutional democracy.

Like the Third Republic in France, the first German Republic was founded in defeat. Military defeat was accompanied by violent uprisings and the forcible overthrow of the Empire and of the monarchical regimes in the member states. One can debate whether or not these uprisings amounted to a true revolution. In any case, in their wake there came into being the first national German constitution that had been proposed from below, rather than imposed upon the country either from above, by its rulers, or from the outside. Despite this, the coincidence between the establishment of constitutional democracy and military defeat encouraged people to associate these events with each other and, in some cases, to attribute the new constitution to foreign influences.

The Kaiser's abdication and the subsequent somewhat half-hearted proclamation of the Republic by the provisional government initially defined the constitutional problem for Germany in 1918. The country was facing many other substantive problems at the same time: the exhaustion of the economy after years of Allied blockade and war, the return of millions of veterans, the imposition of reparations by the victors, the loss of colonies and of territory to her neighbors, negotiation of the Treaty of Versailles, and domestic unrest that flared up in civil war more than once. Much of the internal violence was caused by Communists, who wanted to follow the model of the recent Russian Revolution, and by radicals of the right, who refused to accept the idea of a democratic constitution.

The constitutional problem was dealt with by a popularly elected

National Assembly, which met in the city of Weimar, traditional center of German culture. It performed ordinary parliamentary functions in addition to its constituent duties, that is, it had to create Cabinets, pass circumstantial legislation, ratify the Treaty of Versailles, and so forth. Three-quarters of the members of the National Assembly were in favor of the Republic: the Social Democrats, the Catholic Center, and the liberal Democrats—the parties of the so-called "Weimar Coalition." The National Assembly completed the task of writing the constitution four months after its election. Some of Germany's most distinguished jurists and social scientists, among them men of world renown, participated in the deliberations on the constitution. The document was not submitted to a popular referendum, but was put into effect after its adoption—the vote was 262 to 75—by the National Assembly, which then continued to operate for another year, until the election of the first Reichstag under the new constitution.

The constitution was long and detailed; it contained many procedural provisions and had a high substantive content—higher than that of either the Fourth Republic or the Republic of Italy. It consisted of two major parts, of which the first, running to 108 articles, dealt with the structure and functions of the Reich, while the second, with 58 articles, dealt with fundamental rights and duties of Germans. The constitution provided for proportional representation in the Reichstag, although the details of this were regulated by ordinary legislation. A provision concerning the Cabinet may illustrate the procedural detail of the constitution: "The Reich Cabinet will make its decisions by majority vote. In case of a tie the vote of the presiding officer will be decisive."

We have had previous occasion to refer to the first article of the second part of the constitution. It specified:

All Germans are equal before the law.

Men and women have fundamentally the same civil rights and duties.

Privileges and discriminations due to birth or rank and [formerly] recognized by law are abolished. Titles of nobility will be regarded merely as part of the name and may not be granted hereafter.

Titles may be conferred only when they designate an office or profession; academic degrees are not affected by this provision.

Orders and honorary insignia may not be conferred by the state.

No German may accept a title or decoration from a foreign government.

This part, dealing with fundamental rights and duties, was divided into five sections: "The Individual," "Community Life," "Religion and Religious Societies," "Education and Schools," and "Economic Life."

Two articles from the section on community life can give an idea of the substantive emphasis:

> Marriage, as the foundation of family life and of the maintenance and increase of the nation, is under the special protection of the Constitution. It is based on the equal rights of both sexes.
> The maintenance of the purity, the health, and the social advancement of the family is the task of the state and of the municipalities. Families with numerous children have a claim to equalizing assistance.
> Motherhood has a claim to the protection and care of the state.
>
> Illegitimate children shall be provided by law with the same opportunities for their physical, mental, and moral development as legitimate children.

Another article, from the section on education, is similarly relevant:

> All schools shall inculcate moral education, civic sentiment, and personal and vocational efficiency in the spirit of German national culture and of international conciliation.
> In the instruction in public schools care shall be taken *not to hurt the feelings* of those of differing opinion.
> Civics and manual training are included in the school curriculum. *Every pupil receives a copy of the Constitution* on completing the obligatory course of study. . . .[4]

In the case of the section on economic life, the constitution speaks for itself better than any condensation could:

> The right of private property is guaranteed by the Constitution. Its nature and limits are defined by law.
> Expropriation may be proceeded with only for the benefit of the community and by due process of law. There shall be just compensation insofar as is not otherwise provided by Reich law. . . .
> Property rights imply property duties. Exercise thereof shall at the same time serve the general welfare. . . .
>
> The distribution and use of land is supervised by the state in such a way as to prevent its misuse and to promote the object of ensuring to every German a healthful dwelling and to all German families, especially those with numerous children, homesteads corresponding to their needs. War veterans shall receive special consideration in the enactment of a homestead law.
> Landed property, the acquisition of which is necessary to satisfy the

---

[4] Italics supplied.

demand for housing, to promote settlement and reclamation, or to improve agriculture, may be expropriated. Entailments shall be dissolved.

The cultivation and utilization of the soil is a duty of the landowner toward the community. An increase of the value of land arising without the application of labor or capital to the property shall redound to the benefit of the community as a whole. . . .

The Reich may by law, without impairment of the right to compensation, and with a proper application of the regulations relating to expropriation, transfer to public ownership private business enterprises adapted for socialization. . . .

Every German has, without prejudice to his personal liberty, the moral duty to use his intellectual and physical powers as is demanded by the welfare of the community.

Every German shall have the opportunity to earn his living by economic work. So long as suitable employment cannot be procured for him, his maintenance will be provided for. Details will be regulated by special Reich laws.

The independent middle estate in agriculture, crafts, and trade shall be fostered by legislation and administration, and shall be protected against oppression and absorption.

At the time of its adoption, the Weimar Constitution was widely hailed as the very model of modern constitutionalism. Less than fourteen years later, it was succeeded by Adolf Hitler's totalitarian dictatorship. During the interim, it had been subject to constant amendment, had failed to adapt itself to changes in the grave problems that Germany was facing, had been inefficient as the machinery for making policy, and had failed to generate sufficient consensus on its own merits or on those of constitutionalism in general to prevent its own demise. What happened went directly counter to every intention of the heavy proconstitutional majority that dominated the National Assembly at Weimar.

The question of why the Weimar Constitution failed is usually answered by reference to the tremendous economic and external problems confronting Germany from 1918 to 1932. These, together with German lack of experience with self-government, would have led to the failure of any constitution, it has been said. This is a deterministic, or even fatalistic, explanation. The later success of the Bonn Constitution in the face of even more catastrophic problems suggests that it is wrong. In any case, possible differences in the constitution of the first German Republic might have made the failure less utterly disastrous than it was. The question must, therefore, be dealt with on its merits, that is, in terms of the contribution of the constitution to its own failure. We have previously dealt with its shortcomings with regard to institutions, procedures, and personnel. In addition to these, the composition of the Weimar Constitution undermined its possibilities for success in three ways: Its procedural provisions were too detailed, its substantive provisions too many and contradictory, and its amending process too easy.

In addition to the procedural detail included in the constitution itself, there were the rules of procedure of the Reichstag, taken over intact from its Imperial forerunner. As suggested in the chapter on legalism, the Germans' lack of practice with democratic procedures at the grass roots may have necessitated the inclusion of provisions like the one on voting in the Cabinet. But the legalistic inclinations led to excessive concern with strict observance of provisions of this kind, regardless of whether this served their original purpose. Moreover, these were not the kind of procedures designed to filter down to communal problem-solving at lower levels, both inside and outside of politics proper—no matter how many school graduates were given copies of the constitution. That there are other ways for building up practice with and agreement on procedures at the grass roots is suggested by the experience with codetermination in the Bonn Republic.[5]

Much worse than the effects of procedural detail were those of the excess of contradictory substantive provisions. The substantive fundamentals included in the Weimar Constitution were based on less consensus than those in the preamble to the constitution of the Fourth Republic. This lack of agreement is expressed in the juxtaposition of incompatible values. Thus, the articles dealing with the family confused religious and secular values, and the economic section came out in favor of both private property and socialization and combined bits of several antagonistic ideologies, among them liberalism, Marxism, Henry George's theory of the single tax on land, and traditionalist corporatism. Some of its statements dealt with rather circumstantial matters, like veterans policy and family subsidies. Such items could safely be included in the Swiss constitution, which is no longer the true constitution; here, however, the National Assembly did have the job of creating a true constitution and made a mistake when it did not stick to fundamentals. But was it really possible to keep these substantive provisions out of the constitution? The parties of the Weimar Coalition had been denied political responsibility for so long that they naturally wanted to take advantage of this opportunity to convert their ideological aspirations into constitutional law. They had become so accustomed to the habits of ideologism,

[5] See pages 168-69.

bred by lack of responsibility, that they often paid more attention to formal provisions than to practical achievements. The fact that Socialists, Catholics, and Liberals did not agree among themselves further complicated the situation. It meant that the National Assembly faced the alternative of either ignoring their traditional substantive goals, for the sake of which they had wanted democracy in the first place, or anchoring substantive differences permanently in the constitution and thereby sanctifying their disagreements.

The easy amendability features, finally, thwarted the intention to make any part of the constitution, whether substantive or procedural, truly fundamental. Since any bill passed by a two-thirds majority of the quorum of two-thirds of the Reichstag could be considered a constitutional amendment, nothing was really fixed. This facilitated the end of the Republic in 1933. After Hitler's appointment as Chancellor and an election that returned his Nazi party as the strongest party in the Reichstag, his Cabinet was voted full legislative powers—including, by implication, constitutional amending powers. After that, the distinction between fundamentals and circumstantials completely withered away. All laws, decrees, and orders of the Nazi government had equal value, except that new ones could be assumed to supersede old ones. The Nazi "movement," as its leaders called it, had given so much movement to the constitutional state that "permanent revolution" replaced constitutionalism. From 1933, a condition of flux was to prevail, in which no one could have foreknowledge of the morrow or of the consequences of his own decisions. Germany had had no true constitution in 1918, and the men of Weimar failed to give it one. The lack of fundamental institutions and procedures was carried to its logical and tragic conclusion in National Socialist totalitarianism.

The Bonn Republic

The rebuilders of German constitutionalism in 1948 faced even more difficult problems than their fathers had after World War I, largely because of the twelve years of Nazi rule through which the country had just passed. This time, military defeat had been even more colossal, much of the industrial and transportation system had been reduced to rubble, and the whole country was still under foreign military occupation. The division between the Soviet and Western zones of occupation had lowered the iron curtain right through the middle of Germany when the task of writing a constitution was imposed upon the Germans by the United States, Great Britain, and France. The Allied Military Governors told the Ministers-President of the West German states what to do and how to do it. They set minimum requirements that the constitutional draft would have to meet, limits within which the German constitution-makers would have to stay, and interfered from time to time to correct specific "faults" of the work of the Parliamentary Council at Bonn.

This body consisted of sixty-five members, selected by the state diets in proportion to the strength of the parties there. Its work lasted over a period of about eight months. It had no concurrent parliamentary functions, and the only nonconstitutional decisions it made dealt with the law under which the first Bundestag was elected, and the selection of Bonn as the federal capital. The Basic Law that the Parliamentary Council drafted, after approval by the Military Governors, was submitted to the state diets for ratification, not to the electorate. It was accepted by all the states but Bavaria, with its traditions of local autonomy and loyalty to the Catholic Wittelsbach dynasty.

The Basic Law is a little longer than the Italian constitution, but this is due to the many federal provisions that were not needed in Italy. Its procedural content is lower than that of the Weimar Constitution. For example, proportional representation is not mentioned, nor is the voting procedure of the Cabinet. The substantive provisions have been reduced. But the Basic Law explicitly incorporated five articles of the section of the Weimar Constitution on religion and religious societies. The shortest of these reads: "Sunday and the recognized public holidays remain protected by law as days of freedom from labor and of spiritual elevation." A paragraph on illegitimate children was again included. Otherwise, the section of "Basic Rights" was shifted to the beginning of the constitution, and now contains only nineteen articles. These are still stated in positive and universalist terms, and some of them are quite long. But the section as a whole is shorter and contains fewer contradictions than its forerunner in the Weimar Constitution. By placing it at the beginning of the Basic Law, the Parliamentary Council emphasized its intention to make these rights really meaningful. This same wish was one of its reasons for establishing the Federal Constitutional Court, with its function of judicial review. This motive, finally, also explains the constitutional prohibition against amending the basic principles laid down in the first section of the Basic Law. Other parts of it "can be amended only by a law which expressly amends or supplements the text thereof." Constitutional amendments require two-thirds of the votes in both houses of Parliament. Unlike the Weimar Constitution, therefore, the Basic Law of Bonn is really basic or fundamental.

In the decade since its ratification, the Basic Law has retained the intended stability. Only two major sets of amendments have been passed. One of these rearranged fiscal relations between the states and the federal government and parallels similar amendments that the Swiss and Canadian federal constitutions have undergone from time to time. The other provided for the adjustments needed for the West German defense establishment. The Basic Law was adapted to the great changes in the problems faced by West Germany between 1948, when it was still poor and under military occupation, and 1958, when it had achieved one of the strongest economies in the world and had become the most reliable ally of the United States on the Continent.

The efficiency of politics in the Federal Republic has been the envy of its neighbors. The Basic Law and policies made under it have gained wider acceptance than their counterparts in either Italy or France. The intentions of the founding fathers of the Parliamentary Council at Bonn have been realized to a far greater extent than they could have hoped in their wildest dreams. How can we explain this—so far—very successful experiment in constitution-making?

We have already given some specific answers to this question in the course of the book, among them the provision for the constructive vote of no confidence. But these answers by themselves are inadequate, because they do not explain either why the Parliamentary Council was able to write such provisions into the Basic Law, or why they have been observed rather than circumvented—as was or would have been the case in Italy and France. Nor would it suffice to give the credit to the more limited, more procedural, and more nearly fundamental content of the Basic Law, without accounting for the fact that the constitution-makers at Bonn were able to create this kind of document. The explanation for this must be found in the purely constitutional task of the Parliamentary Council. Circumstantial politics were excluded from its deliberations as much as possible, by contrast with the National Assembly and the French and Italian Constituent Assemblies. True, the members of the Parliamentary Council were party politicians, elected by state diets, which also consisted of party politicians. But even the state diets and the Economic Council—which could, under Occupation supervision, make policy for the Western zones—performed very few of the normal functions of politics while Military Government was still in control. The constitution-makers could not, therefore, be influenced very much by immediate substantive issues, since they themselves had little influence on substantive policy. This enabled them to arrive at consensus on many problems that did not involve partisan advantage. Some of those issues that did—like the election law and selection of the federal capital—they left out of the constitution. As a result, procedures that did not command strong consensus were not included in the Basic Law, but pushed to the level of circumstantials, where they properly belong.

The conditions under which the Basic Law was composed could be expected to have encouraged ideologism and legalism. Ideologism could have been enhanced by the impotence of German politicians to realize their aspirations under the strict controls imposed by Allied Military Government. Legalism might have been reflected in an excessive reliance on the rigid and automatic operation of the machinery of government in accordance with constitutional provisions, which were devised more or less as an academic exercise, without responsible reference to reality, abetted by the retrospective desire to correct all the supposed shortcomings of the Weimar Constitution. However, the more harmful kinds of ideologism were curbed by Occupation fiat through exclusion from politics of Nazis and other opponents of constitutionalism. Only two Communists served on the Parliamentary Council. And legalism in some ways actually contributed to success. Combined with the consensus on revulsion against both Nazi and Communist totalitarianism, legalism made for general agreement on the desirability of subjecting all politics to law, of regularizing it, and then of obeying constitutional provisions strictly. Because France did not pass through a hiatus of politics similar to that in Germany under the Allied occupation, or through totalitarianism, and because of her tradition of "progress on the barricades," similar attitudes could hardly have developed there. The French recognize the irregularity of politics, and like it, while the Germans have reacted with disgust to it. And when parts of politics are subjected to regularization by means of law, strict observance of the letter is not considered as great a virtue in France as in Germany.

West German politics has not achieved perfection by any means—no political system ever does. There is still constant discussion of constitutional changes, encouraged by the explicitly tentative character of the Basic Law. Election laws have been altered frequently, as have parliamentary rules of procedure from time to time. There is much constitutional litigation, and popular familiarity with the procedures of compromise has not been increased very much as a result of formal efforts to this effect. Nevertheless, when compared with the failure of Germany's first democratic constitution, of Italy's first Republic and France's Fourth, and when viewed in relation to the substantive problems that West Germany has been confronting since World War II, the success of the Basic Law appears quite remarkable. It comes closer to being a true constitution than any other German attempt at constitution-making and is likely to serve this purpose even when, and if, Germany is reunited.

Guidelines for Constitution-Makers—IX

Most new constitutions that are likely to be required by old or new communities in the future are likely to place much greater demands on their authors than did those of Sweden and Switzerland. In many cases, the need for creating a true constitution will be even more obvious than in the cases just discussed. Recent constitution-making in France, Italy, and Germany should, therefore, yield the most useful guidelines for the founders of new political systems.

An engineered constitution should be created by a small assembly of experienced politicians, one that does not at the same time have to make decisions calling for a shorter perspective on time than is required for deliberation about fundamentals.

The constitution should be confined to matters commanding the greatest consensus. These are likely to be matters of negative substance—like national independence and the prevention of violence—and procedures for resolving substantive disagreements.

Positive declarations of policy should be kept out of the constitution, first because there is usually very little consensus on them, and second because the passage of time will change both problems and goals.

The constitution should, therefore, emphasize procedures, and these should preferably be derived from practices with which the population is familiar. Where no such procedures are available, or the available ones are inefficient, practice with the new procedures should be widely disseminated.

Constitutional procedures should be kept truly fundamental by making the constitution hard to amend. At the same time, flexibility should be insured by leaving the door open to procedural experimentation on the periphery of the constitution itself.

PART VII

The Future

CHAPTER 25

New Political Systems

While this book is being read, millions of political decisions are being made all over the earth. Most of these are of a routine kind: A judge in Moscow awards damages to a woman employee for her dismissal from a state-owned factory. President Tito of Yugoslavia denounces President Mao Tse-tung of China. The parliamentary delegation of the Swedish Peasant party opposes the latest social security scheme of the Social Democratic Cabinet. The Postmaster General answers a question about the British Broadcasting Corporation in the House of Commons. Three-fifths of the eligible voters in an American presidential election cast their ballots for one of two candidates, while the other two-fifths do not go to the polls. A French finance inspector audits the books of a bakery and finds tax evasions. The West German Chancellor visits the Italian Premier to discuss Euratom and migrant workers. The decisions involved are routine, not because they affect only a few people—they may affect millions—but because they are not intended to lay down fundamentals. This does not mean that they will not have the effect of establishing fundamentals. We have seen how some very circumstantial procedures have on occasion become firmly established and have survived for centuries, although there was no original intention to use them in anything but passing, current circumstances.

In our own time, however, this kind of *ex post facto* conversion of a routine decision into a fundamental choice is not as likely to happen as in the past. Politics is too much bathed in the light of publicity for this to occur. And those who participate in politics are too much aware of the possibility of deliberately making those decisions that are to have lasting effect. Men everywhere are too much conscious of their increased capacity for responsibility to miss any opportunity for shaping their fate themselves, rather than letting it be shaped by circumstances. It is because of this awareness that there has been such a marked increase in constitution-making, especially during the last few decades. This increase in the deliberate creation of fundamentals, in turn, should also increase the attention given by the comparative study of government to the devices by which policy is made, and decrease that currently given to the content of particular policies—like social security in Sweden, labor relations in Germany, French colonial policy, or United States foreign policy.

The need for this shift in focus becomes especially evident in connection with the many new or renovated political systems that are coming into being all over the globe. These will demand new constitutions, no matter how much pessimism about the feasibility of constitution-making may have been evoked by past experience. The three renovated political systems just discussed certainly give little cause for optimism. Yet their constitutional problems seem less difficult in many ways than the constitutional problems of new political systems. After all, in France and Italy, the geographical scope of the nation-state was not an issue after World War II. And even in divided Germany, the desirability of reunification has not been an issue, but only the auspices under which reunification should be achieved. By contrast, in many new political systems, geographical scope is an issue. British India split into the Republic of India and the Republic of Pakistan upon achieving independence, and Pakistan consists of two parts completely separated by India. Egypt and Syria combined in the United Arab Republic, which some groups in other Arab states want to join, while other groups do not. Before and after Southern Rhodesia, Northern Rhodesia, and Nyasaland were federated, there was and has been opposition to this union. Blacks and whites in all three sections disagree about the desirability of federation, continued separateness, joining other neighboring states, and the degree of British supervision. Many similar examples could be cited.

The Unit of Politics

The first issue for potential or actual new political systems, therefore, is whether to join or remain together in one political unit. This issue arises after consciousness of the existence of a political community has arisen. This consciousness, in turn, is the result of recognizing common problems. A community exists where some people are aware of facing problems in common. In this sense, a global community of mankind is today coming into existence. But the question as to whether people who are not at the time members of one political system do indeed face common problems is usually the first issue. Conversely, when an independence movement is started, the first issue revolves around the denial of a community of problems between the colonial state, like Great Britain, and the advocates of independence, like Thomas Jefferson and Mohandas K. Gandhi and their respective contemporaries in the American and the Indian colonies. This issue may be deliberated and resolved by means of violence, of litigation before national or international tribunals, by means of ideologism or of circumstantial pragmatism, or by means of the purposive compromise of material interests. Often it is settled by means of a combination of all of these. Just how it is settled is of great importance for shaping the style of the new political system after it is launched.

The factors that play a role in the establishment of a new political system are resources in relation to goals, and the consensus these goals command. For example, when the resources of the several Canadian colonies were considered inadequate for the achievement of new economic and other goals, on which there was widespread agreement, the fathers of Confederation decided to pool their resources. Their federal movement was pushed along by the knowledge that the mother country would not add enough of its resources, unless the provinces first helped themselves through more efficient use of their own. Similar considerations figure in contemporary efforts for European union, only that it is the help of the United States that is sought this time. In India, under the leadership of Gandhi, there was increasing consensus on the goal of independence from the British Empire. This agreement grew partly in order to deny to British outsiders the exploitation of Indian resources. The Indians felt that their resources should be available to themselves for use in the solution of their own problems. In this way, agreement on the goal of independence was closely related to the new goal of economic welfare, and to an interpretation of reality, according to which this goal could best be achieved by means of planning. Agreement on the goal of economic welfare and on the type of knowledge deemed useful for attaining it was strong enough to lead to the adoption of a form of socialism by the government of the Republic of India. However, after the goal of independence had been reached, the cultural consensus of the population was too weak to prevent establishment of the separate political system of the Islamic Republic of Pakistan. In this instance, the issue generated by the cultural problem of the subcontinent was too divisive to be contained by agreement on other substantive goals and even by the solution of problems raised by these goals. Agreement on the procedures of self-government that had been introduced by the British was also insufficient for this task, the more since the independence goal had already been achieved.

Nationalism

Questions about the degree of consensus in connection with movements for separation or union have been analyzed by students of nationalism and communications. Switzerland and Canada have shown us that cultural homogeneity, either religious or ethnic, need not be a crucial determinant in the founding or success of political systems. On the contrary, issues produced by cultural disunity can be effectively contained so long as there is sufficient agreement on general procedures to be used for the resolution of all kinds of issues. This kind of agreement is sometimes instilled automatically—that is, unintentionally—in the "socialization" of children, for example. Their unconscious use of political procedures at play and in school has been cited in Chapter 22. This suggests that "politicization" occurs as a process paralleling socialization. Children of two families of very different cultures may be raised as neighbors, each according to the customs and beliefs of his parents. They regularly play with each other and, in the course of this, evolve procedures of "fair play," to which they are so firmly committed that this agreement may later be able to contain quarrels between them caused by the cultural differences.

The study of nationalism would do well not to overconcentrate on cultural factors to the neglect of political ones, in an age in which more and more people are getting some experience with practices of self-government. To be sure, in trying to foresee the founding of new political systems or the merging of existing ones in a new union, one has to inquire into racial, linguistic, religious, sectarian, educational, and other cultural identifications. Useful methods for measuring this in terms of communications—transport, postal, radio, press, and so on—have been suggested for this purpose.[1] These same methods could also be applied profitably to more general aspects of consensus.

Such inquiries might begin by asking how much agreement there is on the recognition of problems, because this may be more important than agreement on ultimate goals. For example, each of the several

[1] See Karl W. Deutsch, *Nationalism and Social Communication*, 1953.

members of a future European federal union may be pursuing its "national interest" rather than the goal of union. But in this pursuit, they all recognize that they share certain problems in common, like increasing steel production and insuring defense against the Soviet Union. For solving these problems, federal institutions may be brought into being—some already exist—that will later continue to expand, even though they have by then removed the initial problem. Among other factors, the personnel of the new institutions will facilitate their maintenance.

After inquiring into awareness of common problems, we should ask about the procedures with which citizens of a potential new political system have experience. In the case of European union, procedural agreement would not be hard to find. But in most instances of "backward" or "underdeveloped" areas seeking to become independent political systems, procedural underdevelopment may be at least as marked as economic underdevelopment. Especially in those African and Asian countries, where colonial rule discouraged the development of self-government, consensus will be the strongest on the goal of independence, and not on the methods for resolving disagreements among the population. Moreover, if the European state resisted the independence effort, this movement is likely to be accompanied by much violence. The less self-government is granted; the less gradually participation is extended from a center of authority; and the longer the struggle lasts, the more ideological will the leaders of the nationalist movement become. Comparisons between British and French colonies back up this generalization.

Political Style

The political style of the new system will reflect the nature of the independence struggle. Leaders who used assassination as an instrument in fighting for independence and spent time in jail for violation of colonial regulations are not likely to give up assassination or to be hesitant about throwing their domestic opponents into prison, in order to resolve internal issues. If the European regime was corrupt and responded erratically and pragmatically to "native" demands, the politicians of the new state are likely to make their decisions on similar grounds. If, before achieving their only agreed goal, they have been "chewing their ideological cud" for many years, they are likely to go on making and justifying their decisions in terms of the ideology of independence, long after this has been achieved. The ideology will involve recrimination against both deviationists from the domestic movement and the former imperialist powers on the international plane.

These unfortunate stylistic phenomena will be further aggravated by the personnel of politics. There will be a scarcity of this personnel unless self-government was encouraged by the European administration. The most prominent leaders may be models of ideologism and violence —passive resistance as practiced by Gandhi and his disciples is hard to emulate. If they spent much time at study or in exile in Continental Europe, they may also be very legalistic. With the achievement of independence, they may become afraid of losing their popular support and therefore manufacture artificial and unrealistic new issues, to deflect attention from the real problems the system is facing. Or they may feed on newly important real problems, like denominational or linguistic cleavages, by exaggerating the issues arising out of them. To make things even worse, "they" are not an organized group of leaders, who are agreed upon procedures and goals, but competing individuals and groups.

This picture may appear unnecessarily bleak. However, it describes fairly accurately the situation that has prevailed in many newly independent political systems after removal of the imperial regime. Even where a relatively progressive British colonial administration did provide experience in self-government and in British procedures, as in India or Ghana, political style after independence was characterized by much violence, ideologism, and corruption. Where the colonial regime itself was violent and corrupt, the effect would be doubled. And yet it is usually at this stage of political development that the constitutional problem becomes urgent.

The Value of Constitutions

What kind of advice can we now offer toward the solution of the constitutional problem of a new, politically underdeveloped system? To begin with, we should analyze the problem. This analysis may reveal that the constitution is not wanted as a device for helping the system deal with its substantive problems, but as a façade behind which the anticonstitutionalist rulers can hide, for purposes both domestic and international. After all, the Soviet Union and all of its satellites have elaborate constitutions—which, incidentally, are full of substantive content—but everyone knows of the realities of totalitarianism that are but ill concealed behind this window dressing. Mussolini's dictatorship, too, operated behind the façade of the *Statuto* and the laws establishing the Fascist Grand Council. Is it worth while to concern ourselves with this kind of demand for a mere "paper" constitution? The answer is *Yes,* and for two main reasons. In the first place, no harm can be done by taking seriously the insincere request for a constitution, and there is in any case no way of keeping states out of the world-wide club of proprietors of constitutions. The very fact that totalitarian systems have constitutions ensures that the adoption of one will not by itself lend internal or international authority to any regime. The second reason is even more important: Though no more than a scrap of paper at first, the constitution may later be used for replacing the nonconstitutional regime. This happened to some extent in Italy, when the Fascist Grand Council overwhelmingly passed a motion asking the King to take over "effective command" and the "supreme initiative of decision" from Mussolini.[2] And it is at least conceivable, according to Professor Adam B. Ulam, that something similar might someday occur in the Soviet Union.[3] In an underdeveloped system, the hope for this kind of occurrence would be much more justified, especially after the generation that achieved independence had died. In the meantime, the constitutionalists can always try to use discrepancies between the provisions of the constitution and the facts of politics on behalf of their good cause. West German propaganda has been doing just that in attacks on the Soviet East German regime.

The Model Constitution

Since there is no way to keep a new political system from acquiring a constitution, nor any good reason for doing so, the next question is: What does the model of a good constitution for a new political system look like? Students and practitioners of state government in the United States have actually drafted a model state constitution. They were able to do this because the fifty states, by and large, face fairly similar problems and because their constitutions are certainly not the true fundamentals. Since these factors do not apply to new and underdeveloped political systems, however, it will be much more difficult to answer the question about a model constitution for them. But we can at least suggest a method for arriving at an answer.

First, we would inquire into the procedures of deliberation and

[2] H. Stuart Hughes, *The United States and Italy,* 1953, p. 126.
[3] See Adam B. Ulam, "The Russian Political System," in *Patterns of Government,* Beer and Ulam, eds., 1958, pp. 516 ff.

resolution with which the population—or those parts of it likely to become participants in politics—is familiar. These procedures may or may not be suitable for the efficient conduct of democratic politics. But in order to find out whether or not they are, one has to isolate and describe the procedures. For this purpose, the study of all groups that make decisions about their own problems is recommended. How does the village deliberate about the allocation of pasture land? How does it resolve local quarrels? How do the councils of the chiefs of different tribes "advise and consult"? How does the agricultural coöperative decide how much produce to grow, how to market it, and how to divide its profits? How does the language shape the manner in which people formulate issues, not only in politics, but in ordinary conversation? In terms of two opposed alternatives, many overlapping alternatives, or vaguely, fatalistically, and "non-issue-like"? Do different segments of the population use any of the same procedures? These questions may yield no useful answers at all, and in that event, the task of the constitution-writers is doubly difficult. But it is probable that some procedures will be uncovered that can be adapted for use by a modernizing political system. In any case, even if the results are wholly negative, the inquiry is still indispensable, to avoid making mistakes in the course of designing new procedures. Such mistakes could be committed, for example, by introducing a procedure reminiscent of a primitive one used by a cruel chief, which would therefore be popularly associated with a long-discredited regime. No new political system can ever start with a completely clean slate, as the makers of both the French and the Russian Revolutions discovered to their dismay.

Next, we would want to get a picture of the actual present and potential future pattern of interest identification. This picture will also give an accurate description of consensus at levels less than fundamental, if there is fundamental agreement on the unit of politics. With what kinds of interests do people primarily identify themselves—clan, tribe, race, religion, sect, occupation, level of education, generation, sex, source or level of income, locale, etc.? Do they usually identify themselves with only one major interest, or do they feel that they "belong" to different ones, some of which may be vertically, others horizontally stratified? These questions must be answered before one can construct channels of representation through which interest groups may contribute to central decisions. The existing degree of popular interest in political participation should also be surveyed, so that the earlier guideline, against extending opportunities to participate to groups that do not want them, may be observed. If people were unable to contribute to central decisions prior to independence, it may take some time before they will grasp their new situation of responsibility.

Channels of representation lead to the next set of questions, which are closer to those traditionally asked by the institutional and functional schools: Where, how, and by whom are central decisions to be made? Before these can be answered, we have to inquire into the major substantive problems confronting the new system, and into prevailing concepts of authority. In most cases, problems of economic development will be the most serious ones—hence the term "underdeveloped areas." In most newly independent political systems, there will be agreement on the need for general improvements in the standard of living, although there may be disagreement about the extent to which different sectors of the population are to benefit from such improvements. That is why different interests will want, and should be given, opportunities to contribute to the making of central decisions about the solution of economic problems. This desire was one reason for the earlier inquiry into interest identification. The nature of economic and other problems is likely to be of such proportions that the need for resolution will be emphasized more than the need for deliberation, at least for the first few years after independence. This emphasis is likely to be reënforced by the dominant conception of authority.

After the struggle for self-government and the establishment of the new system has been crowned with success, the leaders of this movement will possess more authority than anyone else. These leaders will be resolute personalities—otherwise they would not have succeeded in the first place. The new constitution, especially where it is more than a façade, should provide for resolution. We have seen that there is a variety of means for doing this—e.g., the organs of resolution in the United States, Great Britain, West Germany, the Fifth Republic, and Switzerland. Which of these types to propose depends on concepts of authority older than those associated with the independence movement—and on circumstances. For example, if an ancient dynasty possesses great authority, constitutional monarchy may be indicated. Where popularity lends authority, ways can be devised for giving the sustained capacity for resolution to a popularly elected head of state; and so forth. Getting guidance from circumstances—e.g., the personality of the probable first incumbent—amounts to confusing circumstantials with fundamentals. It may nevertheless bring long-run success—witness the case of George Washington and the Presidency of the United States.

After resolution has been institutionalized, there should be organs in which representatives of interests can deliberate about resolution of issues proposed to them. Wherever possible, these organs should be given procedures that are both efficient and indigenous, although efficiency should be accorded priority. These procedures should be made popular, preferably by informal means, for example by introducing them at lower levels of self-government, as was done with codetermination, and in schools. The structure of politics should be such that a normal political career is truly political all the way from original entry into it to the possible final achievement of the highest offices in the land. There are different devices for encouraging careers of this type, none of them necessarily involving a rigid distinction between political parties and interest organizations, in the conventional sense. This distinction is also superfluous in constructing election laws or their equivalents. If the country had a rich associational life before it achieved independence, there may not even be any reason for adopting an election law at all, because various established corporate interests have their own accepted procedures for selecting representatives. In most cases, the goal of universal suffrage will be a part of the ideology of independence, so that an election law will be needed. No single electoral system should, however, be recommended. Rather, the important aim to keep in mind is that of giving opportunities for participation in deliberation to self-conscious interest groupings. Whichever election law is adopted, it should be shielded against circumstantial tampering. This protection can best be gained by including the basic principles of the election law in the constitution, which should not be amendable without something approaching a concurrent majority, that is, without consensus that is both widespread and reaches over more than one generation into both past and future.

This raises the question of what else to put into the constitutional document. On the basis of the experience of the developed—and some overdeveloped—constitutional systems surveyed in this book, our answer is: a minimum of provisions about procedures to be observed in relations among, and in the internal operation of, the major institutions; vague and long-range substantive goals, but no more than actually command wide and deep consensus; and negative statements of citizens' rights in terms of procedural prohibition on the government.

Ethnocentrism and Disagreement

There is, of course, no guarantee that a constitution drafted according to these guidelines will succeed. Indeed, because of the risks involved and inability to arrive at adequate agreement, some new political systems have decided not to adopt a constitution, and have instead passed some organic laws on the model of the Third Republic, leaving further accretion of both consensus and its reflection in explicit fundamentals to a process of evolution. Israel is a case in point.

In any case, a constitution that follows these guidelines is likely to have greater chances for success than one which seeks to establish a separation of powers, a "two-party system," and a long list of positive and substantive rights for its citizens. Some modern constitutions, for example, include not only the right but the duty to vote. In underdeveloped and new political systems, this would probably have very unfortunate consequences, by forcing political participation upon people who are neither interested in it nor adequately prepared for it.

Similarly, a two-party or multiparty system may be quite unsuitable for a new state like Indonesia, whose President Sukarno has been experimenting with what he calls "guided democracy," a scheme somewhat reminiscent of European corporatism. Secretary of State Dulles condemned this as smacking of totalitarianism. This naturally offended many Indonesians. From our point of view, Mr. Dulles' criticism can serve as a dramatic illustration of the naïve attitude toward new political systems on the part of citizens of developed constitutional democracies in the West—an attitude to whose popularity political science has contributed more than it should be willing to admit. There is nothing sacrosanct about the various Western types of party systems or other specific institutions.

What is sacrosanct is the norm of individual responsibility. There are many different ways of maintaining and improving situations of responsibility. And the best method for finding out about specific ways in particular circumstances is by asking: What are the problems of the political system? What are the issues? How are they resolved? How are the problems solved? Who is affected by the solutions? What contributions can they make to decisions about the problems?

By judging other political systems in terms of the categories and great achievements of our own, we only promote disagreements, of which there are already too many for comfort in the global community of mankind. That community cannot yet be described as a political system. In our final chapter, we will inquire into the factors preventing such a description, and we shall seek the answer to the question: What kind of consensus does humanity require in order to be able to solve its common problems?

CHAPTER 26

Cosmopolis

When the Greek polis was breaking down, Cynic and Stoic philosophers formulated the goal of the cosmopolis, the universal city, whose citizenry would consist of all wise and good men. Great empires replaced the small city-states, and the cosmopolis of the wise and the good has never been realized upon earth. The notion of the cosmopolis was antipolitical and the product of a philosophy of escape. In our own time, when established political systems are passing through grave crises, new escapist philosophies are conjuring up even wider goals of humanitarianism, without facing up to the fact that the goals of any community of men can be realized only through politics. The problems of our emergent universal community can be solved only by means of politics, if at all. If these problems are not solved, the consequences may be fatal, not merely for a particular political system, but for mankind.

This is the one justification for the comparative study of politics that is ultimate in every sense. Mankind for the first time is becoming aware of the common problems all of its members are facing. The tragic cause of this dawning consciousness of the human community is the possibility of nuclear extermination of all human life. This final catastrophe can be prevented only through politics. But while the human community is becoming a reality, there is still no cosmopolis with institutions and procedures capable of solving this grandest of all problems ever posed to men. There is no international political system. Relations among states on the global sphere are less "systematic" than those between Ireland and Great Britain after establishment of the Free State, or between India and Pakistan after the breakup of the political unity of the subcontinent. International politics has no constitution and little structure. Frightful decisions have to be made in it, whose consequences could undo in a flash all that men have built for themselves over thousands of years—including their political systems and the norm of responsibility. The possibility of universal destruction presents the greatest constitutional problem of them all. We will now analyze this problem, utilizing the categories that have been developed in this book.

"Constitutional History"

The foundations of the present "non-constitution" of mankind were laid during the period when modern national states were founded in Europe. The age was marked by violence, both domestic and international. At the time, Thomas Hobbes, who contributed as much as any philosopher to the theory of domestic tranquility, observed that sovereigns were forever facing one another in the posture of gladiators because they were in a "state of nature" in their mutual relations. The state of nature was a state of war, in which the situation of man is "solitary, poor, nasty, brutish, and short." Hobbes thereby described the situation of irresponsibility that has prevailed in international politics from his day to our own. His contemporary Hugo Grotius tried to reduce international violence by beginning the construction of international law, the nearest thing to fundamental procedures the international community has.

Until World War I, international politics was conducted mainly by a few European states. The rest of the world was either the arena of competition among the great colonial powers, or the scene of efforts to erect modern states on the basis of earlier looser forms of political organization. In Europe, war was waged for limited goals, as an extension of diplomacy "by other means." The procedures of diplomacy were highly formalized, and diplomats were in profound agreement on their propriety. But when a state could not get what it wanted by diplomatic means, it used the other means—violence—instead. War, too, was carried on according to an agreed code, which still had carry-overs from the earlier age of chivalry. This ended when the *World* became engaged in its *First War*. During the last year of that struggle, war was no longer being waged for a limited objective. The conflict was so awful that some idealists sought to make it the "war to end all wars," so that the world could be "made safe for democracy," in the words of Woodrow Wilson. The League of Nations was founded as a result:

THE HIGH CONTRACTING PARTIES, in order to promote international co-operation and to achieve international peace and security by the acceptance of obligations not to resort to war, by the prescription of open, just, and honourable relations between nations, by the firm establishment of the understandings of international law as the actual rule of conduct among Governments, and by the maintenance of justice and a scrupulous respect for all treaty obligations in the dealings of organized peoples with one another, agree to this Covenant of the League of Nations.

The Covenant was a relatively short document, its content mainly procedural and its goals stated in negative terms. It was dedicated to "the reduction of national armaments to the lowest point consistent with national safety and the enforcement by common action of international obligations." Members agreed to submit disputes to the League or to judicial arbitration. They agreed also that they would

> endeavour to secure and maintain fair and humane conditions of labour for men, women, and children . . . entrust the League with the general supervision of the trade in arms and ammunition with the countries in which the control of this traffic is in the common interest . . . endeavour to take steps in matters of international concern for the prevention and control of disease . . . encourage and promote . . . Red Cross organizations. . . .

The League failed. Some states, notably the United States of America, never joined it. Others left it when the League tried to resolve issues in ways counter to their "national interest." World War II, even more horrible in its consequences than the first global conflict, followed. Just before its end, the victorious Allies made another effort to constitutionalize international politics by adopting the Charter of the United Nations:

> WE, THE PEOPLES OF THE UNITED NATIONS, DETERMINED to save succeeding generations from the scourge of war, which twice in our lifetime has brought untold sorrow to mankind, and to reaffirm faith in fundamental human rights, in the dignity and worth of the human person, in equal rights of men and women and of nations large and small, and to establish conditions under which justice and respect for the obligations arising from treaties and other sources of international law can be maintained, and to promote social progress and better standards of life in larger freedom,
> AND FOR THESE ENDS to practise tolerance and live together in peace with one another as good neighbours, and to unite our strength to maintain international peace and security, and to ensure, by the acceptance of principles and the institution of methods, that armed force shall not be used, save in the common interest, and to employ international machinery

for the promotion of the economic and social advancement of all peoples, HAVE RESOLVED TO COMBINE OUR EFFORTS TO ACCOM- PLISH THESE AIMS.

Accordingly, our respective Governments, through representatives assembled in the city of San Francisco, who have exhibited their full powers found to be in good and due form, have agreed to the present Charter of the United Nations and do hereby establish an international organization to be known as the United Nations.

The Charter is almost three times as long as the Covenant. Com- parison of the two preambles shows its stronger substantive emphasis and the tendency to state goals in positive terms. The United Nations was designed to prevent a third world war, on the basis of conditions prevailing in 1945. At that time, there were still more than two great centers of power. No state possessed hydrogen bombs, intercontinental ballistic missiles, or artificial moons orbiting in outer space.

Deliberation in the forum of the United Nations has actually pre- vented the outbreak of military violence on several occasions. At other times, the United Nations itself, in conformity with its Charter, con- ducted military operations, notably when North Korea attacked South Korea. North Korea was a Communist satellite, allied with Communist China, whose government controlled 600 million people but was not represented in the United Nations. The Korean action would have had to take some other form if the Soviet Union had not happened to be boycotting the Security Council at the time of the outbreak of hostilities. This "accident" led to adoption of the "Uniting for Peace Resolution," which makes possible circumvention, by the General Assembly of the United Nations, of obstruction on the part of the Soviet Union in the Security Council.

Since 1950, the world has several times been on the brink of war —over Indochina, the Suez Canal, Lebanon, the Chinese offshore islands, and Berlin. Most of these crises have been debated in the United Na- tions, and the solution of some of them was helped by these debates. Other international conflicts have been resolved by means of traditional diplomacy, outside of the organs of the United Nations. Members of the U.N. have concluded regional treaties as the foundation of more or less stable international alliances. One of these is the North Atlantic Treaty Organization (NATO). It includes states that have been on the verge of violence over some issues, like Cyprus, but nevertheless remained in this political quasi-system, whose members are agreed on one goal of overriding importance—defense against aggression from the Soviet Union. This agreement has been so strong that NATO includes some of the former enemy states whose defeat was celebrated in the Charter. The most fundamental decisions in international politics today are about nuclear war—whether, when, and where to start one, or how to prevent one. These decisions are made only by the governments of the United States of America and the Union of Soviet Socialist Republics. Less fundamental decisions, which still affect millions of human beings, can be made elsewhere, including the United Nations. But "the last words" in international politics are spoken by the United States and the Soviet Union—separately.

"Constitutional Structure"

There are structures in international politics, but there is no single structure. Many different focuses of resolution compete with one another, but no one center for deliberation is generally accepted. There are specialized agencies that give some stability to procedures of deliberation and resolution in their respective fields, like the Universal Postal Union, the International Telecommunication Union, the World Health Organization, and the World Meteorological Organization. However, these specialized agencies cannot be compared with the specialized committees of Continental parliaments, which are used by special interests for regulating their own affairs with the aid of public authority. There is still no agreement on what lends authority to international decisions. And while communications, public health, and meteorological personnel all over the world do have common interests, the members of these world organizations are not interest groups, but states. The specialized representatives of these states often seem to have an easier time with negotiations than their diplomatic colleagues, possibly because they are members of scientific communities and are in agreement on the specialized methods of their field. It is also true that both politicians and policies can gain additional authority, especially in new political systems, if they bear the stamp of approval of a specialized international agency with universal membership. Nevertheless, whenever the particular resolution of an issue proposed by a meeting of one of these organizations goes counter to the intentions of a member state, that state can safely ignore them.

The same is usually true of decisions of the Security Council and General Assembly of the United Nations. Their existence has failed to give structure to international politics. Many of the founders of the United Nations probably did not intend that it should provide this in the first place. This is suggested by the internal construction of the U.N., as set up by its Charter. The Security Council, as the "upper house" of the international parliament, has five permanent members: China, France, the Soviet Union, the United Kingdom, and the United States. The "Big Five" are supplemented, on a two-year rotating basis, by six lesser states as representatives of various regional interests in the world. Any one of the Big Five can veto substantive decisions of a majority of the Council, so that the Security Council cannot resolve issues on which the Big Five are not in unanimous agreement. The veto does not apply in the General Assembly, of which all the eighty-odd "united nations" are members. This was the reason for adopting the "Uniting for Peace Resolution"—to make possible the resolution of deadlocks in the Security Council between the Soviet Union and the other Big Powers. However, the larger body is even less capable of resolving issues in ways that go counter to the interests of the Soviet Union.

Problems

The global community that is not yet a political system faces many substantive problems in addition to the primary constitutional one just outlined. The major economic problem is the fact that poverty, hunger, disease, and lack of adequate shelter plague the majority of human beings, and that they are becoming increasingly aware of these problems. Most of them are not getting the education that would enable them to deal efficiently with the problems they recognize in their own environment. Many of the conventional resources of the world are nearing exhaustion, but the population is increasing at such a rate that the specter of Malthus has been haunting many demographers and statesmen. The Industrial Revolution has affected only small parts of the globe, and those very unevenly. The overpopulated countries of Asia, which have the largest populations and therefore most of the consumers of the earth, produce the least. In some ways, the economic problems of the globe are like those of Italy, "writ large."

Excess population in Italy used to be able to emigrate to the Americas. The excess population of the earth is not likely to be redistributed more evenly without the use of violence, and it will not be able to emigrate into outer space, at least for the time being. The earth's external problems have only recently been recognized as obstacles between ourselves and our goals of exploring and exploiting the universe around us. This is a good example of the way in which new knowledge and the creation of new resources generate new goals and new problems, and out of them unprecedented issues for politics. Something similar happened during the great age of exploration, when the New World was discovered. There, however, the early colonizers faced the additional problem of defense against the Indians; at least the global community has not yet encountered any problems of defense in its efforts to conquer the newest worlds.

The cultural problems of mankind are still more urgent than the external ones. Mankind is divided into its great races—loosely designated by the colors black, brown, yellow, white—and the members of these races are fully conscious of this division. It is also divided into great and small religions and sects, many of which demand the total commitment of their followers, and some of which deny the importance of life on this earth. It is further divided into hundreds of communities of language, and most of the members of each of these *communities* cannot *communicate* with people who speak different tongues. Many of these racial, religious, and linguistic cleavages cut across one another, so that with regard to cultural problems the earth is like Switzerland, writ very large and much more complicated.

The culturally divided Swiss were able to find procedures for the solution of their cultural problems, as well as their economic and external ones. The generality of mankind has not yet solved its constitutional problem.

Issues and Politics

Economic problems have given rise to some of the most divisive issues in the world community. Some of these are disagreements over which states should have access to which resources. Conflicts of this type were particularly common during the age of colonialism that preceded general recognition of the existence of a global community. During that period, European states gained access to the resources of America, Asia, and Africa, to help the Europeans solve their economic problems. In our own time, when colonial areas are gaining independence, memory of this past has been generating issues about the better equalization of economic opportunities—e.g., the nationalization of foreign-owned enterprises and demands for technical assistance. The problem of exploiting new sources of energy, especially nuclear energy, has been recognized as a universal one that could best be solved through international coöperation; hence the founding of the International Atomic Energy Agency under the aegis of the U.N.

The most serious set of issues raised by economic problems today deals with the economic organization of mankind as a whole. The Soviet Communists and their allies proclaim as their primary goal the organization of the global community along first socialist and then communist lines. They assert that the world's limited resources can be exploited efficiently and equitably only by means of such organization. In order to achieve world-wide Communism, the Soviet Union has annexed some states, forcibly put others in the hands of its followers, and seeks to coerce, cajole, or persuade the governments of many other systems to adopt Communism.

The Western political systems, under the leadership of the United States and Great Britain, are also dedicated to the efficient and equitable exploitation and distribution of the earth's resources. But they firmly disagree that Soviet Communism is the way toward that goal. There are disagreements among and within Western political systems about the best form of economic organization, as we saw in the countries dealt with in this book. But there is widespread consensus—which excludes the Communists in these countries—that changes should not be imposed by means of violence. The rest of mankind, especially the "uncommitted" states in Asia, Africa, and the Near East, can choose the Soviet approach or one of the several Western alternative solutions to the world's economic problems. Each of them makes this decision about its internal economic organization, and this choice will be reflected in the stand it takes on the issue of world-wide Communism versus some kind of freer economic organization. That is why both the Soviet Union and the United States are trying to cultivate the economically underdeveloped countries by means of loans and other forms of economic aid.

Issues arising out of cultural problems, particularly racial ones, are closely linked with those just discussed. The colored peoples, many of whom have been under white colonial domination, and some of whom still are, also populate the poorest and most crowded areas. They have so far benefited least from the Industrial Revolution. They stand to gain most from any global economic policy designed to equalize opportunities. A statement by the Commissioner General for Economic Affairs of the Government of India shows this very clearly:

> He warned that disparities in living standards constituted one of the greatest threats to peace and freedom.
>
> In industrialized countries today the average man is ten times as well off as in the underdeveloped countries, and if present trends continue the disparity will increase to 15 to 1 within twenty years. . . .
>
> In the same period Communist countries, which have a standard of living two and a half times higher than that of the underdeveloped countries, would increase their advantage to 4 to 1, he went on.

"The consequences of such an eventuality hardly need any elaboration," he added.[1]

As a result of these disparities, many international issues arising out of economic problems are complicated by disagreements about the solution of cultural problems. The Bandung Conference of twenty-nine Asian and African nations in 1955 illustrated this. People who had been under colonial rule, who were poor, colored, and not Christians, had at least these four reasons for agreeing among themselves and for disagreeing with the white West. In international politics, issues of race, color, or religion no longer play as important a role as they used to. Since the racist regime of Nazi Germany was defeated, and that defeat laid the cornerstone of the United Nations, few states have tried to promote discrimination on these grounds in the international arena, although they may have practiced it officially at home. Nevertheless, in diplomatic alignments and voting alliances in the United Nations, delegates of culturally related states have often voted in "blocks"—for example, the Moslem states, the Arab states, the colored states, the predominantly Roman Catholic states, and similar international interests.

Issues produced by the problems that mankind faces vis-à-vis the rest of creation, including the universe—i.e., its external problems—have only recently begun to be debated in connection with international collaboration, and mainly between the United States and the Soviet Union. The International Geophysical Year was a case in point. This collaboration was made possible by the realization that it would probably benefit both sides and indeed all of mankind. For example, the scientific stations in only one country or only one continent are insufficient for accurately tracking the orbit of artificial satellites. It seems plausible that future trips into outer space will demand resources of such proportions that only international pooling will be capable of solving these problems efficiently.

Some of the most divisive issues in international politics have been raised by the constitutional problem. While the actual outbreak of violence has usually been caused by substantive disagreement, there is at least one case in which war was threatened over a procedural issue: Communist China used this threat because it was denied access to procedures of deliberation and resolution available to almost all of the other states. Within the United Nations, heated controversies have taken place over the intent and abuse of provisions, like the veto of the Big Five and the Uniting for Peace Resolution. Some members have boy-

[1] B. K. Nehru, quoted in *The New York Times,* September 25, 1958.

cotted meetings of organs of the United Nations as a result of procedural disagreements. The Charter made provision for its own periodic review and revision, but the improbability of getting the five permanent members of the Security Council to agree on amendments has so far prevented revision. Nevertheless, changes in the Charter and in the fundamentals of international politics beyond the United Nations are constantly being discussed and written about all over the world.

Success

The success of the global community of mankind in dealing with its problems has not been striking in the past, and the record seems to be getting poorer, as awareness of the existence of the community is becoming stronger. In the nineteenth century, while the pattern of the so-called "balance of power" prevailed in European international politics, there was at least a fair degree of stability. The substantive goals of diplomacy and war were limited, and their rules did not change significantly. This is no longer true. World War II aimed at the *unconditional* surrender of the Axis states. Today, the Communists' professed aim of establishing world Communism removes limits on their own substantive goals and also on those of their opponents. This is so because the West feels compelled to "fight fire with fire."

The procedures of international politics have been changing rapidly and radically. These changes have occurred as a result of improvements in communications and the consequent exposure of international deliberations to the glare of publicity, including television at the United Nations.

Efficiency is being shown only in limited areas, like coöperation among the criminal police agencies of states, suppression of international narcotics traffic, and handling of the problems assigned to the specialized agencies mentioned earlier. In most of the cases in which efficient solution of important international problems occurred, it was achieved not through international institutions and procedures but by one or more states acting outside of these.

The effectiveness, too, of international institutions has been quite low. The United Nations has made few important decisions that were supported by most of its members from both sides of the iron curtain. Yet only such nearly unanimous decisions will be accepted by both "parties." Many resolutions of specific issues, made by strong "bipartisan" majorities in the United Nations, have not been accepted by the member concerned and therefore could not be implemented—that is, they were not real resolutions; e.g., the issue of segregation in the Union of South Africa.

Perhaps the worst failure of the procedures of international politics has been with respect to their adaptability. They have not shown much flexibility in the face of the changes in the world's problems, which have taken place since 1945. Issues are still being stated and deliberated as though hydrogen bombs, I.C.B.M.'s, and artificial moons did not exist. The vocabulary of international politics seems as obsolete today as the political vocabulary of the fifteenth and sixteenth centuries was before thinkers like Machiavelli, Bodin, Hobbes, and Grotius brought it up to date, by forging new concepts, or by giving new meaning to older concepts, like state, sovereignty, natural law, power, war, and peace.

The failure of the "constitution" of the universal community of mankind puts individuals into very poor situations of responsibility, no matter how favorable their situations may be as citizens of constitutional democracies. There is no single focus of deliberation or resolution to which individuals or states can make contributions. Because of this, even channels that are open to contributions to citizens of constitutional democracies are made worthless. The foreign ministers of such systems may operate in complete awareness of their accountability to their electorates, but because the separate foreign policies in the global community are nowhere coördinated, the decisions of diplomats are based on a minimum of foreknowledge of their consequences. The situation of international politicians is so similar to that of gamblers that more than one scholar has applied "game theory" to it.[2] No one has ever gambled with higher stakes. Even worse is the situation of the hundreds of millions of individuals on whose behalf the diplomats act with delegated responsibility. The consequences have meant death for millions in the past and may bring death to all in the future, and yet there are no meaningful contributions the people themselves can make to a stable flow of policy about the problems of survival.

Political Style

The style of contemporary international politics consists of a combination of violence, ideologism, legalism, and pragmatism. Deliberation in terms of compromisable purposive interests is rare indeed. References to force, and its actual employment, have been frequent. The United States and the Soviet Union especially have justified the stands they have

[2] Morton A. Kaplan, *System and Process in International Politics*, 1957, Part IV, "On Strategy."

COSMOPOLIS : : : 453

taken on important international issues, both to their own peoples and in foreign propaganda, by way of their relative military strength—nuclear bombs, strategic bombers, air bases, ballistic missiles, submarines, troops, industrial capacity, and so on. They have deployed their armies and air and naval fleets in order to back up their antagonistic policies in different parts of the world. In the United States, there has been elaborated a whole set of theories preoccupied with violence in one form or another—"national interest," "containment," "massive deterrent," "limited nuclear war," and so forth. The Soviet Communists simply transferred their theory and practice of violence from the national to the international plane.

Meanwhile, both sides have conducted international debates with the vocabulary of ideologies. The Communists have emphasized this more than the West, since their system gets most of its impetus from the ideology of Marxism-Leninism (and until 1953, Stalinism) and since they do have the explicit goal of establishing a world-wide Communist society. But the West has also tried to build consistent systems of knowledge around its opposition to the falsehood of Communism, and it has engaged in much recriminatory ideologism—in connection with events as far back as the Russian Revolution, or as close to the present as the victory of the Chinese Communists and the Korean War. These were problems international politics could not digest, and the memories of the events have consequently been petrified, to be used in connection with every new divisive issue that arises.

The newly independent states are no less ideological in their international conduct. They were excluded from international responsibilities until long after they had become aware of their interest in international problems. And extension of participation, which did not come from one generally accepted center, happened by leaps and bounds, so that all of the conditions of ideological style were present. Representatives of these states, for instance, debated in terms of "colonialism" and "imperialism," when Israel invaded Egypt and again when the United States landed troops in Lebanon, though neither colonialism nor imperialism had much to do with the problems that had generated these conflicts. Anti-colonialism and anti-imperialism have been elaborated into recriminatory ideologies, which flavor the contributions of the newly independent states to international deliberation as though these were still central problems.

As the antithesis of violence, legalism has alternated with it in dominating international discourse. Large and small states justify their actions in terms of the letter of the Charter or of some treaty to which they are parties. Western states, in order to maintain a current situation they consider favorable to themselves, try to stabilize it by means of intricate networks of treaties, which are often incapable of adaptation to changing problems in the most fluid of all communities. The Soviet Union justifies its cruel suppression of the Hungarian revolution with legalistic (and other) arguments. Meanwhile, well-intentioned individuals in the West and in uncommitted nations call for a strengthening of international law, the application of it to individuals instead of its present "subjects" (i.e., states), the elaborate revision of the U.N. Charter, the solution of most international problems by the International Court of Justice or similar tribunals, or the early establishment of "world federalism" or "world government." Much of this is reminiscent of the German leanings toward legalism, which can be partly explained by past experience with violence and the fear of its recurrence. Similarly, in international politics, violence has been so frequent that the effort to subject all politics to rigid adjudication or prior legislation seems understandable, if unrealistic.

Ideologism has its antithesis in pragmatism. In international politics, this appears as the cynical settlement of disputes in terms of immediate goals, without the overt employment of force, but also without reference to long-run goals. After the great states have talked themselves or each other into ideological dead-end alleys, they often find that the only way out, short of a world war, is a pragmatic nonpurposive about-face. The Suez and Hungarian crises, along with Lebanon and the Chinese offshore islands, may serve as examples. The reader can decide for himself which parties to these conflicts acted the most violently, ideologically, legalistically, or pragmatically. Whatever your conclusion, instances of debate in terms of compromisable, purposive, material interests seem few and far between.

Procedure

These shortcomings of style in international politics are the result, not only of lack of substantive consensus, but also of the novel procedures of deliberation that have come into use in this greatest of all communities. We have already mentioned the glare of publicity under which much of its deliberation is carried on. Diplomacy used to be veiled in secrecy—that is why officers entrusted with it are still called "secretaries." In privacy, real deliberation could be conducted. This is not true of "open covenants, openly arrived at" under the klieg lights of a television production. The traditional diplomatic procedures are still being used concurrently with these novel forms, but they, too, are handicapped by other technological developments. Among these are improved communications, which make it possible for home governments to keep their diplomatic negotiators under constant control and instructions. This dependence of diplomats upon detailed directions from their governments gives them fewer opportunities for creative innovation in the conduct of their negotiations. It also reduces their commitment to diplomatic procedure and to the very ancient and honorable profession of diplomacy. If it were not for this dependence, diplomats might feel more committed to the goals of universal welfare and international tranquility than to their respective national interests. Diplomats from small states and men of the old school of diplomacy sometimes still do feel so committed.

The great dramatic conferences, whether or not they are held under the auspices of the United Nations, perform virtually no deliberation. They rather afford opportunities to the participating states to register their wills. That is why they can vote without prior debate—the debates are not designed to persuade. The votes, alas, often make no difference, either. The outcome of the votes is often insignificant, because they do not resolve the issue, since the states affected by the decision will not accept it, unless they have agreed to it in the first place. Deliberation is made difficult because there are no central resolutions about which to deliberate. There is no central resolving organ in the United Nations or elsewhere in the global community. Each of the great states or blocks of states can propose its resolution to an issue under discussion, but once this happens, the others will not engage in a deliberate weighing of alternatives. They will declare their own alternatives, register their opposing wills. True, before this stage is reached, deliberation does take place within the various alliances participating— the NATO states, for example, or the Arab or South American states. Some of the uncommitted members may even engage in real deliberation and let themselves be persuaded one way or the other. But this again is of little significance, because a majority decision need not be effective unless the affected party concurs.

Personnel

One reason for this lack of true deliberation is the composition of the personnel of international politics. The commitment to the rules and goals of diplomacy on the part of the old school has just been mentioned. In the nineteenth century, European diplomats generally came from the same background of nobility, wealth, and public service. Many of them were as much interrelated as the ruling dynasties of Europe, even though they might be temporarily as much at odds as members of the best of families. King George V, Kaiser Wilhelm II, and Czar Nicholas II were cousins. Democracy and totalitarianism in the twentieth century have brought men of different backgrounds to the role of the diplomat, especially in the two most important countries, the United States and the Soviet Union. Many of them are not professional diplomats at all, but successful businessmen or revolutionaries, popular politicians or party bureaucrats. They are committed to substantive achievement in the course of their sometimes brief diplomatic careers, rather than to the established rules of international negotiation with which they have spent a lifetime. Even when, as experienced international lawyers like Secretary of State Dulles, they do have a firm commitment to the procedures of diplomacy, the abuse of these rules by Soviet politicians not similarly committed exasperates them so much that they, too, find purposive compromise hard.

Compromise is also made difficult by differences of legal background. For example, American lawyer-diplomats have come to Four Power conferences, armed with a card file of rebuttals to every conceivable propaganda attack that might be launched by the Russians. In an American school debate or before an American judge and jury accustomed to adversary pleadings, they would undoubtedly have won. But the Russians were not pleading under the same rules—if indeed under any rules—and the conferences were not trials designed to get decisions, from a judge, jury, or anyone else, unless it be the opinions of various publics in the world. And these publics were not always as favorably impressed by the American performance as an American audience would have been.

As the human community is becoming more aware of its existence, it is evolving some universal concepts of authority, but these do not yet play an important role in the making of policy for the international non-system. When men speak, whose works and faces are as obviously wise and good as those of Albert Einstein, Albert Schweitzer, and Mahatma Gandhi, they speak with authority. But they do not speak at conferences of the "Big" Two, Three, Four, or Five. Nevertheless, even in international politics, the outlines of a widely accepted concept of authority are perhaps being sketched out. The first two Secretaries-

General of the United Nations, Trygve Lie and Dag Hammarskjöld, could speak with considerable authority to parts of the world which did not like what they had to say on particular occasions. They made decisions, some of which caused even the two greatest powers to modify their policies. A few of the diplomats of the old school, from small states which do not have much directly at stake in international crises, also wield considerable authority. This was shown, for example, during the Near East crisis of 1958, when states like Sweden, Norway, and Japan tried to bring about compromises between the large Western states and the Soviet Union. It is at least conceivable and certainly to be hoped that improvements in communications and increase in travel will give further content to this outline of an international concept of authority, which will lead those who are affected by central decisions to accept their consequences.

Representation

At present, the prospects for getting wider consensus on a concept of authority do not seem very bright. The blame for this has often been placed upon the fact that "sovereign" states are represented in the United Nations, rather than other types of constituencies. Some advocates of individual liability under international law—which was applied to the so-called "war criminals" after World War II—would also like to see individuals become members of the electorate of international assemblies. Under such a scheme, delegates to the General Assembly of the United Nations from the United States would presumably be directly elected. Similar proposals have been made for the parliament of a future European federal union. In that case, the expectation is that Socialists, Christian Democrats, Liberals, and others from the different member countries would vote together on international party lines, rather than on national and state lines as Germans, Frenchmen, Italians, and so on. Advocates of the direct popular election of members of international assemblies often attribute particular failures of these institutions to the fact that deliberation in them is carried on by agents of governments, who have no supranational—or better, suprastate—commitments. Whether this kind of election scheme would result in great changes seems doubtful. In any case, the present system is likely to last for a while longer. From our point of view, it has the merit of fitting prevailing forms of interest identification. Theorists and politicians have often claimed that most individuals do identify themselves more strongly with groups other than their state. The Marxists assert that the international cohesion of the working and exploiting classes are stronger than the identification of members of each class with their own national state. The Nazis claimed that the Jews were engaged in an international conspiracy. Anticlerical zealots levy the same accusation against the Roman Catholic Church. Some anti-intellectual demagogues in the United States seemed certain that the objects of their wrath were plotting varied horrors with fellow eggheads all over the world. But practice has rarely borne out any of these claims. When the crisis arrived—that is, when organized violence began on the international plane—people with other additional international interests have overwhelmingly sided with their own political system. The best-known instance of this is the support of war votes in national parliaments by Social Democrats in France, Germany, and other Continental countries at the outbreak of World War I, a few days after an international conference of the Socialist parties, in which they had all pledged themselves to oppose war.

Larger political systems have been formed out of smaller ones as the result of either conquest or union, and union has usually been prompted by threats from the outside to the survival of member states with inadequate resources. When the latter course was followed by federal union, the member states have continued to be represented as such for many years after the founding of the new system. In the four federal systems we have studied, citizens still identify themselves with their canton, province, or state, in addition to other interests with which they feel affinities. And these federal systems have what the international community lacks, central organs of resolution. Until the global non-system acquires such an organ, national states will probably continue to be the units represented in the United Nations, and delegates will continue to be appointed by their governments. The main interest alignments in the United Nations will continue to be of countries which take similar stands on issues arising out of the world's substantive problems. On the most important of these issues, the two-camp alignment, which has so often pitted the Soviets against the West, is likely to be repeated frequently in the future, until a bridge of agreement can be built over the great cleavage of the present.

The two-alternative pattern is unfortunate, mainly for one of the reasons that led us to criticize the model of the two-party system: It tends to exaggerate disagreements, which makes deliberation much more difficult than it might otherwise be. This suggests that the two-alternative pattern of politics has merits only in connection with the resolution of issues, not in connection with deliberation. Effective nonviolent resolution is still extremely rare in international politics. And since violent resolution of major contemporary issues could lead to the "extermination of practically everybody"—as the humor of the gallows has called it—the postponement of resolution seems much to be preferred. For this, constant and efficient deliberation, with participation of all interested parties, is required, and the road should be kept open to the introduction of new alternatives. This kind of deliberation is not likely to benefit from the two-camp alignment.

Power

Some may impatiently argue that this whole discussion is futile because it leaves power factors out of consideration. "The two great camps have all the military strength, and they will not accept any decisions by others that go against their own conception of their 'national interest.' The only thing that matters is relative military and economic power." Similar arguments are often used by politicians and military men who predict that the relative power position of the United States and the Soviet Union, given the current rate of armament, will at some time reach a certain ratio that will inevitably lead one side or the other to attack or to have to surrender. These arguments invite us to repeat for the international community the exercise in electronic voting, with which we experimented for democracies in Chapter 19.

Somewhere in Colorado, the United States Air Force is said to have an electronic brain that records all reports from the various radar outposts guarding the air approaches to North America. When this calculator reports enemy planes or missiles, and these reports are verified, we are told, another device is set off, which issues orders to the bombers of the Strategic Air Command, some of which are always airborne, to proceed at once to their predesignated target areas. The Russians presumably have similar installations.

Professor Vassily Leontieff has developed the so-called "input-output table," which shows correlations among all sectors of the American economy. By building this table into an electronic calculator, the effects of changes in one sector of the economy on its remainder can be gauged readily. The Russians, who plan their entire economy centrally, may be assumed to have similar devices.

This suggests that each of the two great camps could construct a military-economic input-output calculator, which would register the current power position of the system at any moment in time. The two "brains" could then be hooked up to a central calculator at the United Nations, which would show not only the present power ratio, but also future trends. The central U.N. calculator, in turn, would be connected with attack-dispatchers in the United States and the Soviet Union. If the adherents of theories of power were right, one side or the other would attack very soon after these devices had been installed. As a matter of fact, since each side receives fairly good intelligence reports about the other, all these electronic gadgets would not really be needed. If American and Russian politicians had been operating on the basis of power assumptions, World War III would already have taken place. Both sides have also been thinking beyond the use of their power to the consequences that its exercise would bring. The U.N. calculator could have the same effect if it were further extended to predict the destruction that war, when unleashed at any particular moment, would wreak.

Much more than power is involved in contemporary international politics. Thomas Hobbes defined power as "present means to obtain some future apparent Good." The future apparent Good pursued by the Soviet Russians is world-wide Communism, that pursued by the West is prevention of this eventuality. The armaments with which both sides have provided themselves as the means for obtaining their antagonistic goals have reached a point of saturation. Their employment, because it would automatically set off employment of the enemy's weapons systems, and because it might contaminate the user's own territory, would be self-defeating. Nuclear weapons are no longer power in the sense in which that word has been used ever since Hobbes's time. Rather, they tend to restrict their possessors' scope of decision. Once the saturation point has been reached, the Big Two are not in a "balance of power," like the two sides of a scale that might be tipped one way or another by an increase in strength or by third parties. It makes better sense to think of international politics as a vast electricity network, for which power is generated in all political systems. The United States and the Soviet Union are the most "powerful" generators connected with the grid. If either of them ceases to generate its share of electricity, the whole network will break down. If either of them generates too much, the whole network will blow up.

This analogy between political and electrical power seems appropriate for another reason, namely the fact that both can be put to many different uses. Any number of different types of consumers can be connected up to an electrical network—industries, homes, schools, churches, communications facilities, railroads, and so on. The electrical power used by all of these consumers is always generated in the same manner and travels through the same high-tension cables, but it can be applied to the solution of many different kinds of problems. This is also true of the means human communities employ to solve their common problems. In a stable political system, the same basic procedures are used for making decisions about a great variety of problems. In international politics, the procedures by which problems are handled are becoming more important for the solution of the problems than the power—in the conventional meaning—wielded by political systems.

The inadequacy of the term *power* for understanding the realities of contemporary world politics points to a parallel between our age and that of Hobbes, Grotius, and Cromwell. They, too, had to grope for new categories that would describe, not only the facts of their times, but also the goals toward which they wanted to transform these facts. That was three centuries ago. Yet we are still using the same concepts today. But the traditional meaning of words like *peace* and *war,* to cite only this example, cannot be used to describe the present relations between the Soviet Union and the United States, nor even the kind of relations that either side wants to bring about in the future. Thinking in old categories about new realities is like trying to repair an airplane with tools designed for a covered wagon. This becomes particularly evident when politicians and political scientists apply the concept of power to international politics. Even this traditional field for "power politics" has been transformed into a vast and intricate grid of mutual interdependence, in which problems rather than power are the raw material of politics. How much truer this is of constitutional and democratic systems should by now have become clear. There can be politics where there is no power in the traditional sense; and there can be an absence of politics where there is all the power in the world. That has been our reason for focusing on the problems men recognize and on the decisions they make about these problems.

Consensus and the Cosmopolis

International politicians do not need electronic calculators to tell them that efforts to resolve by violence the major issues between Communism and the West would result in the death of millions and perhaps billions of human beings and the destruction of so much else that the now conflicting substantive goals of the Communists, the West, or the neutral remainder could never be realized. In the absence of agreement on fundamental procedures of negotiation or on positive values, this negative consensus on the imperative necessity of averting a nuclear world war may perhaps serve as the first layer upon which to build the agreement needed to transform the universal community of mankind into a global political system. We might almost hope for an attack from Mars, so that this negative substantive agreement could be expanded.

Leaders of both the Soviet Union and the United States, and of the third nuclear state, Great Britain, have proclaimed their agreement that a nuclear global conflict should be prevented. They have set in motion negotiations to find out whether nuclear armaments can be controlled, nuclear explosions monitored, and disarmament inspected. The most successful of these negotiations have been conducted by scientists, who could start their deliberations with the deep consensus commanded by the method of their disciplines. However, merely because the scientists agreed on the number of inspection stations required, their governments need not agree either to establish these stations or to cease experimenting with new and more horrible weapons. The decisions that face any community can be depoliticized no more by science than by ideologies or law. The politicians have to, and will, weigh many other factors. Ultimately, some of them may have to decide which to forgo— the realization of their ideological goals or the continued existence of human civilization.

Unless this happens soon, with the decision going the wrong way, there are hopes for building more consensus upon this first thin layer. Perhaps positive agreement on the need for pooling resources for the exploration of outer space will come next. Perhaps the negotiations being carried on about the prevention of nuclear war and the conquest of the universe, aided by skilled negotiators from neutral states, will result in the construction of consensus on the procedures of purposive compromise. Increased contacts among the peoples of opposing systems may also help in this direction.

There is another prospect for reducing the prevailing substantive disagreements, especially those due to economic problems. These issues were first raised in an age of poverty and scarcity, which we in the United States have already left for the age of affluence. Soviet Communism is geared to the overcoming of poverty. But the freeing of new sources of energy, nuclear and solar, and new modes of production, including automation, may lift the Soviet Union and even the underdeveloped areas of the world out of poverty and into affluence. This may not happen for several decades, but technological progress is so rapid nowadays that poverty, disease, and ignorance may well be minor problems within one or two generations. Men will certainly be facing new problems then—boredom, perhaps, may be one of them—but the problems underlying the most divisive issues of the world today would have evaporated. If this should happen, we can only hope that international politicians will drop the old issues and generate new ones, relevant to the new problems of a happier age.

Politicians and political scientists can also play the role of inventive innovators. The possibility of human inventiveness—the one respect in which men and political systems differ from electronic calculators, at least until now—is one of the most hopeful factors that should be considered by those who are concerned with our capabilities for surmounting the present crisis. If the American Founding Fathers had not been as inventive as they were, their descendants and those of later immigrants would not still be living under the most successful engineered constitution in history. The inventors must look to the future, not to the past. Solutions to old problems, couched in the mechanical terms of the age of Newton, will be of little help in solving new problems of the age of Einstein and beyond.

The incredibly rapid pace of progress in global communications is one phenomenon that points to the changes being wrought in the problems of mankind as a whole. Before long, global television will be possible, perhaps with the use of artificial moons as relay stations. This might help to reduce misunderstandings between peoples and their leaders. Cultural differences would still continue to exist, but their divisive effects, too, might be ameliorated through better information about other political systems and their citizens. Education can perform a great mission here, although there is no reason whatsoever to identify literacy with capacity for democratic politics—witness the case of the completely literate and, if anything, overeducated population of the Weimar Republic. But exposure to learning, and to the methods by which responsible scholars approach closer toward the ever inaccessible truth, can also help to create universal procedural consensus. The heroic resistance to oppression by many intellectuals in the Soviet orbit demonstrates that the truth, while it may not make men free, makes them want to be free and responsible for their own future, in terms of their understanding of the world around them.

Knowledge is one condition of responsible living. Another is found in the resources of this earth, whose exploitation is being made ever more efficient. The third consists of available alternatives among which individuals can make choices. As citizens of nation-states, most of us have no alternative international policies about which we can make meaningful decisions. And there are no effective organs of resolution in the international community to whose decisions we can make contributions through channels of representation other than those provided by our states, to which we "belong" as much as Socrates "belonged" to Athens. Our study leads to the conclusion that there will be little improvement in the channels through which individuals can contribute to central international decisions until both resolution and deliberation are more clearly focused at a central spot than they are today. And no effective center of this kind is likely to be created until consensus on fundamental procedures and on substantive values has been strengthened far beyond its present condition.

Consensus is not likely to be strengthened by means of the inclusion of pious declarations in constitutional documents. The Charter of the United Nations is full of such declarations, and its Universal Declaration of Human Rights, which has not been ratified, even fuller. Only the rights that are stated in negative terms are likely to be of much consequence—for example, that "No one shall be held in slavery or servitude . . ." and that "No one shall be subjected to torture." But even in the United States, the negatively stated rights of the Constitution could not be made operative against state governments before more than a century had passed in the life of the central government. Debates about such documents in the United Nations usually result in raising more new issues rather than in demonstrating old agreement. This was true even of the Convention on the Prevention of the Crime of Genocide. Nevertheless, documents of this kind can serve the same purpose that an insincerely adopted constitution serves in some new political systems and under totalitarianism. Advocates of international constitutionalism can use them as a goal and point to discrepancies between them and the practice of anticonstitutional states, in fighting—without violence—for their good cause. And the procedures of international negotiation, which are evolved in the course of debating documents about rights, may later be used in resolving different types of issues.

The strengthening in universal consensus, which must precede the creation of central organs of deliberation and resolution, may yet occur because of the growing awareness of the community of interest in preventing universal extinction. It may take place as a result of solving present economic problems. Or it may come about because better and more frequent contacts among peoples generate increasing agreement on the procedural goal of enabling the individual human being to become responsible for himself. This does not mean that the Communist systems, the Western systems—eight of which we have studied in this book—and the political systems of Asia, Africa, and South America all have to agree on the same economic and cultural values. Their values are likely to remain different so long as their major problems continue to vary. It does mean that they must all agree on the ultimate goal of giving human beings opportunities for making meaningful choices about their lives. Refusal to compromise with those who oppose this goal would be justified by the norms we have established at the outset—and belief in which has motivated this study. But since there is no politician of consequence left in the world who would deny his adherence to the norm of individual responsibility as an ultimate goal, the decision about the insincerity of such professions would be an awful one to have to make—possibly the most awful decision of all that man has ever been forced to make.

This decision, and all the others that will have to be made about the future of humanity, will be a part of the stream of politics. As in the Greek polis once upon a time, so in the cosmopolis that must be created in our time, politics is that which concerns the citizens. We are, all of us, already citizens of the universal city, even before its institutions and procedures have been clearly defined. Its problems concern us all. None of us can escape them. The conclusion may be tragic—in the classical Greek sense: Politics is again the master science.

Select Bibliography

Most of the items in this bibliography add more detailed treatment to the subjects dealt with in this book, the several political systems and topics of comparison as well. The section on "Comparative Government" includes some titles that would normally be listed under the separate heading of political theory. The present arrangement was motivated by considerations of both the particular merit of the work of men like Hobbes and Bentham for purposes of this study, and their general merits, which are derived precisely from their attention to comparative government. Some of the classical studies of comparative government, notably Mr. Lowell's and Lord Bryce's, have been included, because they are of interest to readers concerned with method, and because they offer very good descriptions of the governments of their time.

Next to personal attendance at parliamentary and other political meetings, the reading of verbatim transcripts of such proceedings and of the press gives the best insight into the politics of any system, from a local precinct to the United Nations. If they have the opportunity, readers should go to or read about such meetings, before they make use of the mainly secondary and English items listed in the section on "Political Systems."

Inexpensive paperbound or other reprint editions are available for a number of the books; a bracketed reference to such editions has been added to the individual listings.

I. Comparative Government

Adam, Thomas R., *Modern Colonialism: Institutions and Policies,* New York, 1955.
Allport, Gordon, *Personality: A Psychological Interpretation,* New York, 1939.
Arendt, Hannah, *The Origins of Totalitarianism,* New York, 1951 [Meridian Books].
Beer, Samuel H., and Adam B. Ulam, eds., *Patterns of Government: The Major Political Systems of Europe,* New York, 1958.
Bentham, Jeremy, *Tactiques des Assemblées Législatives,* Paris, 1822.
———, *Works,* John Bowring, ed., London, 1843.
Bretton, Henry L., "Current Political Thought and Practice in Ghana," *American Political Science Review,* LII (March, 1958).

466

Bryce, James, *Modern Democracies,* 2 vols., Oxford, 1921.

——, *Studies in History and Jurisprudence,* 2 vols., Oxford, 1901.

Brzezinski, Zbigniew K., *The Permanent Purge: Politics in Soviet Totalitarianism,* Cambridge, Massachusetts, 1955.

Burckhardt, Jacob, *The Civilization of the Renaissance in Italy,* S. G. C. Middlemore, trans., London, 1921 [Modern Library].

Burke, Edmund, *Reflections on the Revolution in France,* London, 1790 [Liberal Arts Press].

Deutsch, Karl W., *Nationalism and Social Communication: An Inquiry into the Foundations of Nationality,* New York, 1953.

Duverger, Maurice, *Political Parties: Their Organization and Activity in the Modern State,* New York, 1954.

Easton, David, *The Political System: An Inquiry into the State of Political Science,* New York, 1953.

Ehrmann, Henry W., *Interest Groups on Four Continents,* Pittsburgh, 1958.

Elliott, William Y., *The Pragmatic Revolt in Politics: Syndicalism, Fascism, and the Constitutional State,* New York, 1928.

Finer, Herman, *The Theory and Practice of Modern Government,* New York, 1949.

Friedrich, Carl J., ed., *Authority,* Cambridge, Massachusetts, 1958.

——, *Constitutional Government and Democracy: Theory and Practice in Europe and America,* Boston, 1950.

——, *The New Image of the Common Man,* Boston, 1950.

——, and Robert R. Bowie, eds., *Studies in Federalism,* Boston, 1954.

——, and Zbigniew K. Brzezinski, *Totalitarian Dictatorship and Autocracy,* Cambridge, Massachusetts, 1956.

Hamilton, Alexander, James Madison, and John Jay, *The Federalist, or the New Constitution* [Modern Library].

Hartz, Louis, *The Liberal Tradition in America: An Interpretation of American Political Thought Since the Revolution,* New York, 1955.

Hermens, Ferdinand A., *Democracy or Anarchy?* Notre Dame, 1941.

——, *The Representative Republic,* Notre Dame, 1958.

Hobbes, Thomas, *English Works,* Sir William Molesworthy, ed., 11 vols., London, 1839-45.

——, *Leviathan,* London, 1651 [Liberal Arts Press].

Jaeger, Werner, *Paideia: The Ideals of Greek Culture,* 3 vols., New York, 1939-44.

Kelsen, Hans, *General Theory of Law and State,* Cambridge, Massachusetts, 1949.

——, *Society and Nature: A Sociological Inquiry,* Chicago, 1943.

Kohn, Hans, *The Idea of Nationalism: A Study in Its Origins and Backgrounds,* New York, 1944.

Lasswell, Harold D., *Politics: Who Gets What, When, How,* New York, 1936 [Meridian Books].

Leiserson, Avery, *Parties and Politics: An Institutional and Behavioral Approach,* New York, 1958.

Lerner, Daniel, and Harold D. Lasswell, eds., *The Policy Sciences: Recent Developments in Scope and Method,* Stanford, 1951.

Lindsay, A. D., *The Modern Democratic State,* New York, 1947.

Livingston, William S., *Federalism and Constitutional Change,* Oxford, 1956.

Locke, John, *Two Treatises of Government* [Everyman's Library].

Loewenstein, Karl, *Die Monarchie im modernen Staat,* Frankfurt, 1952.

Lowell, A. Lawrence, *Governments and Parties in Continental Europe,* 2 vols., Boston, 1896.

————, *Greater European Governments,* Cambridge, Massachusetts, 1926.

MacIver, R. M., *The Web of Government,* New York, 1947.

Mackenzie, W. J. M., *Free Elections: An Elementary Textbook,* New York, 1958.

Macridis, Roy C., *The Study of Comparative Government,* New York, 1955.

Mannheim, Karl, *Ideology and Utopia: An Introduction to the Sociology of Knowledge,* New York, 1936 [Harvest Books].

Marx, Karl, *Capital* [Modern Library].

————, and Friedrich Engels, *The Communist Manifesto,* Samuel H. Beer, ed., New York, 1955 [Appleton, paper].

Millar, Robert Wyness, "The Mechanism of Fact Discovery: A Study in Comparative Civil Procedure," *Illinois Law Review,* XXXII (1937-38).

Montesquieu, C. L. de Secondat de, *Spirit of the Laws,* Thomas Nugent, trans., New York, 1949.

Neumann, Sigmund, ed., *Modern Political Parties,* Chicago, 1955.

Northrop, F. S. C., *The Meeting of East and West,* New York, 1946.

Parsons, Talcott, *The Social System,* Glencoe, 1951.

Peaslee, Amos J., *Constitution of Nations,* 2nd ed., The Hague, 1956.

Pepper, George Wharton, *Pleading at Common Law and Under the Codes,* Northrop, New York, 1891.

Redlich, Josef, *The Common Law and the Case Method in American University Law Schools,* New York, 1914.

Robson, William A., ed., *The Civil Service in Britain and France,* New York, 1956.

Rossiter, Clinton L., *Constitutional Dictatorship: Crisis Government in the Modern Democracies,* Princeton, 1948.

Rousseau, Jean Jacques, *The Social Contract* [Everyman's Library].

Rustow, Dankwart A., "New Horizons for Comparative Politics," *World Politics,* IX (July, 1957).

Schwartz, Bernard, ed., *The Code Napoleon and the Common-Law World,* New York, 1956.

Shotwell, James T., ed., *Governments of Continental Europe,* New York, 1952.

Snyder, Richard C., *et al., Decision-Making as an Approach to the Study of International Politics,* Princeton, 1954.

Spiro, Herbert J., "Responsibility in Citizenship, Government, and Administration," *Public Policy,* IV (1953), C. J. Friedrich and J. K. Galbraith, eds., pp. 116-33.

Sturmthal, Adolf F., *The Tragedy of European Labor,* New York, 1943.

Truman, David B., *The Governmental Process: Political Interests and Public Opinion,* New York, 1951.

Von Mehren, Arthur T., "The Judicial Process: A Comparative Analysis," *American Journal of Comparative Law,* V (1956).

Watkins, Frederick M., *The State as a Concept of Political Science,* New York, 1934.

Weber, Max, *Ancient Judaism,* Hans H. Gerth and Don C. Martindale, trans., Glencoe, 1952.

————, *From Max Weber: Essays in Sociology,* Hans Gerth and C. Wright Mills, trans. and eds., New York, 1946 [Galaxy Books].

Wheare, K. C., *Federal Government,* Oxford, 1946.

II. Political Systems

SWEDEN

Arneson, Ben A., *The Democratic Monarchies of Scandinavia,* New York, 1949.

Andersson, Ingvar, *A History of Sweden,* Carolyn Hannay, trans., New York, 1955.

Childs, Marquis W., *Sweden: The Middle Way,* New Haven, 1947.

Herlitz, Nils, *Sweden: A Modern Democracy on Ancient Foundations,* Minneapolis, 1939.

Hovde, B. J., *The Scandinavian Countries, 1720-1865,* Boston, 1943.

Myers, Charles A., *Industrial Relations in Sweden,* Cambridge, Massachusetts, 1951.

Rustow, Dankwart A., *The Politics of Compromise: A Study of Parties and Cabinet Government in Sweden,* Princeton, 1955.

Sweden, Royal Ministry for Foreign Affairs, *The Constitution of Sweden,* Sarah V. Thørelli, trans., Stockholm, 1954.

SWITZERLAND

Friedrich, Carl J., and Taylor Cole, *Responsible Bureaucracy,* Cambridge, Massachusetts, 1932.

Herold, J. C., *The Swiss Without Halos,* New York, 1948.

Huber, Hans, *How Switzerland Is Governed,* Zürich, 1947.

Nabholz, Hans, and Paul Kläui, eds., *Quellenbuch zur Versaffungsgeschichte der Schweizerischen Eidgenossenschaft und der Kantone von den Anfängen bis zur Gegenwart,* Aarau, 1940.

Rappard, W. E., *The Government of Switzerland,* New York, 1936.

Sauser-Hall, George, *The Political Institutions of Switzerland,* New York, 1946.

Schweizerische Bundeskanzlei, *Bundesverfassung der Schweizerischen Eidgenossenschaft, Vom 29. Mai 1874, Mit den Änderungen bis 1. Juni 1948.*

Siegfried, André, *Switzerland, A Democratic Way of Life,* Edward Fitzgerald, trans., London, 1950.

ITALY

Carlyle, Margaret, *Modern Italy,* London, 1957.

Croce, Benedetto, *A History of Italy, 1871-1915,* Oxford, 1929.

Einaudi, Mario, and François Goguel, *Christian Democracy in Italy and France,* South Bend, 1952.

——, Jean-Marie Domenach, and Aldo Garosci, *Communism in Western Europe,* Ithaca, 1951.

——, "The Constitution of the Italian Republic," *American Political Science Review,* XLII (August, 1949).

——, Maurice Byé, and Ernesto Rossi, *Nationalization in France and Italy,* Ithaca, 1955.

Finer, Herman, *Mussolini's Italy,* New York, 1935.

Grindrod, Muriel, *The Rebuilding of Italy: Politics and Economics, 1945-1955,* London, 1955.

Hughes, H. Stuart, *The United States and Italy,* Cambridge, Massachusetts, 1953.

La Palombara, Joseph G., "The Italian Elections and the Problem of Representation," *American Political Science Review,* XLVII (1953).

Salvemini, Gaetano, and G. LaPiana, *What to Do with Italy,* New York, 1943.

Sprigge, Cecil J. S., *The Development of Modern Italy,* New Haven, 1944.

GERMANY

Bowen, Ralph H., *German Theories of the Corporative State,* New York, 1947.

Brunet, René, *The New German Constitution,* New York, 1922.

Bullock, Alan, *Hitler: A Study in Tyranny,* London, 1952 [Bantam Books].

Bürgerliches Gesetzbuch nebst Einführungsgesetz, Berlin, 1896.

Golay, John Ford, *The Founding of the Federal Republic of Germany,* Chicago, 1958.

Halperin, S. William, *Germany Tried Democracy*, New York, 1946.

Kirchheimer, Otto, "The Composition of the German Bundestag," *Western Political Quarterly* (1950), pp. 590-601.

Litchfield, Edward H., ed., *Governing Postwar Germany*, Ithaca, 1953.

Meinecke, Friedrich, *The German Catastrophe*, Cambridge, Massachusetts, 1950.

Pollock, James K., ed., *German Democracy at Work*, Ann Arbor, 1955.

———, and H. Thomas, *Germany in Power and Eclipse*, New York, 1952.

Rosenberg, Arthur, *The Birth of the German Republic*, London, 1931.

Spiro, Herbert J., *The Politics of German Codetermination*, Cambridge, Massachusetts, 1958.

Ullmann, R. K., and Sir Stephen King-Hall, *German Parliaments*, London, 1954.

Valentin, Veit, *The German People*, New York, 1946.

Wallich, Henry C., *The Mainsprings of German Revival*, New Haven, 1955.

Watkins, F. M., *The Failure of Constitutional Emergency Powers Under the German Republic*, Cambridge, Massachusetts, 1939.

FRANCE

Brogan, D. W., *The Development of Modern France, 1870-1940*, London, 1939.

Earle, Edward Mead, ed., *Modern France: Problems of the Third and Fourth Republics*, Princeton, 1951.

Einaudi, Mario, and François Goguel, *Christian Democracy in France and Italy*, South Bend, 1952. (See also the other books by these authors in the section on Italy.)

Elbow, Matthew H., *French Corporative Theory, 1789-1948: A Chapter in the History of Ideas*, New York, 1954.

Goguel, François, *France Under the Fourth Republic*, Ithaca, 1952.

Gooch, Robert K., *The French Parliamentary Committee System*, New York, 1935.

Hoffmann, Stanley, *et al.*, *Le Mouvement Poujade*, Paris, 1956.

Jouvenal, Robert de, *République des Camarades*, Paris, 1913.

Lerner, Daniel, and Raymond Aron, eds., *France Defeats EDC*, New York, 1957.

Lidderdale, D. W. S., *The Parliament of France*, London, 1951.

Lorwin, Val R., *The French Labor Movement*, Cambridge, Massachusetts, 1954.

Luethy, Herbert, *France Against Herself*, New York, 1955 [Meridian Books].

Melnik, Constantin, and Nathan Leites, *The House Without Windows: France Selects a President*, Evanston, 1958.

Middleton, W. L., *The French Political System*, New York, 1933.

Thomson, David, *Democracy in France*, New York, 1954.

Werth, Alexander, *France, 1940-1956,* London, 1956.

Williams, Philip, *Politics in Postwar France,* London, 1958.

Wright, Gordon, *The Reshaping of French Democracy,* New York, 1948.

GREAT BRITAIN

Amery, L. S., *Thoughts on the Constitution,* Oxford, 1953.

Bagehot, Walter, *The English Constitution,* Oxford, 1867.

Beer, Samuel H., "Pressure Groups and Parties in Britain," *American Political Science Review,* L (March, 1956).

————, *Treasury Control: The Co-ordination of Financial and Economic Policy in Great Britain,* Oxford, 1956.

Bowen, Catherine Drinker, *The Lion and the Throne: The Life and Times of Sir Edward Coke, 1552-1634,* New York, 1957.

Brogan, D. W., *The English People,* New York, 1943.

Butler, D. E., *The British General Election of 1955,* London, 1956.

————, *The Electoral System in Great Britain, 1918-51,* Oxford, 1953.

Campion, Lord, *An Introduction to the Procedure of the House of Commons,* London, 1958.

Cole, G. D. H., *Guild Socialism: A Plan for Economic Democracy,* New York, 1920.

Cromwell, Oliver, *Writings and Speeches,* Wilbur C. Abbott, ed., 4 vols., Cambridge, Massachusetts, 1937-47.

Feiling, Keith G., *History of England to 1918,* New York, 1951.

Finer, S. E., *Anonymous Empire: A Study of the Lobby in Britain,* London, 1958.

Fortescue, Sir John, *De Laudibus Legum Angliae,* Stanley B. Chrimes, ed., Cambridge, England, 1942.

Franks, Sir Oliver, *Central Planning and Control in War and Peace,* Cambridge, Massachusetts, 1947.

Greaves, H. R. G., *The British Constitution,* London, 1955.

Jennings, Sir W. Ivor, *Cabinet Government,* Cambridge, England, 1951.

————, *Parliament,* Cambridge, England, 1957.

Keir, D. L., *Constitutional History of Modern Britain, 1485-1951,* London, 1953.

Lewis, Ray, and Angus Maude, *The English Middle Classes,* New York, 1950.

McIlwain, Charles H., *The High Court of Parliament and Its Supremacy: An Historical Essay on the Boundaries Between Legislation and Adjudication in England,* New Haven, 1934.

McKenzie, R. T., *British Political Parties,* New York, 1955.

Maitland, Frederic W., *The Constitutional History of England,* London, 1908.

May, Sir Thomas Erskine, *A Treatise on the Law, Privileges, Proceedings and Usage of Parliament,* Lord Campion Butterworth and T. G. Cocks, eds., 15th ed., London, 1950.

Morrison, Herbert, *Government and Parliament: A Survey from the Inside,* Oxford, 1954.

Redlich, Josef, *The Procedure of the House of Commons,* A. E. Steinthal, trans., 3 vols., London, 1908.

Ross, J. F. S., *Parliamentary Representation,* New Haven, 1944.

Smith, Sir Thomas, *De Republica Anglorum,* 1583. L. Alston, ed., Cambridge, 1906.

Taylor, Eric, *The House of Commons at Work,* London, 1951.

Woodhouse, A. S. P., ed., *Puritanism and Liberty; Being the Army Debates 1647-9 from the Clarke Manuscripts with Supplementary Documents,* London, 1938.

Wormuth, Francis D., *The Origins of Modern Constitutionalism,* New York, 1949.

CANADA

Beauchesne, Arthur, *Rules and Forms of the House of Commons of Canada,* Toronto, 1958.

Bourinot, Sir J. G., *Parliamentary Procedure in the Dominion of Canada,* 4th ed., Toronto, 1916.

Brown, George W., ed., *Canada,* Berkeley, 1950.

Careless, J. M. S., *Canada: A Story of Challenge,* Cambridge, England, 1953.

Cole, Taylor, *The Canadian Bureaucracy: A Study of Canadian Civil Servants and Other Public Employees, 1939-47,* Durham, 1949.

Dawson, Robert MacGregor, *The Government of Canada,* Toronto, 1954.

Durham, John George Lambton, *Lord Durham's Report on the Affairs of British North America,* Sir C. P. Lucas, ed., 3 vols., Oxford, 1920.

Forsey, Eugene A., *The Royal Power of Dissolution of Parliament in the British Commonwealth,* Toronto, 1943.

Gérin-Lajoie, Paul, *Constitutional Amendment in Canada,* Toronto, 1950.

Lipset, Seymour M., *Agrarian Socialism: The Cooperative Commonwealth Federation in Saskatchewan: A Study in Political Sociology,* Berkeley, 1950.

Macpherson, C. B., *Democracy in Alberta: The Theory and Practice of a Quasi-Party System,* Toronto, 1953.

Mallory, J. R., *Social Credit and the Federal Power in Canada,* Toronto, 1954.

Morton, W. L., *The Progressive Party in Canada,* Toronto, 1949.

Sharp, P. F., *The Agrarian Revolt in Western Canada: A Survey Showing American Parallels,* Minneapolis, 1948.

Wade, F. Mason, *The French Canadians, 1760-1945,* New York, 1955.

Williams, John R., *The Conservative Party of Canada, 1920-49,* Durham, 1956.

UNITED STATES OF AMERICA

American Political Science Association, Committee on Political Parties, "Toward a More Responsible Two-Party System." Supplement to the *American Political Science Review*, XLIV (September, 1950).

Bailey, Stephen K., *Congress Makes a Law*, New York, 1949.

Binkley, Wilfred E., *American Political Parties: Their Natural History*, New York, 1947.

Bryce, James, *The American Commonwealth*, 2 vols., New York, 1888 [Sagamore Press].

Campbell, Angus, *et al.*, *The Voter Decides*, Evanston, 1954.

Cannon, Clarence, *Cannon's Procedure in the House of Representatives*, Washington, 1939.

Corwin, Edward S., *The "Higher Law" Background of American Constitutional Law*, Ithaca, 1957 [Great Seal Books].

————, *The Presidency: Office and Powers*, New York, 1957.

Galbraith, J. Kenneth, *The Affluent Society*, Boston, 1958.

————, *American Capitalism: The Concept of Countervailing Power*, Boston, 1952.

Gilfrey, Henry H., *Precedents, Decisions on Points of Order, with Phraseology, in the United States Senate, 1789-1913*, Washington, 1914.

Gross, Bertram M., *The Legislative Struggle: A Study in Social Combat*, New York, 1953.

Holcombe, Arthur N., *Our More Perfect Union*, Cambridge, Massachusetts, 1950.

Key, V. O., Jr., *Parties, Politics, and Pressure Groups*, New York, 1952.

Laski, Harold J., *The American Democracy*, New York, 1948.

Lerner, Max, *America as a Civilization: Life and Thought in the United States Today*, New York, 1957.

Lubell, Samuel, *The Future of American Politics*, New York, 1951 [Anchor Books].

Maass, Arthur, *Muddy Waters: The Army Engineers and the Nation's Rivers*, Cambridge, Massachusetts, 1951.

Morris, Richard B., *Alexander Hamilton and the Founding of the Nation*, New York, 1957.

Pennock, J. Roland, "Responsiveness, Responsibility, and Majority Rule," *American Political Science Review*, XLVI (September, 1952).

Riesman, David, *et al.*, *The Lonely Crowd, A Study of the Changing American Character*, New Haven, 1950 [Anchor Books].

Rodell, Fred, *Nine Men*, New York, 1955.

Rossiter, Clinton, *The American Presidency*, New York, 1956 [New American Library].

Schattschneider, E. E., *Party Government*, New York, 1941.

Tocqueville, Alexis de, *Democracy in America*, 2 vols. [Vintage Books].
Truman, Harry S., *Memoirs*, 2 vols., New York, 1955-56.
United States Congress, *Documents Illustrative of the Formation of the Union of the American States*, Washington, 1927.
White, William S., *Citadel: The Story of the U.S. Senate*, New York, 1956.
Wilson, Woodrow, *Congressional Government*, Boston, 1885.
Wright, Benjamin F., *The Growth of American Constitutional Law*, New York, 1942.
Young, Roland A., *This Is Congress*, New York, 1943.

INTERNATIONAL POLITICS

Bentwich, Norman, and Andrew Martin, *A Commentary on the Charter of the United Nations*, New York, 1950.
Clark, Grenville, and Louis B. Sohn, *World Peace Through Law*, Cambridge, Massachusetts, 1958.
Hocking, William Ernest, *The Coming World Civilization*, New York, 1956.
Kaplan, Morton A., *System and Process in International Politics*, New York, 1957.
Kelsen, Hans, *Law and Peace in International Relations*, Cambridge, Massachusetts, 1942.
———, *Peace Through Law*, Chapel Hill, 1944.
Kennan, George F., *American Diplomacy: 1900-1950*, Chicago, 1951 [New American Library].
Kissinger, Henry A., *Nuclear Weapons and Foreign Policy*, New York, 1957.
Leontief, Wassily, *et al.*, *Studies in the Structure of the American Economy*, New York, 1953.
Morgenthau, Hans L., *In Defense of the National Interest*, New York, 1951.
———, *Politics Among Nations*, New York, 1948.
Osgood, Robert E., *Limited War: The Challenge to American Strategy*, Chicago, 1957.
United Nations, *Yearbook on Human Rights, 1945* (and subsequent years), New York.
Wright, Quincy, *The Study of International Relations*, New York, 1955.

Index

Abolitionists, 207
Abraham, 392
Academic degrees, 278, 283 ff.
  honorary, 166
Act of Mediation (Switzerland), 55-56
Act of Settlement (Britain), 113
Act of Succession (Sweden), 47, 386
Act of Union (Sweden), 388
Action, responsible, 39. *See also* Responsibility
Adaptability, constitutional, 41-42. *See also* Success
Adenauer, Konrad, 91-94, 265, 352, 353, 374
Adversary method, common law, 225-30
Africa, British Empire in, 118
"Age of Freedom" (Sweden), 234, 389
Agreement, procedural priority, 394-97
Agreement of the People (England), 32
Agriculture, 50, 134-35, 139-40, 305, 315
  Department of, 305
  See also Economic problems *and* Interest organizations
Air Force Association, 156
Alberta, 134, 205, 208
Albertine *Statuto. See Statuto*
Alcoholism, 49, 51-52, 135-36
Algeria, 101, 102, 104, 107, 108-9, 406
Allied Occupation (Germany), 90, 91, 168, 184, 198, 307, 389, 423-24, 426

Allport, Gordon K., 196
Alsace, 87, 102
Alternatives:
  merits of two, in resolution, 354-57
  in situations of responsibility, 34-36
Amendments, constitutional, 146, 390
  Canada, 130, 133, 137
  France, 96 ff., 267-69
  Germany, 84, 85, 92, 423
  Great Britain, 113-14, 115-16
  Italy, 69-70
  Sweden, 48, 50, 390
  Switzerland, 56-57, 60-63
  United States, 146-47
"America first," 153
American Automobile Association, 156
American Civil Liberties Union, 156
Americans for Democratic Action, 156
American Federation of Labor, 139, 156, 165
American Legion, 156, 306
American Political Science Association, 337
American Revolution. *See* War of American Independence
American Telephone and Telegraph Company, 295
Amnesties, 58
Analogies, 28-29
"Anticipated reactions, rule of," 348
Anticlericalism, 98. *See also* Religious problems
Antirepublicanism, 313
Anti-Semitism, 88, 98

Guildhall, 326
Gustaf IV, Adolf, King of Sweden, 46

Habeas corpus, 128, 225, 271
Haldane, Lord, 136
Halifax, 134
Hamburg, 82
Hamilton, Alexander, 131, 143, 147,
222, 259-60, 264, 270, 289
Hammarskjöld, Dag, 53, 457
Hanover, Kingdom of, 82
Hanseatic Cities, 82
Harcourt, Sir William, 261
Hartz, Louis, 362
Harvard Law School, 222
Helvetic Confederation, 55
Helvetic Republic, constitution (1789),
55
Henry VIII, King of Great Britain,
114, 389
Hermens, Ferdinand A., 347n
High Court of Parliament, 228
Hindenburg, Paul von, 84, 351
Hitler, Adolf, 6, 14, 84, 88-90, 94-95,
186, 187, 188, 198, 327, 347, 351,
421, 423
Hobbes, Thomas, 30-31, 212, 374, 443,
452, 460, 461
Holmes, Justice Oliver Wendell, 110,
220, 411
Holy Alliance, 197
Homer, 145
Honorary degrees, 166
House of Commons (Canada), 130,
131, 136, 138, 241
House of Commons (Great Britain),
113 ff., 173, 229, 241, 259-62, 277,
339-40
committees, 254-55, 319-20
High Court of, 228
question period, 246
Standing Orders, 114, 241
supremacy, 115
See also Parliament
House of Lords (Canada), 131
House of Lords (Great Britain), 113 ff.,
287
life peers, 116
House of Representatives (United
States), 148, 150, 157, 239, 254,
256, 321 ff.
committees, 321 ff.
Minority Leader, 230
See also Congress

Hughes, Charles Evans, 286
Hughes, H. Stuart, 414, 437n
Hume, David, 143-44, 147, 222, 289
Hungarian revolt (1956), 249, 454

I.C.B.M., 452
Ideologism, 188-89, 194-210
Canada, 205-07, 208
France, 198-99
Germany, 188, 197-98
Great Britain, 203-05
Italy, 199-200
Sweden, 202-03
Switzerland, 200-01
United States, 207-09
critique of, 188-89
guidelines for constitution-makers,
210
ideological style and "functional
autonomy," 195-96
Ideology:
and political style, 180-81
and "situation of responsibility," 38
Illegitimacy, 49
Immediate goals, 182
Immigration, 135, 141, 152, 153, 154
"Imperialism," 453. *See also* Colonial-
ism
India, 118, 121, 124, 432-33
Individual decisions, 27-28
Individual responsibility, norm of, 365,
441. *See also* Responsibility
Indochina, 101, 102, 107, 445
Indonesia, 441
"Industrial democracy," 183
"Industrial order," French society, 311-
12
Industrial Revolution, 73, 87, 118, 313,
314, 332-33, 389, 447, 449
Industrialization:
Canada, 135
France, 100-02
Germany, 87
Great Britain, 118-19
Italy, 72-73
Switzerland, 58-59
United States, 152
Inflation of 1924 (Germany), 264
Initiative, popular (Switzerland), 56,
57, 60, 61, 63, 65
Inns of Court (London), 222, 228
"Input-output table," 459
Institutional orders, France, 311-12
Institutional school, 8-10